Sketches of
Negro Life and History
in South Carolina

GORDON, Asa H. Sketches of Negro life and history in South Carolina. 2nd ed. South Carolina, 1971. 337p tab 76-122358. 7.95. ISBN 0-87249-201-X
Valuable both as a topical history and as a primary source. First published in 1922, *Sketches* was an effort, in the era of the "new Negro" of the Harlem Renaissance, to reveal the heritage and life of black South Carolinians. Gordon wanted to dispel the image of the black as "the race nobody knows" and with this book provided a summary of the past and present life of the black in the "Old Palmetto State." The author quotes liberally from other sources and includes one chapter, "The new Negro challenges the old order" by Benjamin E. Mays, which is particularly valuable for its Southern view of the "new Negro" of the Harlem Renaissance. Except for an introduction by Mrs. Gordon and an informative foreword by T. E. Terrill, it is a reissue of the first edition. Recommended particularly for purchase by libraries interested in Southern black history.

CHOICE   JUNE'71
History, Geography & Travel
North America

Sketches of
Negro Life and History
in South Carolina

By

Asa H. Gordon

SECOND EDITION
Foreword by Tom E. Terrill
Preface by Joan L. Gordon

UNIVERSITY OF SOUTH CAROLINA PRESS
Columbia, S.C.

FOREWORD

AMERICAN whites and blacks have lived—and still live —in separate worlds. That separation has meant more than separate restrooms, separate lunch counters, and separate schools. Separation has also meant separate perceptions of the past and the present. Yet American whites and blacks have lived—and still live—in the same world, sharing a common past and present and holding common basic values. This paradox lies at the core of the American experience.

These paradoxical themes flow through Asa H. Gordon's *Sketches of Negro Life and History in South Carolina*, which was first published in 1929. The book was clearly the product of a black man in the United States of the 1920s. Not only does it reflect the mood and ideas of the 1920s, but it also reveals what Professor W. E. B. DuBois called the "double-consciousness" of being both black and American at the same time.[1] Gordon wrote as an American, but a black American. Thus, reminiscent of Benjamin Franklin and Andrew Carnegie, Gordon accepted sound education and hard work as the elemental steps on the upward economic and social climb. Yet he was keenly aware that black men were denied adequate opportunities in their pursuit of happiness.

Gordon was also a Progressive, but a black Progressive. In giving as much attention to economic and social history as to political history, he used the conceptual framework of the "New History" of the Progressive era. He had the thorough optimism characteristic of many Progressives. He pointed with pride to the accomplishments of South Carolina blacks. He was hopeful about the future of race relations, probably overly so. When the South Carolina

[1] W. E. B. DuBois, *The Souls of Black Folk*, introduction by Saunders Redding (Greenwich, Conn.: Fawcett Publications, Inc., 1961), pp. 16–17.

v

Interracial Commission was founded in the late 1920s, he saw a new trend developing in race relations in the state. But that trend developed with excruciatingly "deliberate speed." Like many Progressives and like DuBois, Gordon thought that accumulated facts and forceful persuasion would change minds and human behavior. Thus, he itemized the considerable achievements of South Carolina blacks in order to challenge the fixed assumptions of white supremacy shared by most whites and blacks. Unfortunately, such chapters as "The Negro's Long War Against Ignorance," "The Evolution of the Negro Home," "The Negro in Business in South Carolina," "The Negro Farmer in South Carolina," and "The Gifts of Womanhood in Ebony" had no discernible effect upon the self-image of the blacks or upon the attitudes and behavior of South Carolina whites toward South Carolina blacks.

Whatever his immediate contribution was, Professor Gordon left an important legacy. Most significantly, he gave us an insight into the mind and mood of black leaders in South Carolina in the 1920s. Gordon made it abundantly clear that they were dissatisfied with the status of black men and were determined to change that status. Although they avoided the strident rhetoric of the 1960s, black leaders were hardly complacent. The chapter, "The New Negro Challenges the Old Order," clearly demonstrated their quiet determination. Written by Dr. Benjamin E. Mays, then executive secretary of the Tampa Urban League and now President, Emeritus, of Morehouse College, it reflected the Harlem Renaissance and showed that the South Carolina civil rights movement had local origins. Much of this particular chapter was initially part of a speech delivered at Benedict College in 1926. It is significant that, as Dr. Mays recalls, the Benedict students responded enthusiastically to his address.

Gordon challenged certain historical assumptions. For example, he argued persuasively that slaves were not indolent, content, shiftless Samboes. More than that, slaves made crucial contributions to the economic development of the antebellum South. And he effectively discounted the simplistic view of Reconstruction in South Carolina as the "Tragic Era" several years before Professors Francis B. Simkins and Robert H. Woody wrote their *South Carolina During Reconstruction*.[2]

Finally, Gordon has left us facts about and impressions of South Carolina blacks that might otherwise be lost, and he has shown convincing evidence of some of the unfortunate ramifications of segregation. Not only did segregation hamstring the socioeconomic rise of the South Carolina blacks, but it contributed to creating a delusory climate of race relations. South Carolina whites apparently thought their black neighbors were content with their lot in the 1920s. They were wrong. Clearly, segregation facilitated a climate of serious misunderstanding.

Sketches is an important book for the legacy it left, but it is not and was not intended to be a book of great originality. Much of the general history of the Negro in the United States appeared earlier in such volumes as George Washington Williams' *History of the Negro Race in America, 1619–1880*. Although DuBois's socialist ideas are absent, Gordon obviously imbibed the spirit of his teacher and of the DuBois studies that appeared in *The Atlanta University Publications*.[3] The text has aged with dignity but is not without its wrinkles. For instance, blacks are not inherently superior singers, nor is it true that whites are naturally suited for business and blacks are not.

Hopefully, Dr. Gordon's wish that the black American

[2] See Edwin D. Hoffman, "The Genesis of the Modern Movement for Equal Rights in South Carolina, 1930–1939," *Journal of Negro History,* XLIV, No. 4 (October, 1959), pp. 346–69.

[3] George Washington Williams, *History of the Negro Race in America, 1619–1880* (New York: Arno Press and the *New York Times,* 1968). Some of the Atlanta University studies have been reprinted by the same publishers. *The Atlanta University Publications,* Nos. 1, 2, 4, 8, 9, 11, 13, 14, 15, 16, 17, 18 (New York: Arno Press and the *New York Times,* 1968).

cease being "The Man Nobody Knows" will in part be fulfilled by the reprinting of his book.

Department of History   Tom E. Terrill
University of South Carolina
December 1970

PREFACE TO SECOND EDITION

SINCE the publication of the first edition of this book there has been an increased interest in the history of the Negro. It is proposed that the awakening of this interest began in 1954 with the Supreme Court Decision concerning education and desegregation in *Brown* v. *Board of Education of Topeka*. Gaining momentum with each passing year, interest in Negro history has matured into the current realization of the need for including "Black Studies" in the educational curriculum.

Today's students, as well as the general reading public, realize that there is a need to become knowledgeable about Black history. This realization has resulted in many colleges expanding their curricula to include courses in Black Studies. Such curricular expansions are undoubtedly based on the assumption that knowledge in any discipline increases one's understanding of the tenets of that discipline, thereby curtailing fallacious or biased opinions. This educational process certainly holds true with reference to knowledge in the area of race relations.

My decision to accept the proposal of the University of South Carolina Press to publish a new edition of my late husband's book was largely influenced by the current focus on Black Studies. Further motivation stemmed from the hope that republication would serve four main purposes: (1) to make available to all students, as well as teachers, of Negro history a source of relevant information; (2) to help Blacks develop self-respect and from such self-respect, based on a knowledge of the achievements of one's own race, to acquire respect for the accomplishments of other races; (3) to assist in speeding up the educational processes of informing the reading public about aspects of history either omitted or de-emphasized in current textbooks in an effort to nullify this quotation from the preface to the first edition of this volume: "the Negro is scarcely known at all to the other races of the world—contrary to common opinion, he is not fully known to his white neighbors in the south"; and (4) to preserve for posterity competent research of older works in order to furnish writers interested in historical research an available source of documentary evidence that might otherwise be inaccessible or difficult to obtain. The comprehensive index in this second edition should be of great assistance to historians, bibliographers, genealogists, and students in general.

We feel that the contents of this volume warrant its republication since they reveal significant insights which were to a large measure not envisioned by the "intelligent world" at the time the book was written—but which are today generally accepted. Accordingly, we take the liberty to surmise that our purposes in reissuing this book and the purposes that motivated the author to write it originally very nearly coincide. Furthermore, it is our hope that this second edition will meet the demands of the widening interest of the layman and academicians in Black-oriented literature. It is also hoped that it will be instrumental in achieving better understanding in the realm of human relations.

Professor of Social Science   JOAN L. GORDON
Savannah State College
December 1970

SKETCHES

OF

NEGRO LIFE
and HISTORY

IN SOUTH CAROLINA

By

ASA H. GORDON, A.B., LL.B.

Professor of History, State A. and M. College,
Orangeburg, S. C.

SPECIAL CONTRIBUTORS

DR. D. H. SIMS
President Allen University, Columbia, S. C.

MR. B. E. MAYS
Secretary National Council Y. M. C. A., Atlanta, Ga.

MR. B. B. BARNWELL
Farm Demonstration Agent, Frogmore, S. C.

PREFACE TO FIRST EDITION

IN the well-known publications of a contemporary writer of no small popularity we find Jesus Christ referred to as "The Man Nobody Knows" and the Bible as "The Book Nobody Knows." The Negro race, wherever it is domiciled, whether it be in the vast continent of Africa, in the islands of the seven seas, in the United States at large, in the famous old State of South Carolina, is the race which nobody knows. The Negro does not even know and appreciate himself—his own life and history in the world at large or in any particular country. The Negro is scarcely known at all to the other races of the world. Contrary to common opinion, he is not fully known to his white neighbors in the South.

Just as Jesus and the Bible are only partly known and vaguely understood largely because people do not really desire to know and understand them, so it is with the Negro race. It is much more convenient to accept current notions without investigation. Then, too, the Negro, it must be admitted, has found that he could get along easier if he just allowed people to form opinions about him as they wished, regardless of the truth in the case. He has taken the path of least resistance.

The Negro and his neighbors are awakening to the importance of his history and achievements. There is much literature dedicated to the task of introducing the race to the intelligent world. Distinguished colored writers, such as W. E. B. DuBois, Booker T. Washington, Kelly Miller, Benjamin Brawley, Carter Woodson, James W. Johnson, and many others have dedicated their talents to the work of putting the Negro before the world as a man of achievement and progressive ideals as well as a humble worker and a faithful friend of all, even his enemies. This book is one more attempt to help dispel the current idea so largely accepted that the Negro is a race without civilization and historical background and largely lacking in real, substantial contemporary achievement as a member of modern complex society.

We believe that there is not any group of Negroes anywhere on the earth which can furnish better opportunity for such a study and presentation than the colored population of the "Old Palmetto State." Here a large number of Negroes have played their part with representative fortitude, courage and optimism. Here African culture has met and merged with Anglo-Saxon civilization and produced remarkable characters from the unknown slave workers, who transformed primeval swamps and forests into the waving fields of rice and snowy fields of cotton, to distinguished scientists such as Earnest Just and Kelly Miller, who speak to and have the respectful attention of the world's greatest philosophers in their respective fields.

As the title of this book suggests, it is limited to the Negro in South Carolina. This precludes a discussion of the history and civilizational background of the Negro in the Orient in general, and in Africa in particular, before his advent in America. We assume the reader to be somewhat familiar with this; if not, we recommend volumes of the Journal of Negro History and books on the general history and culture of the Negro by Carter G. Woodson, W. E. B. DuBois, Benjamin Brawley, W. D. Weatherford, Booker Washington, Jerome Dowd, H. Barth, E. W. Blyden, Levi Coppin, Von Luschan, Louis Huot and numerous others. The general literature on the subject is now quite extensive.

It thus appears that it is not our purpose to write a scientific history of the Negro or even an exhaustive historical survey of his civilization in South Carolina, but rather to present "sketches" of his life and history which may serve to advertise his achievements in adapting himself to this civilization and making his characteristic contributions to its further development, and to inspire him and his posterity to greater and finer effort, and to show his friends among the white people that their faith in him has not been unjustified or unfruitful. This is our pleasant task.

True to our title, we have barely sketched many subjects that deserve careful, exhaustive investigation which, in one or two of them, we hope some day to carry out. But this has been impossible for us as we carry on the work of a history teacher with crowded classes in the state college. We hope that our free use of secondary sources has shown a reasonable sense of what is valuable for our purpose and plan. We have attempted to be fair and unbiased in our consideration of the studies of others in the fields we have touched. In some instances, such as the reconstruction period, we felt that delving into primary sources was not really imperative because this has been previously and excellently performed by Mr. A. A. Taylor and others. In self-defense we should say that on account of the urgent request of the publishers that we hasten through the preparation of this book, and because of our own limited time referred to above, we have not investigated primary sources as thoroughly as we would like and we were not able to make more thorough original studies of certain subjects which should have been so treated as there was little or no reliable information previously gathered on them.

In our way, we have attempted to write in the spirit of the "New History"; that is, we have attempted to emphasize social and economic factors as well as the political. We have tried to present a record of the life of the people in mass.

We have conscientiously striven to keep the historical parts of this book strictly loyal to the truth. We have no special interests to serve except the truth. We were and are not interested in promoting any prejudicial propaganda. We believe that a presentation of the unvarnished truth will furnish inspiration for the Negro and should be a source of pride and honor to the entire citizenry of South Carolina. If some parts of the truth are disagreeable to the Negro, or humiliating to the white people, this is to be expected. The ideal of the historian is ever that of the Great Teacher: "Ye shall know the Truth and the Truth shall set you free." If larger freedom, resulting from contact with the truth here presented, is really the result of the perusal of this work by even a small number of those who read its pages, we shall feel that we have not labored entirely in vain however much or little credit may be given us by the critics.

A. H. GORDON,
S. C. State A. & M. College.

ACKNOWLEDGMENTS

We do not present here a book made up entirely of our own writings alone. Parts of two or three of the ten chapters were written by others. These persons were asked to write these particular parts because we felt that they were more competent to write on these matters than any one else known to us in this state. Doctor Sims of Allen University has kindly written a very appreciative introduction for us. Other sections have been written by experts in those fields. Their contributions are noted as they appear in the book. We thank all these special writers for their additions.

We wish also to thank the various authors and publishers who have given us permission to quote from their works. Among the authors we wish especially to thank Dr. Carter Woodson, Mr. William Pickens, Dr. U. B. Phillips, Dean Kelly Miller, and Doctor DuBois. Among the publishers are: The Associated Publishers, Macmillan, Appleton, Doran, The Stratford Company, Neale Publishing Company.

We wish to thank several of our colleagues on the faculty here who have helped us in various ways; especially the president, Dr. R. S. Wilkinson. Some of the other individuals who have assisted us in various ways are: Mr. Robert Kennedy, librarian at the University of South Carolina; Miss Mae Holloway of Charleston, S. C.; Mr. Edward Mickey of Charleston; Misses Henrietta Blackwell and Mozelle Taggart, students, State College. Some others doubtless should be mentioned but time and space dictate that we stop sometime. We here thank them all, the named and the unnamed.

A. H. G.

CONTENTS

Foreword by Tom E. Terrill   v
Preface to Second Edition by Joan L. Gordon   ix
Preface to First Edition by A. H. Gordon   xiii
Acknowledgments   xvii
Introduction by D. H. Sims   xxi

CHAPTER I

THE BLACK MAN'S BURDEN   1

How the Negro slaves laid the foundation of South Carolina's
economic and industrial prosperity by performing the necessary labor where all others have failed. What did the colored
laborers bring to their work which others lacked, causing them to
succeed where all others have failed?

CHAPTER II

THE SLAVES' FIGHT FOR PHYSICAL FREEDOM 13

Contrary to the opinion of some, South Carolina's Negro population was never contented, satisfied and happy in slavery. The
struggle of the colored people to be free largely contributed to
make slavery ultimately a failure as a labor system and was
contributory to South Carolina's secession from the union which
precipitated a Civil War. That war resulted in that coveted
freedom for which some of the slaves fought, bled and died and
never saw but which many received.

CHAPTER III

THE NEGRO'S PART IN THE RECONSTRUCTION OF SOUTH
    CAROLINA 55

Most historians have emphasized the mistakes and crimes of the
Negro leaders during the reconstruction period and ignored their
worth-while achievements. This has resulted in a widespread
current belief that the Negro's participation in politics was a
complete and dismal failure. The facts do not warrant such a
pessimistic or discouraging theory.

CHAPTER IV

THE NEGRO'S LONG WAR AGAINST IGNORANCE 80

One of the brightest\ pages in American history is that which
records the Negro's fight out of dense ignorance into comparative
intelligence. The Negroes of South Carolina have won many battles of importance for the race, the country and the world.

CHAPTER V

THE EVOLUTION OF THE NEGRO HOME 113

The colored people have established their right to a place in
modern civilization by their achievements as home builders if

they have accomplished nothing else. In this chapter we attempt to record the thrilling triumph of the race in this essential. The meager facts and cold statistics seem hardly fitted for such a noble task, but the reader we hope can read it all between the lines.

CHAPTER VI

THE NEGRO IN BUSINESS IN SOUTH CAROLINA 135
If we compare Negro business with white business in this state, that of the Negroes seems conspicuous for its insignificance, but if we think of it in comparison with fifty or sixty years ago, it appears more hopeful. At any rate, the facts are worth recording and the ideals should be broadcast.

CHAPTER VII

THE NEGRO FARMER IN SOUTH CAROLINA 156
South Carolina still remains an agricultural state. Upon the great industry depend her prosperity and her progress. The Negro seems to be striving to help push our state to the front in this old but still necessary vocation.

CHAPTER VIII

THE GIFTS OF WOMANHOOD IN EBONY 174
In the spirit of true chivalry we are grateful to all womanhood for its great sacrificial gifts and stand with bared heads in its presence, regardless of its color or its race, but our hearts throb with surging pride as we think of Negro womanhood remaining so largely loyal, pure and happy, while passing through the fiery furnace of modern race prejudice with Negro manhood.

CHAPTER IX

THE NEW NEGRO CHALLENGES THE OLD ORDER 192
"I's a gittin' weary of de way dat people do," sang Dunbar in one of his poems. The South Carolina Negro is developing that restlessness and dissatisfaction which are characteristic of all progressive people and essential for higher achievements in any group.

CHAPTER X

MANHOOD IN EBONY FACES THE FUTURE 213
History is a record of the past, but it always suggests a forward-looking vista. We cannot resist the temptation to peer thereat for a few fleeting moments.

APPENDIX 235

INDEX 281

INTRODUCTION

THIS book is valuable from several points of view. Professor Gordon has given his life and fine talent to the study of the group with which this book is chiefly concerned. He is eminently fitted for such a task because he has the mental poise and has given more time to investigations, to which the material of this book is related, than perhaps any other person in South Carolina.

I regard the production as a real contribution to the literature which relates to the greatest American, if not world, problem. The book has a fine motive back of it. It is a search for truth.

One of the stubborn factors in the complex race problem is that of wrong attitude. Both groups live within the same political and industrial areas. They come into competition either as individuals or racial groups. But they, in general, are ignorant of each other. "The behavior of the white man is determined by a complex of deep seated prejudices toward the Negro, and by a fixed conception of the proper place of the Negro in the social and industrial order."

The race problem is thus a heritage from an earlier social order. It is the problem of maintaining harmonious and mutually satisfactory working relations between the Negro and the white man. In order to accomplish this, the attitude of both of the groups must be changed, and enlightenment in the form of facts should facilitate the task. In other words, we must change the social order in respect to the problem.

The mental and social attitude of the Caucasian and the mental and social attitude of the Negro need overhauling. The white man needs to be cured of the "superiority" complex, and the Negro needs to be lifted out of the stupor of the "inferiority" complex, and develop a strong racial consciousness that will enable him to make his largest contribution. Theorizing, debating and bulldozing will get us nowhere. "Where ignorance is bliss, 'tis folly to be wise." This book presents the facts so that even he who runs may read.

The locus and limit of investigation present a decided advantage. People at certain stages of development are prejudiced against truth that comes from afar. Negro achievement in New York, Illinois or Ohio is not as significant to whites and Negroes who live in South Carolina as that extracted out of and performed upon native soil.

However, the truth of achievement within this given locus shows that the Negro's progress is not indigenous to any particular soil.

The diagnosis of the social, religious, political and economic phases without prejudice or bias for or against either group is one of the distinct characteristics of the author's endeavors. The author allows truth to speak. It is a scientific record following facts on the highway of investigation, unmindful as to whether that highway leads pro or con.

The viewpoint is that of emphasizing social and economic forces and conditions. This is a history of the people of color in South Carolina in mass and not merely a collection of individual biographies of a few leaders.

The Negro must be able to profit by his mistakes, but he must have scientific information concerning his mistakes. He must be thrilled and stimulated by his achievements, but he must know those achievements. Comparisons are not reliable unless they are made on the basis of scientific data. One of the contributions very unique in this work of the author is the "stock taking." It is truly a historical inventory which will help the citizens of South Carolina and the United States to get a true perspective of civilization's progress in South Carolina during the period covered by this history.

In this work there is a convincing portrayal of how the Negro slaves laid the foundation of South Carolina's economic and industrial prosperity in the performance of tasks wherein others had failed. The reason assigned for this signal victory of which all South Carolina is beneficiary is illuminating.

Some have advanced the opinion that Negro slaves were contented in South Carolina, and that only here and there some exceptional Negro slave would resent slavery. Data and argument in Chapter II are sufficient to convince the open-minded that South Carolina's Negro population was never contented, satisfied and happy in slavery, but struggled persistently to be free, and contributed to the failure of slavery as a labor system.

The economic and social prodigality of slavery is set forth in a very vivid fashion showing that slavery was not baneful alone to Negroes, but also whites. The sequence of slavery is seen in the evils which make up the vexing race problem of our contemporary epoch.

The most wonderful array of facts is brought to the readers of this history to support a thesis to which most historians have presented an anti-thesis. The mistakes and crimes of the Negro in the period of reconstruction in South Carolina, have been emphasized and the real contribution which he made has been either ignorantly or viciously ignored. For instance: "This procedure has resulted in widespread current belief that the Negro's participation in politics was a complete and dismal failure." The facts do not warrant any such conclusion.

Out of the night of ignorance which covered the Negro in South Carolina, he has emerged to the dawn of intelligence, and South Carolina's educational history is criminally incomplete without a chapter on "The Negro's Long War Against Ignorance."

The home is truly denominated as one of civilization's bulwarks. The author is in scientific fashion setting forth a wonderful story of the evolution of the Negro in South Carolina. He shows that the Negro has established his right to a place in modern civilization by his achievement as a home builder.

The Negro's business history in South Carolina suffers from comparison with that of the other group, but the author directs our attention to the status of Negro business sixty years ago and today. The results are worthy of our attention.

The importance of the Negro laborer and farmer to the prosperity and progress of South Carolina in the past, present, and future, is shown in Chapters I and VII. South Carolina is still an agricultural state, and hence the importance of the Negro farmer who constitutes a large part of the farming population of South Carolina.

One of the barometers of group achievement in modern civilization is the status and contribution of woman. The Negro woman in South Carolina has not only been the recipient of all of the maladies inherent in the institution of slavery and its aftermath, but in addition she has been the social target of all groups whose sex propensities led them to exploitation. This optimistic portrayal of "The Gifts of Womanhood in Ebony" is given in Chapter VIII. Truly it is a marvel that she has remained so largely pure, loyal and happy while she passed through the fiery furnace of race prejudice.

The South Carolina Negro population is pleased with achievements, but be it said to their credit, they are not satisfied. They are restless in face of conditions which confront them. They are dissatisfied with their present status. This is characteristic of advancing groups. Let the New Negro challenge the old order sanely and in the spirit of true patriots.

In the closing chapter, the author runs true to form. He uses the past to face the future. The Negro in the Palmetto State has a forward look. How important! How far you have come is important. Which way you are headed is more important. Face the future with clear vision, undaunted courage and a resolute will to achieve all that citizenship has to offer, to inaugurate racial and inter-racial groups, and inter-groups. Co-operation in the pursuit of the ideal is the goal of society. A civilization of brotherly men is efficient in contributing to community welfare.

D. H. SIMS, President,
Allen University, Columbia, S. C.

CHAPTER I

THE BLACK MAN'S BURDEN

"By an' by I'm goin' ter lay down ma heavy load."

THE Negro entered South Carolina through the gates of toil. It is a fact universally known and admitted that he was forced into the United States against his will as a burden bearer. The title of "Burden Bearer" is, therefore, not figurative or far-fetched when applied to him. The mission of the colored race, as conceived and determined by the early settlers, was different from that of the horse, mule and ox only in that he, being human or nearly so, could perform tasks that those animals could not because of their lack of rudimentary intelligence. Slavery came to be prominent in the colony when rice and cotton plantations began to call for a large supply of cheap labor. The Negro slaves were conscripted to take up the burden of cleaning swamps, tending rice fields, and cultivating cotton. These tasks seem to have been too exacting for the constitutions or abilities of other available workers—the poor whites and aboriginal Indians.

It is difficult to say just when Negroes first came into South Carolina. It seems probable that they were here at the founding of the colony, though in small numbers and of uncertain classification. It is certain that the "Fundamental Constitutions" prepared by John Locke to guide the Lords Proprietors in their government of the colony of South Carolina recognized slavery in 1669. The status of slaves was further officially defined in 1682. In 1708 there were in the colony 3,500 whites, 4,120 Negro slaves, and 1,400 Indians. In 1720 there were 9,200 white persons and 12,220 colored slaves. In 1724 there were 14,200 whites and 32,000 slaves. It is not necessary to quote further population statistics to show that the Negro population was increasing faster than the white population. This rapid increase of the Negro

1

population caused no little concern and agitation among the white people and efforts were made to more carefully control the slaves and even to reduce the importation, so as to prevent their too rapid increase. Beginning about 1690 there was much legislation to regulate the conduct and life of slaves.

In 1749 a very high duty was placed upon imported slaves. Brawley thinks that this was partly inspired by a slaves' insurrection fomented by one Cato.[1]

In these early days while slavery was growing so rapidly we find that the rice cultivating industry of South Carolina was also making wonderful strides and great profits for the fortunate plantation owners. This explains why the various laws designed to prevent the rapid increase of slaves were uniformly unsuccessful. It is ever thus—when the laws conflict with the economic interest of the lawmakers, the laws are of no avail.

That the success of the Carolina colony's project of producing rice for the world market was mainly due to the fact that the Negro slave took up the burden of its necessary labor is admitted by every careful student and writer dealing with this period. A quotation from White[2] will serve to illustrate:

Rice was planted in the deep, wet soil of the swamps. It was found that white men lost their health if they tried to work in the swamp lands. Negroes from Africa, however, were able to work in the rice fields without injury to themselves. For this reason large numbers of Negroes were brought from Africa to South Carolina. Without their help the rice could not have been cultivated.

The following description by Phillips is also interesting in this connection:[3]

For the rice harvest, beginning early in September, as soon as a field was drained the Negroes would be turned in with sickles, each laborer cutting a swath of three or four rows, leaving the stubble about a foot high to sustain the cut stalks carefully laid

[1] *A Short History of the American Negro*, page 91.
[2] *The Making of South Carolina*, page 22.
[3] *American Negro Slavery*, pages 90-91.

upon it in handfuls for a day's drying. Next day the crop would be bound in sheaves and stacked for a brief curing. When the reaping was done the threshing began, and then followed the tedious labor of separating the grain from its tightly adhering husk. In Colonial times the work was mostly done by hand, first the flail for threshing, then the heavy fat-pine pestle and mortar for breaking off the husk. Finally the rice was winnowed of its chaff, screened of the "rice flour" and broken grain, and barreled for market.

The ditches and pools in and about the fields of course bred swarms of mosquitoes which carried malaria to all people subject. Most of the whites were afflicted by that disease in the warmer half of the year, but the Africans were generally immune. Negro labor was therefore at such a premium that whites were virtually never employed on the plantations except as overseers and occasionally as artisans.

In Colonial times the planters, except the few quite wealthy ones who had town houses in Charleston, lived on their places the year around; but at the close of the eighteenth century they began to resort in summer to "pine land" villages within an hour or two's riding distance from their plantations.

With this period especially in mind, Brawley[4] says: "The whole system of slavery in South Carolina was very profitable, Negroes being naturally adapted to life in the low lands." All this, and much more of similar import, makes it quite clear that the Negro was the burden bearer who established South Carolina's leadership in this important industry.

The Negro's success in bearing the burdens of the rice industry was only the beginning of his task. One success (!) led to larger responsibilities. The introduction of cotton, later crowned "King," increased the burden for the black man tremendously and indefinitely. The burden of physical labor necessary for the successful cultivation of cotton was early placed upon the broad shoulders of the Negro slave and he, now partially free, still carries it. Writing of the development of the cotton-growing industry so vitally associated with the economic prosperity of the South, Phillips[5] refers to the early efforts in South Carolina as follows:

The first success in South Carolina appears to have been

---

[4]Brawley: *History of the American Negro*
[5]*American Negro Slavery*, pages 152-153.

attained by William Elliott, on Hilton Head near Beaufort, in
1790. He bought 5½ bushels of seed in Charleston at 14s. per
bushel, and sold his crop at 10½ per pound. In the next year
John Screven of St. Luke's parish planted thirty or forty acres,
and sold his yield at from 1s. 2d. to 1s. 6d. sterling per pound.
Many other planters on the islands and the adjacent mainland
now joined the movement. Some of them encountered failure,
among them General Moultrie of revolutionary fame, who
planted 150 acres in St. John's Berkeley in 1793, and reaped
virtually nothing.

The English market came promptly to esteem the long, strong,
silky sea-island fiber as the finest of all cotton; and the prices at
Liverpool rose before the end of the century to as high as 5 shil-
lings a pound. This brought fortunes in South Carolina. Captain James Sinkler, from a crop of 300 acres on his plantation,
"Belvedere," in 1794, gathered 216 pounds to the acre, which
at prices ranging from 50 to 75 cents a pound brought him a
gross return of $509 per laborer employed. Peter Gaillard of
St. John's Berkeley received for his crop of the same year an
average of $340 per hand; and William Brisbane of St. Paul's
earned so much in three years from 1796 to 1798 that he found
himself rich enough to retire from work and spend several years
in travel at the North and abroad. He sold his plantation to
William Seabrook at a price which the neighbors thought ruin-
ously high, but Seabrook recouped the whole of it from the
proceeds of two years' crops.

The gentlemen referred to by Professor Phillips, of course,
did not do the physical labor necessary for their famous
successes themselves—it was done by Negro slaves. From
these early days down to the "bumper" crop of this year
(1928) Negroes have carried on this burden to the great
profit of the whites.

DuBois gives an excellent survey of the Negro's early
contribution in work.

The problem of America in the fifteenth and sixteenth centuries was the problem of manual labor. It was settled by
importing white bond servants from Europe, and black servants
from Africa, and compelling the American Indians to work.
Indian slavery failed to play any great part because the comparatively small number of Indians in the West Indies were rapidly killed off by the unaccustomed toil or mingled their blood
and pooled their destinies with the Negroes. On the continent,
on the other hand, the Indians were too powerful both in numbers

and organization, to be successfully enslaved. The white bond servants and the Negroes therefore became the main laboring force of the New World and with their toil the economic development of the continent began. . . .

In this way the economic organization was provided by which the middle classes of the world were supplied with a cheap sweetening material derived from sugar cane; a cheap luxury, tobacco; larger quantities of rice; and finally, and above all, a cheap and universal material for clothing—cotton. These were things that all men wanted who had anything to offer in labor or materials for the satisfaction of their wants. The cost of raising them was a labor cost almost entirely because land in America was at that time endless in fertility and extent. The Old World trade, therefore, which sought luxuries in clothing, precious metals and stones, spices, etc., for the rich, transformed itself to a world-wide trade in necessities incomparably richer and bigger than its medieval predecessor because of its enormous basis of demand. Its first appearance was in the slave trade where the demand for the new American crops showed itself in a demand for the labor necessary to raise them; thus the slave trade itself was at the bottom of the rise of great commerce, and the beginning of modern international commerce. This trade stimulated invention and was stimulated by it. The well-being of European workers increased and their minds were stimulated. Economic and political revolution followed, to which America fell heir. New immigrants poured in. New conceptions of religion, government and work arose and at the bottom of it all and one of its efficient causes was the toil of the increasing millions of black slaves.[6]

Although "Queen Rice" and "King Cotton" monopolized the major part of Negro slave labor in these early years, he was bearing the burden elsewhere also. Although men, women and children labored in the fields; some of them were required to give early morning and late evening hours to domestic service at the "Big House" of the master. There was food to be cooked for master and fellow slaves, clothes to be washed, babies to be nursed, live stock to be attended to and innumerable and never-ending chores to be done. All these burdens the slaves bore for little and plain food and common and scanty clothing. The Negro did these tasks and developed himself as DuBois points out.

---

[6]DuBois, W. E. B.: *The Gift of Black Folk,* pages 60-62.

Why and how could the Negro bear these burdens? This is a question to cause a philosopher no little reflection. History suggests an answer. It is now generally admitted that the various racial characteristics are the result of environmental influences working to fit groups of people to survive and thrive in their respective geographical locations. The Negroes who came to South Carolina were individuals who had been accustomed to tropical or semi-tropical environments. They were physically fitted to live and labor in the new environment. They had a superior physical endowment for the work at hand and were constitutionally fitted to the climate. It is also true that many of them had previous experience at agricultural labors in Africa or in the Barbadoes, whence so many of the South Carolina Negro slaves were imported. It is a fact often overlooked that many of the Negroes in Africa were in the agricultural stage of civilization at this period, whereas the American Indians were in the hunting and fishing stage. This means that the African Negroes had two advantages over the American Indians which would tend to make them more successful and more desirable as burden bearers for South Carolina, struggling for a foothold. The Negroes were superior physically, being less susceptible to fevers, etc., and they were probably, to some extent, accustomed to the regular and somewhat monotonous toil necessary for agricultural work, especially that involved in the production of rice, indigo and cotton.

Then there were certain disadvantages of the Negro also which were advantages to the white slave owners. It is quite clear to any one who studies the records that aside from their physical and cultural weakness, the American Indians were further undesirable to the early settlers because they were near their fellows in the unsettled regions of the continent bordering on the sections occupied by the plantations.

The Indians, if enslaved and mistreated, could easily escape to the woods near by and foment trouble for the feeble and unprotected colonists by inciting the other Indians, who were fellow-tribesmen of those enslaved, to rise and revenge themselves upon the white intruders. Then, too, some Indian tribes had effective fighting organizations. The Negroes were at a serious disadvantage in this particular. Whether they came from the Barbadoes or from Africa, they were a long way from any possible help from their fellow-tribesmen. Philosophically and wisely they concluded that they must work or be exterminated by rough treatment. They chose the former. The Negro slave's careful and correct, though probably partly unconscious, analysis of the situation and his adoption of diplomacy as a means of survival is no small tribute to his intelligence and forecast his wonderful skill in adapting himself to western civilization. In the light of these facts it is not difficult to understand why the white settlers contended that "one Negro slave was worth four Indian workers." The general solution of the problem which the Negroes somehow reached was something like this: "We are here without our consent and against our wills. We are required to work by a master with complete authority. We are far from friends and relatives. Out yonder are the Indians, of whom we know nothing, and whose attitude toward us we cannot anticipate. We may run the risk of escaping to them and lose our lives. We can either work or die. We choose to work, learn, prosper perchance a little, and possibly escape at last. While we work we propose to flatter our masters and by other diplomatic means get all we can out of them for as little work as possible on our part." That was the philosophy of the Negro slave worker as he took up the unwelcome task of burden bearer for the advancing industrial revolution in the New World in general and in South Carolina in particular. Of course, this philosophy was not consciously formulated in the minds of the slaves, much less put in the writer's phraseology, neither was it publicly expressed in any way for obvious reasons. Yet a study of the records of Negro activity and achievement reveals a line of conduct that could hardly have come from any different philosophy. Then, too, we see the aftermaths of that philosophy in the conduct of the "old school" Negroes of today. It is evident that not all the slaves were guided by this philosophy, however. There were many instances of Negro slaves running away to cast their lot with the Indians, for better or worse. So we find the colonists carefully isolating their Negro slaves from all contacts with the Indians as far as possible under the circumstances. In spite of all their efforts, many Negro slaves made their escape. In South Carolina the Negro slaves were definitely encouraged to dislike and fight the Indians.

The Negro slaves did not refuse to risk their lives by joining the Indians because they were cowardly—not willing to risk their lives for freedom. This is proven by their willingness to join any war in which they were promised freedom as a reward for the risks involved. When the English colony of South Carolina was threatened by the Negro soldiers fighting for Spain, many Negroes joined the Spanish forces when offered freedom to fight with them. This is attested by the fact that very harsh regulations were made to prevent the slaves running away. Among the punishments were the branding and cutting the "hamstring" of the leg. Furthermore, during the Revolutionary War so many South Carolina Negroes joined the British forces upon their offer to give them liberty if they fought for the King, that the colony was forced to duplicate the offer on its own part. Thus it appears that many of the Negro slaves were as true Americans as Patrick Henry when he cried, "Give me liberty or give me death!" All this seems to prove that the Negroes refused to join the Indians largely because they considered such a project so problematic as to be of doubtful expediency and not worth the effort, rather than on account of fear of losing their lives.

We have seen that the Negro apparently brought to his task as burden bearer in South Carolina superior physical fitness, remarkable general adaptability, and a shrewd analysis of his new problems, resulting in a naïve but effective philosophy which enabled him to "carry on" where others failed and ultimately to make a contribution toward the building of modern industrial society in this state.

The Negro slave not only carried on and adapted himself with wonderful efficiency to the new order, but he brought with him into the New World and into South Carolina in particular a new attitude toward work. He lifted work out of its purely materialistic setting given it by the Western mind and placed it in the realm of spiritual values. Just as Jesus Christ made morality more sublime as well as more difficult by broadening its scope to include the psychological plane as well as that of overt acts, so the Negro lifted labor from a mere dirty grind into an agency for achieving the abundant life. The Negro never was, and is not now, convinced of the worth of "labor for its own dear sake." That is an Anglo-Saxon fiction. The Negro is not impressed with the philosophy, "work as a moral tonic." He is not even fundamentally concerned with labor as a necessary agency of acquiring the essentials of physical existence. These theories he accepts and practices in fact as wise policy for a member of Western modern industrialism. But the Negro makes a larger demand on labor than all this. He ever tends to consider labor as some sort of a narrow gate leading to happiness, to richer and fuller enjoyment. The Negro is forever asking why follow the rocky trail of labor if you cannot stop along the way and pick flowers, drink of the refreshing waters of babbling brooks, perchance chase butterflies, laugh and sing with the birds, and turn aside here and there to follow a mysterious by-way leading perhaps nowhere? Why let a drab thing like work interfere with living fully and freely? To the sophisticated, hard-boiled, materialistic business man of the white world this seems at best a naïve interpretation of the great necessity of our civilization. It seldom enters his thought that this attitude may be the ultimate philosophy of labor which the Negro's Oriental environment gave him without conscious effort at reflective thinking. Some would simply pass the matter up by saying that the Negro is crude and uncivilized, and hence knows not the value of work. Even so shrewd a student of his fellow-men as the late Booker T. Washington was perhaps misled in this particular. In answering his critics who said that industrial education was not necessary for the Negro because he knew how to work already from his contact with slavery, Wash-

ington said, "The Negro has 'been worked,' but now he needs
to learn to work." The great leader contended that there
is a vast difference between "being worked" and "working."
As usual, he was in line with Anglo-Saxon thinking, but in
this particular he lost contact with the Negro feeling.

The Negro believes in "having a good time," and "having
a good time" is not synonymous with working, in his opinion.
He tends to rush through his work to arrive at the good time
beyond. Perhaps the ultimate philosophy of work will em-
brace something of both the white and the colored man's
ideas.

This study of work as it relates to the Negro is especially
interesting to the writer, but perhaps time and space limits
dictate that we close the matter with an excellent summary
by the consummate artist of expression, Dr. W. E. Burghardt
DuBois:[7]

To all this we must add the peculiar spiritual contribution
which the Negro made to labor. Always physical fact has its
spiritual complement, but in this case the gift is apt to be forgotten or slurred over. This gift is the thing that is usually
known as "laziness." Again and again men speak of the laziness of Negro labor and some suppose that slavery of Negroes
was necessary on that account; and that even in freedom Negroes
must be "driven." On the other hand and in contradiction to
this is the fact that Negroes do work and work efficiently. In
South Africa and in Nigeria, in the Sudan and in Brazil, in the
West Indies and all over the United States Negro labor has
accomplished tremendous tasks. One of its latest and greatest
tasks has been the building of the Panama Canal. These two
sets of facts, therefore, would seem to be mutually contradictory,
and many a northern manager has seen the contradiction when,
facing the apparent laziness of Negro hands, he has attempted
to drive them and found out that he could not and at the same
time has afterward seen someone used to Negro labor get a
tremendous amount of work out of the same gangs. The explanation of all this is clear and simple: The Negro laborer has not
been trained in modern organized industry, but rather in quite
a different school.

The European workman works long hours and every day in
the week, because it is only in this way that he can support him-

---

[7] *The Gift of Black Folk,* pages 77-79.

self and family. With the present organization of industry and methods of distributing the results of industry any failure of the European workingman to toil hard and steadily would mean either starvation or social disgrace through the lowering of his standard of living. The Negro workingman, on the other hand, came out of an organization of industry which was communistic and did not call for unlimited toil on the part of the workers. There was work and hard work to do, for even in the fertile tropical lands the task of fighting weeds, floods, animals, insects and germs was no easy thing. But on the other hand the distribution of products was much simpler and fairer and the wants of the people were less developed. The black tropical worker therefore looked upon work as a necessary evil, and maintained his right to balance the relative allurements of leisure and satisfaction at any particular day, hour or season. Moreover in the simple work-organization of tropical or semi-tropical life individual desires of this sort did not usually disarrange the whole economic process or machine. The white laborer therefore brought to America the habit of regular continuous toil which he regarded as a great moral duty. The black laborer brought the idea of toil as a necessary evil, ministering to the pleasure of life. While the gift of the white laborer made America rich, or at least made many Americans rich, it will take the psychology of the black man to make it happy. New and better organization of industry and a clearer conception of the value of effort and a wider knowledge of the process of production must come in, so as to increase the wages of the worker and decrease rent, interest, and profit; and then the black laborer's subconscious contribution to current economics will be recognized as of tremendous and increasing importance.

The Negro slave laborer in South Carolina sang as he worked, sang as Negroes usually do. He received little in the way of wages, but he got something out of his work because of this philosophy of labor which the Negro somehow developed. The Negro insisted upon work as a means to play. The economic value of his work was appreciated by the white people, but his contribution to its philosophy has been ignored. However, the gift is here waiting to be received. The acceptance of the gift may yet help to solve some of our vexing modern industrial problems. For, as Joseph Lee[8] says in a contemporary magazine:

---

[8] *World's Work,* Vol. CIII, No. 1 (Nov., 1926).

The causes of unrest are not economic, but spiritual. What we are witnessing is the revolt of men who see life passing away without their ever having lived, who face the prospect of carrying their ideals and aspirations unfilled and unspoken to the grave.

Since play is the most deeply rooted instinct in human nature, the ideal is to have man's work satisfy his play instinct.   But civilization upsets theory, sidesteps play abruptly at the point where the child becomes a man.   There is no place in nine-tenths of industry and business for play.

The artist and the professional man can play while they work, but with foolproof machines and organized business, the majority of people today must live upon the margin left outside their work, or die.   Thus our present civilization must tend to permit a man to earn high enough wages to indulge in play outside of economic production.

As the Negro found a place for play in the drudgery of plantation labor, so he may somehow bring it into modern mechanical or industrial civilization.

The black man as a burden bearer in South Carolina created dollars for others and somehow was able to laugh and sing himself and, through his laughter and his songs, he enjoyed and immortalized his work.[9]   The employers are vastly richer today in dollars and property, but who can say that the employees, the burden bearers, have not, after all, achieved the greater good?   At any rate none can or will deny that he has made a valuable contribution to South Carolina's economic and industrial advancement.

---

[9]Jazz music and the plantation songs or "spirituals."

CHAPTER II

THE SLAVES' FIGHT FOR PHYSICAL FREEDOM

"Go down Moses,
Way down in Egypt land
Tell old Pharaoh
Let my people go."

* * * * *

"Oh, freedom! Oh freedom, Oh Freedom over me!
An' before I'll be a slave;
I'll be buried in my grave,
And go home to my Lord and be free."

* * * * *

All men love liberty and hate the
condition of slavery.—*Julius Caesar.*

A FEW years ago a very interesting little pamphlet was published under the title "Missing Pages in American History."[1] It deals with the activities of Negroes in the various wars of the United States. There are many other pages in American history which are still missing. We propose in this chapter to deal with some of these other "Missing Pages," those pages which should deal with the Negro's fight for physical freedom in South Carolina and the other Southern states. American history is strangely silent on this subject. There are whole libraries of books on the Civil War, its causes and effects. One of the causes of this war—the Negro's fight for freedom—is scarcely touched upon in the usual history. This ignoring of the Negro's own effort to achieve his freedom has resulted in a widespread, in fact almost universal, belief that the colored slaves did nothing at all to procure the great gift of freedom. Many people believe that freedom was a more or less undeserved and perhaps unwelcome blessing which was thrust upon the Negro by the events of history. This theory, plausible because of the absence of these missing pages, is excellent support for the theory of Negro inferiority. In fact, if it were really true that the Negro made no effort to fight for

---

[1] Laura E. Wilkes: Press of R. L. Pendleton (1919).

his own freedom this fact would be positive proof, in the opinion of the writer, that he is in truth inferior as a human being. It is unfortunate for those who would like to prove the Negro inferior, that the facts are plentiful to show that the Negroes did fight for their freedom for a long time and in many ways.

Facts which we expect to call attention to in this chapter seem to suggest that if the slaves had not fought for their freedom there probably would never have been a Civil War and consequently no freedom for the Negro, at least at the time he received it.

The facts upon which we base the opinions just mentioned above are perfectly familiar to every one who has a fair knowledge of the history of the United States. We think that any unprejudiced student of history will admit that if Negro slavery had not existed in the United States, largely concentrated in the southern part thereof, there never would have been a Civil War. It was the existence of slavery, largely in the South, and the agitation over it that caused the two sections—North and South—to develop such strong antipathy for each other that the South finally decided that it would be best for her to secede and "go her own way in peace" if possible. The argument over the principles of secession and local self-government was the immediate *occasion* of South Carolina's fatal step of secession but the remote or fundamental *cause* of South Carolina's great determination to exercise what she deemed to be her rights was her wish to protect her economic interests involved in the institution of Negro slavery.[2]

It is also probably true that slavery would have never become such a serious issue as to precipitate a war between the sections if slavery had not been so largely concentrated in the South and involved such a vast amount of property. It is generally admitted by historical writers of our day that slavery developed in the South rapidly and extensively because the agricultural type of life here was temporarily

---

[2]This point of view is supported by U. B. Phillips, C. G. Woodson and a host of other writers on United States history.

profitable under a slave regime. The apparent economic prosperity based upon slavery muffled the voice of every would-be reformer, muzzled the voice of the pulpit, and stilled the pen of practically every Southern writer. The autocracy of the "Almighty Dollar" ruled supreme and hardly a single "voice crying in the wilderness" could be heard to protest against "man's inhumanity to man" in the form of Negro slavery. It seems to be a well established fact that the invention of the cotton gin, resulting in a greater demand for cotton, was a cause of the increase of slaves in South Carolina and other Southern states because more cheap labor was necessary to cultivate the greater amount of cotton which could be rapidly separated from the seed by this machine and sold at a price cheap enough to appeal to a large market. This is a striking example of how a machine or any other invention may be a great blessing to humanity as a whole and yet a great disadvantage to some individuals or classes. The cotton gin also caused a further concentration of the slaves in the South as the greater demand for slave labor caused the price of slaves to rise and encouraged the people of the North to get rid of all slaves remaining by selling them South.

Enough has been said, all of which is substantiated in the well known writings of most of our American historians, to show that economic influences, growing out of the agricultural civilization of the South, were largely responsible for the growth of slavery in South Carolina and its rise to a place of prominence in the social order of the time. In our opinion this is quite different from saying that the North rejected slavery purely because it did not pay there as in the South. Not only was it true that slavery did not pay in the North but there were two classes of people in the North who furnished heroic reformers, of the material of which martyrs are made, who uncompromisingly opposed slavery on humanitarian grounds irrespective of financial or economic considerations. We refer to the Puritans and the Quakers, especially the latter. It is a significant fact that the only determined opposition to slavery which came out

of the South with sufficient power to attract national attention, such as that of Helper of North Carolina, was based
upon economic consideration.[3] It seems that there was very
little humanitarian propaganda against slavery originating
in the South. It is true that a few distinguished Southern
leaders, like Thomas Jefferson, offered mild opposition to
slavery on these grounds but they were weak and compro-
mising in their protests and the rising tide of economic power
completely swept their opposition away so that by the time
of the Civil War there was scarcely a voice to be heard in
the entire South in favor of freedom for humanitarian reasons.

The question of the placing of the responsibility for
the bringing on of the Civil War at the time it came, which
our discussion here has suggested, is a difficult problem. There
are many theories; most of them are plausible because there
is some truth in them. We dismiss as obviously biased those
theories which claim that the Civil War was caused by the
obstinacy of Abraham Lincoln or the ambition of Southern
political leaders. Some historical writers of no mean reputation, such as Professor U. B. Phillips, of the University
of Michigan, seem to be strongly of the opinion that the
war might have been obviated or at least postponed if it
had not been for the extreme radicalism of the abolitionists
such as William Lloyd Garrison, John Brown and others.[4]
Another theory is that the war came when it did because
leading statesmen, North and South, had come to see and
agree that the economic interests of the slave owners, known
at the time as "Southern interests," could not be longer protected and perpetuated without changing the nature of the
American government; in fact, without revolutionizing the
American social order.[5] The political leaders had come to
agree with Lincoln that "this nation cannot exist half free

---

[3]Helper: *The Impending Crisis;* also see Woodson, page 355.
[4]The writer received these impressions listening to Professor Phillips
lecture on the "History of the Ante-Bellum South" in a Harvard
University summer session course, 1921.
[5]Such was the final conviction of Tombs of Georgia, Calhoun of South
Carolina, and others.

and half slave. A house divided against itself cannot stand."
The Southern statesmen were not willing to follow the Great
Emancipator further and declare, "We do not expect the
house to fall but we do expect it to cease to be divided."
The Southern statesmen seemed to believe that the house
might perhaps stand by becoming all slave or by being transformed into a kind of two-family apartment house. But
Lincoln did not think of a united house in terms of an apartment building. The Southern statesman decided that the
house would have to be divided into two separate homes.
Lincoln interpreted this as an attempt to demolish the house.
The Civil War came out of the clash of opinions and deter-
minations.

Our own theory accepts these latter mentioned theories
as partly true. But further, our theory insists that the
humble, forgotten Negro slave figured in all this consciously
and unconsciously, directly and indirectly, because, all along
the line, from 1619 to 1860, he was fighting for his freedom.
These "missing pages" of American history which we here
propose to sketch will record the ways in which he fought.
It will be our task here to show how the Negro's fighting
spirit, constantly in action, though often in strange and
peculiar ways, was often the inspiration and always the ally
of those influences and events which all serious and reputable
historians admit to be the things which made freedom for
the Negro ultimately inevitable.

William Pickens, one of the most distinguished of the
younger group of Negro leaders in the United States, a Phi
Beta Kappa graduate of Yale, and a native son of South
Carolina, once made a remark in a lecture which I heard, to
the effect that "the first abolitionist was the runaway slave."
His remark is full of philosophy. The runaway slave was
obviously the cause of the famous Fugitive Slave Law. Also
the Fugitive Slave Law was the never failing, perpetual inspiration of the inexorable abolitionists. The fugitive slave
made slave property uncertain.

Almost at the instant that slavery was introduced into
South Carolina slaves began to run away. The fugitive slave

was a real courageous fighter. This is readily realized when
we admit there are many more ways of fighting than physical
conflict. The fugitive slave reasoned that this method of
abolishing his personal slavery was the safest and surest
method usually open to him. It was far from easy and safe.
The early slaves in South Carolina found difficulty in deciding whither they might safely run away and hide. The
Indians were near by, but the black slave could not be sure
of a sympathetic reception for him from these wild red men.
However, many of the first fugitive slaves went to the Indians
and threw themselves upon their generosity and kindness.
In many instances these fugitives were freely received and
generously treated and cared for. Many of them inter-
married with the Indians and some of their descendants were
among the greatest leaders of the Indians.†

The love of freedom was so strong in some of the slaves
that they ran away even though they had no definite place to
go; they ran away and died in the forests and mountains
if they could not live on the grains, wild fruits and birds
which they could find out in these hiding places. As soon
as the slaves somehow got some vague ideas of the geography
of the country and some idea of the direction in which they
could discover friends who would help them to escape, they
began to run away toward the North into the states above
the Mason and Dixon Line and even into Canada. The slave
who undertook to escape from slavery in South Carolina by
fleeing to the North was evidently undertaking a long, tedious
and very dangerous journey. With the methods of travel
available in those early times and with the handicaps of a
fugitive from the clutches of the law, backed by almost solid
public opinion throughout the length and breadth of the
South, the distance to freedom must have indeed seemed great
to the lonely black slave meditating and planning his escape
from some plantation in this state. It is true that the escaping slave could always depend upon co-operation from the
majority of his fellow-slaves, but he could not be sure of all

---

†The wife of the famous Osceola is an example. Brawley: *Social
History*, page 92.

of them. Some of the slaves felt that they were running too great risks in attempting to help their fellow sufferers to escape so they refused to do so. Therefore the fugitive had to be very careful because one mistake in reference to who was a friend or enemy among his fellow slaves might cause him to be captured and returned to a revengeful master before he was fairly started on the rocky road to freedom.

The slave owners developed a good system of apprehending the slaves because they realized that this habit of running away was one of the most subtle and dangerous methods of fighting slavery that the well nigh helpless slaves could command. As soon as it was detected that a slave had escaped, a descriptive advertisement of him was scattered far and wide as quickly and efficiently as the methods of communication available at that time would permit. Rewards of no mean value were offered for the capture of these fugitives, sometimes dead or alive, and a vigorous search and pursuit were immediately initiated. Dreadful bloodhounds trained especially for the purpose, and men little less bloodthirsty than the hounds, were put upon the trail. The fugitive was hotly and relentlessly pursued. The slave chasers felt no scruples against killing the slave as they would a fleeing rabbit or deer if he could not be captured alive or if he put up a dangerous resistance when cornered. Many escaping slaves lost their lives in fierce conflicts with bloodhounds or in desperate efforts to overcome the handicaps offered by cold, rain, rivers, mountain-passes and many other obstacles perhaps never known or recorded. In *Uncle Tom's Cabin*, Harriet Beecher Stowe gives a masterly and realistic description of the heroic escape of "Liza" to the land of freedom. This is a good example of what hundreds of unknown slaves went through in their fight for freedom by way of the Underground Railroad. If anyone can read the story of the heroic struggles made by the slaves who attempted to run away from slavery without being willing to admit that the fugitive slave was *fighting* for freedom *with skill and courage*, we know not how to classify such a man. The slave undertook a journey more dangerous than Lindbergh's recent transatlantic flight.

The successful runaway slave was not only an abolitionist in the narrow sense in that he abolished his own personal slavery, but in a larger and more important sense he helped the abolition movement by calling out from the slave-owning class attempts at retaliation which were so cruel and inhuman that they advertised the whole system as infamous. The fugitive slaves agitated slave owners and goaded them into acts and policies which ultimately injured their cause and tremendously aided the abolition movement. As stated above, it is obviously a fact that the fugitive slaves were the cause of the Fugitive Slave Law which was responsible for an enormous amount of friction between the North and South and was really one of the important immediate causes of the Civil War. The fugitive slaves, perpetually fighting for their freedom, kept before the friends of humanity this open sore upon the body of the American democracy.

The romance of their never ceasing fight furnished inspiration and concrete material for multitudes of anti-slavery propagandists with less influence and skill than Harriet Beecher Stowe, but nevertheless with some effect. The fact that the slaves were willing to take the risks involved in attempting to escape in the face of the great odds against them was consistent and impressive proof to the abolitionists that these slaves were men worthy to be free and therefore sufferers in a state of slavery. Other evidence along this line was the great skill shown by many of the slaves in their methods of eluding the white officers of the South and effecting their freedom in spite of the carefully laid plans of the "superior" whites. The Underground Railroad saw many flashes of genius along its busy lines. As examples of skill and fortitude often displayed by fugitive slaves, we quote below the stories of "Henry Box Brown" and William and Ellen Craft, who though they did not escape from South Carolina, were doubtless matched by many who left this state.

The marvelous escape of Henry Box Brown was published widely in papers when the anti-slavery agitation was being carried on. In point of interest his case is no more remarkable than any other; indeed, he did not suffer near as much as many. He was a piece of property in the city of Richmond. He seemed to be a man of inventive mind, and knew that it was no small task to escape the vigilance of Virginia slave hunters, or the wrath of an enraged master, for attempting to escape to a land of liberty. The ordinary modes of travel, he concluded, might prove disastrous to his hopes; he therefore hit upon a new invention, which was to have himself boxed up and forwarded to Philadelphia by express. Size of box was two feet wide, two feet, eight inches deep and three feet long. His food consisted of few small biscuits. He had a large gimlet which he intended to use for fresh air if necessary. Satisfied that this would be far better than to remain in slavery, he entered the box. It was safely nailed up and hooped with five hickory hoops, and addressed by his friend, James A. Smith, a shoe dealer, to Wm. Johnson, Arch street, Philadelphia, marked "This side up, with care." It was twenty-six hours from the time he left Richmond until he arrived in Philadelphia. The notice, "This side up," did not avail, for the box was often roughly handled. For a while the box was upside down and he was on his head for miles. The members of the "vigilance committee" of Philadelphia had been informed that he would be started. One of the committee went to the depot at half past two o'clock in the morning to look after the box, but did not find it. The same afternoon he received a telegram from Richmond. "Your case of goods is shipped and will arrive tomorrow morning." Mr. McKim, who had been engineering this undertaking, found it necessary to change the program, for it would not be safe to have the express bring it directly to the anti-slavery office. He went to a friend who was extensively engaged in mercantile business who was ready to aid him. This friend, Mr. Davis, knew all the Adams Express drivers, and it was left to him to pay a trusty man $5.00 in gold to go next morning and bring the box directly to the anti-slavery office. Those present to behold the resurrection were J. M. McKim, Professor C. D. Cleveland, Lewis Thompson and Wm. Still. The box was taken into the office. When the door had been safely locked, Mr. McKim rapped quietly on the lid of the box and called out, "All right." Instantly came the answer from within, "All right, sir." Saw and hatchet soon removed the five hickory hoops, and raised the lid of the box. Rising up in his box, Brown reached out his hand, saying, "How do you do, gentlemen?" He was about as wet as if he had come up out of the Delaware. He first sang the psalm beginning with these words: "I waited patiently for the Lord, and he heard my prayer." At the home of Lucretia Mott he received a cordial reception, and was entertained for some time, when he went to Boston.

The success of this undertaking encouraged Smith, who had nailed him up in the box, to render similar service to two other young bondmen. But, unfortunately, in these attempts the undertaking proved a failure. The young men, after being duly expressed and some distance on the road, were, through the agency of the telegraph, betrayed, and the heroic young fugitives were taken from the box and dragged back to helpless bondage. Smith was arrested and imprisoned for seven years in a Richmond penitentiary. He lost all his property, was refused witnesses on his trial, and for five long months, in hot weather, he was kept heavily chained in a cell 4 by 8 feet in dimensions. Mr. Smith had, by his efforts, aided many to gain their liberty. He received five stabs aimed at his heart by a bribed assassin. But all these things did not move him from his purpose. After his release he went North and was united in marriage at Philadelphia to a lady who had remained faithful to him through all his suffering.[6]

* * * * * *

William and Ellen Craft were slaves in the state of Georgia. The desire to become free became so strong that they commenced planning to escape. Ellen, being fair, would pass for a white man, and was to act the part of master, while William was to be the servant. She dressed in a fashionable suit of male attire, and was to pass as a young planter. But Ellen was beardless. After mature reflection her face was muffled up as though the young planter was suffering from a face or toothache. In order to prevent the method of registering at hotels, Ellen put her right hand in a sling, put on green spectacles, and pretended to be very hard of hearing and depended upon her faithful servant. Ellen, disguised as a young planter, was to have nothing to do but to hold herself subject to her ailments and put on the air of superiority. The servant was always ready to explain in case of inquiry.

They stopped at first class hotels in Charleston, Richmond and Baltimore, and arrived safely in Philadelphia, where the rheumatism disappeared, her right arm was unslung, her toothache was gone, the beardless face was unmuffled, the deaf heard and spoke, the blind saw. The strain on Ellen's nerves, however, had tried her severely, and she was physically prostrated for some time. Her husband, William, was thoroughly colored, and was a man of marked ability and good manners, and full of pluck. They were sent to Boston, where they lived happily until the Fugitive Slave Law was passed. Then slave hunters from Macon,

---

[6]Nichols and Crogman: *The Progress of a Race*, Chap. V, pages 98-101; 103-104.

Georgia, were soon on their track, but the sympathy of friends in Boston would not permit their being returned to Georgia. It was, however, considered best for them to seek a country where they would not be in daily fear of slave capturers, backed by the United States Government. They were therefore sent by their friends to Great Britain.

In England the Crafts were highly respected. After the emancipation they returned to the United States with two children, and after visiting Boston and neighboring places, William purchased a plantation near Savannah, and lived there with his family.[7]

Such incidents as these greatly enraged the slave owners and encouraged the abolitionists. One very important fact which should not be overlooked in discussing this fight for freedom put up by the fugitive slaves is the fact that many of the bravest and best officers for the Underground Railroad were Negroes. Among them was William Still, who was chairman and secretary of one of the branches. In the preface to his book on the Underground Railroad, Mr. Still describes his own work as follows:

In these records will be found interesting narratives of the escapes of men, women and children from the present House of Bondage; from cities and plantations; from rice swamps and cotton fields; from kitchens and mechanic shops; from border state and gulf states; from cruel masters and mild masters; some guided by the North star alone; penniless, braving the perils of the land and sea, eluding the keen scent of the bloodhound as well as the more dangerous pursuit of the savage slave hunter; some from secluded dens and caves of the earth, where for months and years they had been hidden away awaiting the chance to escape; from mountains and swamps, where indescribable sufferings and other privations had patiently been endured. Occasionally fugitives came in boxes and chests, and not infrequently some were secreted in steamers and vessels, and in some instances journeyed hundreds of miles in skiffs. Men disguised in female attire and women dressed in the garb of men have under very trying circumstances triumphed in thus making their way to freedom. And here and there, when all other modes of escape seemed cut off, some, whose fair complexions have rendered them indistinguishable from their Anglo-Saxon brethren, feeling that they could endure the yoke no longer, with assumed airs of impor-

---

[7] Ibid.

tance, such as they had been accustomed to see their masters show when traveling, have taken the usual modes of conveyance and have even braved the most scrutinizing inspection of slave holders, slave catchers, and car conductors, who were ever on the alert to catch those who were considered base and white enough to practice such deception.

Doubtless South Carolina furnished her full quota of these heroes. Many other colored agents of the systems did valient work. We cannot mention them all, but the grand old warrior "Sojourner Truth" should always be mentioned in such a record.

We deem it fitting and proper to speak chiefly in this work, especially in this chapter, about the efforts of Negroes themselves in achieving their freedom by the method of running away, but we must here make it clear that we do not wish to ignore or minimize the wonderful assistance given the Negroes in this fight by their courageous self-sacrificing white friends. For example, Calvin Fairbanks, who spent over a decade in a Kentucky prison for helping slaves to escape, described his own sufferings as follows:

I was flogged, sometimes bowed over a chair or some other object, often receiving seventy lashes four times a day, and at one time received 107 blows at one time, particles of flesh being thrown upon the wall several feet away.

Captain Walker, a white engineer engaged in railroad construction in Florida, aided slaves to escape and for this "crime" was branded with the capital letters "S.S." on his right hand. This incident called forth the following poetic lines from the abolitionist poet, John Greenleaf Whittier:

"Then lift that manly right hand, bold plowman of the
    wave,
Its branded palm shall prophesy Salvation to the Slave;
Hold up its fire-wrought language, that whoso reads
    may feel
His heart swell strong within him, his sinews change to
    steel;
Hold it up before our sunshine, up against our Northern
    air.
Ho! men of Massachusetts, for the love of God, look
    there!

Take it henceforth for your standard, like the Bruce's
    heart of yore;
In the dark strife closing round ye let that hand be seen
    before." [8]

This poem is a small extract from the literature which
the fugitive slaves inspired. If any one doubts the great
problem the fugitive created let him read the newspapers and
magazines published in South Carolina, in the South, and all
over the country while this fight was going on.

It can be seen from all this that the fugitive slaves were
not only consciously fighting for their own individual freedom, but they were sometimes consciously and sometimes unconsciously fighting for the cause of the ultimate general
emancipation of all the slaves, since the practice of slaves
running away caused the famous Fugitive Slave Law to be
enacted which helped bring on the Civil War and it made
property in slaves uncertain or uneconomical. The Negro
officers of the Underground Railroad and other Negro assistants of fugitive slaves, of course, realized that they were
working in the ranks of the abolitionists.

The Negro slaves of this state also fought for their freedom in more direct and definite ways. Many fought for freedom through hard labor and rigid economy. Some fought for
freedom by what Doctor DuBois calls the "appeal to reason."

Very early in the history of slavery in South Carolina
some of the slaves began to fight for freedom by trying to
purchase themselves or their relatives. It was a real fight
for a slave to purchase himself, not to speak of any of his
people. This difficulty grew out of several things. The slave
had to work most of the time for his master and therefore
had only "spare" or "overtime" to work and accumulate
money with which to buy himself. Many of them worked for
miserably low wages on Saturday afternoons, on Sundays,
and on holidays. It often took a very long time for the
worker to save enough to buy himself or a loved one. The
wages were scarcely over $20.00 per month as a maximum;
slaves found it difficult to earn more. Many fought it through
to a successful conclusion and thereafter enjoyed a few fleet-

---

[8] Ibid., page 92.

ing years of comparative freedom. In a few exceptional cases unusually generous or far-sighted masters would allow their slaves to hire themselves from their masters. All they could earn above the amount they paid the master they were at liberty to use in any way they chose. The greatest desire of most of the slaves being freedom, they usually saved to buy themselves.

This act of giving the slave the opportunity to buy himself was not always due to humanitarian or Christian sentiments. In some instances, it was due to the fact that the slave owners realized that slave labor was an economic failure and they planned, by offering the slaves the great blessing of personal freedom, to make him approximate the efficiency and economy of a free laborer. The scheme was not a bad one, judged by results procured in several instances. This point is well explained by Booker T. Washington as follows:

When he (the master) allowed them (the slaves) to buy their own freedom, it was a practical recognition that the system was economically a mistake, since the slave who could purchase his freedom was one whom it did not pay to hold as a slave. This fact was clearly recognized by a planter in Mississippi who declared that he had found it paid to allow the slaves to buy their freedom. In order to encourage them to do this he devised a method by which they might purchase their freedom in installments. After they had saved a certain amount of money by extra labor, he permitted them to buy one day's freedom a week. With this much capital invested in themselves, they were then able to purchase, in a much shorter time a second, a third and a fourth day's freedom, until they were entirely free. A somewhat similar method was sometimes adopted by certain freedmen for purchasing the freedom of their families. In such a case the father would purchase, for instance, a son or a daughter. The children would then join with their father in purchasing the other members of the family.[9]

Illustrative of their fight for freedom through the method of purchase is the wonderful story of George and Susan Kibby, of Saint Louis, told by Trexler as follows:

In 1853 Kibby entered into a contract with Henry C. Hart and his wife Elizabeth L. Hart to purchase their Negress named

---

[9] Washington, B. T.: *The Story of the Negro Race*, Vol. I, page 194.

Susan, whom he wished to marry. The price was eight hundred dollars. The contract is devoid of all sentiment and is as coolly commercial as though merchandise was the subject under consideration. Kibby had two hundred dollars to pay down. He was to pay the remainder in three yearly installments, and upon the fulfillment of the contract Susan was to receive her freedom. In the meantime Kibby was to take possession of Susan under the following conditions: "Provided, however, said Kibby shall furnish such security as may be required by the proper authorities, to such bond as may be required for completing such emancipation, so as to absolve . . . Hart and wife from all liability for the future support and maintenance of said Susan and her increase. This obligation to be null and void on the part of said Hart and wife, if said Kibby shall fail for the period of one month, after the same shall for the time become due and payable, to pay to said Hart and wife said sums of money as hereinbefore specified, of the annual interest thereon, and in the event of such failure, all of the sum or sums of money whether principal or interest, which may have been paid by the said Kibby shall be forfeited, and said Kibby shall restore to said Hart and wife said Negro girl, Susan, and such child or children as she may then have, such payments being hereby set off against the hire of said Susan, who is this day delivered into the possession of said Kibby. And said Kibby hereby binds himself to pay said sums of money as hereinbefore specified, and is not to be absolved therefrom on the death of said Susan, or any other contingency or plea whatever. He also binds himself to keep at his own expense a satisfactory policy of insurance on the life of said Susan, for the portion of her price remaining unpaid, payable to T. J. Brent, trustee for Mrs. E. L. Hart, and that said Susan shall be kept and remain in this County, until the full and complete execution of this contract."

Attached to the back of this contract are the receipts for the installments. The first reads thus: "Received of George Kibby one mule of the value of sixty-five dollars on within contract Feb. 1st, 1854, H. C. Hart." The fifth and last payment was made on December 3, 1855—two years lacking six days following the date of the contract. Accompanying the contract is the deed of manumission of Susan, likewise dated December 3. Thus Kibby fulfilled his bargain in less than the time allowed him.[10]

In and around Charleston there were many cases to equal these in pathos and tragedy. In fact, in almost every locality

---

[10] Quoted by Weatherford: *The Negro From Africa to America*, page 175.

of the state there can be found a few very old persons who can tell you wonderful stories of how men and women struggled and sacrificed to "buy" their freedom, which really belonged to them by natural rights.

The Negro slaves in South Carolina made a fight for freedom through appeals to the sense of fair play and feeling of common humanity which the Southern white people always possessed. Of course the nature of slavery was such that it encouraged the slaves to be interested on the question of freedom. Diplomacy on the part of the slave dictated that he not be radical on the question of abolition of slavery, yet there were some Negroes who did not hesitate to condemn the system and to denounce their own masters for wrongfully holding them in bondage. Many of these brave pleaders for freedom practically became martyrs for their frank opposition to the prevailing regime, but their sacrifice was a worthwhile contribution in the Negro slave's fight for freedom. The Negroes also presented a kind of mute appeal to reason by conduct worthy of freemen. Many a slave convinced his master that he ought to be free because he conducted himself with such manly and honorable bearing that the master's reason suggested that it was folly to deprive such a man of his freedom. The Negro slave who displayed the essential qualities of manhood in so far as they could be displayed under the limitations of the life of a slave was a tremendously effective argument in favor of emancipation to any reasonable man. Such individuals among the slaves were proof that the theory of racial inferiority was a fiction. As this belief in the Negro's hopeless inferiority was one of the fundamental pillars of the slave owner's philosophy, when this theory was exploded the whole system seemed to weaken.

The character of the Negro was continually disturbing the tranquillity of the minds, the solace of the consciences and the satisfaction of the souls of the slave owners. All this constituted a part of the Negro slave's marvelous *fight* for freedom.

The slave rightly drafted the Christian religion to help him challenge the justice and righteousness of slavery. When a Negro slave professed and adopted the religion of Jesus Christ he thereby became a "brother in Christ" of his master and oppressor. The Negro was not slow to impress the master with the fact that slavery was incompatible as a relationship between fellow Christians. The Negro was, even as he is today, too diplomatically polite to be offensively rude, but how could the sensitive slave owner hear his fellow Christian, the slave, singing "Everybody talkin' 'bout Heaven ain't goin' dare" without feeling that he was being gently rebuked for holding the singer in bondage contrary to the teachings of Him who taught his disciples to pray "Our Father" and demolished the argument for racial inferiority with the matchless story of the Good Samaritan? This was indeed subtle but very effective fighting for freedom. We may illustrate how this subtle method of fighting for freedom accomplished results by quoting a statement from the pen of Henry Laurens, distinguished South Carolina statesman and leader. Writing to his son this great South Carolinian expressed himself as follows: "You know, my dear son, I abhor slavery. I was born in a country where slavery had been established by British kings and parliaments, as well as by the laws of that country ages before my existence. I found the Christian religion and slavery growing under the same authority and cultivation. I nevertheless disliked it. In former days there was no combating the prejudices of men supported by interest; the day I hope is approaching when, from principles of gratitude as well as justice, every man will strive to be foremost in showing his readiness to comply with the golden rule." What caused Laurens, born and nursed in the cradle of the slave regime, to "abhor slavery"? Some may say that it was his great innate love of freedom. There may be something in that, but the writer is constrained to believe that the character of the Negro slaves and their half mute appeal for freedom had much to do with converting this great man and many others of his way of thinking. The attitudes and actions of many men, like Laurens in South Carolina, resulted in the freeing of many Negroes and many of these free Negroes used their liberty to fight more effectively for freedom for all.

It must be said that a few of the free Negroes failed to catch the vision of the righteousness of general abolition and themselves entered into the support of the slave regime by purchasing and holding slaves themselves as far as their means and ability would permit them. It is said that about 130 Negroes in and around Charleston owned 390 slaves at one time before the Civil War.[11] But these Negro slave owners were hopelessly in the minority and were insignificant internal opponents of the Negro in his self-directed fight for freedom. They were merely the exception that proved the general rule that the freedom of the Negro was achieved like that of all free peoples, because he fought for it, assisted by friends of the other races. It should be noted also that many of the Negroes who held slaves did so to keep them from being sold into other hands where they would receive less sympathy. This idea was given the writer in conversation with Miss Mae Holloway in Charleston. Her family owned slaves.

Although the writer believes that the line of conduct which we have discussed thus far is clearly a part of the Negro slave's fight for freedom, there are doubtless those who think that most of this is a belabored or far-fetched argument. However, there is yet to be recorded the story of more definite fighting—unmistakable physical fighting—which the Negro slaves engaged in to procure the coveted prize of freedom. The Negroes started fighting physically for their freedom as soon as they were captured on their native soil in Africa. Many of them died there fighting; others died in conflict on the sea. Still others began fighting as soon as they landed in America. A few fought single-handed and a few joined the Indians and battled with them.

It is a fact that the majority of the Negro slaves who finally came to South Carolina did not engage in physical conflict to procure their freedom because, as we have said previously, they did not consider that a safe or efficient method under the circumstances which prevailed. If they engaged in open rebellion the chances were ten to one that they would be destroyed. The slave regime was well organized and forti-

[11] List of Charleston tax payers, 1860.

fied against rebellion. Those who showed signs of chronic determination to appeal to physical resistance were cruelly punished and ruthlessly eliminated. A distinguished Negro writer has expressed this idea as follows: "A long, awful process of selection chose out the listless, ignorant, sly and humble and sent to heaven the proud, the vengeful and the daring. The old African warrior spirit died away of violence and a broken heart."[12] But "the old African warrior spirit died" hard and was instrumental in causing much bloodshed before its heart was broken. In fact, the Negro slaves in South Carolina kept on fighting physically from time to time until Abraham Lincoln hit slavery the knockout blow with his famous Emancipation Proclamation and millions of former slaves all over the South jubilantly sang, "I Thank God I'm Free At Last!"

Brawley, DuBois, Woodson and other Negro writers agree that the Negroes who first came into North American territory as slaves were far more warlike and prone to rise and fight single-handed, if necessary, for their freedom, than those who came along later, when the process of selection which DuBois referred to in the quotation above had been in operation long enough to produce its deadly work.

As early as 1711 we have definite records of slaves who had run away organizing and fighting their masters.[13] The next date that attracts our attention in reference to this matter is 1720.[14] At this time we find that a few Negroes organized and killed a white man, a white woman and a Negro boy. It seems that the first well organized rebellion conducted by South Carolina slaves was attempted about 1730. Holland describes this attempt as follows:

The first open rebellion which took place in Carolina where the Negroes were actually armed and embodied, is traced as far back as the year 1730. In the month of August of that year, a conspiracy was detected, the plan of which had been long secretly agitated. Two methods had been proposed in order to carry it into execution; one, that the Negroes in each family, in the dead

---

[12]W. E. B. DuBois: *John Brown.*
[13]Holland: *A Refutation of Calumnies, etc.,* page 63.
[14]Ibid.

of the night, were to murder all their masters and the white men of every family in the neighborhood in which there were no Negroes. There was so much distrust and want of confidence, however, among them, that they resolved to adopt the other proposition, which was, that they should assemble in the neighborhood of the town, under the pretense of a "Dancing-Bout," and, when proper preparations were made, to rush into the heart of the city, take possession of all the arms and ammunition they could find, and murder all the white men, and then turn their forces to the different plantations. Such was the secrecy with which this conspiracy was conducted, that it was discovered only a short time previous to its projected explosion, and many of the Negroes had actually assembled. As soon as the discovery was made, the citizens, by private orders and without noise, rendezvoused at their respective points of alarm, and immediately marched to the place where the Negroes were collected, and without the slightest opposition took the whole of them prisoners. The ringleaders of the rebellion were immediately executed, and the remainder returned to their daily labor and obedience.

In the year 1739, there were no less than three (3) formidable insurrections among our slaves, in which many valuable lives were lost and, during the fury and devastation of which, the most detestable outrages were committed.

They were all, however, instantly quelled, and the measure of retribution was full to overflowing. These insurrections were all fomented by the Spaniards in St. Augustine, who clandestinely gave protection to all the fugitive slaves from this colony, and by sending their Priests as emissaries among our Negroes created among them such wild and visionary ideas of liberty and freedom, as finally plunged them into open rebellion.[15]

Hewitt gives us the following interesting account of this insurrection:

At this time (about the year 1740), there were above 40,000 Negroes in the province. Long had liberty and protection been promised and proclaimed to them by the Spaniards at Augustine, nor were all the Negroes in the province strangers to the proclamation. At different times Spanish emissaries had been found secretly tampering with them, and persuading them to fly from slavery. Five Negroes, who were cattle hunters, at Indian Land, some of whom belonged to Captain McPherson, after wounding his son and killing another man, made their escape. Several

---

[15] Ibid. (Holland).

more attempting to get away were taken, tried, and hanged at Charles Town.

While Carolina was kept in a state of constant fear and agitation from this quarter, and insurrection openly broke out in the heart of the settlement which alarmed the whole province, a number of Negroes having assembled together at Stono, first surprised and killed two young men in a warehouse, and then plundered it of guns and ammunition. Being thus provided with arms, they elected one of their number captain and agreed to follow him, marching towards the southwest, with colors flying and drums beating, like a disciplined company. They forcibly entered the house of Mr. Godfrey, and having murdered him, his wife, and children, they took all the arms he had in it, set fire to the house and then proceeded toward Jacksonborough. In their way they plundered and burned every house, killing every white person they found in them and compelling the Negroes to join them. Governor Bull, returning to Charleston from the southwest, met them, and observing them armed, spread the alarm, which soon reached the Presbyterian Church at Wiltown, where Archibald Stobo was preaching to a numerous congregation of planters in that quarter. By law of the province, all planters were obliged to carry their arms to church, which at this critical juncture proved a very useful and necessary regulation. The women were left in church trembling with fear, while the militia, under the command of Captain Bee, marched in quest of the Negroes, who by this time had become formidable, from the number that joined them. They had marched about twelve miles and spread desolation through all the plantations in their way. They halted in an open field, and began to sing and dance, by way of triumph. During these rejoicings, the militia discovered them, and stationed themselves in different places around them, to prevent them from making their escape. One party advanced into the open field and attacked them, and, having killed some Negroes, the remainder took to the woods and were dispersed. Many ran back to their plantations, in hopes of escaping suspicion from the absence of their masters; but the greater part were taken and tried. Such as had been compelled to join them, contrary to their inclination, were pardoned, but all the chosen leaders and first insurgents suffered death.

All Carolina was struck with terror and consternation by this insurrection, in which above twenty persons were murdered before it was quelled.

The following document is important and informing in this connection. We insert it complete:

PETITION AND REPRESENTATION

to His Majesty of the present state of the Province.

To The King's Most Excellent Majesty.

The Humble Petition and Representation of the Council and Assembly of your Majesty's Province of South Carolina upon the present state of the said Province:

Most Gracious Sovereign:

We, your Majesty's most dutiful and Loyal Subjects, the Members of your Majesty's Council, and the Members of the Common House of Assembly of this your Majesty's Province of South Carolina, now met together in General Assembly, to take under consideration the dangerous situation in which the Province now is, most humbly beg leave to represent to your Majesty, that it is with the utmost grief and concern we find this Province greatly reduced and weakened, by a series of Calamities and Misfortunes which have attended it for some time past. The Small Pox, in the year 1738, succeeded by a pestilential fever, in the year 1739, whereby numbers who had escaped the first were carried off by the last. That again succeeded by an insurrection of our slaves in which many of the inhabitants were murdered in a barbarous and cruel manner; and that no sooner quelled than another projected in Charles Town, and a third lately in the very heart of the settlements, but happily discovered time enough to be prevented. Wrestling with difficulties at home, we see ourselves at the same time exposed to dangers from abroad, to enemys very near, and by far too numerous and powerful for us; and that the many succours which your Majesty has been graciously pleased from time to time to give us, and what we, weak and as we are, have been able to do for ourselves, comes far short of your Majesty's Royal Intention and expectations from thence.

It is with great reason, we apprehend, that that part of our calamity, proceeding from the frequent attempts of our Slaves, arises from the designs and intrigues of our enemys, the Spaniards in St. Augustine and Florida, who have had the ruin and destruction of these, your Majesty's Colonies of South Carolina and Georgia, long in view. Witness the great preparations made at Havanna and St. Augustine, about three years ago, for a powerful descent on these Provinces; and since that, in time of profound peace also, a proclamation published at St. Augustine, in his Catholic Majesty's name, promising freedom and other

encouragement to all slaves that should desert from your
Majesty's subjects of this province and join them. In consequence of which proclamation many have already deserted, and
others encouraged daily to do the same; and even those who have
committed the most inhuman murders are there harboured, entertained and caressed. Such, may it please your Majesty, was
the situation of this Province when General Oglethorpe applied
to us to assist your Majesty's Forces in attacking St. Augustine.
Induced by the assurances we had from that general, and the
Commodore of your Majesty's Ships of War, together, met in the
harbour of Charleston, of the great probability there was of
success, and by the advantage, we were sensible would thereby
accrue to your Majesty's subjects of this Province and Georgia,
and for the glory of your Majesty's arms, in reducing a fortress
which stands an eye-sore to the British Dominions in North
America; and as such has been before attempted by this Province,
but without success, we exerted ourselves and cheerfully voted
such a supply of forces as that general thought sufficient to
succeed in that expedition; together with a great quantity of
provisions, artillery, warlike stores, vessels for transportation,
arms and presents for 500 Indians, and many other necessaries;
but considering the uncertainty of warlike events, and that the
enemy might be stronger than that the general had represented
them to be, we added 200 men more. The whole expense amount-
ing to a greater sum than our present circumstance could well
bear. With this additional reinforcement, we had the greatest
reason to hope for success; and more especially, as to all this, was
afterwards added, your Majesty's great supply sent to the general, of warlike stores proper for such an undertaking. But so
it has fallen out, that with hearts full of sorrow and anxiety, are
we now obliged to represent to your Majesty, that this attempt
proved altogether unsuccessful, and the troops sent from this
Province, by express orders dated the 4th instant, from General
Oglethorpe to their commanding officer, ordered to withdraw
from before St. Augustine, and to carry off or destroy the cannon
made use of by them against the enemy. Whether the bad success of this expedition proceeds from the misconduct, or from
any other cause, we shall not presume to judge. But, may it
please your Majesty, such being the issue and event of this
unhappy expedition, in which all our hopes were placed, we are
now exposed to a powerful enemy, roused with resentment and
encouraged by our disappointment, are become more formidable
than ever, and if not speedily prevented by a superior force, may
soon turn their arms against us. And what a tragical scene an
attack from a foreign enemy must produce, when at the same time

our whole force will be scarce sufficient to guard against that within us, is but too apparent.

Exposed as we are to present danger from the Spaniards, consequences more fatal to us, as well as to the whole of your Majesty's Dominions in America, are to be apprehended in case of a rupture with France, from the wonderful progress made in these few years by that nation in their grand and long projected scheme of opening a communication between their Canada and Quebec settlements and those on the great river, Mississippi, to the bay of Mexico. A scheme, great to them, but dangerous to the British Dominions, as has been heretofore set forth by two several representations made to your Majesty from this province since the year 1734. This communication being now opened, by that means, they have an army of between 3,000 and 4,000 men on our backs; and have of late built new forts and reinforced those formerly built; by which there is great reason to apprehend that they are able not only to prevent the progress and extension of the British Settlements in North America, but to invade some of what is already settled.

As we have heretofore humbly represented to your Majesty, this Province and that of Georgia have the most to fear, and not only on account of their being the weakest and most exposed to their enemies, but on account of their situation, and the great advantage which the French must consequently have by becoming masters of them. The country between these Colonies and the French Settlements and Garrisons on the Rivers Mississippi and Mobile, being plain, flat and open, not intersected by the large Applatachian Mountains; we have therefore no other barrier but a few Nations of Indians, far inferior in number to theirs. Next to them are the Chickasaws, a bold and brave people. Strict friends to your Majesty's subjects of this Province; but not now in number above 400 men; with them the French have lately made an insidious peace; and in their security thereupon, many of them have been cut off by the Choctaw Indians. These Choctaws are very numerous, and under the immediate influence and direction of the French. This, together with the many former attacks upon that brave nation of the Chickasaws, leave no room to doubt of their intention to exterpate that people, as they have already done the Notches, with a view manifestly to make their next attempt on the Creeks, the only remaining barrier, in that case, between us and the French. In that nation, the French have long had a fort, called the Alabama fort; which they have lately reinforced; and by repeated intelligence from our traders, are now using their utmost endeavors, by offers of great presents as well as threats, to withdraw our people from our interest, and to engage them to destroy our traders now amongst them. In which, were they to succeed, terrible must be the fate of these, your Majesty's Provinces of South Carolina and Georgia; who unless supported must fall a prey to them and their numerous Indians, whose devastations and crueltys this Province has heretofore fatally experienced: and they in that case become masters of what they have had long in view, to wit a settlement and ports on this eastern part of the American continent, so absolutely necessary for the support and advantage of their back Settlements, and of great use to their Sugar Islands in America, which at present depend almost wholly upon the English Colonies for lumber and provisions; but as they are now situated have no other opening but from the Rivers Mobile and Mississippi, at the extremity of the Bay Appalatchee, in the entrance of the Gulf of Mexico, which renders their traffic from these Colonies not only tedious but dangerous; and then once having secured a settlement on this shore and a communication opened to their settlements on those rivers; we have reason to apprehend they may become masters of all Florida and its coast quite down to these great rivers, including St. Augustine itself, if it remains unconquered by your Majesty, and that large tract of fertile and rich soil called the Appalatchees, formerly conquered by the inhabitants of this Province from the Spaniards. Such, may it please your Majesty, seems to be the great schemes of the French, part of which are already executed and performed; and what are to come, we can easily foresee, but are of too high and extensive a nature for us to prevent.

Expectations and hopes arising at first from the settlement of Georgia being now vanished and gone by, the drooping and languid condition of the few inhabitants which still remain there, our own inhabitants and fortunes greatly reduced and impoverished by a long series of calamitys and misfortunes heretofore unknown, we have nothing left but to fly to your Majesty for protection. And full of gratitude for the many favours heretofore conferred in this Province, and confiding in that glorious disposition and spirit so lately evidenced and made appear to us in the early care taken of these your remotest subjects in America, by the assistance of so many of your Majesty's ships of war, the good effects of which we have already, in many instances, experienced.

We most humbly and earnestly implore your Majesty's most royal and paternal protection and assistance against our enemies by land, and particularly those in St. Augustine; who, no doubt, by our disappointment now bid defiance to the power and force of this Province, and from whence we sustained so many losses and injuries, by the reception from time to time of our deserted Slaves and even of those who have committed the most barbarous and cruel murders of their masters. And we most humbly pray your Majesty that in case this fortress should remain unconquered, then in any future peace to be concluded, between your Majesty and the King of Spain, provision may be made for the restoration of our Slaves already deserted, and for our security against such evils for the future, as also for the great expense which has attended this Province in consequence thereof.

All of which we most humbly and earnestly submit to your Majesty's royal consideration.

In the Upper House of Assembly the 26th day of July 1740.

JOHN FENWICKE.

In the Commons House of Assembly the 26th day of July 1740.
By Order of the House
WILLIAM BULL, Junr. Speaker.

These insurrections caused the famous "Negro Act" of 1740 for discouraging the importation of slaves to be made.[16] No doubt minor affairs of similar nature took place from time to time and individual Negroes were now and then fighting for personal freedom. But the next conflict of great importance in which Negroes took occasion to fight for their own freedom was in the Revolutionary War. Every student of history knows that many Negroes from South Carolina and the other colonies fought on both sides in this great war for freedom. In this war, as in most of the others in which they fought, the Negroes were not fighting for exactly the same reason that the whites were fighting. Let us take the explanation as given by Doctor DuBois in a chapter on "Black Soldiers," in a recent publication:

In all these wars the Negro has taken part. He cannot be blamed for them so far as they were unrighteous wars (and some of them were unrighteous), because he was not a leader, he was for the most part a common soldier in the ranks and did what he was told. Yet in the majority of cases he was not compelled to fight. He used his own judgment and he fought because he believed that by fighting for America he would gain the respect

[16]C. G. Woodson: *The Negro in Our History*, page 92.

of the land and personal and spiritual freedom. His problem as a soldier was always peculiar, no matter for what America, and no matter for what her enemies fought, the American Negro always fought for his own freedom and for the self-respect of his race. Whatever the cause of war, therefore, his cause was peculiarly just. He appears therefore, in American wars always with double motive, the desire to oppose the so-called enemy of his country along with his fellow white citizen and before that, the motive of deserving well of those citizens and securing justice for his folk. In this way he appears in the earliest times fighting with the whites against the Indians as well as with the Indians against the whites, and throughout the history of the West Indies and Central America as well as the Southern United States we find here and there groups of Negroes fighting with the whites.

The writer of this book heartily agrees with DuBois that most of the Negroes, certainly the South Carolina Negroes, who fought in any of the wars before the Civil War always had an eye single to their own freedom as the chief result of their fighting. In the Revolutionary War many Negroes were deserting the colonies and going over to the English side because they were promised their freedom if they did so. Thomas Jefferson put the number at 20,000. The result was that they were offered their freedom by the colonies also if they remained loyal and fought with their masters for the cause which they espoused.

An example is the defense of Fort Moultrie as described by Laura Wilkes:

Early in 1776 it was decided to fortify Charleston against a probable attack from the enemy's guns. Negroes were drilled in extinguishing fires, placing ladders and in meeting other emergencies that would arise were the city to be shelled. They (Negroes) took lead from the roofs of houses and churches and melted it into bullets that the supply of ammunition might be increased. As the city is near the sea it was necessary to place defenses about the harbor by which it is approached. It was therefore decided to erect breastworks on Sullivan's Island, in Charleston Harbor. This piece of land is a low sandy bar on the right of the inlet. At the time of the war it was covered with marshes, thickets and many trees. This point was selected because it had a deeper channel than that made by the other island in the neighborhood, and because the British ships were sure to pass that way if they made an effort to storm the city. A fort put up here was laid out in four bastiles. A fascine battery was also erected. Most of this work was done by Negroes, a large force being called in from the outlying plantations. Under the direction of Col. Moultrie "these men ably assisted the whites." They dovetailed the spongy palmetto, whose bullet resisting power is so well known, into a number of pens, connected with each other. These were filled with sand, making a parapet sixteen feet thick and high enough to shield the defenders and their guns. By April 26 one hundred guns were in operation.

On May 31st the expected British fleet, after having made several unsuccessful attacks off the coast of Virginia and North Carolina, appeared twenty miles off the mouth of the Ashley River. This was followed by some weeks of extra preparation on the part of the Charlestonians. The defenses were attacked on the fifteenth of June, at which time a division of Clinton's force opened fire upon the fort, where the Negroes were still at work even when the action began. In the city the blacks, who had been previously trained, took charge of the fire apparatus. So furious was the assault of the Americans that at no time were Clinton's men able to land upon Sullivan or Fort Moultrie, as the point was afterward called. An advance guard of some eight hundred men of both races defended the island at its lower extremity, while there was a force of four hundred and thirty-five in the fort. It was Clinton's plan to proceed to Charleston from this point, but neither the first nor the second division of the British fleet ever effected a landing. Badly crippled, they sailed away up the coast toward New York, where a large force of George III was concentrating. This victory brought security to South Carolina and to Georgia for the next three years. Much of it, if not most of it, was due to the efforts of Negroes.

When the Negroes clearly understood that if they helped in the cause by fighting on the side of their master they would procure freedom they entered the war and fought bravely, gaining the commendation of their white friends, North and South. Charles Pinckney, distinguished white South Carolinian, paid his tribute to the Negro soldiers in the Revolutionary War as follows:

They were, as they still are, as valuable a part of our population to the Union as any other equal number of inhabitants. They were in numerous instances the pioneers and, in all, the laborers of your armies. To their hands were owing the erection of the greatest part of the fortifications raised for the protection of our country; some of which, particularly Fort Moultrie, gave at that early period of the inexperience and untried valor of our citizens, immortality to American arms; and, in the northern states numerous bodies of them were enrolled into and fought by the sides of the whites, the battles of the Revolution.

The next important chance for the Negro to fight for his freedom, while the white people fought for something else, came along with the War of 1812. The Negro slaves of South Carolina had nothing particular at stake in this war. A few volunteered and fought because they believed that they might in the process somehow get free or aid the general cause of the abolition of Negro slavery. The Negroes of Alabama and Louisiana were much more prominent in this war than the Negroes of South Carolina.

It should be remembered that Negroes from South Carolina fought in practically all the wars carried on against the Indians. Some of these Negroes fought with the Indians and others fought on the side of the white people. It all depended upon which promised the Negro most freedom.

We have quoted DuBois and others to show that as time went on the Negro slaves were more and more convinced that physical resistance was not their way out to freedom; due in part to their own keen perception of the situation as well as to the ruthless policy of selection which the slave owners consciously and unconsciously pursued.

As we have said before the Negroes never ceased to fight physically and directly, although they could not be sure of success or certain of any large amount of co-operation from their fellow slaves. There were always some Negroes who sang, "Before I'd Be a Slave, I'll Be Buried in My Grave," in all seriousness and earnestness. They were just as much in earnest as Patrick Henry was when he made his famous statement, "Give me liberty or give me death."

We have mentioned above the earlier attempts made by South Carolina Negro slaves to procure their freedom. After the period around 1740 there seem to have been comparatively few insurrections led by Negroes themselves. This was doubtless due to the fact that the incidents before, during, and after, the Revolutionary War, provided opportunity for the more enterprising and courageous among the slaves to procure their freedom by a less dangerous method than that of insurrection. Holland thought it was due to the efficiency of the Act of 1740. However, in 1816, the Camden insurrection took place. We reproduce a description of this insurrection as given by Francis G. Deliesseline, Esq., as published by Holland:

In compliance with your request I send you a narrative of the projected conspiracy of the blacks in Camden, and its neighborhood, in the year 1816—the professed design of which was to murder all the whites, and free themselves. A long lapse of time has erased from my memory many of the particulars, but I am enabled to give you the following outline:

About the middle of June, 1816, Col. Chestnut, a citizen of Camden, and an aide-de-camp to Gov. Williams, was informed by a favorite and confidential slave, that propositions of dangerous character had been to him, in relation to projected insurrection among the blacks—and that the time and place of rendezvous had been already appointed. His master, placing the most unreserved confidence in his fidelity, directed him to attend the meetings of the conspirators, previous to the development of the plot, and, at the same time, to conduct himself with the most guarded discretion. . . . A communication was immediately had with Governor Williams, and Colonel Chestnut received the necessary instructions with regard to the defeat of the conspiracy. These were communicated to none other than the town council; and such was the secrecy with which the whole affair was conducted, that on the morning of the 1st or 2nd of July, the young men chosen to arrest the ringleaders of the conspiracy were assembled under the pretense of a fox chase, and despatched under the command of leaders, who were enjoined to the utmost secrecy. They were perfectly ignorant of the nature of the service they were on, until the moment they were ordered to arrest the conspirators, most of whom were at work in the fields, many miles apart. Their movements were so secret and simultaneous, that the arrests were made almost at the same instant of time, and without any intimation on the part of those respectively arrested, of the fate of their confederates. The same caution was subsequently used, at their trial, to conceal the name of the informer who was likewise in custody. The most satisfactory testimony, independent of that of the informer, and regulated by the most rigid rules of evidence sufficiently established their guilt; and the first gang who were executed died ignorant of the informer. They all confessed their crimes, and the most intelligent of them acknowledged that they had no causes of complaint against their individual masters, and advised their surviving brethren of the futility of any further attempt. They expressed themselves surprised with the mild and humane manner of the proceedings instituted against them, and freely acknowledged that they had anticipated immediate death in case of a discovery. Two brothers engaged in this rebellion could read and write, and were hitherto of unexceptional characters. They were religious, and had always been regarded in the light of faithful servants. A few appeared to have been actuated solely by the instinct of the most brutal licentiousness, and by the lust of plunder, but most of them by wild and frantic ideas of the rights of man, and the misconceived injunctions and examples of Holy Writ.

The scheme had for its object the conflagration of a part of the town—the massacre of all the white male inhabitants, and the more brutal sacrifice of the female. Their plan was entrusted to a few only, and they left its development and consummation to chance; relying on the presumed disposition to rebellion on the part of the blacks of every description.

The night of the 4th of July was appointed for the explosion—great anxiety had been exhibited among the younger and more ardent associates in the revolt, in the different meetings that were held, to precipitate the period of attack, and begin the work of desolation and slaughter some time before. But the cautious and calculating judgment of the more cunning and elder, urged as reasons for deferring it, that there was a scarcity of provisions—that the crops not yet made would be lost in the confusion that would ensue, and that famine would accomplish what force might not be able to effect. They confidently relied, also, upon the usual indulgences among us on a day celebrated as a great national jubilee; and it was finally determined, that the night of the 4th of July should be appointed as the time for the re-enaction of the horrors of the Sicilian Vespers. The different commands had been regularly assigned to particular leaders, and all had been allotted, except that of commander-in-chief. This was reserved for him who should first force the gates of the arsenal. To strengthen the possibility of success, the Negroes from the circumjacent country were invited, under various pretenses, to Camden that night. The fidelity of a favorite domestic, as I have already stated defeated their flagitious scheme, and consigned the ringleaders of the revolt to a premature and ignominious grave. The legislature of the state purchased the freedom of the informer, and settled a pension upon him for life.

Although many were known to have been concerned in the insurrection none but the chiefs of the revolt were executed. As well as I can recollect, the whole number hung was six.

We wish to call attention next to the most conspicuous attempt by Negroes to gain their freedom by physical fighting which ever took place in South Carolina and perhaps the greatest one in the entire history of slavery in these United States. We refer, of course, to the slave insurrection led by Denmark Vesey of Charleston. Professor Benjamin Brawley, a native South Carolinian, born at Columbia, who has written much on Negro history, literature and art, has published the best short story of this insurrection with which we are familiar.

The chief source of original information available to me, however, is the record of this insurrection in the little book, "The Status of the Negro in South Carolina" (1822-1823), a copy of which was loaned to the writer by Professor Yates Snowden of the University of South Carolina. Our record here is based upon information procured mostly from that source.[13]

This "Intended Insurrection" was almost wholly due to the work of Denmark Vesey and it is therefore proper to pay some attention to him here as an example of the Negro leaders who at various times attempted to arouse their comrades to fight physically for freedom.

Denmark Vesey was a native of St. Thomas. He was brought to Charleston by one Captain Vesey, who engaged in the slave trade between St. Thomas and San Domingo.

Denmark Vesey was described as handsome, active and unusually keen intellectually. He doubtless procured ideas of freedom and was enthused to strive for a place among free men by contact with the white people as he became a kind of favorite of the officers on Captain Vesey's ship before he was brought into slavery in South Carolina. The name Denmark was a corruption of Vesey's original given name—Telemaque.

---

[13]Holland.

One early indication of shrewdness that Denmark Vesey gave was in connection with his sale by Captain Vesey to a man in San Domingo. It seems that Denmark feigned insanity with such success that the official examiners, in accordance with the law, required the seller to take him back. For twenty years he proved an excellent investment as a slave for his master, Captain Vesey.

Captain Vesey made his home in Charleston, where, in the year 1800, Denmark won $1500 in a lottery game on East Bay Street. Six hundred dollars of this he invested in himself—he purchased his freedom. The other he apparently used wisely as we see him from that time able to take care of himself financially and support his large family comparatively well. He had much time and energy left which he used in planning the insurrection which bears his name.

It was in the planning of this insurrection that Vesey proved himself to be an able leader and a shrewd, efficient worker. His plans were comprehensive, far reaching and well worked out. He demonstrated his possession of one of the characteristics of a successful leader—the ability to gather around him a group of able, loyal supporters. His project failed only because all such schemes led by the slaves or the freedmen were doomed to fail. Yet it did not fail in a large sense because it resulted in bringing about conditions which ultimately hastened the break between the North and South resulting in the Civil War and freedom for the Negro.

Early in his life in South Carolina Vesey conceived the idea of leading an insurrection or revolution of the slaves to the end that they might all procure their freedom. For twenty years he worked and planned. Fortunately for Vesey, the law that Negroes should not hold separate meetings to themselves was not strictly enforced around Charleston. He took advantage of this to meet frequently with a congregation of Negroes who had a church organized in the outskirts of Charleston. Here Vesey addressed the slaves and tried in every way to get them to make a physical fight for freedom. He told them that they deserved to be slaves if they would not rise and fight like true men for their coveted freedom.

He studied and familiarized himself with the conditions in Haiti, he corresponded with the leaders there and passed the information and inspiration which he secured on to the men he addressed in the meetings.   Finally this black abolitionist decided to leave off his trade altogether and spend all his time planning the insurrection which was not only to free the Negroes but bring vengeance upon the whites for their injustice in keeping the Negroes in slavery.   His plan as finally evolved contemplated the destruction of all the lives and much of the property of the white people of Charleston.

In December, 1821, Vesey began recruiting the personnel for the leadership of his intended insurrection.   He was very careful in selecting these leaders and procured some excellent persons for his purpose.   Among those trusted by Vesey were Ned Bennett and his brother Rolla, Peter Poyas, Jack Burcell, Gullah Jack, Monday Gell, Lot Forrester, Battean Bennett and Frank Ferguson.   All these were men of influence and ability which they demonstrated as the insurrection gained in power.   In selecting his aids Vesey, through Peter Poyas, had explicitly advised against attempting to recruit "those waiting men who receive presents of old coats, etc. from their masters."   He also excluded women and men who had a reputation of being generally talkative.

The plan did not contemplate getting Negroes involved all over the state but only in an area between 75 and 100 miles from Charleston.

The plans for the details of the insurrection were comprehensive and detailed.   Arms were provided by taking collections from those participating at the meetings held at frequent intervals.   Members of the insurrection who were tradesmen, such as blacksmiths, carpenters, etc., were commissioned to prepare weapons of every kind such as spears, spikes, daggers, etc.   Many of these weapons were found when the insurrection was discovered.   The members were instructed to take all hatchets, axes, hoes, etc., that they could procure in any way from the houses of the white people.

It seems that the original date set for the insurrection to

take place was Sunday, July 14, 1822. However, certain events caused the date to be changed.

The plot moved along smoothly it seems until May 25th when a slave by the name of William Paul revealed it to another slave belonging to one Colonel Prioleau, through whom it passed to this master. The Colonel at once informed the mayor of Charleston, who immediately took measures to protect the white people of Charleston and apprehend the leaders if possible. Other slaves began to inform their masters and so it rapidly became apparent to Vesey and the other leaders that changes must be made as the original plans were now understood. The fear of Peter Poyas as to the probability of betrayal by a slave of the domestic variety was justified. On June the 15th, Jessie Blackwood, a messenger of Vesey, who was trying to get in touch with confederates in the plot out from Charleston, was halted twice and forced to return. This convinced Vesey that his plans were known and he determined to change them again if possible. The date had already been changed from July 14th to June 16th.

As soon as Vesey knew that his plan was frustrated he began to destroy all papers, etc., that might incriminate any one. He showed great ability in concealing evidence of the plans and plots he had so ably brought up to a high state of perfection. The great loyalty of some of his aids was illustrated by the statement of advice to confederates made by Peter Poyas just before he died, having been convicted of complication in the plot: "Do not open your lips, die silent as you shall see me do." Many of them kept his advice courageously.

The balance of the story is tragically brief. The plot was rapidly and fully revealed, as indeed it was doomed to be from the beginning. As has been stated elsewhere all such attempts were ordained to fail because the white slave owners had been shrewd enough to organize the system of self-defense. They shrewdly played off the domestic servant class of slaves against the less favored ones and caused many of the free Negroes also to believe that it was to their interest to inform the whites of any unlawful attempts of the slaves to change the social order. Of course, much of this apparently so well planned, probably developed naturally and without definite effort of the masters. Naturally, a few of those free Negroes, who themselves were slave owners, were interested in maintaining the status quo. Vesey's plot, like all the others engaged in by Negro slaves to procure their own freedom, including the one led by the white man, John Brown, was an exhibition of poor judgment as to a method of abolishing slavery, but they all show that the Negro was a real human being who was willing to risk his life fighting for freedom though his chances of success were slim indeed. He thus exhibited that he possessed his share of that courageous character of which true heroes, pioneers, and real martyrs are made.

It is our honest opinion that Denmark Vesey and the other thirty-four of his confederates who were found guilty and forced to pay the death penalty, deserve to be numbered among the world's great martyrs for human freedom. As was said of John Brown, so it must be said of them: their bodies lie moulding in their graves, but their souls will ever go marching on as long as men find liberty as dear as life.

It may be interesting to note here that 131 persons were arrested in connection with this great plot. Some sixty of these were finally acquitted, a few were transported, and others imprisoned.

Of course, the immediate effect of the insurrection was to increase the nervousness of the slave owners, due to their fear of the slaves, fears which all oppressors experience. It caused some of the free Negroes to believe that the insurrection had injured them and retarded the movement toward freedom. As we have suggested elsewhere, in our opinion, the verdict of history is·that it helped accomplish Abolition because it was a contributory cause of the Civil War. We agree with the hymnologist—it was God moving "in a mysterious way His wonders to perform."

Denmark Vesey's insurrection was the last important direct physical fight which Negroes of South Carolina made for freedom. It, along with all the other fighting which we have briefly described, had performed its mission in helping to bring on the final great fight for freedom—the Civil War. The white people of the country apparently tried to convince themselves and spread the propaganda over the world that the rebellion in the South was not a fight in defense of slavery, but a war over certain principles of democracy. The Negroes, as a whole, were not misled by any such sophistry. They knew that the war would settle the question of their freedom one way or the other.

It is one of the ironies of history that the Negroes were forced to plead, even in the North, for an opportunity to fight in a war which they caused and was for their benefit. Many people of the North, unable to appreciate fundamental causes and misled by propaganda, really thought that they were fighting only to preserve the Republic, without realizing that the institution of slavery was the vital issue. Lincoln was too much of a diplomat to tell these persons the ugly truth, because he sympathized with their ignorance and needed their help. There were some Negroes also who believed that the Civil War was not an effort to settle their status in the Republic, but a question of disagreement between the white people. The important fact which we wish to emphasize here is that the Negroes who sought to participate in this war and who did finally participate in it, did so, in the majority of cases, because they believed that they would help the cause of Abolition—personal and general.*

Although the Negroes found that neither the North nor the South desired their services as soldiers when the Civil War first began, they persisted in their effort to be allowed to fight for their freedom, until their plea was finally answered. The official records show that 178,595 colored men were finally enlisted in the Union army, and had the pleasure of fighting for their freedom and that of their fellow slaves. Many Negroes who joined the Union army were fugitives from slavery in the southern states. In the South the Negroes were first used only as laborers. Indeed, it was, or should have been, more than the people of the South could stand to ask

---

*Woodson, DuBois, Brawley, all agree here.

3

the Negroes to fight against their own freedom.   Just as
the war was about to close the Confederacy planned to enlist
large numbers of Negroes to fight on their side.   The surrender of Robert E. Lee and the collapse of the South before
this plan could be put into operation saved the Negroes from
being called upon to apparently defend the slave interests.

Many people wonder why the Negro slaves in South Carolina and other southern states did not rise in rebellion while
the white masters were away at war with the northern armies
to keep these same Negroes in bondage.   Much sentimental
and imaginative oratory has been spent upon the supposed
loyalty of those Negro slaves.   It seems to me that the slaves
acted as they did partly because of the fact that the selective
process which we described above had weeded out the more
war-like members of the slaves and partly because they were
"playing safe."   They were not sure that the North would
win and emancipate them and they knew that in case the
Union forces should lose and they had assisted the North, or
even openly sympathized with them, their lot would subsequently be hard indeed.   On the other hand, if they remained
apparently loyal and freedom came through the success of
northern arms they had nothing to lose.   The Negro's conduct was good diplomatic policy.   Of course, there were many
whose ignorance was so great that they were easily misled
by the subtle propaganda of the slave owners into believing
that the "Yankees" were the enemies of the Negroes as well
as of themselves.   There also was a small group of Negroes
who were interested in the success of the South because they
themselves were slave owners, and were therefore economically
interested in maintaining the slave régime.   The vast majority of the Negroes were with the Union forces in heart, soul
and prayer, whatever may have been their apparent sympathy
or conduct.

The Negroes of South Carolina played a very conspicuous part in the Civil War in this state.   Here they fought for
freedom nobly and well.   One of the most striking examples
of the way in which the Negro slaves finally were allowed
to fight for freedom in this state is connected with the Union

general, Hunter. This officer was sent into South Carolina with a greatly insufficient force and was refused reinforcements. He solved the problem by enlisting Negroes who had volunteered to fight with him. For this action he was severely criticized. Being accused of having enlisted "fugitive slaves" without authority, he replied as follows:

To the first question, therefore, I reply: that no regiment of "fugitive slaves" has been, or is being, organized in this department. There is, however, a fine regiment of loyal persons whose late masters are fugitive rebels—men who everywhere fly before the appearance of the National flag, leaving their loyal and unhappy servants behind them, to shift as best they can for themselves. So far, indeed, are the loyal persons composing the regiment from seeking to evade the presence of their late owners, that they are now one and all endeavoring with commendable zeal to acquire the drill and discipline requisite to place them in a position to go in full and effective pursuit of their fugacious and traitorous proprietors.

The experiment of arming the blacks, so far as I have made it, has been a complete and even marvelous success. They are sober, docile, attentive and enthusiastic, displaying great natural capacities in acquiring the duties of the soldier. They are now eager beyond all things to take the field and be led into action; and it is the unanimous opinion of the officers who have had charge of them, that in the peculiarities of this climate and country, they will prove invaluable auxiliaries, fully equal to the similar regiments so long and so successfully used by the British authorities in the West India Islands.

In conclusion, I would say, it is my hope—there appearing no possibility of other reinforcements, owing to the exigencies of the campaign in the peninsula—to have organized by the end of next fall and to be able to present to the government from 48,000 to 50,000 of these hardy and devoted soldiers.[17]

This reply of Hunter was read in Congress and created considerable merriment on the part of the anti-slavery Republicans. Where Hunter led, others followed, and soon many thousands of Negroes were enlisted in South Carolina as well as in other places where the battles of freedom were being fought. One of the famous battles in which the Negroes performed nobly was in the attempt to take Fort Wagner. This

---

[17]W. E. B. DuBois: *The Gift of Black Folk,* pages 103, 104.

battle is eloquently described by a white man of the Confederate side as follows:

The carnage was frightful. It is believed the Federals lost more men on that eventful night than twice the entire strength of the Confederate garrison. . . . According to the statement of Chaplain Dennison the assaulting columns, in two brigades, commanded by General Strong and Colonel Putnam (the division under General Seymour) consisted of the 54th Massachusetts, 3rd and 7th New Hampshire, 6th Connecticut and 100th New York, with a reserve brigade commanded by General Stephenson. One of the assaulting regiments was composed of Negroes (the 54th Massachusetts) and to it was assigned the honor of leading the white columns to the charge. It was a dearly purchased compliment. Their colonel (Shaw) was killed upon the parapet and the regiment almost annihilated, although the Confederates in the darkness could not tell the color of their assailants.

At last it was seen that Negro troops could do more than useless or helpless or impossible tasks, and in the siege of Petersburg they were put to important work. When the general attack was ordered on the 16th of June, 1864, a division of black troops was used. The Secretary of War, Stanton himself, saw them and said:

The hardest fighting was done by the black troops. The forts they stormed were the worst of all. After the affair was over General Smith went to thank them, and tell them he was proud of their courage and dash. He says they cannot be exceeded as soldiers, and that hereafter he will send them in a difficult place as readily as the best white troops.[18]

It was in this great battle that the courageous Sergeant William H. Carney won highly deserved immortal fame by saving the colors from disgrace and placing them on the height, although he paid dearly for it. His comment is immortalized in story and song: "Boys, the old flag never touched the ground." Many more of the "missing pages of American history" might be filled with the stories of the heroism of Negroes fighting for freedom along with their white comrades who were also fighting for freedom, though the latter did not realize or admit it. We have said enough

---

[18] Ibid., pages 123, 124.

to show that the Negroes of South Carolina fought well for their freedom. It is a melancholy fact that while monuments in honor of the white Confederate soldiers stand in almost every town and hamlet of South Carolina, one must travel hundreds of miles, to Boston Commons, to find, standing on northern soil, a proper tribute to Negro soldiers and their leaders. We quote the inscription on General Shaw's monument:

THE WHITE OFFICERS

Taking Life and Honor in Their Hands—Cast Their Lot with Men of a Despised Race Unproved in War—and Risked Death as Inciters of a Servile Insurrection If Taken Prisoners, Besides Encountering All the Common Perils of Camp, March, and Battle.

THE BLACK RANK AND FILE

Volunteered When Disaster Clouded the Union Cause— Served Without Pay for Eighteen Months Till Given That of White Troops—Faced Threatened Enslavement If Captured— Were Brave in Action—Patient Under Dangerous and Heavy Labors and Cheerful Amid Hardships and Privations.

TOGETHER

They Gave to the Nation Undying Proof That Americans of African Descent Possess the Pride, Courage, and Devotion of the Patriot Soldier—One Hundred and Eighty Thousand Enlisted Under the Union Flag in MDCCCLXIII-MDCCCLXV.

In concluding this chapter we wish to remind the reader that we have only suggested the mass of evidence to prove that the Negroes themselves played an important part in making their freedom inevitable: *by becoming fugitives, by purchasing a little freedom and then using it to work and fight for more, by agitation and the "appeal to reason," by insurrections, and fighting physically in every important war.* All these actions on the part of the Negro caused slavery to be an everlasting, burning issue which caused the secession movement, which in turn led to warfare and emancipation.

When, finally, the great Emancipation Proclamation came from the pen of Lincoln, the Negroes of this state and of all the states had a right to be proud of their own achievement, as well as grateful to Almighty God and the Union soldiers. *Abraham Lincoln wrote the Proclamation, but the circumstances which furnished him the occasion and made his action a necessity, were brought about by long years of fighting for freedom by Negroes in South Carolina and elsewhere.* We do not mean that there were not other influences, but they were subsidiary to the fighting spirit of the Negro.

When the Civil War came to a close, the Negro entered a new life. He had secured physical freedom for which he had so long hungered. The Negro did not realize, in this, his first great hour of triumph, that the fighting had just begun in the long war for his complete emancipation. He sang happily, but alas! prematurely: "Hallelujah—trouble over."

CHAPTER III

THE NEGRO'S PART IN THE RECONSTRUC-
TION OF SOUTH CAROLINA

The evil that men do lives after them;
The good is oft interred with their bones.
—Shakespeare.

IT is not our purpose here to present an exhaustive study of the Reconstruction of South Carolina. We merely wish to further suggest some other "missing pages of American History" by emphasizing the part played by Negroes in this much misrepresented period. At the beginning we wish to express our debt to A. A. Taylor's[1] study of this subject which will be obvious to the reader as he peruses this chapter.

Elsewhere we have called attention to the fact that the United States Congress, feeling that the State of South Carolina (along with the other ex-Confederate states) was not making an honest effort to recognize the results of the Civil War in reforming its government, decided to place the state under military control and force another plan of reconstruction. The plan applied is familiar to every student of United States history as the "Congressional Plan." This plan embraced the Civil Rights Bill, giving the freedmen all the civil rights of citizens. It also embraced the Fourteenth Amendment, which each ex-Confederate state was required to accept and approve before it could be readmitted into the Union. Thus the Negroes were given the power to vote and help destroy the "Black Codes" and other legislation prejudicial to their interests which the white people of this and other southern states had passed to "revitalize slavery."

Thus the political phase of reconstruction has attracted far more attention than the social and economic phases.

---

[1]A. A. Taylor: *The Negro In South Carolina During the Reconstruction.*

Just as the white people of the North had previously found themselves unable to complete the task of freeing the Negroes physically without the aid of the latter in the armies of the Republic, so now they found it impossible to preserve the Negro's freedom and assure his progress without his own assistance. DuBois puts the thought excellently as follows:

Thus Negro suffrage was forced to the front, not as a method of humiliating the South; not as a theoretical and dangerous gift to the freedmen; not according to any preconcerted plan but simply because of the fruits of war made it necessary to keep a freedmen's bureau for a generation and to use the Negro vote to reconstruct the southern states and to insure such legislation as would at least begin the economic emancipation of the slave.

In other words the North being unable to free the slave, let him try to free himself. And he did, and this was his greatest gift to this nation.[2]

A white man, Post, who styled himself a "Carpet-bagger," approved this view:

Read the history of the time without prejudice and you will realize that Congress had but one alternative. It must either permit restoration of Negro slavery in its essentials, or else enfranchise the freedmen for their own protection against the efforts of the master class to re-enslave them. Congress did the latter, rightly as I viewed it then and view it yet—rightly upon democratic principle, and rightly also out of the national and local necessities of the case. It was done by receiving South Carolina back into the Union under her "Black-and-tan" Constitution of 1868, as that truly democratic document was derisively called.[3]

These statements are obviously true in reference to South Carolina. The Negroes comprised the majority of the population of this state, and therefore were very influential in the subsequent government of the state until they were disfranchised several years later. Thus it happened that the proud old state of South Carolina was placed "under the rule of Negroes and adventurers from the North" from 1868 to 1876. As anyone who was familiar with the ideas and attitudes of

---

[2] W. E. B. DuBois: *The Gift of Black Folk*, pages 211, 212.
[3] *Journal of Negro History*, Vol. 10, page 34.

the white people of the state might expect, these white people observed the work of these new rulers with a scrutinizing eye single for the mistakes only. Naturally, there were a plenty of mistakes to be seen. These have been published to the world with emphasis and reiteration.

It may not be out of place therefore for us to try to present both sides of the question, with special care to present the Negro side in a true light. The question of whether or not it was wise to give the Negroes the ballot is the one which causes the most discussion and illustrates most strikingly the difference of opinion between the white people of South Carolina and most of the thoughtful Negroes in and out of the state. We may illustrate this by giving here two quotations, both from South Carolinians, one white and one colored. First we present the opinion of a white writer, the author of a text-book on this state's history used in some schools:

In 1867 the country that had so long borne the honorable name of the Commonwealth of South Carolina was called Military District No. 2. Soldiers were put in entire control of the people. Judge A. P. Aldrich, of the Superior Court, received a written order from a Federal officer that he could no longer sit as judge. Judge Aldrich opened his court, and read the order aloud. Then laying aside his gown he directed the sheriff "to let the court stand adjourned while justice is stifled"—then in the following year (1868) a negro government was formed. Every Negro man had the right to vote and to hold office. White men who had helped the Confederacy could not vote. This meant that almost all of the white people of the state were cut off from taking part in the government.

The period from 1868 to 1874 was known as the time when South Carolina was under the "Rule of the Robbers." All power was in the hand of the negroes and a few white men from the North and West.[4]

But the colored fellow citizen of this writer, who is also the author of a book, has an altogether different opinion of this same matter which opinion he expresses as follows:

It was the ballot in the hands of the Negro that saved the nation from unspeakable humiliations, established beyond question its supremacy and sovereignty, destroyed forever the menac-

---

[4]White: *The Making of South Carolina,* page 291.

ing and dangerous forms of state rights, and preserved "the jewel of liberty in the family of freedom," thus fulfilling in a most signal, unexpected, and remarkable manner Lincoln's prophecy that "they would probably help in some trying time in the future to keep the jewel of liberty in the family of freedom."

Under the desperate and chaotic conditions existent in the South at this time, it is not surprising that in the selection and election of men to carry out the work of reconstruction serious blunders were made; that some thieves and plunderers forged to the front and filled some of the offices. It is the universal experience in governmental affairs that under normal conditions, in times of profound peace, bad men and thieves have been elected to offices and have betrayed their trusts. It was unavoidable, it could not have been otherwise during the Reconstruction era. The circumstances were propitious for this. The South had gone far beyond her financial ability in the prosecution of a disastrous and wasteful war. She had no public moneys, and her private fortunes were wrecked; a billion dollars in slave property had evaporated. Money was needed to operate state and local government. Taxes were assessed. Bonds were issued. From 25 to 75 per cent of the par value of these bonds remained in the safes and lockers of bondholders in the North; in fact the northern bondholders got a larger proportion of money which should have been used to run these state governments than it was possible for the "carpet-baggers" to steal.

Those southern leaders who attribute the poverty of the South following the war to the stealings of "carpet-baggers" are unwise in their utterances. This poverty was due more to the waste of war, the unsettled conditions, and the low price of southern bonds than to the stealings of the "carpet-baggers." Much stealing has been done since the passing of these conditions; millions have been stolen in later years by defaulters, embezzlers, grafters, and boodlers.

But after all that may be charged against the blundering and plundering of the carpet-bag governments in the South, it is probably true that the Tweed ring in New York City actually stole and squandered more of the people's money than all the "carpet-baggers" in the South combined.

It is so-called carpet-bag government; such were Georgia, Tennessee, and Texas; others were so controlled for only a short time, as, for instance, Louisiana, Mississippi, Virginia, Alabama, and Arkansas, for three or four years; North Carolina for about six years; and only Florida and South Carolina for about eight years. So it will be seen at a glance that the so-called dishonest carpet-bag government of the South was neither so general nor so extended in time as southern leaders pretend.[5]

We cannot know the truth about this matter by just reading or presenting these opposing views by partisans. It is necessary for us to examine, as far as we may, the actual personnel and works of this remarkable Reconstruction legislature of South Carolina. We must also take into consideration their problems, so that we may measure their success or failure not alone by the actual results they produced, but by these results judged in the light of the circumstances which necessarily conditioned their achievement. It is true, as the last writer quoted remarked, that the newly made Negro and "carpet-bagger" legislators were compelled to labor in post-war conditions and under the disadvantages naturally growing out of hostile environment and a highly unfavorable background. Both classes were largely without political experience and previous educational opportunity which every democracy should guarantee its citizens.

As we have suggested above, the critics of the work of Negroes in South Carolina during the Reconstruction are legion. Some of them, such as John S. Reynolds, have presented many facts along with their criticisms. These facts though presented by prejudiced writers will eventually establish the truth. We shall use some of them here.

One of the choice bits of unfriendly propaganda has to do with the character of the Negro personnel of the Reconstruction government of South Carolina during the rule of the "Carpet-baggers," Negroes, and "Scalawags." The general impression the reader gets from most of the southern white writers is that all these men were ignorant, dishonest, incapable, and malicious. This is false. This testimony of Louis F. Post seems to ring true:

Some of the Negroes were self-sacrificingly honest, many were above the average level of legislative intelligence, some were men of education, not a few were deliberately and brazenly dishonest, and most of them bore testimony in their color of the natural possibility of miscegenation. The body as a whole was

---

[5] W. A. Sinclair: *The Aftermath of Slavery,* pages 88-89.

in a legislative atmosphere so saturated with corruption that the honest and honorable members of either race had no more influence in it than an orchid might have in a mustard patch.[6]

It may not be out of place to mention here a few of the Negro leaders in the political life of South Carolina during her reconstruction under the Congressional plan. First we mention A. J. Ransier who was lieutenant governor for a while. According to Post, he "presided with dignity" although he was probably not an able politician or statesman and certainly must not have been much of a success as a manager of his personal finance as he finally descended to the humble position of street sweeper in Columbia, the city where he once presided over the state senate. A pathetic story is told of him to the effect that one day while cleaning the streets of the city he picked up a sheet of an old newspaper which carried a news item in which his name was mentioned as "Lieutenant-Governor in the Chair." Among the early state senators were Robert Small and Beverly Nash. Both of these men achieved no small amount of local fame and were men of more than average ability. Later they held other important official positions. There are others who perhaps require special mention. Samuel J. Lee, a member of the legislature, was admitted to be one of the best criminal lawyers of the state. Bishop Isaac Clinton who was treasurer of the town of Orangeburg was so highly respected that at his death business was suspended in his honor; the whole town, white and black, participating in paying him this signal honor. Mr. George Harriot, who was superintendent of education for his county, was kept in office a long time, even after the Democratic party came into power. Honorable Thos. E. Miller remained in office up until the disfranchisement of his people. In fact, he was there to oppose that act and to embarrass the leaders in that movement, especially Senator Tillman. Francis L. Cardoza, educated at universities in England and Scotland, was for a long time a leader in the South Carolina legislature. He organized the forces of the Negroes and one

---

[6]A "Carpet-Bagger" in South Carolina: *Journal of Negro History,* Vol. 10, page 17.

act of his showing his general interest in his fellow members was the fact that he had copies of the *New York Tribune* distributed among all the members of the Constitutional Convention in order that they might be better informed for their work. Kelly Miller, a native South Carolinian, who lived in the state during this period described the situation in part as follows:

Negroes filled all stations in the government, with the exception of governor, which was always accorded the white race. The Lieutenant Governor, Secretary of State, Treasurer, Legislators, and Congressmen were plentiful. As a boy, thirty miles away, my eyes and ears were just about beginning to be opened. I used to hear of the fabulous happenings going on in Columbia. I had relatives who went from Fairfield County as representatives and senators. They would tell me that Negroes often lit their cigars with five-dollar bills. Nowhere on earth did Negroes ever exercise so much political power as in Columbia. Nor did they ever revel so extravagantly in the excrescences of power. Every Negro boy in the state was dreaming of a political career. Had I been ten years older I would have been in the thickest of the fray. But the bubble must soon break. Babylon must needs fall. South Carolina is the only state that admitted Negroes to the State University. Of course, the whites left. Professor Richard R. Greener had the distinction of being the only Negro to be appointed professor in this famous institution. I was with him in Columbia many years later when he could only stand at a distance and point out the room which he used to occupy. After the overthrow of reconstruction, when the whites regained control, all records of the Negro regime were destroyed as if there had been an interregnum.

Many of the Negroes cast down from the seats of power cut a sorry figure. As many as could sought berths in the department service in Washington. When I was in Charleston last month I heard an eye witness tell of a former lieutenant governor becoming a street sweeper. Columbia dropped from the heights to the depths so far as the Negro was concerned. How did the mighty fall! But South Carolina has had the experience, and that is worth something. After the downfall in '76, some of the old liners held on to a lingering hope. General Robert Small, Thomas Miller and George W. Murray were elected to Congress from the blackest districts. But the rise of Tillman put an end to all of this. The Negro now has been driven from every vestige of political power. He makes no further effort, not even to function seriously in quadrennial election of Republican delegates.[7]

The Negroes we have mentioned were exceptionally intelligent as one would expect of the leaders. The majority of the Negro members of the legislature were ignorant and so were many of the other Negro officers of this period. It may be doubted whether they were much less ignorant than the majority of the white members of this and other southern state legislatures. In all countries that are experimenting with democracy the masses are ignorant and politically incompetent and must be led by a few exceptional persons.

The character and intelligence of the Negro leaders could not count for much because of the influences surrounding them. The white people who were in the legislature with the Negroes and who filled other political offices throughout the state really set a poor example for the Negroes and led them into much of the corrupt politics which they practiced.

The best way to judge the character of the Negroes who took part in the Reconstruction is to examine the results of their work. It is charged that they devoted most of their time to devising means of extracting money from their fellow citizens in the form of high taxes which they in turn spent with criminal extravagance. It is said that in an environment of poverty and economic ruin these politicians lived and moved in luxury and reveled in graft. It is claimed that individuals grew rich following no other occupation besides that of "legislatin'." This is a half truth and therefore a very plausible lie.

The poet was profoundly right who wrote the familiar lines:

> Truth crushed to earth shall rise again—
> The eternal years of God are hers;
> But error wounded writhes in pain
> And dies among her worshipers.

As time passes more and more of the truth concerning the Negro's part in the political and economic reconstruction of South Carolina is coming to the attention of the reading pub-

---

[7]Kelly Miller: *"These Colored United States—South Carolina."—New York Messenger,* December, 1925.

lic and being accepted by a larger and larger number of people, white and colored. When Negro writers first began presenting some of the facts concerning this period which are favorable to the Negroes they were "voices crying in the wilderness" of doubt. These writers were considered as radicals and their contentions were dismissed as mere Negro propaganda. Times have changed. The facts which we shall present below are now admitted by most writers, though not widely heralded.

What is the truth about the claim that the Reconstruction governments were honeycombed with thieves and robbers? The facts show that much money was stolen and many resources squandered for illegitimate purposes. The fact which is often overlooked is that the situation was such that large sums of money were also needed and used for legitimate purposes. The war had been very destructive and money was needed to replace much government property which had been destroyed or stolen. There was no way to get the necessary money except by taxing the people, but they were already very poor and experiencing that dissatisfaction which comes from the feeling of economic prostration. In the midst of these conditions the "carpet-baggers," mostly white; and the "scalawags"—all white, who were the real leaders in the Reconstruction government, found it necessary to spend much money to establish order by employing officers and soldiers. They also found it necessary to provide funds for a public school system which existed only in name on paper before this time in South Carolina. We wish to emphasize the fact here that this Reconstruction government was not Negro rule or domination as it is generally called. It is true that the white people who were at the head of affairs were forced to depend upon Negro support to "carry on." Negro influence was powerful in shaping the policy. It is impossible to produce any reliable evidence to show that Negroes made any great effort to get revenge upon the white people or to rule them oppressively. The white people simply objected to the Negroes, so lately slaves, having any authority at all. These white people would not have been satisfied if the Negro legislators had unexpectedly proven themselves to be superhuman and achieved a perfect government. These people did not want a democratic government with the Negro playing his part and enjoying his rights as a man. They desired a "white man's government," however incompetent, with Negroes reduced to a servant class, with no rights "a white man need respect." Of course, there were some white people more liberal than this, but this reactionary view prevailed every time the Negro vote was eliminated.

With all these handicaps and disadvantages the Negroes made a fine showing. Our point here is excellently summarized by a native South Carolinian, W. A. Sinclair:

No one would, perhaps, challenge the correctness of the principle that wars are unusual occurrences and therefore they call for the exercise of unusual powers, not only in conducting them but also in the settlement of complex and perplexing questions growing out of them. A nation's life or sovereignty is paramount.

So it was with the Civil War, and so it was with reconstruction. And with reference to Negro suffrage, it is all-important to consider these fundamental truths connected therewith.

The giving of the ballot to the Negro became the necessary means for the accomplishment of the rehabilitation of the southern states; and the use of the ballot in the hands of the Negro was effective in achieving the following results: First: It established the sovereignty of the nation. Second: It utterly destroyed all that was vicious, mischievous, and menacing in the doctrine of state rights. Third: It made effective the thirteenth amendment, and enacted the fourteenth and fifteenth amendments to the Constitution of the United States—giving rise to the strange paradox, unique in the history of the world, that the ballot of the ex-slave had become necessary to save the face of a conquering nation, preserve the fruits of victory, and assist in the enactment of laws which made his own freedom secure; and it wrote his own citizenship ineffaceably into the constitution, the organic law of the land. Fourth: It was effective in causing the adoption of free constitutions for the southern states, the establishment of orderly government in them, and, in a word, rehabilitating them and restoring them to practical and proper relations with the Union. Fifth: It gave the South its first system of free public schools, a benefaction and blessing of incalculable value.

It is not, therefore, too much to say that the glory and the power of the republic today—the foremost and most powerful nation in the world—may be traced to the use of the Negro as a soldier and as a voter in the most stormy and perilous hour of its existence. He was unquestionably the deciding factor. "The truth is the light," and in the light of the truth these facts blaze forth.

It must, therefore, appear evident to every serious, patriotic American who has more regard for liberty and Union than for race hatred and caste prejudice, that the bestowal of the ballot on the colored people, under the circumstances, and at the time, and in the manner that it was bestowed, was not only not a crime, but, on the contrary, was perhaps the sublimest act of enlightened statesmanship.[8]

These good accomplishments which were certainly due in part at least to Negro influence would seem to partly recompense the state of South Carolina for the money which was lost or stolen and the uncouth manners in the legislative halls which replaced the polished though worthless activity of the aristocrats who had formerly ruled at Columbia and led the state into rebellion, war, and economic ruin. It must be remembered that this reconstruction legislation was good enough to last the state of South Carolina up to the present time to a large extent. It is a significant fact that most of the legislation enacted under the influence of the Negroes still remains in force, except that which allowed the Negroes their rights as citizens, this part being largely nullified by the ignoble disfranchisement laws. We shall conclude this matter with a statement by one of the Negro leaders in the South Carolina Reconstruction legislature. We quote from a speech made by Hon. Thomas E. Miller, answering an argument by Mr. Tillman in the South Carolina Constitutional Convention in 1890, whereby most of the Negroes of South Carolina were disfranchised:

The gentleman from Edgefield [Mr. Tillman] speaks of the piling up of the state dept.; of robbery and speculation during the period between 1869 and 1873 in South Carolina, but he has not found voice eloquent enough nor pen exact enough to mention those imperishable gifts bestowed upon South Carolina

---

[8] Sinclair: *The Aftermath of Slavery,* pages 102-103.

between 1875 and 1876 by Negro legislators—the laws relative
to finance, the building of penal and charitable institutions and,
greatest of all, the establishment of the public school system.
Starting as infants in legislation in 1869, many wise measures
were not thought of, many injudicious acts were passed. But
in the administration of affairs for the next four years, having
learned by experience the result of bad acts, we immediately
passed reformatory laws touching every department of state,
county, municipal and town governments. These enactments are
today upon the statute books of South Carolina. They stand
as living witnesses of the Negro's fitness to vote and legislate
upon the rights of mankind.

When we came into power, town governments could lend the
credit of their respective towns to secure funds at any rate of
interest that the council saw fit to pay. Some of the towns
paid as high as 20 per cent. We passed an act prohibiting town
governments from pledging the credit of their hamlets for money
bearing a greater rate of interest than 5 per cent.

Up to 1874, inclusive, the state treasurer had the power to
pay out state funds as he pleased. He could elect whether he
would pay out the funds on appropriations that would place the
money in the hands of the speculators, or would apply them to
appropriations that were honest and necessary. We saw the
evil of this and passed an act making specific levies and collections of taxes for specific appropriations.

Another source of profligacy in the expenditure of funds
was the law that provided for and empowered the levying and
collecting of special taxes by school districts, in the name of the
schools. We saw its evil and by a constitutional amendment
provided that there should only be levied and collected annually
a tax of two mills for school purposes, and took away from
the school districts the power to levy and to collect taxes of
any kind. By this act we cured the evils that had been inflicted
upon us in the name of the schools, settled the public school
question for all time to come and established the system upon
an honest financial basis.

Next, we learned during the period from 1869 to 1874, inclusive, that what was denominated the floating indebtedness, covering the printing schemes and other indefinite expenditures,
amounted to nearly $2,000,000. A conference was called of the
leading Negro representatives in the two Houses together with
the State Treasurer, also a Negro. After this conference we
passed an act for the purpose of ascertaining the bona fide floating debt and found that it did not amount to more than $250,000
for the four years; we created a commission to lift that indebted-

ness and to scale it. Hence when the democratic party came into power they found the floating debt covering the legislative and all other expenditures, fixed at the certain sum of $250,000. This same Cardoza, knowing that there were millions of fraudulent bonds charged against the credit of the state, passed another act to ascertain the true bonded indebtedness and to provide for its settlement. Under this law, at one sweep, those entrusted with the power to do so, through Negro legislators, stamped six millions of bonds, denominated as conversion bonds, "fraudulent." The commission did not finish its work before 1876. In that year when the Hampton government came into power, there were still to be examined into and settled under the terms of the act passed by us and providing for the legitimate bonded indebtedness of the state, a little over $2,500,000 worth of bonds and coupons which had not been passed upon.

Governor Hampton, General Hagood, Judge Simonton, Judge Wallace and in fact, all of the conservative thinking Democrats aligned themselves under the provision enacted by us for the certain and final settlement of the bonded indebtedness and appealed to their Democratic legislators to stand by the Republican legislation on the subject and to confirm it. A faction in the Democratic party obtained a majority of the Democrats in the legislature against settling the question and they endeavored to open up anew the whole subject of the state debt. We had a little over thirty members in the House and enough Republican senators to sustain the Hampton conservative faction and to stand up for honest finance, or by our votes to place the debt question of the old state into the hands of the plunderers and speculators. We were appealed to by General Hagood, through me, and my answer to him was in these words: "General, our people have learned the difference between profligate and honest legislation. We have passed acts of financial reform, and with the assistance of God, when the vote shall have been taken, you will be able to record for the thirty odd Negroes, slandered though they have been through the press, that they voted solidly with you all for the honest legislation and the preservation of the credit of the state." The thirty odd Negroes in the legislature and their senators by their votes did settle the debt question and saved the state $13,000,000.

We were eight years in power. We had built school houses, established charitable institutions, built and maintained the penitentiary system, provided for the education of the deaf and dumb, rebuilt the jails and court houses, rebuilt the bridges and re-established the ferries. In short, we had reconstructed the state and placed it upon the road to prosperity and, at the same time, by our acts of financial reform, transmitted to the Hampton government an indebtedness not greater by more than $2,500,000 than was the bonded debt of the state in 1868, before the Republican Negroes and their white allies came into power.[9]

In this matter of the reconstruction of South Carolina the "sound and fury" which has been created and kept up, most of it "signifying nothing" of truth, has distracted attention from the economic and social phases of reconstruction. All possible stress has been placed upon the political side of it. The average person thinks, as A. A. Taylor suggests, that the Negroes of the state of South Carolina during the Reconstruction did nothing at all but engage in politics and military affairs. If one thinks about the matter just a little he can easily see that this could not be true. This treatment of the Reconstruction period is practically all of the old school historical writing. Most of the world history and practically all of the innumerable national histories have usually been devoted largely to political and military affairs. Only recently has there come to the front a tendency to relegate military and political affairs to their proper place as of secondary importance in any real history of civilization. The political and military activities are the most conspicuous parts of a people's life, but not the most important. Certainly we can get no proper or adequate grasp of the Negro's part in the reconstruction of South Carolina unless we take into consideration his contribution and work along other lines than in politics and economics. We must see what he was doing socially, economically, educationally, and religiously.

In a previous chapter we spoke of the Negro being humanly imitative of the white people among whom he lived. Especially is this true in his social life, using the phrase "social life" here, as before, in the narrow sense. During the Reconstruction period this social life of the Negro, like the life of the nation as a whole, was democratized to a certain extent. Of course the Negroes who had absorbed the ideas

---

[9] W. E. B. DuBois: *The Gift of the Black Folk,* pages 243-248 (quoted from occasional papers of Negro Academy, No. 6).

of the aristocracy and who had been encouraged to develop the aristocratic complex continued their attempt to maintain their "superior" status. As time went on it became increasingly clear that to most of the white people all colored people were considered in the same light. All Negroes were considered as inferior and not deserving the treatment accorded to white people. This attitude on the part of the responsible whites tended to encourage the Negroes to unite and minimize their differences. In certain localities, in Charleston in particular, the aristocratic influences were more strongly entrenched and were correspondingly more difficult to eradicate.

But even in the "City by the Sea" the careful observer can detect a growing group consciousness, a social self-respect, and a feeling of comradeship, which means the ultimate triumph of democracy. There are still many Negroes in Charleston and elsewhere who believe in the principles of aristocracy and their dissatisfaction with the present arrangement in the South is not rooted in their belief in democracy, but in their conviction that the caste system as now organized fails to recognize all the aristocrats, especially themselves, who are due special considerations suitable to their proper "station in life," and their extraordinary inherited talents. There are still many Negroes who believe in the value of "blue blood," though the test tubes of the scientists fail to reveal anything extraordinary about it. At this point the following from the pen of a distinguished South Carolina Negro author, is interesting and informing:

The story of the free Negroes in Charleston is one that is full of interest and charm. In all of the older established cities, there was a small band of free Negroes who lived in self-satisfied complacency in a little world below the whites and above the slaves. They enjoyed existence with a keenness of relish, which freedom has almost wholly destroyed. It is a glorious experience to have a mass of people below you, even if there are others above you. The free colored people had their own churches and schools, and enjoyed a certain area of recognized privileges which gave them an established place in the city's economy. They were assigned the bulk of the industrial and mechanical work as carpenters, painters, bricklayers, tailors and marketmen. The whites encouraged their social separateness from the slaves, as a means of ruling by division. The line of demarcation coincided almost wholly with the color line. As a result, there grew up between the two shades of color an almost impossible barrier. Many of the free Negroes were owners of slaves, and easily assumed the attitude and hauteur of the white master.[10]

The abolition of slavery meant a sweeping and profound change in the economic status and problems of the Negroes in South Carolina. As we pointed out in an article on "The Slaves Carry On in Civilization," the Negroes of South Carolina absorbed the ideas of the western civilization of which they were a part. They saw that the white man in this civilization placed great importance upon the ownership of land and gained great power through it. As soon as the Negroes were freed they began to express their desire to own land and they also began to work toward that end. The Government, seeing this demand, made some effort to assist. Much land came under the direct supervision of the United States Government as a direct result of the post-war legislation. Although most of this land eventually came back to the owners, Negroes procured some of it. About $750,000 was appropriated for the land commission of the Reconstruction government to use in purchasing land for the freedmen, but most of it was stolen and never performed the service which was intended. The commissioners seem to have been responsible for the graft which made this worthy attempt abortive. The Negroes did finally come into possession of much land through purchase from the Government and from individuals, mostly white, who were forced to sell a part of their land to procure funds or capital necessary to carry on their operations. Some white people sold their land at reasonable prices because they doubted that it could be properly cultivated with free Negro labor. It is a fact that the ownership of the land made the Negro farm laborer much more efficient. As long as the Negro worked on the white man's land he found

---

[10] Kelly Miller: Article in *The Messenger*, December, 1925.

that there was more truth than poetry or music in the old song:

> See dat pecker-wood
> Settin' on de rail
> Learnin' how ter figger
> All fer de white man
> Nothin' fer de Nigger.

Thus the Negro began to protest against his exploitation in the gang system on the large plantations. When assured that there was something in it for him in that he would be paid a fair wage or because he worked his own land the freedman developed rapidly as a free laborer. Even the white people, who had been unfriendly and pessimistic, were gradually brought around to admit that the Negro free laborer was doing much more to reconstruct the southern states economically than he would ever have accomplished as a slave laborer. We read an editorial in the *Daily News* which contained the following:

> The experiment of free labor has been tried but a short time, and we would not undertake to speak confidently as to the final result; but notwithstanding much discomfiture and distress and failure, there is much in the experience of the past that opens a charming prospect in the future.[11]

The editor further goes on to say that the Negro had learned that freedom and idleness are not synonymous and that his ultimate freedom required that he learn to labor more efficiently. We could produce more evidence of the same kind to support this fact but it is hardly necessary here as the fact is almost obvious. Travelers, magazine writers and preachers all could be quoted to support the view that the Negro farm laborers were making a valuable contribution toward the reconstruction of the state.

As the majority of the newly freed Negroes were grossly ignorant their desires were few and inexpensive. It is a well known fact that people increase in efficiency as workers as they increase in intelligence and consequently have more and more expensive desires and demands. Intelligence lifts

---

[11] *The Charleston Daily News.* Editorial, December 15, 1866. (Univ. of S. C. Library.)

the standard of living and so calls for a more productive labor programme on the part of the individual worker so that he may hold his own as his group moves on to a higher and higher plane. The facts reveal that the Negroes in mass did not care to work more than a part of the week for although their wages were pitifully small they could make enough in three or four days each week to satisfy their immediate desires. In addition to this there were two things which definitely discouraged the Negroes from working. First, there were the "Black Code" provisions, which we have referred to before, which prohibited working at certain trades and other occupations calling for education and, of course, for higher wages.

Before the Civil War resulted in freedom for the Negro slaves the vast majority of them in this state had worked for their masters as plantation laborers. After emancipation these planters still needed the work of the slaves. They were not convinced that the Negro was worthy of his hire as a free laborer and they were unwilling in practically all instances to pay him. Naturally the Negroes declined to continue to work for nothing although they were faced with starvation as the alternative. These former slaves were unable and unwilling to migrate. After all, only a comparatively small number of them could go in for politics, though one gets the impression from the average anti-Negro writer on this period that all the Negroes strove to achieve a parasitic life as politicians. The large majority of the Negroes soon returned to work on the plantations. They became wage slaves instead of chattel slaves.

Some Negro freedmen did not go to work immediately because they believed that they would get land of their own and become independent farmers. In 1862, as a result of the Acts of Forfeiture, large amounts of land especially around St. Helena Island and Port Royal became the property of the federal government. It was rumored that this land and much more similarly procured by the government would be issued to the freedmen. They each hoped for "forty acres of land and a mule" as a gift from the government to start them out as free men. Then the ex-slaves knew that the government procured a large amount of land on account of the non-payment of taxes. A governmental commission procured an appropriation of $750,000 to obtain land for the Negroes. All this did not benefit the Negroes because of dishonesty in administration.[12] All this was some disappointment to the Negroes but they finally went to work. That these ex-slaves worked faithfully and well if not with maximum efficiency is attested by many worthy witnesses. For example, the editor of the well known South Carolina newspaper, the *Daily News*, expressed himself as follows:

The Negro has begun to understand that freedom does not mean idleness; and hence want as well as the influence of superior sagacity and ability has contributed as well to his industry as to his good order.[13]

While the above statement is patronizing and grudging in its praise it goes far with one familiar with the situation. The writer, talking with an old colored citizen of Charleston (Jan. 5, 1927) by the name of Gregory, was told that the general propaganda that the Negroes did not work and would not have worked without the "Black Code" regulations was in his opinion "bunk" because it was evidently true that the Negroes had no other way to procure a living. Mr. Gregory further stated that the Negroes were compelled to work for very low wages, which was very discouraging to them. The truth is, the freedmen were offered work at wages that were very much below the amount of income necessary to maintain a standard of living equal to that of the poor whites. The Negroes naturally tried in every way to avoid working for such wages. The whites were anxious to have the ex-slaves begin working at such low wages that they could be kept perpetually in debt and so reduced to the new form of slavery known as peonage. If the Negroes could not be induced to work for such low wages the planters proposed to get the same result by having them to farm as share-croppers. In this system the plantation owners co-operated with the mer-

---

[12]A. A. Taylor: *The Reconstruction in South Carolina.*
[13]*Daily News*, December 15, 1866. (In Univ. of S. C. Library.)

chants who furnished the "cropper" with his supplies in such
a way that the Negro's share was never sufficient to pay his
debts. The supplies were sold "on credit" at profiteering
prices and in addition the bookkeeping was so manipulated
that the poor ignorant Negroes were totally unable to escape
ruthless exploitation in most instances. Even those Negro
farmers, comparatively few in number, who somehow managed
to be able to rent land and farm more or less independently
could not escape this credit system altogether. Even Negro
farmers who owned land found it difficult to escape.

Where the wage system prevailed the poorer Negroes on
the whole had a better chance to keep free of debt and somehow save some money. Orangeburg County, in one of the
leading cotton districts, is typical in this connection. In
this county, where the state A. & M. college is located, and
where the writer has lived and taught several years, the average wage paid the farm laborer was $8.00 per month. If he
worked by the day he received 50 cents per day. Out of this
miserably small wage many of the Negro workers managed
to save something and finally get a start up the ladder of
financial prosperity. This performance is a wonderful tribute
to the ability and capacity to sacrifice on the part of the
Negroes. Of course, it is quite true that the purchasing
power of $8.00 was quite a deal greater in terms of the neces-
sities of life than an equal amount today, but it represented
a very low wage even then.

In the share-cropping system the majority of the Negroes
worked on some such arrangement as this: the planter furnished the land and all supplies and received one-fourth to
one-third of the crop. A different arrangement is described
by Chancellor Johnson of Marlboro as follows:

I have a good many tenants, white and black. I furnish the
stock, food for them; pay one-half of the blacksmith, fertilizer,
bagging and ties account, and furnish ginning facilities; the tenant
has his garden and potato patch free, does all the work, from
repairing fences and ditches to preparing the crop for market,
my advances are repaid and the crop is equally divided. The
tenants generally get at the rate of eight to ten bales for each
mule they work, grain for their family supplies and enough to

make their meat. I get the same amount of cotton and more than grain enough for the next year's crop. I have had some tenants over ten years.[14]

In all the systems where Negroes worked for deferred income other than money they were tempted, and usually yielded, to buy up to the limit of their credit, mortgaging their future incomes. They were led into relative extravagance and ended in economic slavery-peonage.

From the point of view of the land owners the share-cropping system was ultimately unsatisfactory because the share-croppers took no interest in any work that was not connected with the particular crop they would share. They naturally had little or no interest in attempting to keep or build up the place and its equipment or improving the productivity of the soil. The result was that the plantations subjected to this devastating régime were soon reduced to bare land with dilapidated fences and buildings. When the old farm became practically worn out, the share-croppers, like the Arabs of old, were ready to "fold up their tents and silently steal away," leaving the planter with something of a white elephant upon his hands.

These same evils prevailed to a certain degree among the tenants on the rented farms. The renter was careless about the land and the buildings because he could leave at any time and he did not care to build up or improve the place for the landlords or some renter who might take his place at any time.

It should be mentioned here, too, perhaps that the general methods of farming in the state at the time were backward, uneconomical and inefficient—in a word unscientific. There were a few striking exceptions to this among both white and Negro farmers who owned their own land and so were interested in building up their own property.

We have said more about the Negroes as farm workers than space will permit us to record about Negroes in other pursuits, but we feel that this is justifiable on account of the

---

[14] A. A. Taylor: *The Negro in South Carolina During the Reconstruction,* pages 62-63.

fact that most of the Negroes worked on the farm, as we stated before.

Compared to the comparatively few Negroes who went in to "live by legislation,"—going into politics—there were great numbers in domestic service, for the whites mostly, though a few worked for more affluent members of their own race. It is a peculiar fact, yet a fact easily explained, that most of the Negroes of the domestic servant class or common day labor class preferred to work for white people, especially of the aristocratic families, than to work for members of their own race. This was a result of the propaganda of the whites during slavery which encouraged the Negro servants to consider it beneath their dignity to work for a poor white person and unthinkable to work for a free Negro. The idea of the aristocratic whites in fostering this was to strengthen their own position by giving them a practical monopoly on the service of Negroes. It also served to engender hatred between the Negroes and poor whites and divide the Negroes into classes unfriendly and non co-operative with each other. The Negro servants and common laborers have not yet recovered from the evil effects of this subtle propaganda. Mostly women and children worked at domestic service such as nurses, maids, cooks, housekeepers, etc. However, there were not a few men as butlers, yard men, personal servants, etc. These servants were very poorly paid in terms of the medium of exchange, but they usually received their board and lodging which on the whole was probably better than they could have provided for themselves on any possible wage available for them at that time. Many of them shared the food and lodging of their employers and were given the cast-off clothing, which was usually of good material, or at least better than they could have bought new. But the extremely low money wage which they received made it well nigh impossible for many of them to save any money or make any progress economically. It seems miraculous that many of them managed to educate their children, or at least start them on the road. Many a Negro leader of today, with a fine education obtained at Oberlin, Yale, Harvard—such leaders as Wm. Pickins, R. S. Wilkinson and others, were given their start by hard-working mothers or fathers who literally "bore the burden in the heat of the day." These mothers and fathers worked without any hope that they personally would ever "lay down their heavy load" of unrecompensed toil but they saw the triumph of their children from afar and they toiled unceasingly that their posterity might have a better, fuller, and freer life. They were the real "unsung heroes" of the Negro race in this and every other southern state. Their bodies now lie moulding in humble graves, but their unconquerable souls will forever go marching on!

There were many more Negroes engaged in various trades and industries than ever dreamed of entering politics. The Negroes in Charleston, Columbia, and Beaufort were especially prominent in this respect. In Charleston a large part of the Negro aristocracy, blue-blood and otherwise, were recruited from this class. Such family names as the Leslies, the DeReefs, the Halls, the Gordons, the Grants, the Birnies, the Shrewsberrys, the Wilsons, the Mickeys, the Morrisons, the Hollaways and others are examples.

Then there were Negroes who followed business and the professions and so achieved prominence and wealth and rendered great service to the race. For example, in Columbia there were: James S. Mobley, Bishop Clement, William Taylor and others. At Beaufort there were such men as Robert Smalls, Thos. Miller and J. I. Washington, Sr.

We must not forget that Negroes were also busy, outside of politics, in carrying on the religious and educational development of their race. Then there was much activity in the carrying on of the secret societies such as the Humane and Friendly Society of Charleston, which was organized, I believe, in 1808. We shall not discuss the activity of the Negro in these departments of his life during the Reconstruction period as these subjects are treated more extensively under different chapter headings and some by different writers more competent than the writer of this chapter.

In conclusion of the discussion emphasizing the evident fact that the most important activity of the Negroes during

Reconstruction was not political, though most noise has been
made about that, we wish to present testimony of the following figures from the United States Census records of 1890,
showing that 223,496 Negroes were engaged in agriculture,
fisheries, and mining; 44,755 in domestic and personal service; 12,198 in manufacturing industries; 7,043 in trade and
transportation, and 2,048 in professional service.[15]   Since
this discussion of the Negro in South Carolina has approached
the problem from a different point of view to most of the
studies, except that of Mr. A. A. Taylor, to which we referred
and to which our obligation is apparent, it may not be out
of place for me to summarize my main conclusions, which substantially agree with those of Mr. Taylor and Mr. Louis F.
Post, author of "A Carpet-Bagger in South Carolina."   If
some of our conclusions seem insufficiently supported by evidence rehearsed here we refer the reader to the works of these
men, especially Mr. Taylor's work, where we are confident
he will find justification for all we have not ourselves demonstrated.

The Negroes in the reconstruction of South Carolina were
busy in other ways than in politics.   After the first brief
period of rejoicing over freedom when little work was done
the vast majority of the Negroes went to work at the gigan-
tic task of economic reconstruction and social and religious
advancement and improvement.

The white people of the aristocratic class of the state
were given a wonderful opportunity to reconstruct the state
and restore it to its rightful place in the Union through the
liberal policy inaugurated by President Johnson.   This opportunity was not used but instead the white leaders began
an attempt to restore the old régime as nearly as posible,
which involved the practical re-enslavement of the Negroes,
which was almost accomplished by the infamous "Black Code"
laws.   Congress was not willing to see the greatest blessing
of the war thus prostituted and consequently took over the
problem of reconstructing the state, a task which it found
it impossible to perform without the aid of the Negroes, as

---

[15] U. S. Census Report, 1890, Part 3.

the white people for the most part refused to co-operate.
The Negro was therefore given the ballot and protected in
his new rights by the power of the Federal Government executed through military rule for a short time. On the whole
Negroes conducted themselves with wonderful moderation and
with a reasonable amount of efficiency. There was much mis-
rule and exploitation through the state government, but a
great part of this was due to the evil leadership of some of
the "carpet-baggers" and "scalawags." Much good was accomplished, probably enough to far outweigh the evil. It is
indisputable that the Negroes helped to accomplish three
things of great and permanent value to all the people of South
Carolina; that is, they established a public school system in
the state vastly more democratic than any before or since
it, they adopted a constitution more democratic than any
before and caused the state to be readmitted into the Union,
and, finally, they demonstrated the capacity of the Negro
part of the population to produce a reasonable number of
political leaders of ability and character. Through the dirty
work of the old Ku Klux Klan and the cheating methods of
unscrupulous white politicians, the Negroes were unjustly and
unnecessarily eliminated from politics in the state because the
whites desired to monopolize all political positions and use
their political advantage to exploit the Negroes economically.

During the Reconstruction period the Negro, with characteristic courage, fortitude and optimism, was able to
"carry on" economically, educationally, and religiously. In
fact, great progress was made in all these fields and though
the Negro was seriously wounded in the political conflict he
came out with his head "bloody and unbowed" and still singing:

> It matters not how strait the gate,
> How charged with punishment the scroll,
> I am the master of my fate;
> I am the captain of my soul!

CHAPTER IV

THE NEGRO'S LONG WAR AGAINST IGNORANCE

Education is the fine net which democracy uses
in fishing for human talent.—*H. G. Wells.*

> Prone in the road he lay,
>   Wounded and sore bestead:
> Priests, Levites passed that way,
>   And turned aside the head.
> They were not hardened men
>   In human service slack:
> His need was great: but then,
>   His face, you see, was black.
>   —*Nicholas Worth.*

THE statement that the story of the South Carolina
Negro's struggle to acquire education is one of the great
romances of modern history is probably trite, but it is certainly true. If the thirst for knowledge and education is a
human characteristic, the Negro slaves who came to South
Carolina were certainly obviously and profoundly human.
The Negro's acquisition of education and a fair degree of
intelligence, like his acquisition of freedom, would have been
an impossibility without his own efforts. In the first place it
was obviously essential that the Negro should have the capacity or "native ability" to be educated before the process
could begin, and, secondly, the Negro had to have a strong
enough desire for knowledge to inspire him to make tremendous sacrifices to procure it under the serious disadvantages
he must overcome. In meeting these fundamental conditions
or requirements the Negroes of South Carolina were con-
spicuously successful.

In addition to the Negro's capacity to learn and his thirst
for knowledge urging him on to work and fight for it, several other influences worked together to aid the cause of the
beginning of the education of the slaves even before the Civil
War. It was argued by some who wished to salve their consciences by justifying the slave régime that slavery was a

blessing to the slaves because it gave them a chance to be civilized.* It soon became obvious that the Negroes could not profit to any extent by contact with "Christian" civilization unless they could at least read and write. The early slave owners therefore began to teach the slaves, or have them taught to read and write. This was in line with the theory of the Protestant religious faiths, which prevailed in this state, since they all advocated the reading of the Bible by all true followers of Christ. The religious leaders were committed to this principle and they severely criticized any slave owners who did not have their slaves taught enough to read their Bibles and other religious literature deemed necessary for them.

Some slave owners taught the slaves or encouraged them to get education because they found that the slaves who could read and write and attend to simple business matters were more valuable servants. Their economic interests being thus served, these masters insisted on their right to educate their slaves even after laws had been passed to prohibit the education of slaves or free persons of color.

The free Negroes saw the great value of education and provided schools for themselves and for their children. Many of the free Negroes who came from the Islands of the Atlantic east of Charleston were partially educated before they came to America and they encouraged the South Carolina Negroes to fight for education in every possible way. These free Negroes established schools for their children. Many slave children came to these schools for free Negroes, as there was no serious effort made to distinguish which children were free and which were of slave parents.

One important influence in making the Negro slaves anxious to get education was the fact that they were compelled to show written "passes" in order to be allowed freedom in visiting after a law was passed regulating this very closely.[1] The slaves, however, knew that if they could learn to write

---

*This idea is often seen in the literature of the period—even in one of Phillis Wheatley's poems.
[1] A law to this effect is quoted later in this chapter.

4

they could easily deceive most of the officials on account of the ignorance of many who could hardly read themselves,[2] and on account of the carelessness of some.

It seems to us that the Negro's fight against ignorance in this state falls naturally into three parts: the period before 1861, the period during the Civil War and its immediate aftermath, extending through the Reconstruction era, and the period from the Reconstruction to the present. Of course, one does not find these periods sharply defined or radically different at any special point, but the division is a convenient one for the writer and the reader.

A good deal has been written about the education of the Negroes of South Carolina before the Civil War. We have at least two reliable and authoritative sources of information on this period: a brief paper by Dr. C. W. Birnie, *"The Education of the Negro in Charleston, South Carolina, before the Civil War,"* published in the *Journal of Negro History,* January, 1927; and the larger, more general and better known work of Carter G. Woodson, *"The Education of the Negro Prior to 1861,"* published in 1919 by the Association for the Study of Negro Life and History. These two sources are our main dependence for the facts behind our story of this period, though we have received much valuable information from individuals and miscellaneous newspapers, magazines and books.

We have already called attention to the fact that the first educational efforts for Negroes by the whites came through religious sources. The Society for the Propagation of the Gospel in Foreign Parts was organized in London in 1701. This was a missionary organization especially designed to help the Indians and Negro slaves in the American colonies. The society did work in most of the colonies, but the most effective work of its early history was in South Carolina. Rev. Samuel Thomas, at the Goose Creek Parish, began the work of teaching the Negroes about 1695. He was so successful that ten years later he recognized twenty Negro

---

[2] Birnie, C. W.: *The Education of the Negro in Charleston, South Carolina, Before the Civil War,* Journal of Negro History, Vol. 7, No. 1.

communicants able to read and write.[3] Doubtless there were many others who had learned as much though not officially connected with the church in any way. Reverend Taylor was able to interest several persons in his work to the extent that they took the responsibility of seeing that the work was carried on after he left.

In 1731 we find that Rev. E. Taylor at St. Andrew's parish advanced the cause of education for the Negroes in that he not only gave religious instruction, but gave instruction in other branches of knowledge usually taught in the elementary schools. Rev. Alexander Garden opened a school in 1743, which ultimately had nearly forty students enrolled. In the reports of the S. P. G. in F. P. we find this information about this school which is very interesting as well as informing:

This organization hit upon the plan of purchasing two Negroes named Harry and Andrew, and of qualifying them by thorough instruction in the principles of Christianity and the fundamentals of education, to serve as schoolmasters to their people. Under the direction of the Rev. Mr. Garden, the missionary who had directed the training of these young men, a building costing about three hundred and eight pounds was erected in Charleston, South Carolina. In the school which opened in this building in 1744, Harry and Andrew served as teachers. In the beginning, the school had about sixty young students, and had a very good daily attendance for a number of years. The directors of the institution planned to send out annually between thirty and forty youths well instructed in religion and capable of reading their Bibles to carry home and diffuse the same knowledge to their fellow slaves. It is highly probable that after 1740 such schools were attended largely by free persons of color. Because the progress of Negro education had been rather rapid, South Carolina enacted that year a law prohibiting any person from teaching or causing a slave to be taught, or from employing or using a slave as a scribe in any manner of writing.[4]

The same things happened in other parts of the state though not to the same extent that they were practiced at

---

[3] *An Account of the Endeavors Used by the Society in the Propagation of the Gospel in Foreign Parts,* pages 13, 14.

[4] Birnie, C. W., *Journal of Negro History,* Vol. 12, No. 1.

Charleston. It is true that all over South Carolina, especially in the larger and older towns, such as Columbia and Orangeburg, there were Negroes who were getting a little education on account of the interest of their masters, the zeal of missionaries and the help of free Negroes and slaves who somehow had procured some information.

By 1790 the education of Negroes in Charleston had advanced to such a point that Rev. Thomas Frost suggested the organization of a society which should have as one of its functions the maintenance of schools for Negro children.[5] Several other societies [6] were organized a little later. While all these societies had other additional aims, too much praise cannot be given them for what they did for education at no small financial cost to their members. One of these societies, the Bonneau Library Society, is deserving of special mention and commendation for its definite educational effort in the face of many discouragements. The records, minutes, and other documents still extant dealing with the affairs of this society show that its members were men of no small degree of intelligence.[7]

The educational progress of the Negroes of South Carolina, free and slave, was seriously crippled after the Vesey insurrection in 1822. Laws were passed thereafter severely restricting the opportunities for Negroes to get education. About 1835 the following law was passed which speaks for itself:

An act to amend the law relating to Slaves and Free persons of Color.—Be it enacted by the Honorable, the Senate and House of Representatives now met and sitting in General Assembly, and by the authority of the same. If any person shall hereafter teach any slave to read or write, or cause or procure any slave to read or write, such person if a free white person upon conviction thereof shall for each and every offense against this act be fined not exceeding One Hundred Dollars and imprisoned not more than six months; or if a free person of color shall be whipped not exceeding fifty lashes, and fined not exceeding

[5]*Brown Fellowship Society,* later known as Centenary.
[6]*Humane and Friendly,* 1802; *Minors Moralist,* 1803, etc.
[7]Birnie, C. W., *Journal of Negro History,* Vol. 12, No. 1.

Fifty Dollars, at the discretion of the Court of Magistrates and Freeholders before which such person of color is tried; and if a slave to be whipped at the discretion of the court; not exceeding fifty lashes; the informer to be entitled to one half of the fine and to be a competent witness. And if any free person of color or slave shall keep any school or other place of instruction for teaching any slave or free person of color to read or write, such free person of color or slave shall be liable to the same fine and corporal punishment as are by this act imposed and inflicted upon free persons of color and slaves for teaching slaves to read or write.[8]

This law, strict as it was, did not stop the Negroes from attending schools and getting education, but it did retard the movement by making it more dangerous and difficult for friendly masters, missionaries, and free Negroes who wished to help Negroes, slave and free, to procure some education.

The following paragraphs from Doctor Birnie's essay on Negro Education in Charleston before the Civil War are very interesting and informing and will serve as a conclusion of our discussion of the period:

To give a complete list of all the schools in Charleston between 1790 and 1860 would be an impossibility. These herein mentioned have been brought to light only after research into family records and papers and by correspondence and conversation with the few survivors of those days. One of the most famous colored teachers of his time was Thos. S. Bonneau. He kept a school from about 1803 until his death about 1828 or 1829. His school was so large that he was compelled to employ assistants, one of whom was Mr. William McKinlay and the other Mr. F. K. Sasportas. Later this school was carried on by Daniel Payne, who afterwards became a bishop in the African Methodist Episcopal Church. Thos. S. Bonneau seems to have been a man of great force of character. He left his impress not only on the people of his time, but for many years after. He died when forty-seven years of age, and so much was he appreciated by his former pupils that a monument was erected to his memory. This monument can yet be seen in the cemetery in which he is buried. The teaching profession has been represented in every generation of his lineal descendants.

Other schools for Negroes rendered valuable service in the early part of the nineteenth century. One Mr. Munns or Munz

---

[8]Ibid., footnote, pages 17-18.

kept a school which was quite popular for some time. In 1820, Mrs. Stromer, a woman of color, founded a school which was continued until the Civil War. She was one of the first teachers in the schools for freedmen that were established after emancipation.

One of the largest and best known of these ante-bellum schools was conducted by Mr. W. W. Wilburn, a white man, on Coming Street, opposite Bull Street. He was paid a regular salary, not having to depend at all on tuition. The financial affairs of this school were managed by a Board of Trustees elected by the patrons. The earliest of these trustees of whom we have records were Benj. Huger, Joseph Sasportas and William McKinlay.

Among other schools may be mentioned those taught by the following: Simeon Beard on Wall Street; Edward Beard on Coming Street near Duncan Street; Wm. Feerette on Market Street; Wallace, a white man, on Beaufain Street; Mood, on Beaufain Street; Seymour, on Gorge Street; Andred Miller, who kept school about 1830; Kegney, a white Roman Catholic, who had a school at the corner of Radcliffe and St. Phillip Streets; Fannie Bonneau, on Coming Street; Amelia Barnett, on Mary Street; Mary Witzel, a white woman, on Anson Street; Kittie Soloman, who is said to have been a Haytian refugee; and Henry Frost, on Magazine Street.

The churches, especially the Episcopal, took active part in Negro education. They had Sunday Schools for Negro children immediately after the closing of the white Sunday Schools. Both classes were taught by the same teachers. About 1840, the Diocese of South Carolina opened a school at St. Stephen's Church on Anson Street, which is still used for the same purpose.

The instruction given in these schools compared very favorably with any in the city, the teachers in a number of cases being young men who earned their way through college by teaching. Some of these students after they had finished at these schools employed tutors who taught them many of the higher branches which they were pursuing at the Charleston College.[9]

We hope that the brief sketch so far given will serve to let the reader understand how the Negroes of South Carolina procured quite a bit of education before the Civil War. We hope the reader will not fail to reflect on the cost of this education in money and courage and realize its significance as a tribute to the Negro's great determination to free himself

[9]Ibid., pages 18-20.

from the curse of ignorance in so far as he could do so by his own efforts.

The Civil War had not progressed very far before large numbers of Negroes became attached to the Federal armies in South Carolina. Many of these Negroes were fugitives or the property of "fugitive masters" who feared retaliation by the Federal soldiers. These Negroes appealed to the army officials for help. The people of the North soon became interested in their plight and began to form organizations to help them in every possible way; especially to relieve those suffering from poverty and sickness. Among the organizations formed to meet this urgent need were the following: The New England Freedmen's Aid Society, the New York National Freedmen's Relief Association, the Pennsylvania Freedmen's Relief Association, and others less prominent. These organizations found at once that they could not meet the challenge without attempting to educate the Freedmen in some way and to some extent. In fact, the original call sent out for aid suggested educational effort, as is shown by General Order No. 9, issued by Sherman, February, 1862:

> The helpless condition of the blacks inhabiting the vast area in the occupation of the forces of this command, call for immediate action on the part of highly favored and philanthropic people. . . . Hordes of totally uneducated, ignorant and improvident blacks have been abandoned by their constitutional guardians, not only to all the future chances of anarchy and starvation, but in such a state of abject ignorance and mental stolidity as to preclude all possibility of self-government and self-maintenance in their present condition. . . . To relieve the Government of a burden that may hereafter become insupportable. . . . a suitable system of culture and instruction must be combined with one providing for their physical wants. In the meantime. . . . the service of competent instructors will be received whose duties will consist in teaching them, both young and old, the rudiments of civilization and Christianity.[10]

The New York National Freedmen's Relief Association adopted the following rules, February 22, 1862:

---

[10]Jackson, Luther: The Educational Efforts of the Freedman's Bureau and Freedman's Aid Societies in South Carolina, *Journal of Negro History*, Vol. 8, No. 1, pages 5-6.

1.   They (the Freedmen) must be treated as free men.

2.   They must earn their livelihood like other free men and not be dependent upon charity.

3.   Schools and churches should be established among them, and the sick shall be cared for.[11]

Some of these organizations began the actual work of education as early as 1862. The men and women who volunteered to come down and help the Freedmen were people of excellent character, in fact they were of the material of which martyrs and heroes are made. They were worthy of the name "Gideonites," which was applied to them. They honored the institutions of Harvard, Yale, Brown, Andover, and Cambridge, from which many had but recently been graduated. To give them just praise we must fall back upon a quotation from the matchless Negro writer W. E. B. DuBois. Speaking of the work of these early pioneers in the work of Negro education, he said:

This was the gift of New England to the freed Negro; not alms, but a friend; not cash, but character. It was not and is not money these seething millions want, but love and sympathy, the pulse of hearts beating with red blood—a gift which today only their own kindred and race can bring to the masses, but which once saintly souls brought to their favored children in the crusade of the sixties, that finest thing in American history, and one of the few things untainted by sordid greed and cheap vainglory. The teachers in these institutions came not to keep the Negroes in their places, but to raise them out of the defilement of the places where slavery had wallowed them.[12]

We should not pass over this early educational effort without mentioning the American Missionary Association. In the opinion of the writer there is no other voluntary organization in the country to which is due as much credit as to this organization as a pioneer in education for the Negroes in this and other southern states. In the fall of 1862 this association sent thirty-one teachers into the work.

The work of these pioneers was sponsored by such men as William Cullen Bryant, Wm. Lloyd Garrison, Francis

---

[11]*Annual Report of the New York Freedman's Relief Association,* 1866.

[12]DuBois, W. E. Burghardt: *The Souls of Black Folk,* page 100.

G. Shaw, and Edward Everett Hale.   The Federal Government, through its officials, especially S. P. Chase, sympathized with and encouraged the work.[13]

One may ask, "What part did the Negro play in all this heroic effort for his uplift?"   In answer to this we may say that the free Negroes of the North helped to finance it and their leaders, such as Frederick Douglass, used their influence in every possible way to push the movement ahead.   The Negroes of South Carolina, the Freedmen, in whose behalf the effort was being made, did their part to make it a success by responding with all possible enthusiasm and speed.   Their faith in education was almost if not quite pathetic and they hesitated at no sacrifice in order to procure it for themselves and for their children, as they considered it the open door to all the manifold blessings of civilization.

The effort at Port Royal attracted national and international attention and so became known as the Port Royal Experiment, which appellation indicated the lack of confidence in the capacity of the Freedmen to be educated and to take a respectable place in modern civilization.   Although the vast majority of these early teachers were white people, some were Negroes.   A brilliant example of this is a colored woman of Philadelphia, Charlotte S. Foster.   She was well prepared, being a graduate of the state normal school at Salem, Massachusetts.   She gave up an opportunity to live in Europe, and, like her white co-laborers, denied herself the congenial society of cultured New England and worked faithfully, happily, and effectively among the lonely Freedmen of South Carolina.

The outstanding effort in this section was that of Luna M. Towne, also of Philadelphia.   She played a very important part in the founding of the famous and effective Penn School, so called after the Pennsylvania society which supported the work.   This school effectively taught reading, spelling, writing, and arithmetic.   It has continued to progress and im-

---

[13]Jackson, L. P.: The Educational Efforts of the Freedman's Bureau and the Freedmen's Aid Societies in South Carolina 1862-1867—*Journal of Negro History,* Vol. 8, No. 1.

prove its service until today the Penn Normal and Agricultural Institute is recognized as one of the most effective and serviceable schools of its type in the country.

There were several other schools founded in this period which achieved notable success. Elizabeth Hyde Botume, appointed and supported by the New England Freedmen's Aid Society, established an industrial school at Beaufort, S. C. The women's American Baptist Home Mission Society supported Rachel Crome Mather in an attempt to found a school, which appears to have been more of a social service organization.[14]

It should be mentioned here that these early schools not only began to satisfy the Negro's quest for "book learning," but the contact with the "best blood" of New England which was made possible by the democratic life of these early apostles of true Americanism in South Carolina, resulted in improving the Negro in every worth while way,—religiously, economically, and socially. As that profound philosopher DuBois said in the quotation given before, these people brought more than alms, they brought the inspiration of real Christian fellowship.

Before proceeding further with this narrative of educational effort among Negroes of this state it may be well for us to mention the most important governmental agency involved which was, of course, the famous Freedmen's Bureau, established by act of Congress, March 3, 1865. Speaking of this organization as it pertained to educational effort in this state, L. P. Jackson says:

The organization of the Freedmen's Bureau as affecting South Carolina consisted of a commissioner at Washington, an assistant commissioner for the State at large with headquarters at Charleston, and sub-assistant commissioners—one for each of the five districts into which the State was divided. Furthermore, there was a subdivision of each district with agents in charge. For the educational work of the Freedmen's Bureau there was a corps consisting of a general superintendent on the commissioner's staff, a state superintendent correspondingly on

[14]Taylor, A. A., *The Negro in South Carolina During the Reconstruction*, page 85.

the assistant commissioner's staff at Charleston, and the various sub-assistant commissioners and agents who combined the supervision of schools with their other duties. The personnel of this hierarchy consisted of General O. O. Howard, commissioner; J. W. Alvord, general superintendent of education; General Rufus Saxton, General R. K. Scott, Colonel J. R. Edie, successively assistant commissioner; and Reuben Tomlinson, Major Horace Neide, Major E. L. Deane, successively state superintendents of education. These officers, beginning with the lowest, made to their respective chiefs monthly, quarterly or semi-annual reports which were finally submitted to the commissioner at Washington who was required to make "before the commencement of each regular session of Congress, a full report of his proceedings."[15]

The Freedmen's Bureau was remarkably successful in attracting into its personnel for educational efforts so many persons who were loyal and conscientious in their efforts to uplift and develop the Negroes in accordance with the liberal, progressive and democratic ideals of its founders and supporters. A characteristic and remarkable achievement of the organization was its success in co-operating perfectly with the various private organizations engaged in the same educational effort, all jealous of their freedom and reputation and zealous in their competition with rivals. There were at least three different classes of these private organizations. First, the non-sectarian organizations such as the New York National Freedmen's Relief Association; the New England's Freedmen's Aid Society; the Pennsylvania Freedmen's Relief Association; the London Freedmen's Aid Society and the Michigan Freedmen's Relief Association. Secondly, the denominational organizations, such as The American Baptist Home Mission Society, the Presbyterian Committee of Missions for Freedmen; the Freedmen's Aid Society of the Methodist Episcopal Church; the Protestant Episcopal Freedmen's Commission; the Friends Association of Philadelphia for the Aid and Elevation of the Freedmen. Thirdly, the unique "semi-denominational" American Missionary Association finally more or less definitely associated with the mis-

---

[15]*Journal of Negro History*, January, 1923, page 13.

sionary or world service department of the Congregational
Church.

The private organizations were primarily interested in
Christian missionary work, and their educational work was
considered as subsidiary to this primary work, but knowledge could not be limited to orthodox religious ideas as the
slave owners had previously discovered; and the truth, as
ever, tended to make the Negroes free in every way. The
friendliness of all the private organizations toward the Freedmen's Bureau was perhaps largely due to the fact that all of
them hoped for financial aid and support through this influential organization. At any rate, we find all of them receiving
more or less substantial help and encouragement from this
source.

It is impossible, within the space limitation imposed upon
us in this book to mention all the schools founded and fostered by the Freedmen's Bureau in this state. It is necessary
that we mention some of the leading schools founded by the
bureau and the private organizations.

We turn first to Charleston. Here we find that educational effort began before the Freedmen's Bureau was ready
to function. On March 4, 1865, schools were opened in this
city by James Redpath an appointee of Colonel Woodford,
commander at Charleston. The schools were opened to both
races, but the Negro children came in much larger numbers
than the whites. The children were divided according to
racial affiliation—the colored in rooms to themselves. Teachers were both white and colored, but mostly native South
Carolinians. As soon as the white people of Charleston
came into full possession all the Negro teachers were ousted
and native whites retained. It is a peculiar fact that these
white people of Charleston continued to teach in the Negro
schools, excluding the colored, much longer than any such
system continued anywhere else.

One of the oldest and most influential private high schools
in South Carolina is the Avery Normal Institute, organized
by F. L. Cardoza, October 1, 1865. This school was supported by the Congregational American Missionary Associa-

tion and was called Avery because a philanthropic minister by that name gave $10,000 of the $25,000 necessary to construct a new building for the school at its present site. This school has a long and honorable history and a reputation for efficiency surpassed by few high schools of the South. The present principal is Mr. B. F. Cox.

Other schools established in Charleston were Shaw Memorial Institute, named for the famous Col. Robert G. Shaw, the hero of Morris Island; the Wallingford Academy, founded by Jonathan C. Gibbs, and the Morris Street school.

After Charleston comes Columbia as an important center in the struggle of the Freedmen to procure education. Columbia's red-letter day was November 6, 1865. At this time a school was opened in the basement of a Negro Church at which 243 pupils immediately enrolled. Several other schools were soon founded, using both white and colored faculties where they could be provided. However, 1867 saw the opening of the Howard School through the effort of the New York Society co-operating with the Freedmen's Bureau. Six hundred students attended this school the first year and it made such a good impression on the local community that the *Columbia Phoenix* said of its work:

We were pleased with the neat appearance and becoming bearing of the scholars—and the proficiency exhibited in the elementary branches was respectable.

This school has always had a reputation for progressive work. For a long time it was the only public high school in the state. The present principal is Prof. I. M. A. Myers, secretary of the Negro State Teachers Association (1927).

The most important institutions established at Columbia, however, were those of the private organizations. One of the first of these institutions was Benedict Institute, as it was first called, but now known as Benedict College. This college was founded by the Baptist Home Missionary Society in 1870. As was true in the case of practically all these early institutions for the higher education of Negroes in this and other southern states, Benedict College was made possible by the generosity of a northern white philanthropist. In the case of Benedict the good angel was Mrs. Bethsheba A. Benedict of Pawtucket, R. I. The ideals of Benedict College, as expressed by her founders and early promoters, were very worthy. The purposes of the Institute were: "to educate young men of the Baptist faith for the ministry, to prepare efficient teachers for the colored people, and to train all the students in the essentials of Christian citizenship."* The emphasis was always placed upon thorough academic work at Benedict and higher and higher courses have consistently been added. The college has enjoyed the leadership of excellent friends of the Negroes such as Timothy Dodge, Lewis Colby, E. J. Goodspeed and Doctor Antisdel, the present president. Along with all the denominational schools dedicated to the "higher education" of Negroes in the South, Benedict has had a hard and continuous struggle for adequate financial support to procure buildings and other material equipment and salaries for efficient, well trained teachers, white and colored. In spite of this great handicap the school has established an enviable reputation among the Negro colleges of America. It has a very good modern building for the teaching of science and a modern building for the normal practice work. It is not easy to overestimate the value of this institution's work in preparing many of the most successful Negro leaders in every field activity in South Carolina.

We plan to more definitely emphasize the part played by Negroes in their own behalf in this connection later in this chapter, but we cannot speak of the founding of Allen University, which we should mention now, without calling attention to the fact that its significance is in great part due to the fact that it was one of the earliest efforts on the part of the Negroes to help the Negro procure independent educational facilities under complete Negro control. Allen University was established in 1880 by the African Methodist Episcopal Church under the leadership of Bishop W. F. Dickerson and other leaders of the denomination. Payne Institute, a small school belonging to this church, which

---

*From the *College Catalogue.*

had been founded at an earlier date (1870), was consolidated with the new school. The aim of Allen from the beginning was to offer the Negroes opportunity to procure "higher education" of all types under the inspiration of Negro leadership. Two of the early presidents who did much to foster the work and advance it were J. C. Waters and J. W. Morris. Both these men were forceful characters, and had studied law at the University of South Carolina when it was democratic—open to all citizens of the state. The college soon established a theological course. Allen was unique among the early colleges for Negroes in all the South in that it had for several years a flourishing department of law from which about fourteen young men received degrees in law before the department was discontinued. A man of most commanding influence in the development of Allen was O. A. Straker, professor of law and dean of the college. It was during his administration that the young men did such excellent work in law and other higher branches, thus laying the foundation for the greater Allen which followed. Another outstanding leader who served as president of Allen for several years was Dr. Robert W. Mance. It was during his administration that the new academic building containing a beautiful auditorium and dining hall was built. Bishop W. D. Chapelle, chancellor, did Trojan service in collecting money for Allen from the Negroes of the state. The present president of Allen University is Dr. David H. Simms, a graduate of Oberlin College, the youngest college president in the state, a man whose pleasing personality, great ability and progressive ideals assure a bright future for Allen.

The third focal point of educational activity for and by colored people of South Carolina is Orangeburg, the present home of the writer. One of the best known colleges for Negroes in America is Claflin University. This school obtained its charter from the State Legislature in 1869. It was founded as the chief educational project of the South Carolina Conference of the Methodist Episcopal Church. Like Allen, Claflin emerged from the consolidation of smaller schools; namely, the training school at Camden and the

Baker Theological Institute at Charleston. The college purchased the building and grounds of an old white school known as the Orangeburg Female College. T. W. Lewis and A. Webster, South Carolina ministers of the Methodist Episcopal denomination, were influential leaders in the founding of Claflin. The origin of the name, like that of Benedict, is traced to the generosity of a northern friend, Mr. Lee Claflin of Massachusetts. As the name "university" suggests, Claflin began with a great ambition—it planned to offer all the opportunities of "higher education" to the colored people, in fact, to all people, of the state. In 1872 the Federal Government, co-operationg with the state government, established the State College of Agriculture and Mechanics' Institute, as a department or division of Claflin. There was included an experimental farm of over 100 acres. In 1877 a normal school was established in connection with Claflin. In 1890 we find the school functioning prosperously in all departments. Much of this early progress of Claflin was due to the effective work of the president, Edward Cooke. After the administration of President Cooke the development of Claflin was greatly accelerated and long sustained under the wise leadership of Dr. L. M. Dunton, who is one of those friends of Negroes we have referred to. He labored at Claflin over forty years and really built the institution. Doctor Dunton always showed profound interest in the general welfare of the colored people of Orangeburg, and the entire state of South Carolina. It must be admitted that his able financial leadership is responsible for the excellent physical plant at Orangeburg which constitutes the home of Claflin. Doctor Dunton gained such prominence in education and was so liberal in his support of public education in Orangeburg, that when the new school for colored children was built a few years ago it was called the "Dunton Memorial School." He also invested much time and money in an effort to procure a colored playground for the children of this city. After nearly a half century of service, Doctor Dunton resigned and the faculty of Claflin became entirely Negro, under a colored president, Mr. J. B. Randolph. Under the new administration Claflin has been forging ahead and adding to her prestige and power as a great factor in the educational progress of the Negroes of this state.

It is certainly not possible and perhaps not desirable that we mention all the schools that have been established in South Carolina for the uplift of the Negro people. We shall mention a few of the more outstanding ones in what we may call the second and third class; that is, in reference to their size and influence. At Camden there was the Browning Industrial Home and Mather Academy for Girls. It was the property of Mrs. Mather, of Boston, who later gave it to the Woman's Home Missionary Society of the Methodist Episcopal Church. At Mount Pleasant there was the Laing Normal and Industrial School, founded by Cornelia Hancock, of Philadelphia. The school was owned and supported by Pennsylvania Quakers. It was here that Abbey D. Monroe poured out her soul to help the Freedmen.

There are in South Carolina today several small schools that are quite widely known and which are doing excellent work of a secondary nature in the smaller towns at strategic locations in the state. We must mention several of these. Practically all these schools were founded between 1868 and 1870. One of the best known is the Schofield Normal and Industrial School at Aiken, established by Martha Schofield. Miss Schofield came to South Carolina in search of better health and became interested in the uplift of the Freedmen so she persuaded her father, an influential Quaker, to interest the Friends of Pennsylvania in establishing this school. At Greenwood there is Brewer Normal, Industrial and Agricultural Institute, a project of the Congregational American Missionary Association. This school represents the efforts of this great association in a part of the state far removed from its other older school, Avery, in Charleston.

The Board of Missions of the Presbyterian Church is well represented by the Brainerd Institute at Chester and the Goodwill School at Mayesville. Mention of this little mission school at Mayesville gives us an opportunity to give a dramatic illustration of what these missionary efforts often

mean in terms of Wells' definition of education, quoted at
the beginning of this chapter. Here is a paragraph from a
brief biographical sketch of the life of the Negro woman
who is recognized as one of the greatest leaders of her sex
and race in America today:

When Mary was about eleven years old, a little school was
opened near Mayesville by the Board of Missions of the Presbyterian Church, and she was one among the first who walked the
four miles to school and back. Her mother said, "We have to
make some of the children go, but it seems that Mary, little as
she was, kinda understood what it all meant. She was that happy
to go and was the first one out on the road with her little bucket
on her arm—anxious to get started. In a few years the little
school had done its best for Mary, and Miss Emma Wilson, her
beloved teacher, told her one day that Miss Mary Crissman, a
dressmaker in Denver, Colorado, wanted to pay for a girl to go
to school to Scotia Seminary, and that she, Miss Wilson, had
chosen Mary as the one to go, because she had done so well in
school.

This is the record of the beginning of the educational
career of Mary McLeod Bethume, president of the Daytona-
Cookman College, Daytona Beach, Florida; president of the
National Federation of Colored Women's Clubs; an orator
and educator of international reputation—one of the truly
great women of the modern world.[16] The life and work of
Mrs. Bethume is sufficient justification for all the mission
schools in South Carolina.

At Winnsboro there is the Fairfield Normal Institute,
supported by the Northern Presbyterian Church. At Trenton there stands the Bettis Institute or Academy, founded by
Reverend Alexander Bettis, a Negro ex-slave. It stands like
Allen University, Columbia, as a great monument to the zeal
of the Negroes for self-help in education.

We must not fail to mention in this connection the wonderful work of Elizabeth E. Wright, who founded the Voorhees Normal and Industrial School, located at Denmark. The
story of the work of this young Negro woman is indeed a

---

[16]Information procured from Mrs. Bethume's private secretary, 1927
(Author).

romance touched with tragedy in the field of education. This woman caught the vision of service for the boys and girls in her native state of South Carolina while she was a struggling student at Tuskegee Institute. She was one of the many who have been inspired by the life and work of the famous "wizard of Tuskegee." She first attempted to establish her school, modeled upon the Tuskegee idea, in Hampton County but opposition of the people there to education of Negroes resulted in her buildings being burned. She moved to Denmark and there secured some co-operation from certain local white people and through hard sacrificial service which soon cost her life, she succeeded in interesting the white people of the North in the project. The development of Voorhees has been remarkable. From practically nothing the school has grown until today it has an annual enrollment of 550 students, a faculty of thirty-seven men and women, a plant consisting of 400 acres, and several buildings, and an annual budget of more than $50,000. One notices at Voorhees that the spirit of the founder is a vital influence though she lived and labored there a comparatively short time. Its history is an eloquent tribute to the Negro's initiative and self-help in this great fight for intellectual achievement and freedom.

Another school which we must mention but cannot take space to discuss is Friendship College, which is the property of the Negro Baptists of the state. It supplements the work of Benedict and Morris colleges.

Lest we forget, we turn to the question: "What part did the Negro play in all the struggle and sacrifice for his uplift?" In the first place, he convinced his white friends who came from the North and pioneered this work that he was worthy, appreciative and willing to sacrifice along with them. Without this response on the part of the Negro their work would have been a complete failure. It was perhaps not so difficult to get Northern friends, young and old, able and otherwise, to volunteer for this great work when it was first presented as a challenge to their missionary impulse, but when these volunteers, many of whom had no stronger motive than curiosity or love of adventure, met the difficult problem of the work, many of them failed to measure up to the great demands of the occasion. It was the Negro's help that held the ones who stuck to the task when it revealed itself as a work for martyrs and saints. The early apostles of education for the Negroes of South Carolina entered the state feeling that they were pioneering not only for democracy and human fellowship, but for the Kingdom of Heaven. They had profound faith in the capacity of the Negro and a courage born of faith in God. The Negroes justified their faith by working like Trojans to master their problems, whether intellectual, moral, religious, or industrial. The Negro contributed no small amount of financial aid out of their great poverty.[17]

One not well versed in the actual problem which faced these leaders may ask what made their efforts so difficult if it is true that the Negro on ·the whole, was satisfactorily responsive? The answer comes out of a fuller explanation of economic and psychological aftermath of the war. During the slave régime the white people of the South, in the large, had attempted to solace their own consciences and justify their institution before the civilized world by the propaganda that the Negroes were fundamentally and inherently inferior and therefore totally unfit to function successfully as free men in the modern Western civilization.[18] The white pioneers from among their late enemies, the Yankees, were working on an entirely different hypothesis: namely, the Fatherhood of God and the Brotherhood of man, which implied the equality of races and the competency of the Negroes to absorb civilization and "carry on" as participants therein. As might have been expected under these conditions the white people, natives of South Carolina, generally opposed these efforts for the uplift of the Negro carried on in absolute defiance of their traditions, such as eating and associating with Negroes on terms of social equality, and which, if successful, would disprove their theory. The scientific student can easily understand the naturalness, and one

---

[17]*A. M. A. Annual Report,* 1864, etc.
[18]Snowden, Yates: *Status of Negro in South Carolina,* 1823, part 5.

is tempted to say inevitableness, of the Southern attitude though he may see its injustice and doubt its wisdom or necessity. Thus it happens that the white people of the state, in large, made no effort to help the Negroes educationally, refused to co-operate with the "Yankees," and, in fact, put every possible stumbling block in their way until it became apparent that the success of Negro education was inevitable. In some instances they have not yet fully accepted the inevitable gracefully or philosophically. The general attitude of that group toward the Northern workers is summed up in this quotation from one of the "Yankee" teachers, referring to the Southerner:

Gentlemen sometimes lift their hats to us, but the ladies always lift their noses. It is a fact unpleasant to record that the white men of the South not only fail to exhibit the widely heralded Southern chivalry toward the white women who came from the North to carry on this work, but they actually suffered some things that were unlawful and unworthy in a civilized state. For example: At Orangeburg, the Superintendent of Education reported that a night school was fired into on one or two occasions, and the attempt to discover the perpetrators of this outrage was without success. A. M. Bigelow, a teacher of the colored school at Aiken, was compelled by curses and threats to leave the town in order to save his life. In the town of Walhalla, a school conducted by the Methodist Church was taught by a lady from Vermont. A number of white men tried to break it up by hiring a drunken vagabond Negro to attend its sessions, and accompany the young lady through the village streets. The attempted outrage was frustrated only by the intercession of a Northern gentleman. At Newberry, about the same time, the man who was building a school for the freedmen, was driven by armed men from the hotel where he was staying and his life threatened. These occurrences the superintendent reported as "specimen cases."[19]

But there were a few leaders of the white people of South Carolina who favored the uplift of the Negroes and many of them rendered service as sacrificial and heroic as that of the people from the North. We quote the following anent this point from L. P. Jackson's study:

[19]Luther P. Jackson: Educational Efforts in South Carolina, *Journal of Negro History*, Vol. 8, No. 1, page 31.

A correspondent of the *New York Times* reported that in Columbia "the whites extend every possible facility and encouragement in this matter of education." There is one instance of actual initiative in the education of the Freedmen in the case of Reverend Toomer Porter of the Episcopal Church in Charleston. This gentleman went North to solicit the necessary funds and while there visited Howard and President Johnson. For this deed the Charleston *Courier* remarked that it was "a much more substantial and lasting token of friendship to the colored race than all the violent harangues of mad fanatics." Finally in enumerating here and there cases of favorable attitude, Governor Orr's remarks cannot be overlooked. To the colored people at Charleston he said, "I am prepared to stand by the colored man who is able to read the Declaration of Independence and the Constitution of the United States. I am prepared to give the colored man the privilege of going to the ballot box and voting."[20]

Indeed it is apparent after little thought that if white people had not at least been partly tolerant to efforts, the program would not have been as successful as it was; in fact, it probably would have failed absolutely. A perusal of facts recorded in available documents persuades the writer to remark that the Northern white people were partly responsible for some of the difficulties they faced. For example, they often referred to "Old Jeff Davis" in a disrespectful manner, and greatly rejoiced to have the Negro children sing "Marching Thru Georgia," "John Brown's Body," and similar songs. This was not diplomatic to say the least. Of course it was all very natural but none the less harmful on that account. The Negroes, too, added fuel to the fire by referring to the "Rebels" and greatly rejoicing over freedom and ostentatiously celebrating the Fourth of July and the First of January. All this, too, was quite natural but exceedingly irritating.

We have already several times referred to the fact that the Negroes of South Carolina helped themselves financially a great deal while their friends were leading them. A great many of the schools organized by the Freedmen's Bureau were financed to a large extent by the Negroes who furnished the land and helped buy equipment. In all the private schools,

---

[20]Ibid., page 32.

including those established by the various Freedmen and societies of the denominations and associations in the North, the Negro students paid tuition in money or service. In the case of most of them the Negro patrons were called upon to render financial assistance at intervals. They usually responded generously, considering their poverty-stricken condition.

Another important way in which the Negroes helped the cause was by serving generously and efficiently as teachers and administrators along with the white people. They willingly worked in subordinate positions for small pay in order to serve. These early Negro teachers are due the same praise that we willingly bestow upon their white co-laborers. Although most of these Negro teachers at first worked with the white people and under their direction, there were some who branched out on their own initiative and became founders of schools or independent agents of some of the societies. A good example of the latter was Mrs. C. M. Hicks, who was sent South by a New York society. She established a school at Anderson. Apparently commenting upon a visit to her school, a local newspaper, *The Anderson Intelligence,* spoke as follows:

We were gratified with the proficiency and success attained and trust that they will persevere in their efforts to make better citizens and become more worthy of the high privileges now granted to the race. This school is presided over by a colored female who is intelligent and capable and devotes all of her energies to the school.

Some of the other Negro teachers who labored and sacrificed in these early pioneering days we must mention briefly. Charles Hopkins conducted a school at Greenville which succeeded in getting the confidence of the white people to the extent that they contributed $230 toward its maintenance. Frank Carter founded a similar school at Camden. One of the most interesting of these men was the full-blooded African, Lymus Anders. He was not a teacher. In fact he never procured much education himself as he was illiterate until after the war. He managed to learn to read and write, and became possessed with such passion for education that he led a movement to procure a school for his people. In this he was successful. Two white leaders from Massachusetts came down to teach and became so impressed with Anders that they called him by the nickname "Black Yankee." Two others were Ned L. White and one "Uncle Cyrus," who labored at St. Helena. We should not close this part of our sketch without some reference to one who has been called "the brightest light among the Negro teachers" of this period—F. L. Cardoza. This scholar, for such he was, descended from the free Negroes of Charleston. He received his early education in the schools for the children for free Negroes in that city. Later he was sent to Europe, where he obtained an education superior to most of his contemporaries of South Carolina, white and colored. He believed in thorough classical education and his influence was great, almost inestimable, first as a teacher and educational leader of Charleston, and later as a politician and statesman, shaping the destiny of the state in an educational way.

We shall have to be content to let this much of our sketch serve to bring our story up to about the close of the reconstruction period. I know of no better summary of the fact we have tried to present than the conclusions of Luther P. Jackson, which we quote from the end of his study, *The Educational Efforts of the Freedmen's Bureau and Freedmen's Aid Societies in South Carolina*, 1862-1872:

> Notwithstanding the fact that the efforts put forth failed to reach our modern ideal of the education of all people, yet the movement did accomplish at least these three things: (1) By penetrating almost every county or district in the state the school served to awaken the Negroes to the need of education and to demonstrate to all persons that it was practicable to educate them. (2) It led up to the establishment of the public school and left for this system material equipment in the form of school buildings and furniture; and, (3) greatest of all, the combined efforts of the Freedmen's Bureau and Societies left the state with institutions of higher grade—principal source of teachers for the common schools.[21]

---

[21]Ibid., page 40.

It remains for us to sketch briefly and inadequately the Negro's fight against ignorance as continued since the reconstruction era. We wish merely to suggest how he has "carried on" in the enormous and never-ending task he began in slavery, and renewed before the smoke of battle cleared away from the plains and valleys of the old "Palmetto" State.

In our chapter on the Negro in the reconstruction of South Carolina, we have expressed our opinion that the Negroes made a contribution to the progress of American democracy in South Carolina in that they made an attempt to establish a democratic system of education in the state. For a while they kept the state university open to all the people, but after the elimination of the Negro in South Carolina politics this policy was discontinued. The new regime inaugurated by Wade Hampton professed to be friendly to the Negroes and claimed to stand for real democracy but the facts of the administration of this leader and his followers proved these professions to be mostly the "sounding brass and tinkling cymbals" of the politicians' platitudes and promises. From that time on the Negroes began to fare badly in public educational facilities. More and more money has been put into education, and indeed the Negroes have been receiving larger and larger amounts as the years pass, but, comparing the Negro's actual receipts with what he should receive, we find the state has been far from just to the Negro, not to speak of generous and philanthropic. In spite of inadequate support from his state government and only sporadic co-operation from his white neighbors in non-official capacities, the Negro of this state has forged steadily ahead educationally because of three main reasons: namely, the natural evolutionary, ever-increasing efficiency of the schools founded before the Civil War and during the reconstruction period, the inadequate support appropriated from the public funds, and the ever-increasing heroic sacrifices of the Negroes coupled with the continued generosity of Northern philanthropists.

In our reference to the work of the state government we do not mean to imply that the State of South Carolina

is the "worst sinner in Jerusalem" among the former slave
states of the South, but it is simply the correct statement
of an unpleasant historical fact which a very cursory survey
of the facts in the annual reports of the state department
of education will more than substantiate. Yet the state government has done much to help dispel the cloud of ignorance
among the Negroes.

As we stated above, the State of South Carolina, like
all the other states of the United States, North and South,
is ever spending larger and larger amounts of money for
public education each year. Every year since the Negroes
disappeared from politics most of his money spent in South
Carolina has been spent on the education of the white children, yet much is spent for Negroes. The first attempt to
establish universal, free education was begun in this state
in 1868 when the constitution, framed and adopted at that
time, provided for it. Very little was actually done. In
1870 there were only 18,000 Negroes enrolled in all the
schools of the state. The first appropriation for the schools
of the state was $50,000. Gradually the numbers increased
and more money was invested especially when the Negroes
became influential in the reconstruction government, but a
great part of the money appropriated for education in that
period was wasted on account of corrupt politics and inefficient management. In 1890 there were still about 301,262
illiterates out of a total "colored" population of 470,232![22]

We insert here the statement of "expenditures" from a
recent (1924) report of the state superintendent of education (Hon. J. H. Hope). We place this statement here
for several reasons. First, it will show the great progress
made in the support of education since 1868 and, as it com-
pares with those conditions of the previous year, it will show
the progress from year to year. Secondly, it will serve as
an example of how the white children are given every advantage over the colored. In this connection it is well to
remember that the school population of the two races in the
state is about equal. Thirdly, these figures will suggest how

---

[22]U. S. Census reports, 1890, Vol. II, on population.

far we have to go before we approximate the ideal of adequate educational facilities for all the children of the state at public expense.[23]

ExPENDITURES

Salaries of Teachers:	1922-23	1923-24
White men..................$	1,366,276.71	$ 1,512,599.12
White women..............	4,850,638.51	5,470,389.91
Total	6,216,915.22	6,982,989.03
Negro men................	211,195.27	235,652.39
Negro women.............	634,713.91	727,503.11
Total	845,909.18	963,155.50
Total salaries for both races	7,062,824.40	7,946,144.53

Furniture and Apparatus:		
White ....$	188,155.02	$ 319,948.24
Negro	22,983.09	20,146.51
Fuel and Incidentals:		
White	839,736.87	1,012,492.58
Negro	63,178.13	43,867.48
Libraries:		
White	1,310.03	26,859.61
Negro	85.59	220.48
Transportation of Pupils:		
White	88,903.94	173,805.50
Negro	53.00	196.25
Grounds, Buildings, Repairs, Rent:		
White	1,970,944.22	2,156,296.64
Negro	187,033.63	372,564.68
Bonds (White):		
Interest	400,529.18	557,775.56
Sinking fund and retirement..	326,855.48	331,690.83

	Scholastic Year	
Item	1922-23	1923-24
Total Expenditures for All Purposes:		
White	10,034,349.96	11,561,849.99
Negro	1,119,142.62	1,400,150.90
Grand total of all expenditures for both races.....$	11,153,192.58	$12,962,000.89

[23]Fifty-sixth Annual Report of the State Superintendent of Education, page 3.

While these figures unquestionably show quantitative progress, they are disquieting, not to say alarming, to any lover of true democracy who believes in universal education without regard to race or class. We feel that a history is no place for propaganda however worthy the cause may be, and so we merely state it here as an historical fact that the Negroes of South Carolina do not feel when they read such figures year after year that they are getting what the late Woodrow Wilson was pleased to call "even handed justice." It seems to the colored people that the facts show that the white people of South Carolina are not, as a whole, committed to the principle of democratic public education. Indeed the figures show that the Negroes of the state would be in a deplorable plight indeed if it were not for assistance rendered by outside agencies of a philanthropic nature and some aid from the federal government.

The meager financial support accorded the Negro public schools of South Carolina by the state has been greatly supplemented by the generosity of Julius Rosenwald, a philanthropic multi-millionaire who became interested in the rural education of Negroes in the South through the late Booker T. Washington. The so-called Rosenwald plan of co-operating with the Southern states and the colored people to the end of better education for Negroes in the rural districts was probably born in the fertile brain of Booker Washington. It has the chief ear-mark of his genius—diplomacy. It avoids the errors of the early efforts of Northern philanthropy in that it makes a prerequisite that there be an apparent co-operation among the state government, the local white community, and the Negroes. To get Rosenwald's financial assistance all three must show their interest and approval by investing in the project.

The American principle of free public education is protected in the provision that the property must belong to the state. In actual operation it appears that the plan usually results in the Negroes themselves investing most of the money. In the opinion of the writer the plan has been, on the whole, a blessing to the Negroes, but it is not without dangers, not

the least of which is that it is in part used as an excuse for
the Southern states to shift their rightful responsibility for
the education of Negro youth to other shoulders. In South
Carolina the Rosenwald plan has resulted in much inspiration and aid in the field of Negro education. A perusal of
the report of the state agent for Negro schools (J. B. Felton, 1927) will reveal the vast assistance rendered the cause
of Negro education in this state by outside agencies without
which the agent admits "results would have been quite different." Mr. Felton, the state agent for Negro schools, has
been enthusiastic in his effort to aid in improving the
opportunities for Negro youth of the state. His leadership has been especially effective in advancing the project
of procuring a large number of Rosenwald rural schools
for South Carolina. It is greatly to his credit that South
Carolina has recently been one of the leaders in that
work.

Before concluding this chapter we must make brief record
of the most important and promising development in Negro
education in South Carolina. We refer to the recent growth
of the State A. & M. College here at Orangeburg. We have
previously referred to the beginning of this institution as a
department or division of Claflin University. There soon
developed a sentiment in the state among both white and
colored people that the industrial and higher education of
the colored citizens should be divorced from Claflin and carried forward in its own institution. This sentiment was in
line with the American principle of public education and was
supported by influential politicians in the state. The result
was that in the state legislature an act was passed in 1896
which created the State A. & M. College as an independent
institution at Orangeburg with a campus and plant adjoining
that of Claflin. Hon. Thos. E. Miller, an outstanding statesman of the reconstruction period, was elected the first president. Six trustees were also elected. An excellent faculty of
colored men and women was appointed and work began Sept.
27, 1896. At this beginning, "The plant consisted of 135
acres of land, eight small buildings, a barn, a small dairy

herd, and a few farm animals."[24]   The school has always
attracted a large number of students.   The first year the
enrollment was over 1,000.   The teaching staff was able and
hard working but far too small and equipment was woefully
lacking.   In 1911, Dr. Robert Shaw Wilkinson, a native of
Charleston and a graduate of Oberlin College, who had been
on the faculty as professor of physics from the founding of
the college, was elected president.   From this time on the
story of the college is one of progressive and ever expanding
service.   Doctor Wilkinson has procured the financial support of the state legislature in the form of ever increasing
appropriations.   This new attitude of the state legislature
began under the administration of Cole L. Blease, who has
been friendly to President Wilkinson and the State College,
though by many not considered a friend of the Negro in
general.   Other governors and leading politicians of the state
have usually supported the college more and more.   Of course,
it is obviously true that the college has never received the
amount of financial support that is justly due to the only
school in the state devoted to the public education of the
Negro in the higher branches, but it has consistently advanced
under the leadership of Doctor Wilkinson.   It has gradually
eliminated all the grammar school work and concentrated on
high school, normal, and college work in the academic department with ever advancing efficiency and higher standards in
the agricultural, mechanical and vocational work.   This progress is largely due to the leadership of the president, beyond
question the outstanding leader of Negro education in South
Carolina.   Under Doctor Wilkinson's leadership the faculty
of the college has been enlarged and strengthened until today
(1927) there are more than sixty persons on the faculty
composed of individuals representing, in their training, the
greatest institutions and colleges of the country such as Yale,
Michigan Agricultural College, Ohio State College, Oberlin
College and leading Negro institutions such as Atlanta and
Howard universities and Hampton Institute.   Perhaps the
most obvious and outstanding contribution of his administra-

---

[24]*The Wilkinsonian,* 1926 (College Annual).

tion has been his success in procuring ever larger and larger appropriations for buildings and other material equipment of the college. When he assumed the presidency of the institution in 1911 it was receiving about $10,000 from the state. Now the annual appropriations run around $150,000 or more. Any one intimately familiar with Doctor Wilkinson's administration of the state college, as the writer is, must be impressed with the continued good order, cleanliness, and promptness that always characterize this institution in all its efforts. Few institutions anywhere have as well kept buildings or maintain as excellent general conditions with the financial resources available.

The State College is the center of educational extension work in farm demonstration, home economics, and vocational education throughout the state. This extension service is largely procured through the co-operation of Smith Hughes and Smith Lever agencies, the General Education Board, Rosenwald Fund, etc.

Perhaps the most illustrious graduate of the State College so far is the great biologist, Ernest Just, at Howard University. Hundreds of others less conspicuous have received excellent training at this college and are now engaged as tradesmen, farmers, teachers, preachers, and in influential positions in South Carolina and throughout the country.

Negroes have contributed to the success of this, South Carolina's most promising educational project, by furnishing some of the teachers and by paying a large part of the expense of carrying forward the college through registration fees and other funds. The school is important and deserves the relatively large amount of space we have given it here because it is "the capstone of the public school system for Negroes in this state."

We close this chapter as we began by saying that the story which it attempts to sketch is a great romance. Our sketch is very incomplete and much that could be said is necessarily omitted. We can only hope that the facts presented here suggest certain great achievements by the Negroes and indicate the improvements that may be made.

This fight to abolish ignorance has really only begun among the Negroes of this state. It must continue with ever increasing power and effectiveness until we have an intelligent colored citizenry and educational facilities sufficient to keep it so through all the coming years.

CHAPTER V

THE EVOLUTION OF THE NEGRO HOME
(In South Carolina)

> No mother can love more tenderly or be more deeply
> beloved than the Negro mother. Robin tells of a slave
> in Martinique who, with his savings, freed his mother
> instead of himself.
>
> "Everywhere in Africa," writes Mungo Park, "I have
> noticed that no greater affront can be offered a Negro
> than insulting his mother." "Strike me," cried a Man-
> dingo to his enemy, "but revile not my mother!" . . . .
> The Herero swears "By my mother's tears!" . . . . The
> Angola Negroes have a saying, "As the mist lingers on
> the swamps, so lingers the love of father and mother."[1]
>
> *Wilhelm Schneider.*

THE evolution of the home life of any civilized people is inextricably interwoven with the story of the womanhood of the race or group concerned. This chapter is closely allied to another chapter in this book—"The Gifts of Womanhood in Ebony." The two chapters in a sense supplement each other. Yet the home is evidently impossible without the father. It is also impossible without the various social organizations which co-operate to make it worth while.

In a sense, any home is, in part, an idealistic conception— a reality resting partly in the spiritual world.

The foregoing remarks have served, we hope, to suggest to the reader something of the difficulty before the historian who essays to write on "the evolution of the home" among any people. It is an undertaking which involves dealing with those important but elusive realities which we call moral, spiritual and idealistic—"the great imponderables" of "the immaterial world." He reasons falsely who thinks that he has exhausted the theme of the evolution of the home when he has collected the statistics of houses builded, property bought and sold, incomes earned and spent, necessities and luxuries used, and individuals married and divorced. It is

---

[1] Atlanta University Publication No. 13, *The Negro American Family,* Atlanta University Press, Atlanta, Ga., 1908.

113

now universally agreed among sociologists that the most important function of the home is to provide a proper place for the nurture and development of children. All that is necessary for this important task is included in that wonderful word—home.

The writer does not wish to establish the impression that he underestimates the importance or influence of the house and the other physical elements of the child's environment as factors in its development. These are tremendously important. The experience of the fact so artistically and simply expressed in these old lines is the experience of the writer:

> I remember, I remember,
>   The place where I was born
> The little window where the sun
>   Came peeping in at morn.
>
> It never came a wink too soon
>   Nor brought too long a day
> But now I often wish the night
>   Had borne my breath away.

We hope we have made it clear that in this chapter we expect to attempt to deal with the development of the home as an ideal, as well as a physical shelter and a legal and social organization. It is a difficult task. In *The Souls of Black Folk* DuBois asks the profoundly baffling question: "How shall we measure progress?" Trying to write the history of the home among a people is like trying to report the real service of a teacher or a preacher which, in turn, is like trying to describe the beauty of a lily, the fragrance of a rose, the inspiration of a smile, the tragedy of a tear, the pathos of a groan and "the pessimism of a sigh." These things are beyond the reach of written words yet "how human and how real" they are! *After all they are the essence of history.*

Over twenty years ago (1908) the department of history and sociology at Atlanta University, under the direction of Dr. W. E. B. DuBois and co-operating with the John F. Slater fund, published, through the *Atlanta University Press,* the pamphlet with the title "The Negro American Family."

At that time the editors of that study called attention to the dearth of scientific data on the subject. Unfortunately the passing of over two decades finds us in the same condition. Very little of scientific value is on record, or at least available for the use of the general historian on this subject of the Negro home in South Carolina. Here is a great and interesting field of investigation for the student of sociology wishing to make a real contribution to scientific knowledge. As that is not within the scope of this work we must write the best historical survey we can with available information.

The reader will recognize our debt to the Atlanta University publication named above; especially when we speak of general conditions which are reflected in South Carolina. Many of the facts about Negro home life in this state have been gathered by the writer himself while living and working as a teacher in a South Carolina college for the better part of the last decade. Much of our information about the Negro's efforts before the Civil War was obtained by the author through conversations with members of the older families; especially Miss Mae Holloway, of Charleston, a representative of one of the oldest families in the state. She also kindly permitted us to investigate a scrap book containing many original documents.

Our topic, "The Evolution of the Negro Home," suggests that the institution has grown. The Negro's home, like his civilization, did not originate in the United States; certainly not in South Carolina. His is the African Negro home as adapted to the civilization of South Carolina.[2]

Another influence which we cannot ignore if we wish to present a true, not to say appreciative, account of the growth of the Negro home is the unpleasant influence of slavery upon the Negro's home life.

For convenience we shall group our discussion around three influences; namely, the moral and idealistic principles at the basis of the Negro's home life, the economic and social

[2]Frasier, E. Franklin: *Opportunity* (Magazine), Vol. 5, No. 6, pages 165-166.

influences which have affected his struggle and the houses
he has builded and used in the various stages of his development.

The home is built upon the ideals of love, courtship and
marriage. Any one who is at all familiar with African customs, traditions and practices knows that they differ somewhat from ours here in America. Of course, it goes almost
without saying now that one cannot generalize on Africa as
a whole on account of the great variety of civilizations existing in that vast continent. However, the general statement
which we have made is possibly true; especially in reference
to the native Negroes. It is generally known that polygamy
is widely practiced in Africa. It therefore goes without saying that the monogamous relationship is not as highly praised
or prized among the native Africans as it is among us.[3] This
open and frank practice of polygamy explains, in part at
least, the Negro's difficulty in apparently conforming to the
strict requirements of the monogamous standards that the
white people claim to love and foster with more or less success. If we search for the causes of this polygamy in Africa
we shall find them rooted in economic and social problems.
According to Ellis and many other authorities it is customary to pay parents a certain amount for the bride. A
number of wives, therefore, tends to advertise the master as
a man of wealth and importance.[4] The wives perform much
service of great value and are looked upon as economic assets
for that reason.

When a man has several wives one of them is usually
recognized as the "headwife." The others occupy more or
less subordinate positions; often being slaves. These secondary wives, if we may call them that, are not expected to
be as chaste as the head or favorite wife. In fact the con-
fining of the sex-experience to the husband alone does not
seem to be considered by these people as important as it is
by us. They are said to have, in some sections, one custom

---

[3]Dowd: *The Negro Races.* Kingsley: *Travels in West Africa,* page
336.
[4]Spencer: *Sociology.*

which seems very immoral to us; that is, the custom of temporarily lending one's wife to a friend or visitor.[5]

It must not be concluded from this that the Negroes have no morality; it simply means, as we have mentioned before, that their standards are different from ours. Many writers, especially white men steeped in the prejudices and orthodox dogmatisms of occidental civilization, make the mistake of condemning these people simply because they are different. An example of this is W. D. Weatherford who speaks of the Negroes of the United States as having "inherited a loose moral life."[6]

A cursory survey of the studies and writings of such writers as Ellis, Ratzel,[7] Kingsley,[8] Nassau,[9] Leonard,[10] Harris,[11] and Sweinfurth[12] will convince the honest seeker after truth who is open minded that most of the Africans who had advanced considerably in civilization such as the Yorubas, the Vais and Zulus, had worked out ideals of love, courtship and marriage which were excellently suited to their environment. Of course, the student or observer in our day can see that many improvements were needed and that their systems were far from perfect. The same criticisms can be applied to our present practices. We have not the time or space here to quote extensively from the literature referred to but it will substantiate our statement here that the facts of history show that DuBois was correct in a general observation made nearly twenty years ago to the effect that the Negroes were brought to America as slaves with moral ideals far *different* from those of the white people of North America but which were nevertheless useful and practical in the environment wherein they were developed.[13] The statement is applicable to the Negroes of South Carolina. The Negroes

[5]Ellis: *Yoruba Speaking Peoples*, pages 153-4.
[6]Weatherford: *The Negro from Africa to America*, page 42.
[7]Ratzel: *History of Mankind.*
[8]Kingsley: *Travels in West Africa.*
[9]Nassau: *Fetichism in West Africa.*
[10]Leonard: *The Lower Niger and Its Tribes.*
[11]Harris: *Africa Slave or Free.*
[12]Sweinfurth: *Heart of Africa.*
[13]*Atlanta University Publication* No. 13, Page 18.

were moral in so far as they lived up to these ideals. There is little doubt, as we have stated before, that they were as moral as the white people judged by the standard of performance rather than by high sounding precepts.

Elsewhere we have made an attempt to show that the Negro was able, to some extent, to carry on in civilization in spite of slavery, we mentioned his more or less successful effort to achieve the white man's actual *practice* in several moral and marital customs even if he did not accomplish the white man's artistry in "seeming to be what he is not" in this field. Here we wish to elaborate just a little more on the stumbling block which slavery placed in the path of South Carolina Negroes struggling to achieve new ideals and different, perhaps better, practices along these lines.

In many parts of Africa chastity on the part of the unmarried female had been appreciated and required but for a short time only, due to the general oriental custom of early marriages. Among the white people of South Carolina, as with most American white people, the marriage date being later, the period of chastity is presumably longer. In order for the Negro slaves coming into this state to adopt this new idea of a much longer period of chastity there should have been a very different line of procedure from the one actually adopted. The exigencies of the regime of Negro slavery in South Carolina were not such as to encourage idealistic sex morality or idealistic morality of any kind for that matter. The Negroes were classed as property and not as persons and citizens. It was not possible with that classification to give or assure the slaves legal rights or a legal status at all inconsistent with that of property. There was no such thing as a legal marriage among the slaves. A slave could not procure a divorce on account of immoral conduct on the part of his mate. Slaves were mated and separated as the whims or interests of their masters dictated.[14] The inevitable consequence was to give the Negroes "low moral standards."

The three essential concomitants of the slave regime in

---

[14]Cromwell, John W.: *The Negro in American History*, page 6.

South Carolina which caused it to be extremely difficult for the Negroes to acquire and practice the fundamental ideals of wholesome family life were these: there was no legal marriage, there were no legal family relationships, and parents had no legal control over their children. These principles, as they worked out in practice, are illustrated by the following quotations from writers who were dealing with the subject of slavery in South Carolina:

The houses for the field-slaves were about fourteen feet square, built in the coarsest manner, with one room, without any chimney or flooring, with a hole in the roof to let the smoke out.[15]

The huts of the slave are mostly of the poorest kind. They are not as good as those temporary shanties which are thrown up beside railroads. They are erected with posts and crotches, with but little or no frame work about them. They have no stoves or chimneys; some of them have something like a fireplace at one end, and a board or two off at that side, or on the roof, to let off the smoke. Others have nothing like a fireplace in them; in these the fire is sometimes made in the middle of the hut. These buildings have but one apartment in them; the places where they pass in and out serve both for doors and windows; the sides and roof are covered with coarse, and in many instances with refused boards.[16]

On a very large plantation there were many exceptionally small Negro cabins, not more than twelve feet square interiorly. They stood in two rows with a wide street between them. They were built of logs with no windows—no opening at all except the doorway, with a chimney of sticks and mud; with no trees about them, no porches or shade of any kind. Except for the chimney—the purpose of which I should not readily have guessed —if I had seen one of them in New England I should have conjectured that it had been built for a powder-house, or perhaps an ice-house; never for an animal to sleep in.[17]

The above descriptions are accounts of physical environments wherein home life was impossible to develop, yet more or less unavoidable in the slave regime in South Carolina and elsewhere. But other matters should be mentioned which were even more deplorable. Much suffering was brought upon

---

[15]Angelina Grimpe Weld: *Slavery as It Is,* page 56.
[16]Ibid. (Weld).
[17]Ibid. (Weld).

the Negroes because of the immorality of the masters. A quotation from the pen of a man who lived in South Carolina for fourteen years is pertinent here:

As it relates to amalgamation, I can say, that I have been in respectable families (so-called), where I could distinguish the family resemblance in the slaves who waited upon the table. I once hired a slave who belonged to his own uncle. It is so common for the female slaves to have white children, that little or nothing is ever said about it. Very few inquiries are made as to who his father is.[18]

The above facts and citations suggest that the Negroes found it very difficult to practice the white man's code of morals, especially as it applied to the evolution of the home life, even if they were persuaded that they were correct and attempted to adopt them. Of course there were counteracting influences that helped the Negroes to advance along these lines. They were taught in the churches, both directly and indirectly, about the moral ideals and family obligations as understood by the white people. They had the benefit of the examples of many of the master class who were honorable and upright in their own family relationships. The white women of South Carolina who belonged to the master class produced many noble characters who taught the slaves the true ideals of family life both by precept and by example. One can get an idea of the better type of masters from these lines from the pen of a Southern white man who has written much on the question of Negro slavery:

Each plantation had a double head in the master and the mistress. The latter, mother of a romping brood of her own and over-mother of the pickaninny throng, was the chatelaine of the whole establishment. Working with a never flagging constancy, she carried the indoor keys, directed the household routine and the various domestic industries, served as head nurse for the sick, and *taught morals and religion by precept and example.* Her hours were long, her diversions few, her voice quiet, her influence firm. *Her presence made the plantation a home; her absence would have made it a factory.*[19]

---

[18]Ibid., page 97.
[19]Phillips: *American Negro Slavery,* page 323.

Many of these Southern white women really did an inestimable service for the Negroes in putting before them a high example and in insisting that the slaves live up to these ideals even better than their own husbands and sons did. There is much truth and pathos suggested in the words of a sister of James Madison, who said: "We Southern ladies are complimented with the names of wives; but we are only the mistresses of seraglios."[20]

We must not omit the fact that the Negroes themselves read and studied the moral problems of their conditions and in many instances arrived at semi-independent solutions. The Negro slaves, though considered of weak mental power by the masters, did no little thinking for themselves. The Negro slave who was compelled to stand by silently while some woman he loved—wife, daughter or sweetheart—was taken from him by his master to be used perhaps for immoral purposes did some thinking on the problems of love, courtship and marriage for himself. In a few instances—that is, few comparatively—masters mated Negro men and women without regard to the slaves' personal feeling but with an eye single to profits in the form of slave children for the owner. One must ignore the obvious fact of the humanity of the Negro to doubt that these instances, however few, would cause the Negroes to think intensely on the injustice of it all. They served to force the Negroes to have very definite ideas about the moral ideals which the white people advertised as theirs.

Nearly every writer of any note on the subject of Negro slavery in the United States has referred to the striking fact that the Negroes were greatly influenced by their contact with the white people. If their contact was close and sympathetic the Negroes were greatly benefited in case the masters were really worth while men. Where the slaves had little contact with the better class of masters, as in the coastal lands, large rice plantations of the Carolina-Georgia coasts and on St. Helena Island, the Negroes remained very little Americanized and very backward in all the requirements of this

---

[20]Goodel: *Slave Code*, page 111.

occidental civilization. This influence, or rather the effect of the lack of contact, is shown in the peculiar dialects developed by the Negro slaves who had little opportunity for contact with the better classes of the white people. Of course, Negroes in general have experienced no little difficulty in mastering the English language under the limitations of the slave regime and the poor educational facilities provided in the South since the abolition of slavery. Any one who hears the Negroes on St. Helena Island or on the islands near Charleston will realize at once how much other Negroes have been aided by closer association with the white people and slightly better and more adequate educational facilities. As in language, so in the development of the ideals of home life— the Negroes made more "progress" who had superior advantages of contact with the better whites.

Although the special influence which we have mentioned was greatly beneficial to the Negroes it seems true that the total influence of slavery on the Negroes in South Carolina was to weaken their true morality since it destroyed their African system of morality and failed to put a better system in its place in an effective way. Because the Negroes could not practice the high ideals of Christian monogamy or even approximate them in the slave regime, they gradually developed disregard for the system taught them which they observed was not really practiced by most of the white people who confessed it and had no such handicaps as the Negroes to prevent them from carrying it out if they so desired. So the Negroes came out of slavery far behind the civilization in which they were living so far as sex morality is concerned.

The question arises: What progress has been made along this line since the abolition of slavery? It is not possible to get facts of a scientific nature to demonstrate anything definite on this matter. Any one familiar with the situation in this state, as the writer is, can detect a gradual improvement along this line even within the last decade. The difficulty comes to the front when the investigator attempts to get documentary facts for all that period of time between the abolition of slavery and the present time. A perusal of newspapers and magazine articles, books and sketches published throughout this period reveals facts which indicate gradual improvement. Most of the observations on the sex behavior of the Negroes made by the Southern white people during the period under discussion are not dependable in that they present the subject in a light entirely too pessimistic, due partly to the effort on the part of these people to discredit the Negroes in this particular as a means of justifying lynching and partly to their ignorance of the better class of Negroes.[21] Statistics of illegitimate births, etc., in this state are scarcely in existence in a scientific sense and what we have are totally inadequate to serve as the basis of historical statements. The best we can do, then, is to state that it is a fact that most of the white teachers in Negro schools who have had an excellent opportunity to observe the Negroes and compare their progress in sex behavior with that of the whites agree that the Negroes have made much progress along this line. This is agreed to by white teachers on St. Helena Island and at Benedict College in Columbia. There is also a large group of Southern white people of the liberal persuasion who agree with this point of view. We may mention Mrs. McGowan of Charleston, chairman of the state interracial committee; Mr. T. B. Lanham, state secretary of the Y. M. C. A.; Professor Josiah Morse of the University of South Carolina, and many others of like prominence who have put themselves on record in public addresses as in agreement with this view.

For almost a decade the writer has been teaching in a co-educational state institution in South Carolina and in close contact with the administration of a co-educational denominational school just across a fence. It is our experience that the young people in these schools show progress or improvement along this line even within this short time. My contemporaries here and at Claflin College and at Allen University in Columbia all agree that sexual ideals are improving and that sex behavior is better. Some of these teachers have been dealing with Negro students in this state

---

[21]Dowd, Jerome: *The Negro in American Life,* page 120.

for twenty-five or thirty years, such as Professor N. C. Nix of State College, for example.

It is the opinion of practically all white and colored leaders of this state that miscegenation of an immoral nature is on the decline in this state. This is due to a higher moral standard on the part of Negro women as well as to their greater freedom. The Negro women also have more effective protection by their men. It may also be due, in part, to the improvement in morality among the Southern white men. On the whole, however, it seems to be a fact that most people competent to judge think that it is due to the improvement of morality among Negro women and girls, or, at least, to an increasing race pride among them. Still another source of information which tends to strengthen the writer's conviction that there is improvement in the sense of greater conformity to American morals in this particular is the general opinion of the better class of Negro ministers and church officials in general. The average Negro minister in this state today will state it as his honest opinion that "our people are improving in sex behavior." The same is, in general, true of doctors, dentists, and lawyers who have an excellent opportunity to observe and understand these conditions.

The Atlanta University publication on "The Negro American Family" came to this general conclusion about twenty years ago:

While, then, the tendencies are hopeful, still the truth remains; sexual immorality is probably the greatest single plague spot among Negro Americans, and its greatest cause is slavery and the present utter disregard of black women's virtue and self-respect both in law courts and in custom in the South.[22]

A white man, none too friendly to colored people as revealed by his book, all his protestations to the contrary notwithstanding, substantially agreed with this in 1926. He used the following words which may be applied to conditions in South Carolina although the writer had in mind Negroes of the South as a whole:

---

[22]A. U. Publication No. 13, page 41.

Since an elevated family life is fundamental to the progress of any people, the most important task of the Southern Negro has been the bringing together and binding together of those blood relations which constitute the human family. The task has been difficult because neither the family traditions handed down from Africa, nor the family conditions imposed upon him as a slave to the white man, have been favorable to the development of family virtues or family stability; and further because of the demoralizing environment in which generally he has been compelled to live.

In view of his handicaps we can but admire what he has accomplished in the elevation of his home life within the short period of his emancipation. Nor can we fail to view with charity the faults which his family life still retains and extend to him a helping hand by providing better housing conditions, and better protection to his home in his effort to overcome those faults.[23]

We wish next to direct attention briefly to the influence of the economic situation upon the home life of the Negroes of this state. The first thing that comes to one's attention in this connection is the well known fact that most of the Negroes in this state have some of the female members of the family, especially the mothers, in domestic service. These workers usually get practically nothing for their work—food and shelter sometimes, at other times scarcely that. It is common for girls and women to get two or three dollars per week and even less in actual money. Because of these low wages the Negro women who cook early developed the habit of demanding their own "keep" and taking (often without definite agreement) additional food for their husbands and other members of the family at home who are deprived of the wife's and mother's service while they are away working for the white people. This necessity of the Negro women and girls working in domestic service for "sweat-shop wages" has far-reaching evil effects upon the home life of the Negroes in this state. So here again we can apply an observation made by the writer we just quoted above dealing with Southern Negroes in general:

Negro children in cities have little opportunity to grow up strong physically or morally. In many cases the mother works

---

[23]Dowd: *The Negro in American Life,* pages 101-102.

away from home. The percentage of Negro females in the South who work for a living is about four times as great as that of white females (41.3 per cent for Negro females and 11.8 per cent for white females). The mother who works away from home has neither the time nor the disposition to be a home-maker. Infants, being left alone, learn to crawl and walk much earlier than white infants, and learn to talk much later. Children from four to ten years old often have the daily care of the younger ones. The mother rushes off to work and often leaves nothing for the children's breakfast except leftovers from the last meal. Often the only regular meal is at night when the mother brings home her basket or hurriedly buys something at the market. At times the children have not enough and, as often, too much to eat, and they seldom have food of the right sort. Milk is rare in the average Negro home; hence the frequency of rickets. Children and adults often sleep three or four in a bed; they have no night robes and go many days without a change of underwear. There is a general absence of privacy in the home, and when the parents are away the children take to the streets, where they come in contact with moral degenerates and acquire familiarity with all the vices and vulgarities.

The period of infancy of the Negro child is short. Among urban Negroes, parental care hardly extends to the age of fifteen. Before that time the boys usually leave home, tired of parental restraint and longing for independence and for wages to spend on themselves. The girls also leave home at an early age, lured away by the love of flashy dress, the dance, and travel. They secure employment which takes them away from home, or they marry, or they fall victims to the glare of the red lights.

Under these untoward conditions, the ties that bind the members of a family together will be weak.[24]

Dowd was speaking of Negroes in the larger cities and there are not any large cities in South Carolina, but the evils he referred to are evident in one form or another in the small towns and large towns of this state. The Negroes who live in the rural districts do not escape these evils, except those who are independent farmers who rent or own their land. The poor Negroes in the rural communities and on the large plantations fail to have any family life because of this habit that the white people have of paying Negro women and girls practically nothing for service and because the

[24]Ibid.

small income of their Negro husbands and brothers and sons makes it necessary for them to earn whatever they can.

Some writers, because of ignorance or maliciousness, have insinuated that Negro men have largely been content to let their women folk support them because they were lazy and had no chivalry or sense of family obligation, no love for their wives and children, and little appreciation of the value of family unity and dignity.[25] There is about as much truth in this as there would be in the same statement made about poor white men who are compelled to let their women add to the family income.

Any one familiar with the facts of Negro life in this state knows that most Negro men such as skilled laborers, professional men, business men and others in fairly good circumstances financially take pride in supporting their women folk in the same way that the better class of white people do. Just as in parts of Africa today the native Negro men refuse to let the women folk work for the white European residents in Africa because these Africans have no confidence in the morality of the white employers, so the Negro men in the South, who are able, keep their women folk from working in domestic service for the whites partly for the same reason. Thus we find a large number of colored girls in the schools and colleges of this state who are proud of the fact that they have "never been compelled to work in service for the white people." These Negro girls are trying to escape this domestic service not only because it is drudgery with little pay but also because it, in many instances, precludes a high moral life or reputation on the part of the participants.

All wages of colored people in this state are deplorably low. This fact injures home life beyond estimation. If working people do not receive high enough wages to support them in decency when they work, they are tempted not to work and to attempt to get these things by stealing or other immoral practices. All this almost inevitably leads to immorality, sexual and otherwise. Immorality and poverty go hand in hand. It is perhaps not inevitable that the slave or pauper

---

[25]Odom: *Social and Mental Traits of the Negro.*

be immoral but it is almost a certainty that both will be so to some extent.

The small income received by the Negro workers, male and female, is largely responsible for the habit of early marriage among the Negroes of this state. These early marriages are in turn responsible for many maladjustments. This practice results in large families. The large families cannot be provided for and educated on the small wages of their parents. A vicious circle of poverty is established out of which it is extremely difficult for the Negroes to escape. Individuals here and there escape, sometimes by personal effort and sometimes as a result of good fortune. These few manage to carry on and eventually lift the race economically.

Anent this point the *Atlanta University Press* published the following answers to questions concerning the rearing of children in South Carolina:[26]

Some few properly reared. Most are allowed to come up as best they can; to have their own way. A majority of our boys and girls do not attend school. A large number do not attend any Sunday School.

I should say they are totally ignorant and this is one of their weakest points.

Children are very well cared for and attend school very largely but there should be some improvement along this line.

Imitating the whites in desiring small families. The high cost of living and the increased number of what were formerly regarded as luxuries, that only the rich were to have, but now must be supplied in even the more humble homes, had the same effect among our people as among the whites in making many of them consider a large number of children a burden. More colored children have school training and home instruction now than at any former time.

This is better because they are better trained, clothed and fed. Not brought up in one-room houses.

---

[26]DuBois and Dill: *Morals and Manners Among Negro Americans,* Atlanta University Publication No. 18, page 88.

Quite a number of mothers in service, thus leaving children to care for and rear themselves during the very time they need watching. Many children attend school from such homes, having to prepare themselves. In many such cases the children are taught at home to defend themselves at all hazards.

More than a decade has passed since these statements were made but the writer feels that they represent the conditions today.

The next question which comes up is, what has the South Carolina Negro achieved along the line of home or rather house ownership? The writer agrees that the ownership of the house is one of the best tests of progress in the development of home life. It is a platitude that houses do not make homes but it is usually true that the ownership of the house is a powerful factor in building a home, although some now question its necessity or wisdom.[27]

We have previously hinted at the fact that the slave system as a whole did not attempt to provide housing facilities for homes for the slaves but merely sought to provide the essential shelter or protection from the weather. No attempt was made to provide for comforts or conveniences which are so necessary for *home* life. The slave "huts" or "cabins" were, as a rule, fairly substantial—they protected from the weather, but the slaves were usually too crowded, as we have shown, for the development of wholesome moral and spiritual family life. As we have also tried to show, the home is built upon ideals. There was little room or inspiration for ideals in the slave cabins. Although "Uncle Tom's Cabin" was the home of the "first saint in ebony the world ever saw,"[*] it was not in this respect typical. As a rule the cabins were necessarily and inevitably breeders of sickness, crime, and immorality. It must be admitted, however, that the rural slave quarters perhaps did not exceed the modern city slums as breeders of crime, disease and death. Indeed the modern city quarters are in some instances unquestionably worse.

[27]Oven, Chandler: *The Passing of Private Houses,* Editorial, *The Messenger,* Aug., 1927.
[*]Doctor William Crogman.

In this matter of housing for the slaves it is difficult to make a general statement that would cover all cases. The following quotation from a long letter written about 1822 by Robert J. Turnbull, a wealthy and prominent planter, is perhaps representative of the better conditions: "Their [the slaves'] dwellings consist of good clay cabins, with slag chimneys, but so much attention has been paid of late years to their comfort in this particular, that it is now very common, particularly on the Sea Islands, to give them substantial frame houses on brick foundations and with brick chimneys. Many are of opinion that they enjoy more health in open temporary cabins with ground or dirt floors. But this does not correspond with the experience of those who willingly incur the expense of better buildings."[28] The darker side of the picture has been presented in previous quotations taken from the Atlanta University publication.[29]

All this goes to show that the slave "quarters," however excellent or poor, did not measure up to the requirement of a home. The reasons why this was true are so well summarized by Doctor DuBois that we must give them here though it is somewhat of a repetition of what we have already stated or implied:

The house of the slave, which I have sought to show in its various relationships and degrees of squalor, had certain general characteristics which we must notice carefully. First, there was the lack of comfort; the Negro knew nothing of the little niceties and comforts of the civilized home—everything of beauty and taste had disappeared with the uprooting of the African home, and little had been learned to replace them. Thus, even to this day, there is a curious bareness and roughness in the country Negro home, the remains of an uncouthness which in slavery times made the home anything but a pleasant, lovable place. There were, for instance, few chairs with backs, no sheets on the beds, no books, no newspapers, no closets or out-houses, no bedrooms, no tablecloths and very few dishes, no carpets and usually no floors, no windows, no pictures, no clocks, no lights at night save that of the fireplace, little or nothing save bare rough shelter.

---

[28]Holland: *A Refutation of the Calumnies,* etc., Charleston 1823.
[29]A. U. Publication No. 13.

Secondly, and closely connected with the first, was the lack of hygiene; every nation has its habits and customs handed down from elders, which have enabled the race to survive. But the continuity of Negro family tradition had been broken and the traditions of the white environment never learned; then, too, the rules and exactions of the plantation favored unhealthy habits; there ensued a disgusting lack of personal cleanliness, bad habits of eating and sleeping, habits of breathing bad air, of wearing inadequate clothing—all such changes and abuses in everyday life for which the world's grandchildren must eventually pay.

Thirdly, there was in the slave home necessarily almost an entire lack of thrift, or the ordinary incentives to thrift. The food and fuel were certain, and extra faithfulness or saving could make little or no difference. On the other hand, cunning and thieving could secure many a forbidden knick-knack, far more than honest cultivation of the little garden spot which each family often had. The thriftiest slave could only look forward to slavery for himself and children.

Fourthly, there was the absence of the father—that is, the lack of authority in the slave father to govern or protect his family. His wife could be made his master's concubine, his daughter could be outraged, his son whipped, or he himself sold away without his being able to protest or lift a preventing finger. Naturally, his authority in his own house was simply such as could rest upon brute force alone, and he easily sank to a position of male guest in the house, without respect or responsibility.

Fifthly, and correlated to the last, was the absence of the mother. The slave mother could spend little or no time at home. She was either a field-hand or a house-servant, and her children had little care or attention. She was often the concubine of the master or his sons, or, if unmolested in this quarter, was married to a husband who could not protect her, and from whom she could at any time be parted by her master's command or by his death or debts. Such a family was not an organism at best; and, in its worst aspect, it was a fortuitous agglomeration of atoms.[30]

Anent the brighter side of this picture we may say with truth that the Negro slaves, especially the more or less favored domestic servants, got some of these advantages that were not in the slave cabins by living in the houses of the masters a good part of the time. There at the "Big House," in town and country, the slaves saw what a house should be if it really served as the place for a home and so they caught

---

[30]Ibid.: A. U. Publication No. 13, pages 48-49.

the ideals which in later years, when freedom came, they put into effect.   Then, too, the characteristic optimism of the Negro managed to squeeze some joy out of the quarters any way.   He celebrated the holidays and vacations, such as he had around his cabin.   Something of this is indicated in the following poem by Russel which purports to be the prayer of "Brudder Brown," who was asked, at the Christmas celebration, to "beg a blessin' on dis dance":

O Mashr! let dis gath'rin fin' a blessin' in yo' sight!
Don't jedge us hard fur what we does—you knows it's Christmus night;
An' all de balunce ob de yeah we does as right's we kin.
Ef dancin's wrong, O Mashr! let de time excuse de sin!

We labors in de vineya'd wukin' hard and wukin' true;
Now, shorely you won't notus, ef we eats a grape or two,
An' takes a leetle holiday—a leetle restin' spell—
Bekase, nex' week we'll start in fresh, an' labor twicet as well.

Remember, Mashr—min' dis, now—de sinfulness ob sin
Is 'pendin' 'pon de sperrit what we goes an' does it in;
An' in a rightchis frame ob min' we's gwine to dance an' sing,
A-feelin' like King David, when he cut de pigeon-wing.

It seems to me—indeed it do—I mebbe mout be wrong—
That people raly ought to dance, when Christmus comes along;
Des dance bekase dey's happy—like de birds hops in de trees,
De pine-top fiddle soundin' to de blowin' ob de breeze.

We has no ark to dance before, like Isrul's prophet king;
We has no harp to soun' de chords, to holp us out to sing;
But 'cordin' to de gif's we has we does de bes' we knows,
An' folks don't 'spise de vi'let-flower bekase it ain't de rose.

You bless us, please, sah, eben ef we's doin' wrong tonight;
Kase den we'll need de blessin' more'n ef we's doin' right;
An' let de blessin' stay wid us, untel we comes to die,
An' goes to keep our Christmus wid dem sheriffs in de sky!

Yes, tell dem preshis anjuls we's a-gwine to jine 'em soon;
Our voices we's a-trainin' fur to sing de glory tune;
We's ready when you wants us, an' it ain't no matter when—
O Mashr! call yo' chillen soon, and take 'em home! Amen.[21]

Negroes in South Carolina began to build, own and enjoy houses that were far superior to the typical slave cabins long before slavery was abolished.   That is true especially in reference to the free Negroes who lived in Charleston, in Beaufort and a few less conspicuous and smaller places.

---

[21]Iwin Russel: Poems, 1888, pages 5-7.

These Negroes obtained a sufficient income to buy land and build houses because many of them were skilled laborers such as masons, carpenters, shoe-makers, etc. Quite a few of them had no little education. Some of the best carpenters and builders, even contractors, in Charleston before the Civil War were Negroes. While in Charleston on a visit trying to get facts and information for the writing of this chapter, the writer of this book talked with an acquaintance who was there (1927) living in a house which had been in possession of her family for over 100 years, according to her statement.* These houses were often built by the same workmen who constructed the houses of the white people and so they closely resembled them. They contained all the conveniences and comforts known to house builders at that time. The importance of owning the house is illustrated and emphasized in the case of these free ante-bellum Negroes. The fact that they owned their houses helped them to build real homes embracing all the word "home" implies. One often wonders at the culture and refinement that these early homes achieved. It must be said that these were exceptions. The rank and file had not these conditions and opportunities—they lived on the plantations as slaves in the quarters.

Since the abolition of slavery in South Carolina there has been a steady increase in house ownership by Negroes. During slavery the Negro observed the white people and saw the advantages of house ownership quite clearly and he set out to acquire property just as he began to earn more wages than were absolutely necessary to feed and clothe him and his wife and children. Many of the first houses they bought or built were the typical old log cabins having the one advantage of the inspiration which comes from ownership. Gradually the planters began to develop the habit of leaving the "big house" on the plantation vacant as they discontinued active management of their plantations, left them rented to the former slaves, and moved to town to go into business or live in ease on the rent incomes where these were large enough. The Negroes finally moved into these forsaken "plantation

*Miss Mae Holloway.

mansions." At times they bought these old houses which represented a great advance on the part of the Negroes in the matter of house ownership. Negroes in South Carolina own over 135,551 homes today. About 64,000 of these are farm houses. Nine-tenths of all these homes seem to be free of mortgage.*

It is perhaps not of great value to present statistics of houses owned and controlled by Negroes. But when one thinks of the small incomes of Negroes in this state and then turns to consider the comparatively large amount of this income they have put into the houses, where they strive to build homes, one must admire the Negroes and admit that they are fast assimilating one of the finest ideals of this western civilization—the building of modern houses as the basis of a finer and ever progressive family life. *It is a far cry from the slave cabin or the one-room log cabin to a modern bungalow, yet many Negro families have covered that distance since the Emancipation Proclamation.*

---

*United States Census Reports, *Negro Population in U. S.*, 1890-1915.

CHAPTER VI

THE NEGRO IN BUSINESS IN SOUTH CAROLINA

ANY one who has made a study of the various civilizations of the world, including some investigations of their origins and their characteristics, must be impressed with the fact that the chief contributions made to modern civilization by the white people of the occident consist of material blessings growing out of their wonderful achievements in the fields of applied science, mechanical contrivances or inventions, and economic organization. In religion we look to the Oriental Jews for a contribution. In philosophy we must turn to China, Greece, and India for the best. In law and government we go back to Rome and Babylon. In art and theoretical science we are led back to Chaldea, Egypt, and Africa. In the realms of applied economics, business building and administration the white man of the West has unquestionably led. Unfortunately, his leadership has been able but selfish and ruthless.

The Negro came to South Carolina as a conscripted burden bearer harnessed by the white people in their effort to carry forward their economic program. As these white men conceived it, in the main, the place of the Negro was not to include any participation as a business man—he was only to be a servant. Slavery did not consciously provide an opportunity for the Negroes to learn business or accumulate capital to engage in it. In theory the slave was a beast of burden and incapable of being a business man. This attitude on the part of the white man was the first serious handicap the Negro faced when he began to live as a Freedman in this business age and function as a citizen in a civilization founded on economics.

The next handicap of the Negro came from within himself. The Negro, like most Oriental people, does not seem to be naturally fitted for business of the western type as well

as the European white man. It simply means that in this
particular he seems to be inferior just as the white man, in
general, is inferior to the Negro in certain specific things such
as singing, for example.

In spite of these handicaps the Negro early began to
learn business and participate therein. His first business
experience came to the Negro because the master class soon
learned that there was much of their business which the
slaves could handle. In most instances Negroes handled the
business intrusted to them very well. This gave them confidence and courage.

The Negro's keen analysis of the white man's civilization
and his determination and ability to adjust himself to it
caused him to early appreciate the fundamental importance
of business and inspired him to enter that field as soon as
he could. It thus happened that in all the slave states free
Negroes began to do business more or less successfully long
before the abolition of slavery. We are particularly interested
in what the Negroes in South Carolina did in those early
days to get a foothold in the business world.

We must here turn again to the city of Charleston to
find facts which will show what was actually being accomplished by Negroes in business before the Civil War. The
writer took some time on several trips to Charleston to get
certain facts through conversations with members of some
of the oldest and most distinguished Negro families in the
state. We are fortunate to get to talk to a few of the
remaining persons who were contemporaries of these pioneers
in Negro business in the old Palmetto State. Some of them
were in the businesses mentioned themselves. Of those who
gave us valuable information supporting some of the statements on early Negro efforts in business in Charleston we
mention the following: Dr. John A. McFall, who has many
very old and valuable documents which I examined; Miss Mae
Holloway, who has a very valuable scrap book, carefully
kept and arranged, containing records of the transactions of
her family for over 100 years. The following copies of
documents found in the Holloway scrap book indicate how

careful this man was in various transactions and they also show his varied business relationships.

(1)

CORPORATION TAX FOR 1825

Original, No. 34.........................Richard Holloway

On Free Coloured Persons

	Dollars	Cents
3300 dollars valuation of lots & building	24	75
Lots without well or cistern.......... 40 dollars		
Negroes per head....................150 dollars		
Capitation, mechanic from 21 to 50 years 10 dollars		
Do. male from 21 to 50 years.... 8 dollars		
Do. female from 18 to 50 years.. 5 dollars		
Dogs, each .... 4 dollars		
Horses, each .... 5 dollars	10	
Every two-wheeled chaise, chair, sulky or other carriage with or without top, each .... 5 dollars	10	
	44	75

Received Payment May 12, 1825

Jas. Bennett, City Treasurer,

E. Roach.

(2)

Received January 9, 1858, of Mr. Charles Holloway, in advance $4.00 for one-quarter tuition of Mifs Catherine Holloway, due this date April 6, 1858.

$4.00   F. Pinckney Bonmeaw.

(3)

Charleston, June 7, 1827, received of Mr. Richard Holloway $42.00 for interest due on man Jack.

$42.00   Ann Mitchell.

(4)

Extract of certificate given to Richard Holloway and signed by mark at which time he could not sign his name, which he could do subsequently.

City of Charleston:

To all whom it shall concern of the quorum in and for the said state and notary public by lawful authority duly sworn, admitted and commissioned and residing in the city and state aforesaid.

Do hereby certify that in this day of the date hereof personally came and appeared before the said N. P. Richard Holloway, a seaman, a free Mulatto man who being duly sworn on the Holy Evangelist of Almighty God did depose, testify and declair that he was born in Essex County in the state of Maryland, one of the United States of America and has always been in the employ of citizens of the U. S. of America and has taken the oath of alegience to the same and that he acknowledges no other nation or country. The above mentioned Richard Holloway, a free Mulatto man, is about twenty years of age, 5 feet 8 inches high, black woolly hair, brown eyes, yellowish complexion, no small-pox marks.

his
Richard (x) Holloway
mark

Given under my hand and seal of office at Charleston, this twelfth day of January, in the year of our Lord one thousand seven hundred and ninety seven and in the 21st year of independence of the United States of America, 1797.

J. H. Mitchell (2 No.),
Notary Public.

British Consul's Office,
State of South Carolina.

I do hereby certify to all whom it may concern that John Mitchell, Esq., who has signed and sealed the within certificate and affidavit is a justice of the quorum, in and for this said state and notary public by lawful authority admitted and commissioned and residing and practicing in the city and state aforesaid, and that all due faith, credit and authority is and ought to be had and given to all his certificates and proceedings as such.

Given under my hand and seal of office at Charleston this thirteenth day of January, in the year of our Lord one thousand seven hundred and ninety seven in the thirty-seventh year of His Majesty's Reign.

Benjamin Moore, Vice Council.

These are to certify that the bearer, Richard Holloway, a Mulatto man, served on board of the Catherine near 10 months during which time he always behaved with sobriety and good conduct while under my command.

Job Gardner,

Great Hermitage Street.   London, April, 1797.

General information was given the writer by Messrs. Birnie, Percell, Jervay, Morrison, Mickey, Harleston, Means, Gregory, and Reverend Lowery, now of Columbia.

It seems that the slave owners of South Carolina soon began to despise all manual labor and even considered the participation in business or trade as degrading and beneath the dignity of the master class. The slaves who often attended to these matters for them learned the methods of business and often made some profits on their own account which the masters, or rather some of them, allowed the slaves to keep. In various ways some of these slaves procured their freedom and entered business on their own resources. These men were partly responsible for the early start in business by the Negroes in Charleston. Many Negroes, some of French extraction, came from the West Indies Islands especially to engage in business in South Carolina and the other Southern states.

No reliable statistics are available from which we may compile general facts of great importance about these early efforts in Negro business but we have some estimations which we pass on for what they are worth. We shall take time and space here to mention some of the most outstanding efforts of the early Negro business men. Their efforts were worthy of mention because their accomplishments were the results of great ability and incessant labor conquering in spite of great disadvantages.

One of the earliest efforts along this line was in the fish business. One C. C. Leslie finally developed a wholesale fish business known all over South Carolina and parts of Georgia and other states. Mr. Leslie ran up against the competition of white concerns later in his career and was able not only to hold his own but to come out of the conflict as victor. The business which he established is still successful in a large way.

In connection with the fish business it is said that the first Negro woman (perhaps the first woman of any race) in business in South Carolina was represented by the sign "Joe Cole and Wife—Fish."[1]

Another line of business in which Charleston Negroes achieved no little success was that of cotton sampling and

---

[1]From Dr. McFall.

shipping. Messrs. Richard and Charles Birnie, Joe Wilson, and several others were leaders in the cotton shipping business. The Negroes gained considerable reputation for their work in this line and played a large part in making Charleston prominent as a cotton shipping center. The men who engaged in this business made such a success of it that they rose to places of prominence in the group of free Negroes. They were able to build good homes for themselves and give their children very good educations.

As early as 1805, according to the statement of an old resident of Charleston (Mr. Percell), there were colored men of French extraction engaged in the dry goods business, especially in the business of importing silks, etc. In this connection we should mention the fact that Negroes took part in the effort to establish the business of silk culture in South Carolina. Of course their business, like that of the white people who made similar attempts, finally failed, but they met with as much success as could have been expected under the circumstances. It is clearly seen that their ill fortune was due to the same reasons that the white people failed in the same business; namely, the environmental conditions, geographical or climatic and otherwise, not suitable for the production of silk.

Negroes were active in the general shipping business around Charleston. Some of them owned and operated boats with a capacity of about seventy-five tons. Mr. E. G. Harleston, father of the artist, was active in this business for many years and is still able (1927) to remember much about it and can hold one in a very interesting, informing and entertaining conversation on these matters. The Negroes interested in this business were instrumental in bringing about the organization of a Negro pilots' association. This organization is still in existence. It is over fifty years old. Perhaps the first mercantile establishment among Negroes in Charleston was operated by a somewhat eccentric man by the name of McCall, who had a furniture store not long after the Civil War. He is said to have been the first Negro to ride a bicycle in South Carolina. He also seems to have been a jeweler and did considerable work in this line. He had the reputation of not letting any bargain pass if he could possibly make the purchase. The story is told around Charleston that he bought his own coffin at a sale because he considered it a bargain. Of course, Negroes followed practically all the trades known to our industrial civilization. They were leaders in building and construction, especially in carpentry, and were able to do considerable contracting, which makes it proper to speak of the leaders as business men. Those engaged in this business were too numerous to mention, but some of them were the Holloways, the Westons, the Morrisons, and many others. These men not only built their own homes in many instances, but were responsible for the construction of many of the best homes of white people in Charleston. Something similar may be said of the Morrison home. Most of these men seemed to have been good business managers and left considerable property in possession of various members of their families. This is proof of their business ability and success.

Colored people got a fairly early start in Charleston in the undertaking business. This business probably grew out of the livery stable business. One or two families were in this business before the Mickey's, but they are the leaders now. For a long period of time colored men in Charleston, as well as in many other cities of the state, have had a considerable amount of capital invested in the undertaking business.

Pharmacists began their operation of drug stores in Charleston at an early date. The Peoples' Pharmacy was perhaps the first Negro business of this kind in the state. The Evans Pharmacy, in Columbia, was probably the next. The McFall Drug Store, at Charleston, is one of the oldest of these stores. The owner, Dr. John A. McFall, was the third man in the state to put considerable capital in such a business.

It is proper to record and worth remembering that the colored people carried on much business in connection with their churches and secret societies, especially the former. There are several very old secret societies in Charleston.

Probably the oldest of these is the Brown Fellowship Society,* which still maintains an office at 2 Green Street. The Humane and Friendly Society also has a long and honorable history. There are several others. All transacted no little business and some have accurate financial records of these transactions covering long periods of time.

Although Charleston was the center of practically all early business among Negroes in the state, there was no little effort in other places in South Carolina. A good example of these efforts showing what has been accomplished outside of Charleston by some of the earlier Negro business men is that of the Dibble family in Camden. The family is known all over the state, and its achievement in the mercantile business is of historic importance. The older members of this family have not only achieved no small success in a financial way, but have given their children excellent educational opportunities. One of the sons, Eugene, who was a schoolmate of the writer at Atlanta University, is now one of the most distinguished of the younger medical doctors of the race. He is director of the Hospital at Tuskegee Institute, and recently (1927) toured the world with Principal R. R. Morton. We could give examples similar to this from all the leading communities of the state, but that is not compatible with the general plan of this book.

A place of great interest, which has experienced a development in Negro business very similar to that of Charleston, is Beaufort. Some day we hope that careful scientific investigation will be made in this old town to bring to light and preserve the facts along this line. The information available to me is not very definite or well authenticated for the purpose of this book. We merely call attention to facts well known to persons familiar with Negro business in this state.

Perhaps we should mention Columbia as it attained importance as a center of Negro business in the state, due partly to the fact that it was and is the capital. During the Reconstruction period many Negroes who benefited by and through

---

*Now known as The Centenary Society.

connection with the Government, or by serving members of their race who were connected with the Government, accumulated much property and capital. Their superior economic status enabled many of them to go into business. The Taylors (Joseph and William), Mobley, Cooper and Clement deserve to be mentioned. William Taylor was especially successful in the grocery business.

According to A. A. Taylor, Negroes operated forty-nine stores of importance in South Carolina in 1880. These were distributed as follows: 25 on the Coast, 2 in the lower Pine Belt, 16 in the upper Pine Belt, and 3 in the Piedmont Region." †

The different kinds of businesses were fairly well represented among Negroes, except manufacturing and banking. The former, Negroes have never entered to any extent in this state; the latter, only to a small extent and not very successfully.

We have roughly and briefly sketched the efforts of Negroes in this state in the early days to get a foothold in the business world. We have not been able to present the facts with a wealth of statistics, prepared by scientific investigators, but we are convinced that the impressions we have tried to pass on to the reader are conservative and true.

We shall now attempt to suggest what progress has been made and indicate the present condition and problems of Negro business men in this state. Our statements on this part of the subject are based partly on the ideas of my contemporaries who are familiar with Negro business, especially Mr. John M. Maxwell, Orangeburg; Mr. Dibble, Camden; and Mr. I. S. Levy, Columbia. The other source of information is a study which I made with the assistance of the college classes in economics in Benedict and State colleges. The teacher of economics at Benedict College assisted in a survey of Negro businesses in Columbia. These surveys were made in three places—Orangeburg, Greenville, and Columbia. They were not complete, and, of course, no conclusive find-

---

†*The Negro in the Reconstruction of South Carolina.*

ings for the state could be based upon them.   The following list of questions was used in getting or attempting to
get certain information from about all the important Negro
business in the cities named:

Present name of business?
Address?
When first organized?
Sketch of important developments since organized.
Is the business individual or corporate?
Capitalization?
Amount actually paid in?
Amount actually invested in equipment, current supplies and
stock.   (Include in this building, trucks, autos, etc.)
Total business—daily, weekly, or annually.
In case of banks and insurance companies, statements.
Annual profits (net on invested capital).   This may be given
monthly or weekly.
Number of persons employed in the business.
Average weekly wage.
Number of employees in family (whole or part time).
What proportion of the patronage of the business is colored?
What per cent white?
Is race prejudice a handicap to the business in any way?
Any other special handicaps?
Is the relationship to governmental authority satisfactory?
(That is, license, taxation, police protection, etc.)
Comments of the investigator:
Impression of the general appearance, impression of the busi-
ness as to cleanliness, "Up-to-dateness," etc.

Date...............   Signed...................,
                                                Investigator.

We place before the reader here a summary of results
obtained from the investigations made in Columbia, Orangeburg, and Greenville.   The figures were compiled and
analyzed by Mr. Thomas Brier of the senior college class

(1927) of the State College. Mr. Brier also supervised the investigations in Greenville, his home town:

COMBINED STATEMENT OF PARTIAL SURVEY OF NEGRO
BUSINESSES IN THREE TOWNS

	Orangeburg	Columbia	Greenville	All
Businesses interviewed.....	16	19	14	49
Individual businesses.......	16	15	9	40
Mutual companies..........			1	1
Stock companies and cor- porations		4	3	7
Capital paid in individual or corporations.........$	75,000.00	$132,968.00	$ 76,650.00	$304,618.00
Invested in equipment......	86,700.00	32,334.74	116,300.00	235,334.74
Total business, annually....	69,650.00	64,660.00	190,622.23	325,932.23
Number of persons em- ployed	29	160	69	204
Persons of family employed	11	12	2	25
Salary paid member's fam- ily ....$	68.00	$ 13.00	$	$ 81.00
Average weekly wage, all..	180.00	223.00	765.75	1,168.75
Total weekly wage including salary of family........	*	*	*	1,249.00

Net profit.............$10,262.00

The patronage of these businesses for all places was reported approximately 75% colored and 25% white.

In reference to the question, "Is race prejudice a handicap?" there were many variations. Some said that prejudice was the cause of the colored people patronizing their business! Others said that it kept them from selling to the general public. Then there were those that said that the Negroes themselves were prejudiced or jealous of their own people. All of the places interviewed expressed the opinion that their relationship to the Government was "good."

The kind of businesses interviewed in the above cities were undertaking, banks, insurance companies, tailors, grocers, druggists, theaters, newspapers, printers, dressmakers, shoeshine parlors, dry goods stores, shoe repairers, real estate companies, pressing clubs, confectionery stores, and cafés.

A rather striking fact was revealed by the answers to the question, "Is race prejudice a handicap in any way?" Most

---

*Data inconclusive or not obtained on account of poor records, etc.

of the business men seemed to think race prejudice in the state of South Carolina helps their businesses rather than injures them. The prejudice and discriminations seem to force the Negroes to work together in a business way in many cases, where they probably would not if these discriminations were not practiced against colored people. For example, we find a great number of Negroes more or less successful in the restaurant business. The development of this business is largely due to the fact that Negroes are excluded by law from the regular restaurants for the white people. Negroes were compelled to buy lunches and meals from side windows of white restaurants, or even eat in the kitchens, before they developed their own places for this service. Even now, many first-class white eating places will only serve Negroes on condition that they take the food with them, or order it sent to their homes or other places away from the business. As self-respect and race pride increases among Negroes such practices become disgusting and unbearable. The Negroes have met the issues by establishing their own cafes, restaurants, and ice cream parlors. Of course the places owned and operated by the Negroes themselves are, with few exceptions, far inferior to similar places operated by white people. This is due largely to lack of capital by the Negroes. It must be admitted, however, that these colored businesses of the type under discussion are inferior partly on account of ignorance, carelessness, and general lack of efficiency on the part of Negroes who operate them. The segregation laws of the state force the Negroes for the most part to patronize their own enterprises in this class, whether they are efficient and attractive or not. In certain of the large towns, such as Charleston and Columbia, a few of the places operated by white people comply with the law by separating white and colored by some kind of screen or partition, and thus gain patronage of the few colored people who are able to pay prices charged and who do not have too much race pride to refuse to be "Jim Crowed."

Some other lines of business which Negroes claim to have found more profitable because of segregation, discrimination, and "Jim Crowism," legal or customary, are: the undertaking business, motor transportation, barbering, insurance, banking and general merchandising. In fact, almost all businesses operated by Negroes feel the effect of this system in the state. It may be worth while to say a word here in reference to several of these businesses.

There are a great many successful undertaking establishments among colored people in this state, such as the Mickey's in Charleston; Bythewoods in Orangeburg, and others.

The fact that Negroes have developed separate religious organizations in this Christian (?) country encourages the growth of this business among Negroes. Colored people now almost universally use their own companies for this service because it is almost necessary if they are to maintain their self-respect.

The manifestations of race prejudice as it affects Negro business enterprises are peculiar and inconsistent. White people practically never use, in any way, the services of a Negro undertaking establishment. But this is far from true in reference to the barbering or tonsorial business. Many Negroes have conducted successful and profitable tonsorial parlors designed for white patrons. Of course the law requires that whites be served in separate rooms or compartments. The result is that we find many Negroes operating shops exclusively for white people. Here pecuniary gain encourages the Negro to comply with the segregation policy of the South though few of them really agree with the policy, not to speak of the philosophy, of segregation. In both the undertaking and barbering businesses white people practically never compete with Negroes for Negro patronage. One of the heritages of slavery in South Carolina is the belief of the average white man that it is disgraceful to engage in any business which would require him to "serve" a Negro in such manner as a barber or undertaker serves his customers.

In connection with the barbering business, a recent manifestation of race prejudice appeared in an attempt on the part of a county representative in the South Carolina state legislature to make it illegal for a Negro barber to "bob" the hair of white women or otherwise wait upon them in tonsorial parlors. This was made on the plea that such service by Negroes might lead to undue familiarity and so result in social intermingling or illicit sex relations. The proposition was not enacted and seemed to have been taken by many of the Palmetto solons as a joke; one remarked that, in his opinion, it was more dangerous for Negroes to shine white women's shoes.

According to the perverted ideas of these whites, it is altogether fitting and proper for a Negro to be servant to a white person but it is outrageous that any white person should act as servant for a Negro. This is the attitude of the average white South Carolinian in the year of our Lord 1928. There are some indications that this attitude is slowly changing as shown in the automobile transportation business. We find that white taxi drivers are more and more "condescending" to carry Negroes. They usually do this apologetically, which often embarrasses the Negro customers. Negro taxi drivers also find that the antipathy of the white people against riding with Negroes as passengers on equal basis with them often causes trouble with both his white and colored patrons.

In such businesses as insurance, banking, and merchandising, the Negro business man finds himself up against the keenest kind of competition on the part of the white people. In all these enterprises the white people are definitely and aggressively out for the "Negro business." The white people here have one tremendous advantage over their colored competitors; that is, the white business man can be certain that the Negro will be mostly confined to the support of his own race, the colored people, while he, the white man, can get customers from both races. White people in South Carolina will not, as a rule, insure their lives in Negro companies. They will not deposit their funds in Negro banks. White insurance companies and banks, while eager to get the Negroes' money, will not freely lend it back to Negroes. Of course, it may be said, with much truth, that white people do not insure in Negro companies and deposit in Negro banks for the same reason that many Negroes do not; namely, the white ones are stronger and safer. Granting this to partly account for the fact, we still insist that prejudice also plays a part. Whatever the cause, it puts the Negro business man at a serious disadvantage in the keen competition of the modern business world.

Bearing out the truth implied in the above statement to the effect that the white people of South Carolina will, to some extent, patronize Negro business enterprises when they compare in strength, service, and efficiency with similar white concerns in this state is the fact that many of the best Negro mercantile establishments have a large proportion of white patronage. I was told by a young Negro business man connected with the best and largest colored grocery business in the town where the writer lives that much more than 50 per cent of their patronage comes from white people. We feel that, after all, this is the exception to the general rule. Even in the mercantile business the Negro business man must, in the large, depend upon his own race for support. Of course more and more as years pass Negroes are going to be able here in South Carolina to go out and compete for business along almost all lines without regard to race friction. But that good day is not yet here.

An interesting fact concerning the competition of white people with Negroes for Negro business is that the Negro patrons are taking advantage of the situation to force the white business men to respect them and give the courtesies due men and women. Here in the little town of Orangeburg we overheard a telephone conversation of a colored girl connected with a colored establishment whose trade is valuable to merchants. Her remarks were something like this: "We notice the fact that your agent in calling (over the phone) at this office persistently refuses to address our purchasing agent, who is a married woman as 'Mrs. ——.' We have noticed this for quite a while and resent it as an unnecessary discourtesy. If you desire our trade, we think that the least you can do is to treat our officers with common, decent courtesy." It seems that there was much apologizing at the other end of the line, which, however, the writer was not privileged to hear. It is deplorable that television was not prevalent so that one could have seen the facial expression of the man at the other end. This little incident is recorded here because it shows how the Negro in business is up against race prejudice even on the part of salesmen, who certainly should ordinarily keep such harmful antagonisms out of their customers' sight.

One is surprised as he surveys Negro business enterprises in South Carolina to see so few Negroes in the business of "filling stations"—retailing gasoline, oils, and auto accessories. Careful inquiry reveals the fact that race prejudice places handicaps in the path of the Negro in this popular and lucrative business. The writer has been told by several colored men who have attempted to operate this particular business that even the wholesale jobbers in gasoline seem to be unwilling to have them succeed in this field. The result is that a Negro operating a filling station often finds it difficult to get regular, efficient and honest service from the jobbers. This is probably due to the fact that the big supply companies, finding that the majority of their customers are white and resenting the competition of Negroes in this field, co-operate with these white persons in a sub rosa way so as to discourage the Negroes. A careful scientific study needs to be made in connection with this business.

Although few of the business men interviewed by my investigators in Columbia, Orangeburg, and Greenville, mentioned it, I believe that the manifestations of race prejudice other than those mentioned play a large part in accounting for the comparatively insignificant achievements of the Negro in business in this state. It is perhaps necessary to explain in some detail my impression here.

We have already strongly and plainly hinted at the fact that although some white people support Negro business enterprises when they are more convenient or efficient than similar white ones, the general rule is to the opposite; namely, white people boycott Negro businesses and therefore limit the Negro business man to the support of his own race. The patronage of the Negroes is the less desirable because they constitute the poorer customers. Furthermore, the Negro business man does not get all the patronage of his own race because the colored people do not retaliate with the economic boycott which they could use effectively. Negroes, for the most part, will trade with or buy from a white man just as quickly as from a colored man. In some instances they prefer to trade with the white people for several reasons, among them the following being most potent: white people usually own the most reputable, respectable, and efficient business places; the white business enterprises have more capital, are better housed, and constitute the popular mediums for doing business; thirdly, the Negroes are jealous of each other and, on account of suffering from an inferiority complex, they often prefer to trade with white people, choosing to accept "Jim Crow" service and "regulations" rather than to be identified with the Negro businesses. *In the fourth place, Negroes do not realize the great importance and necessity of economic solidarity and prosperity.* All these circumstances mentioned immediately above are due to the effects or aftermath of slavery and race prejudice.

Race prejudice, by the application of the segregation principle in business areas, operates to exclude the Negro business men from the more desirable sites. Go to any city or town in South Carolina and you will find the Negroes are generally forced to do their business in the "colored district" of the town which is usually the least desirable part of the business district. Usually Negro business is relegated to the "fringe" of the white business district. In Charleston, and here and there in other cities and towns, we find only a few Negroes doing business on "Main Street." In many instances where Negroes cling to Main Street it is simply because they own property there and have not yet been driven out. They find it difficult to "carry on" in these places.

Race prejudice prevents Negro business men from being freely accepted in the business circle of the white people of the towns. The white "Board of Trade" ignores his exist-

ence as a rule or ostensibly considers his puny efforts as a
"huge joke." To them the Negroes are indeed "Toy Business
Men."* Negroes cannot function in the United States
Chamber of Commerce and their own National Business
League is another "huge joke."* In the larger towns the
Negroes struggle along with their own "business league," etc.

There are other ways in which race prejudice affects
Negro business in this state adversely but we must call attention to a weakness of another type, a weakness which we
regret exists but which we must record as a part of the
work of the historian presenting a faithful record of what
has been and is. Negro business in this state is seriously
handicapped on account of the lack of capital. The Negro
group is poor. Dr. W. E. B. DuBois has rightly said that
"Of all miseries, the greatest is to be a poor race in a rich
country." This is the plight of the Negro business man in
South Carolina. The Negro's poverty is all the more restrain-
ing and oppressive because he has not learned to use the
corporation as a form of doing business. There are several
reasons for this. There are few Negroes trained for the organization and management of corporations. The writer does
not know of a single Negro in the state who is a graduate
from a reputable school of business administration. Negroes
must co-operate financially through the use of corporations
if they are to succeed in amassing sufficient capital to finance
business able to compete with any effectiveness at all with
the vast enterprises of the white people. As the statistics
in the little investigation we made strikingly demonstrate,
Negroes in the state have not yet begun to trust each other
with their money which they have to invest.

Some beginning has been made along this line in two
kinds of businesses: banking and insurance, especially the
latter. With a few statements about these two types of
businesses we turn to the hopeful side of Negro business in
this state. When the Freedmen's Aid Bank failed, Negroes
in the state suffered great losses, through its local branches,
as did the colored people in other states. As is generally

---

*A term used by a Negro writer in *The Messenger.*

known, this deplorable incident blighted the budding faith of Negroes in banks and other financial institutions, especially those operated by and for their own race. It was quite a while before they began to use any banks again, and a still longer time before they began to trust their own banks. However, several banks have been established at different times within the state. Several have also failed. These bank failures seem to be due, in most instances, to the fact that the Negroes lack experience* and support from their own people. Of course they receive scant co-operation from the white bankers. At present there are only two or three Negro banks operating in the state. These banks are performing or have opportunity to perform a great service. Negro business cannot amount to very much until there are more and stronger Negro banks because modern business of the large scale type is run on credit and the banks are the modern sources of credit. It has been demonstrated that Negro business men cannot get adequate credit from the white banks. The white banks favor the white business enterprises in spite of the fact that they often have deposits of colored customers which amount to a great deal in the aggregate. Through the white banks the funds of the colored people are used to strengthen the white competitors of their own struggling business men. It is to be hoped that an increasing number of colored men in the colleges and universities of the state will see the challenge of the business world and enter it with brain, training and a zeal for racial welfare which will improve banking and through it stimulate all other Negro business attempts.

We next turn to insurance. Here we find much progress being made. Negroes are gradually being educated to buy the service which insurance of various kinds provides. They are also learning to buy it from their own companies, domestic and foreign. They ought to buy more. We cannot understand why Negroes should continue to deal with white insurance agents who do not respect them.

When the writer was a student in social science at Atlanta

---

*Julius Rosenwald says "Negroes are not prepared for banking."

University some years ago, we carried out a brief study of
Negro business in Georgia. One fact we noted was that
Negroes in that state used manufactured products to a great
extent but we produced very few of these commodities in our
own factories. This is strikingly true in South Carolina
today. Here is an open field for our young men and women.
We hope that more of them will enter this field so that a
later historian of the Negro's efforts in business in this state
will have something to record along this line.

If one reads the list of businesses investigated in these
three towns we studied in South Carolina, he finds mentioned
the kinds of businesses most Negroes in this state are engaged in. Of course, there are a few other persons operating businesses not mentioned, especially in Charleston, where
we, unfortunately, were not able to make a study of contemporary business conditions in time for this publication. The
fact is, there is a vast list of businesses that Negroes in this
state ought to operate in large numbers but which they have
not entered. Here is a distinct challenge to the Negro college men.

Speaking of college men reminds me to record a criticism which came to the writer from a young business man
who rendered us some assistance in an investigation we made
in Charleston. His contention is that the Negro college
man has so far proved practically a complete failure in the
business world; that "he is a liability rather than an asset."
Facts are hard to find to rebut this opinion. Our schools
have failed to furnish trained and efficient helpers for business men. Recently the colleges have added commercial departments which train clerks, bookkeepers, and stenographers.
But most of the young people coming out of these courses
are not well trained and most of the girls make poor stenographers and secretaries, because they are deficient in such
elementary fundamentals as spelling, writing, and good clear
English. Our college men have not received adequate training in economics, and have not been inspired to devote their
lives to *service* through business. Those who enter business
have the predatory idea or "profit motive" instead of a pas-

sion for service. It is up to the colleges to meet the crying need of Negro business in this state—the need for trained, efficient, constructive leadership—leadership with a long vision, big ideas, and a passion for human welfare achieved through economic uplift which, after all, is the most potent form of salvation of which we know in this present world.

In this brief sketch of Negro business in South Carolina we have attempted to be constructively critical, and hopefully prophetic of the better day as well as accurate in the few historical statements we have been able to make. The reader will doubtless feel that more statistics and facts should have been gathered, but if we have left the impression that any great achievement is yet to be produced in the field of Negro business in this state, the writer feels that the unvarnished truth is told.

CHAPTER VII

THE NEGRO FARMER IN SOUTH CAROLINA

THE Negro population of South Carolina is still predominantly rural. Therefore any history of the Negro in this state which fails to emphasize the life, work and problems of the colored tillers of the soil cannot be called a history of Negro life and achievement in this state. Scattered all through this book, in almost every chapter, there are references, direct or indirect, to the Negro farmer, his work and influence. However, in this chapter we propose to deal with him specifically.

As Mr. Barnwell points out in the latter part of this chapter,* the Negro farmer of this state labors under all the difficulties of the Southern farmer of both races and, of course, has constantly wrestled with the additional difficulties which harass the Negro farmers of the South, difficulties due to that incubus of southern civilization—race prejudice.

That the Negro farmers of this state have made progress and built an honorable and valuable place for themselves in the economic order of the state is a patent fact. Here and there one could find a few Negro farmers among the colored people before the war. But the great masses of Negroes lived in the rural communities or on great plantations where they worked for planters as slaves or at the best as unskilled farm laborers.

In this chapter we are chiefly concerned, not with Negro farm laborers, but with Negro farmers who own and operate farms or rent and operate farms—independent business men in the field of agriculture.

Among the free ante-bellum Negroes, in certain sections of the state, were a few conspicuous examples of Negro farmers. We cite a few instances here.

*A part of this chapter was written by Mr. B. B. Barnwell of Frogmore, St. Helena Island, a graduate of Hampton Institute and one of the most efficient farm demonstration agents of the state.

The outstanding example of this is James Pendarvis, who lived in St. Paul's Parish during the latter part of the eighteenth century. Pendarvis was a large planter and at one time held as many as 200 slaves. There was also one Mrs. Persons, perhaps some way related to Pendarvis,[1] who was reported in the census returns of 1780 as having 136 slaves. There were also other cases less conspicuous in different parts of the state. Some of these free Negroes came into possession of their land, slaves, and other property by gifts from their white relatives. Others were descendants of free Negroes who migrated into South Carolina from the West Indies. A few doubtless procured their property by working as skilled or semi-skilled laborers.

Directly after the Civil War there followed a brief period of economic chaos which of course affected agriculture as it did everything else. The few Negroes who possessed property in land and slaves were somewhat prepared to farm, but those who had been slaves had nothing, not even land, and were therefore in poor condition to undertake independent farming, for it takes some capital to embark upon this occupation. The result of this condition was that the vast majority of the former slaves were forced to become farm laborers. For quite a while some refused to work at all, hoping to receive lands and other capital free. The famous rumor that all the land formerly belonging to the white people would be confiscated and parceled out to the former slaves, each receiving "forty acres and a mule," received extensive credence and was not an insignificant factor in the apparent slothfulness of the post-bellum Negro farm laborers. The agencies for the reconstruction of the state of South Carolina realized the importance to trying to supply the Freedmen with farm lands. The government undertook to co-operate with private and semi-public organizations in every possible way.

On account of the great expense of the war, many of the white land owners were unable to keep up the relatively

---

[1] Phillips, U. B.: *American Negro Slavery*, chapter on *Ante-bellum Free Negroes.*

high taxes on their vast land holdings and it passed into the domain of the commonwealth on account of failure of original owners to meet these expenses.   Although most of this land finally passed back into the hands of the original owners, the Negroes who were able acquired much of it.   A few planters voluntarily sold out their large plantations when they found it almost impossible to operate them according to the plans and ideas of the recent slave regime.   The reconstruction government established a land commission which was given the authority to administer the large sum of $750,000.   The purpose of this fund was to buy land for the Freedmen.   It appears that the fund was grossly misused and the government as well as the Freedmen defrauded of a vast amount of this money.[2]

It very soon became apparent to the Negroes who wished to farm that they must buy their own land and otherwise capitalize the business.   This they began to do.   Since that time there has been a steady increase of farm land owned and cultivated by Negro farmers in this state.   Of course, during periods of migration and other economic disturbances, there have been certain periodic reactionary movements, but the tendency has been progressive.   An example of a reactionary period is given by Mr. Barnwell in his statement toward the latter part of this chapter.

The progress of the Negro farmers in this state is in fact remarkable when we face the disadvantages and discouragements they have continually been forced to meet and overcome.   The Negro farmer has inherited the problems of the state and the section.   First, he was compelled to begin his farming operations on the poor land depleted of fertility by the unscientific methods of the ante-bellum agricultural regime.   In addition to poor land there was the far more serious handicap of lack of credit and all other forms of financial assistance and co-operation with the white people except upon such terms as would practically re-establish Negro slavery in the form of peonage, which condition is by no means eliminated even today.

[2]A. A. Taylor: *The Negro and the Reconstruction of South Carolina.*

Furthermore, the Negro farmers were handicapped at this early stage because of their ignorance. Because of their ignorance they often did not appreciate the value of modern machinery and scientific methods. In the days of slavery the Negro farm laborer had been in most instances kept in perfect ignorance because the whites believed correctly that "if you educate the Negro, you unfit him for a slave." As Professor Phillips has conclusively demonstrated in his writings on the economic phases of slavery, the slave regime favored an unscientific method of farming resulting in the rapid depletion of the fertility of the soil and an increasing inefficiency of the farm laborers.[3]

The Negro farmers still are largely ignorant and out of touch with scientific methods. This condition is being improved to some extent by the comprehensive programs of agricultural education planned and partly carried out by the educational system of the state, aided by the Federal Government.

It is quite obvious to any observer of the agricultural situation in South Carolina today that the state has suffered because the Negro farmers have not progressed more rapidly. When one looks for the fundamental causes of this deplorable failure of the colored farmer as a class, he finds some of the chief drawbacks to be: the general economic backwardness of the entire South as reflected in low wages and generally inefficient methods of production, marketing and financing. The credit system as operated in the State of South Carolina tends to keep the Negro farmer poor, ignorant and non-progressive; especially if he is a renter. Even if he is a land owner he finds it difficult to "tide himself over" the lean years without credit; yet if he uses it he is likely to reduce himself to the state of a peon. As pointed out elsewhere, peonage is still practiced here in South Carolina.[4] Its recent existence in Georgia has been widely advertised by the infamous Williams Farm incident.[5] However,

---

[3]Phillips, U. B.: *American Negro Slavery*, chapter on "Economic Failure of Slavery."
[4]Carter G. Woodson: *The Negro in Our History*, pages 435, 436.
[5]Dowd, Jerome: *Negro in American Life*.

Georgia is not the only sinner in the South in this matter. Perhaps the greatest disgrace in this matter belongs to Mississippi, but South Carolina is far from innocent. Peonage exists in South Carolina because of the uncurbed, selfish greediness of many of the small town merchants who through this credit system manage to keep the vast majority of Negro farmers in debt permanently without any prospect of ever getting ahead financially. These small town merchants are really the backbone of the peonage system in this state and in the other southern states where it exists.

The failure of the local governments to function effectively for the protection of the life and property of Negro farmers has also been one of the chief disadvantages. Mob violence and political intimidation, robbing the Negro farmer of his right to vote and share in local government and make his contribution to community development have had the effect of discouraging the colored farmer, driving the more progressive and efficient ones away or, at least, leaving them with little ambition to make the greatest possible progress. It is a deplorable fact that if a successful Negro farmer educates his children, male and female, in this state they usually refuse to return to the farm and stay because the manifestations of race prejudice are so very disagreeable that they prefer to go to cities and make their living at other occupations. The one exception to this is the fact that some of the girls return to the rural communities to teach in the better rural schools, especially the Rosenwald schools, and some of the young men return to teach agriculture in these schools and act as farm demonstration agents. As a rule, we do not find the Negro farmer able to get his boys to study scientific agriculture with the intention of returning to the farm as a farmer and living in the "old home" community on his farm. Even the farmers' boys who study for the various professions such as medicine, dentistry, etc., rarely ever plan to return to the old home community and serve their native folks. All this is discouraging to the Negro farmer. It is partially the result of race prejudice.

It can be clearly seen from this that the renaissance of

Negro agriculture in South Carolina for which our colleague, Mr. Barnwell, prays must wait for the disappearance of the Ku Klux Klan spirit (not only its unmasking) in the rural districts, the eradication of political intimidation of Negro citizens, and the elimination of the credit system supporting peonage.

The low wages paid farm laborers together with the discouraging factors in the present social order to which we referred above have all tended to retard the progress of the Negro farming class in this state. Even if the common, unskilled farm laborer in this state wished to save and invest some part of his earnings to the end that he might some day become an independent farmer he has found that the low wages paid would scarcely suffice to keep body and soul together, not to speak of accumulating capital for the future business of farming. The poor protection actually given the life and property of Negroes in the rural districts cooperates with poverty to deprive the Negro farm worker of all ambition and hope of ever becoming an independent farmer. It is a remarkable tribute to the optimism, skill and courage of Negro character that even a few gradually come forward from these conditions to slowly swell the ranks of the Negro farmers of the state.

The condition which we have been describing above is deplorable not only from the point of view of the Negro rural population of this state but is regretted by every loyal South Carolinian, white or black, who has economic training enough to appreciate the danger, or state pride and loyalty enough to be more interested in the prosperity of the commonwealth than the degradation of the Negro race. But the policy of the state has been unenlightened in this matter. Political leaders, teachers, and even preachers, facing the natural outcome of this policy of oppression perpetrated upon the Negro farmer, have sought some well nigh hopeless way out—such as attracting white immigrants here to take the places vacated by discouraged, disgusted Negroes leaving for more friendly fields of labor. During the height of the migration of Negro farm laborers from this state, which took place a few years ago, one of our most influential white papers, the *Columbia State,* published an editorial advocating something like this.   The present writer sent the editor his reflections on the editorial, which were published in that paper, without comment, as follows:

To the Editor of the *State:*
    Are the Negroes of South Carolina a Potential Asset to the State?
    This question suggested itself to me after reading your editorial in today's issue of the *State* on "Time for Organized Action in South Carolina."   We agree with that sentiment as stated in the subject.   We think, however, that other action than that indicated might also be helpful in solving the problem.
    You quote approvingly the following: "It is recognized that the only permanent solution of the labor problems created by the heavy outflow of the Negroes is to be found, not in bringing in white laboring families to take the place of the Negro families lost, but rather in attracting white families who will buy the land, cultivate it themselves and thus become a permanent and valuable asset to their respective communities."
    Is it not possible and practical, by giving the Negroes now present in this state larger educational and economic opportunities, to so inspire and satisfy them that they will, in larger numbers, be content to "buy the land, cultivate it themselves and thus become a permanent and valuable asset to their respective communities?"   Would this not be a far cheaper and wiser policy for the South in the long run?   If it is true that a large number of small farmers owning their own farms, living in independence and satisfaction and making their contribution to the general welfare along all lines of citizenship is preferable to the present situation, why not use the Negroes already present to create that situation rather than send to Europe or elsewhere at great expense for aliens who, although they may be easily assimilated, are not as well adapted to the South just now as the Negroes who are already here?
    We can think of only one reason why these questions should be answered in any other way but favorably to the retention of the Negroes under the conditions suggested.   It may be argued that such Negro citizens are not desirable; that this is to be a white man's country, unless the Negro is content to remain permanently, in the mass, a body of laboring people without property, education, political rights and economic privileges.   It cannot be said that the Negroes are incapable of producing such persons for in many instances Negro farmers, with limited education

and little encouragement and opportunity, have already bought their farms, cultivate them and are valuable assets to their respective communities. The *State,* we think, does not hold that Negroes should be kept as a group of unskilled laborers simply because of previous conditions of servitude and race relationships.

It may be said that the Negro is leaving, regardless of what may be done. But we believe that more would remain if they felt that the way were opened as we intimate it should be.

I further explain my idea here by saying that justice to the Negro rural worker is necessary to establish a reputation for the state which would encourage or at least not discourage progressive prospective citizens thinking of South Carolina as a civilized community striving to attain modern democracy.

The Negro farmer in South Carolina has made considerable progress in several ways. First, he has come into possession of a considerable amount of good farm land.[6] Negro farmers now own many thousands of acres of farm land in this state, some of it being of the very best. Secondly, the Negro farmer has made progress in home building. While the majority of the homes of colored farmers of the state are not much more than shelters from the weather, there are many real homes with all modern conveniences available for a twentieth century farm home—such conveniences as electric lights, running water, and power driven machinery of all kinds. These homes are not only up-to-date establishments from the point of view of physical plants but also measure up to the highest standards of morality and intelligence. Thirdly, Negro farmers of this state have made a little progress in scientific farming. In this connection great assistance has been given by the following men who have served successfully as head of the agricultural department of the South Carolina State A. and M. College here at Orangeburg: B. F. Hubert,[7] F. M. Staley, and C. D. Haynes. These men have helped train large numbers of young men who have gone

---

[6]There were 18,336 Negro owners of farms in South Carolina in 1925 (U. S. census).

[7]Mr. Hubert headed the department for almost ten years.

forth year after year during the last two decades, spreading
the gospel of "clean living, high thinking, and efficient production." B. F. Hubert, now president of the Georgia State
Industrial College, did pioneering work along this line and
established a morale for the development of scientific agriculture. Today we have in South Carolina the following
men working in the places indicated, trying to increase the
happiness and efficiency of Negro farmers in this state:

Arthur Daniels, Allendale; D. T. Robinson, Society Hill;
H. E. Sutton, Barnwell; B. J. Reddish, Blackville; J. S. Shank-
lin, Burton; T. F. Curry, Batesburg; James M. Jones, Trenton;
P. C. Leggette, Marion; D. T. Taylor, Gresham; J. H. Chapman,
Plezer; F. N. Clemmons, Jefferson; H. G. Brewer, Hartsville;
T. T. W. Bowen, Latta; Milbia Johnakin, Orangeburg; J. T.
Simpson, Easley; L. N. Scott, Eastover; D. J. Johnson, Johns-
ton; Thos. F. Hill, Fair Forest; J. L. Brewer, Timmonsville;
E. L. Avery, Fort Mill; William Jennings, Orangeburg; R. A. E.
Fladger, Lake View; W. A. White, Gray Court; G. B. Fladger,
Latta; Robert McBryde, Little Rock; E. T. Fleming, Lynchburg;
D. C. McDuffy, Marion; William B. Campbell, McCall; R. F.
Bowler, Darlington; R. C. Collier, Minturn; J. S. Roberts,
Mullins; J. A. Holman, McClellanville; E. F. Floyd, Newberry;
H. A. Chiles, Traveler's Rest; R. F. Gladden, Newberry; S. M.
Young, Newberry; Roy Gordon, Eloree; T. W. Cooper, Rus-
sellville; J. H. Rumph, Pineville; Foster Burton, Neeces; Robert
D. Dean, Saluda; Eugene McCottry, Ridge Spring; Roosevelt
White, Simpsonville; Easterling Walker, Pamlico; Leonard P.
Young, Tillman; Asa Thompson, Whitney; E. J. Bradley,
Wisacky; Acy Outten, Summerville.

Aside from the work of the agricultural colleges and the
Smith-Hughes vocational teachers, probably the greatest
development of the Negro farmer has come partly as a result
of the passing of the Smith-Lever Law in 1914. The work
of the county farm and home demonstration agents, under
the Smith-Lever Law, encourages the adult farmer to demonstrate for himself the science of farming. There are sixteen
counties, or about one-third of the state, now enjoying the
benefit of the service of the county agents. The same opportunities that are offered the adult farmers are also offered
the boys and girls, who have a greater opportunity to become

better farm and home makers, through the advice and service rendered by the extension workers.

The following organization heads up the extension work under the Smith-Lever Act, with Mr. H. E. Daniels as state supervising agent for men's and boys' work, Miss Dora E. Boston (1927-8) as state supervising agent for women's and girls' work, both with headquarters at the State Agricultural College for Negroes:

Allendale County, Rosa Gibbs; Banberg County, E. D. Jenkins; Beaufort County, Benjamin B. Barnwell and Mabel Price; Charleston County, Connie N. Jones; Clarendon County, William Thompson; Darlington County, Mabel Howard and S. C. Disher; Florence County, Jessie J. Wilson; Greenville County, Delphenia Wilkinson; Orangeburg County, G. W. Daniels; Richland County, J. E. Dickson and Francis Thomas; Spartanburg County, W. C. Bunch, and Sumter County, J. C. Maloney.

It seems to us that there is an encouraging amount of progress along the lines indicated above among the Negro farmers of this state. We give below a statement on the Negro farmer of South Carolina prepared especially for this chapter by Mr. B. B. Barnwell, Smith-Lever agent in Beaufort County, whose work certainly gives him the opportunity to know many of the facts and the right to speak with some authority on the subject.

The Negro Farmers in South Carolina. According to the census report of 1920, there were 109,010 colored farmers in the State of South Carolina. The census report of 1925 showed that there were only 90,578 colored farmers in the state, a decrease of 18,529 during the five-year period.

How These Farmers Were Classed. The above report also showed the following classifications: 14,476 colored farm owners in full, 3,892 colored farmers who owned their farms in part, 34 colored farmers who were managing farms for some one else, 72,179 who were tenant farmers. Of the 72,179 who were classed as tenants, 11,389 were known as cash tenants, 32,368 as croppers and 28,422 were classed as other tenants.

Causes of the decrease of colored farmers might be grouped as follows: (a) Cotton Boll Weevil, (b) Failure to adapt themselves to new condition, (c) Inability to obtain credit to operate their farms, (d) Fluctuation of prices, (e) Opportunities to earn big wages in Northern industries, (f) A failure to appreciate the value of co-operation.

The Cotton Boll Weevil. The effect of the cotton boll weevil on the average colored farmer can hardly be measured in dollars and cents. The growing of a non-perishable crop that finds a ready demand with a fair or good price has a peculiar fascination for the average farmer regardless of race or creed. While it is very true that the average colored farmer did not get rich growing cotton, he was sure of enough, either in cash or credit, to carry him from one year to another. Coming as it did and when it did, the average farmer could not adjust himself quickly enough to ward off disaster and when the boll weevil swooped down on him, he gave up in despair.

Failure to Adapt to New Conditions. The experts had made a study of the effect the boll weevil would have on the cotton farmers, and had suggested such ways out as rotation, diversification, and co-operation. Being somewhat conservative and not always intelligent enough to follow advice, the average colored farmer did not succeed and again he found himself in despair and ready to move on.

Failure to Obtain Credit can be counted as another reason why the average colored farmer was forced to move on. The failure of the cotton crop affected the entire financial system of the community and the average cotton farmer had nothing that he could offer that would bring in cash to meet his demands in the immediate future. The Federal Land Banks are helping the situation, but only to a limited extent because most of the farms being operated by colored farmers are not of sufficient size to enable them to secure an organization. Then too, if they desire to buy a farm, not many are able to furnish the first payment in order to avail themselves of the Federal Land Bank aid. I trust that in the near future this bank will devise some policy that will be designed to help the small farmers; for, although I may be mistaken, I believe there is a decided advantage for most of the Negro farmers in the operation of smaller farms, say from 25 to 50 acres.

Fluctuation of Prices. With the destruction of the cotton crop, many farmers tried to grow other crops for market, but in this case the law of supply and demand had its effect as it always will with crops that are in some case highly perishable. There has been a wide variation in prices on such crops as Spanish peanuts, oats, wheat, sweet potatoes, watermelons, and rye; while tobacco has done a little better. Prices have also varied on live stock.

Opportunity to Earn Big Wages in Northern Industries has been another reason why a number of colored farmers have left their farms. Of course, this is largely true with the younger generation. From poverty, a number of these farmers are earning from three to ten and twelve dollars a day.

Failure to Co-operate could be given as still another reason why some farmers have been forced to give up farming. In fact, the success of farming depends on the co-operation of one farmer with another and of one group of farmers with another group. As an illustration: last spring during the potato season in Beaufort County, farmers had been shipping their potatoes single handed and since most of them did not raise enough on their plots to make up a carload, they were paying $2.10 a barrel. After some effort, I was able to get these farmers to ship on the same day from the same place. One day we sent off three carloads of potatoes and instead of paying $2.10, we only paid 78 cents a barrel for freight. We were able to save $587.40 on this lot alone. The same has been true in the marketing of peanuts and in the buying of fertilizers and other farm supplies. In unity there is not only strength for the farmers but there is also progress and prosperity.

Successful Negro Farmers. There are hundreds of Negro farmers who are making a success of their farming operations. I am sure in every county of the state there are striking examples of this assertion. In Anderson we had Mr. Hammond, who died recently and left a well equipped farm of more than 600 acres.   He left a comfortable home and boys and girls who have received their education from the earnings of his farm.

In Orangeburg County, at Eloree, there resides Mr. Williams, another successful farmer who owns hundreds of acres of land and a home with all modern conveniences.   He has educated his children from the earnings of his farm and he is still making money.

In Beaufort County we have Robert Lawrence, a very successful potato grower.   He makes from two to three thousand dollars from his farm each year.   One of his sons is a graduate of Tuskegee Institute and he has two of his boys who are partners with him in his farming operations. Then there is Ben Chaplin of St. Helena Island, Beaufort County, who started with three acres and today he owns about forty acres and he is a very young man.   He has improved his home, is sending his children to school and is making more money each year from his farm.   I could name hundreds of others but it is not necessary.   I only name these as examples.   Most of these have started out with practically nothing and by their thrift and economy and with the aid of the extension work they bid fair to accomplish more.

SUGGESTIONS

1. Most of the colored farmers of the present day have had very limited educational opportunities.   The successful farmers must see to it that their children are well educated to and not from the farms.

2. Each colored farmer must practice greater thrift and economy in his farming operations; enlarge his farming operations by careful saving and not by going into debt foolishly.

3. Negro farmers must get all the scientific information they can, remembering that the farm and home agents are only too glad to serve them.

4. Negro farmers must learn to co-operate more with their neighbor farmers.   "In unity there is strength."   They must co-operate in establishing community enterprises not only for themselves but for their children.

5. The Negro must strive to own farms and larger farms, remembering that the man who owns a farm owns a part of heaven's greatest gift.

6. The farmer must be an asset to his community by making his just contribution toward its uplift and its progress.

7. Our farmers must remember that in nearly every community we are now getting good schools. We must send our children in order that they may make of themselves better citizens.

8. We should remember our State college at Orangeburg, which is the center of both agricultural and technical learning. Not only should we send our children, but attend the short courses that are offered to help farmers to improve their condition.

9. We have an excellent school here on St. Helena Island known as the Penn School. It is one of the greatest schools of its kind anywhere. Farmers will do well to see it. We also have other schools that are helping the farmers, such as the Voorhees School at Denmark, the Beaufort County Training School, and numbers of others.

I hope that during the next five years we shall have more than one hundred thousand colored farmers in our state of South Carolina who will be prosperous and who will be making their just contribution toward its progress and its uplift.

*   *   *   *

We conclude this chapter with the following additional information prepared especially for this book by Mr. H. E. Daniels, state supervisor of Smith-Lever Extension Agents for Negro Farmers in South Carolina:

The census of 1920 gives information about colored farmers in South Carolina showing that they own farm land to the extent of 1,146,396 acres. This is an average of nearly 63 acres to the farm. The values of the farm property owned by Negroes were placed at $59,839,583 in 1920; at $22,112,291 in 1910.

As stated by Mr. Barnwell, the estimate of the Department of Commerce published October, 1925, gives the total number of Negro farmers as 90,578, a loss of nearly 20,000 since 1920.

These 20,000 contain certainly some owners—how many no one really knows. If we estimate it at 15 per cent, it would mean that about 3,400 farmers have lost their farms. Considering the deflation of values and the depression of farming since 1920, it would not surprise us if 15 per cent have had to give up their homes and farms, and sometimes lose heavily in money, as well as suffer the disappointment of blighted hope and foiled ambition. It is rather cause for rejoicing that 85 per cent or more have been able to weather the storm and difficulties during the past five years. If we accept the shrinkage in farm owners as around 2,200 to 3,400, we should then have a loss of Negro farm tenants of 16,000 to 17,500. It is probably quite safe to say that the number of Negro farm tenants has decreased from 16,000 to 18,000, and now stands at about 71,000.

Those of us who know how hard the life on the farm has been, how low the standard of living, how poor the rewards of farm labor for the years since 1920, cannot feel sorry that those 20,000 farmers have left the farms. Wherever they and their families have gone, they have probably been at least as well off, most probably much better off, at least for food and clothes, and shelter, than if they had stayed on the farm. Their going has probably brought some relief to themselves and to their families. It has relieved the pressure on those who have remained. Work at the North, work in Florida, work on railroads and public roads, has been a great blessing to many of our colored farmers, who would have almost starved on the farm. Let us hope others will follow them, rather than any of those should, in the present unsettled condition of agriculture, come back to the farm.

The important question is, what is being done among the 90,578 farmers who remain, and for their wives and children, who together constitute a farm population of 528,292—nearly one-third the people of the state? Practically one-half of the agriculture of the state is in their hands. If they prosper, everybody else prospers. If they suffer, everybody else suffers.

In all agricultural efforts everywhere the two matters of outstanding importance are: (1) the relation of the farmer to his land. Does he own or rent it? (2) the relation of the farmer to science. Does he know the results of scientific experiment? Can he secure them and put them into practice?

In the matter of ownership of farm land, the record of the Negro in South Carolina is worthy of all praise. To have come in less than two generations of freedom from nearly nothing to ownership of 1,000,000 acres, worth $35,000,000 to $40,000,000 is a mighty achievement—heroic indeed, when the obstacles are considered. The Negro is like every other human being—he desires to own the land he toils over—but the way to ownership has not always been easy.

The Federal Land Bank system lends money to persons who own farms, or are about to become owners, to assist in the purchase and improvement of farms, and to replace debts already contracted for those purposes, with a debt on the more favorable terms of a longer period of payment and a lower interest rate. The system has been of incalculable benefit to farmers generally in the United States, and the Negro farmer in South Carolina has benefited by it to some extent. The farmers who borrow from the Federal Land Banks are organized into associations, of which there are twelve for Negroes.

I do not say it is easy for a colored farmer to borrow from the Federal Land Bank. That source of credit is the largest single source, and the point I want to make is, that colored farmers have used and are using it, in hundreds of instances through their own associations. Probably no one has ever added up the full amount of their borrowings from the Land Bank, but I feel sure that it will total not less than a half million dollars. How much they have borrowed from state banks and individuals for the purpose of buying farms, I do not know, but it will amount to several millions, probably to eight or even ten millions. Of course their lives are made bitter by this debt. The Bible says, "The borrower is servant unto the lender," and our sad experience tells us it is the truth. Yet upon the whole, the bitter hardship of years of toil and self-denial is sweetened by hope that some happy day the home or farm will be free from debt. The road to ownership is not easy; it is a stiff uphill climb, but a good company is traveling that way, and there are helping hands in the friendly banks and bankers. Industrious thrifty Negro farmers need not be afraid to set out upon it. "In due season ye shall reap, if ye faint not." In general, my conclusion is, that it is easier now than it ever has been before for a colored farmer to own his farm.

The Negro farmer in South Carolina has a far better opportunity today to learn the science of farming than he has ever had. Farmers' bulletins are his for the asking. If he can read, all the treasure houses of scientific knowledge are wide open to him. Farm papers are cheap. I asked a good colored farmer how many farm papers he took, and he answered "four." That man has built as good a barn as I know in his country, has a large two-story house, and has for years kept careful accounts on his farm. He is a careful, in many respects a scientific, farmer.

There has been steady growth among Negro farmers in producing cash crops and food and feed supplies resulting from contact with extension workers and organization. We may close this statement with an example of the progress Negro farmers are making in cash crops and food and feed supplies as a result of the contact they have had with extension workers.

Sam Glover, R. F. D. No. 2, Orangeburg, S. C., by advice and assistance from the extension workers, began demonstration in 1916 on a farm of twenty-five acres of land in a low state of cultivation, with one horse and no livestock of any consequence. He lived in a house worth about $300; his first demonstration was three acres of corn and peas and the results were very gratifying.

The following year it was increased to ten acres in cotton, five acres in corn and five acres in small grain, resulting in good yields. The next year he added twenty-five acres to his farm and the entire farm was then run as demonstration. Following constant advice and assistance from extension workers on the ideas of soil building, crop rotation and pedigreed seed, today he owns 125 acres of land in a high state of cultivation with a modern home worth $3,000; two Jersey cows; fifteen head of swine, including two brood sows and one pure bred boar; three head of horses; improved farm implements; one automobile; 450 bushels corn; wheat sufficient for 1928; has sold eighteen bales of cotton; has eight tons of hay for sale above what is necessary to carry him through 1928. His wife and daughter sold $330 worth of vegetables, chickens, eggs and butter in 1927. The entire farm with modern improvements is valued at $8,000.

He has a life insurance policy with the Metropolitan Life Insurance Company for $3000. One of his daughters graduated from State College and is now teaching in the rural schools of Orangeburg County, carrying out the lessons learned at the State College in developing rural people. He has also three children in State College at present as a result of contact with extension workers; has a bank account, if no misfortune befalls him, to insure his 1928 crop without debt.

What is true of Sam Glover's progress is equally true of a large number of Negro farmers in South Carolina, who have come in contact with Negro extension workers.

We think the facts justify us in saying that the story of Samuel Glover is representative of the Negro farming group as a whole in South Carolina—it is the story of slow but sure progress being made against great odds because of the Negro's ability and willingness to "carry on" though the path is rocky and the final reward far away. Though no heralds proclaim it from the housetops, the Negro farmer is a hero and he will not fail; one day he will reach the goal of prosperity.

NOTE: See "Appendix No. 1" for further information on the subject treated in this chapter.

CHAPTER VIII

THE GIFTS OF WOMANHOOD IN EBONY

"She walks in beauty like the night
Of cloudless climes and starry skies,
And all that's best of dark and bright
Meet in her aspect and her eyes."

WE know of no womanhood anywhere in all the world
to which the above quotation can be more appropriately and truthfully applied than the Negro womanhood of
South Carolina. The gifts of womanhood in ebony as found
in this state have been numerous and of vital importance.
It is often said without full appreciation of its fundamental
truthfulness that no race or nation can rise above its womanhood. This is illustrated in the case of the colored women
in America and we propose to briefly sketch its demonstration in South Carolina. The gifts of Negro womanhood, as
indeed is true of the gifts of all womanhood, have not been
fully appreciated because they have been overshadowed by
the supreme gift of all—motherhood. Once at least, Calvin
Coolidge uttered profound philosophy complimentary to
womanhood of all races everywhere: "No man was ever
meanly born. About his cradle is the wonderful miracle of
life. He may descend into the depths; he may live in infamy
and perish miserably, but he is born great." It seems strange
that men took so long to learn that man could not be born
great of women who were less. Thus we wish to state here
at the beginning of this inadequate sketch that all the mighty
achievements of the colored people in this state would obviously have been impossible if Negro womanhood had not been
inherently great. All the way from the Negro slave's physical
fitness and mental power to bear the burdens of slavery and
adapt himself to western civilization, to his artistic genius
and spiritual power demonstrated by his "sorrow songs" and
his present moral challenge of the "old order," he has been
proving that his womanhood was and is consummately great.

174

First, then, let us say that the first noble gift of Negro womanhood to South Carolina was her gift of greatness transmitted through the laws of inheritance to the Negro manhood of the state.

We stated above that the other gifts of Negro womanhood have been overshadowed by the greatest gift—the gift of life through the miracle of motherhood; the gift of greatness through the profound mystery of inheritance. Yet in silence and tears this slave of slaves, Negro womanhood, has been giving other gifts, queenly gifts.

The second great gift of Negro womanhood to South Carolina is the gift of labor. While a large part of contemporary white womanhood of America was playing the grand part of "the decorated darling of western civilization," Negro womanhood was in the rice swamps and cotton fields of South Carolina doing constructive work toward the building of this civilization. She was helping to provide the "wherewithal" necessary to support many of the objects of the white man's benighted, narrow "chivalry." The Negro womanhood of South Carolina still works more than any other. In a recent publication one of our greatest American writers has stated our contention so well for Negro womanhood in America as a whole that it perfectly describes this phase of the subject for this state. We quote as follows:

Yet these black women toil and toil hard. There were in 1910 2,500,000 Negro homes in the United States. Out of these homes walked daily to work 2,000,000 women and girls over ten years of age—one-half of the colored female population as against a fifth in the case of white women. These, then, are a group of workers, fighting for their daily bread like men; independent and approaching economic freedom! They furnished a million farm laborers, 80,000 farmers, 22,000 teachers, 600,000 servants and washerwomen, and 50,000 in trades and merchandising. In 1920, 38.9% of colored women were at work as contrasted with 17.2% of native white women. Of the colored women 39% were farming and 50% in service.[1]

It is not necessary for us to give statistics showing the number of colored girls and women of South Carolina who

---

[1] W. E. B. DuBois: *Darkwater*, pages 179, 180.

work in the fields and factories of the state.   It is not necessary for us to call attention to the multitudes who wash
clothes, nurse babies, cook and perform other household
drudgery for a mere bagatelle of wages in order that the
pseudo-aristocratic white womanhood of the state may wallow
in unearned luxury.   It is not necessary for us to call
attention to the thousands of colored women and girls of this
state trying to eke out a living teaching school in the rural
districts and small towns of the state[2] and many more trying
to escape the drudgery and moral danger of domestic service
and yet earn a living by entering the various occupations in
the commercial and business world slowly opening to women
everywhere.   All this is well known and taken for granted.
It is the too familiar demonstration of Negro womanhood
literally *giving* labor, an overflowing measure of it, to build
up the economic prosperity of this society in which she can
scarcely hope to share decently, not to say justly.

Doctor DuBois calls attention to the fact that Negro
women have led the way in showing the American man that
women can attain economic independence.[3]   This is well
proven in South Carolina.   Of course, it must be admitted
that colored women have not led in this matter because they
were more intelligent or progressive than white women, but
they were forced by necessity either to earn their own living
or to supplement the efforts of their men either because the
latter were unable or unwilling to carry the whole load.   However, the fact that the Negro woman has, in the mass, supported herself has naturally made her more independent.
One sufficient example of this is shown in the attitude of the
average Negro woman toward the institution of marriage.
Every one knows that colored women feel less dependent upon
marriage for support than most white women in South Carolina today.   Very seldom do we hear of a Negro woman going
into court trying to get alimony from a husband who no
longer desires to support her.   With remarkable self-respect

[2] Report of South Carolina State Superintendent of Education, 1924.
[3] W. E. B. DuBois: *Darkwater,* chapter on "The Damnation of
Women."

and confidence the average Negro woman who has failed to hold the affection of her husband lets him go his way in peace while she plunges into the economic world to support herself and the children. She succeeds in many instances. Of course, it may be justly claimed that one reason why Negro women do not try for alimony is because they know the Negro men not to have any income worth fighting to share. This is partly true, but we feel that it does not fully explain the facts.

We think it is not necessary to say more suggestive of the great gift of labor which Negro women have continuously been making in South Carolina from their introduction into the state up to the present day.

Another great gift of Negro womanhood is the gift of lingering love. Beginning in the dark days of slavery, every possible temptation has been placed before Negro womanhood in this state to seduce it from loyal love to Negro manhood. Slavery placed the Negro man in a very difficult position. It was hard for Negro women to love and cherish a slave husband. It was extremely difficult for the girl to be true to her slave lover when she was flattered and tempted by the attentions of the powerful men of the master class.[4] It goes without saying that many of the girls and women failed to pass through the almost superhuman strain imposed upon them in this connection.[5] We hold that it is remarkable that as many as did maintained love for their men and came through the testing with untarnished character and unquestioned virtue. Negro women developed character rather than merely maintained innocence. We believe that Negro womanhood is stronger today because it stood the test of exposure and struggle imposed upon it in those trying days of the regime of chattel slavery.

The love of Negro women for their men and their race in general not only lived in the midst of slavery but it has lingered through the aftermath of that iniquitous system.

---

[4] Baddy: "Negro Womanhood's Greatest Needs," in *Messenger Magazine*, February, 1928.
[5] Ibid.

Without the protection of any adequate laws; in fact, with exploitation of her virtue encouraged by the laws against intermarriage of the races in this state, the Negro woman has, in the main, remained loyal to her race men. This she has done at some disadvantage from an economic point of view. White men have been anxious to use colored women for immoral purposes because the laws to which we referred above relieve them of legal responsibility and at the same time the economic burden imposed by the Negro concubine was and is far lighter than that likely to be imposed by the white mistress. The Negro man was not able to retaliate because the white man has continuously maintained superiority in fighting equipment, except possibly during the brief period during which the Congressional Plan of Reconstruction was in force in South Carolina and several other southern states. Thus the lingering love of the Negro woman has been largely a voluntary, in a sense a sacrificial matter. It is hardly possible to pay too high a tribute to the Negro women of this state for the record they have maintained in this respect.

In sketching the life and history of the Negro in this state we have mentioned the contributions of many individual men. It seems fitting and proper that we mention a few of the most outstanding women of color who were born in this state and who have given much to the world. Beyond question the greatest woman of color who has yet come out of South Carolina is Mary McLeod Bethume. The nation and the world claim her now, but she belongs to South Carolina in a peculiar and unique way, since here she was born and reared.

Mary McLeod Bethume justifies the American philosophy of the inherent greatness of many individuals born among the lowly. Because of the inherent greatness of her soul and because of assistance rendered by missionaries from the North whose noble work we have approved elsewhere in this book, this black woman is a living testimonial to the fact that a colored girl born in South Carolina has a chance to achieve greatness. She makes no claim to be a self-made woman, but she comes about as near to that as any person we have in the history of the state or the world. She was born in the midst of poverty and ignorance, the arch enemies of human progress and achievement. Yet she achieved success and honor. She was born July 10, 1875, at Maysville. We quote the following brief summary of her life and work from "Who's Who in Colored America," published in 1927:

She was born of slave parents who were unable to give her an education. In 1888 a school teacher (white) gave her an opportunity to enter Scotia College, where she finished in 1895 and won a scholarship permitting her to study at Moody Bible Institute.

After teaching school for a while in South Carolina, Haines Institute, Augusta, Ga., and in Palatka, Fla., she came to Daytona in 1904 and there started the Daytona school. Her cash capital was $1.50, her first enrollment five pupils, and her plant a rented cottage.

In 1923 her school merged with the Cookman Institute of Jacksonville, Fla., becoming co-educational and operating under the auspices of the Methodist Episcopal Church.

She has held the office of president of the Florida State Teachers' Association, vice-president of the National Wage Earners' Association.

Mrs. Bethume was the leading spirit in establishing a home for delinquent colored girls at Ocala, Fla. She has served as president of the Southeastern Federation of Women's Clubs, and in 1924 at Chicago, was unanimously elected as president of the National Association of Colored Women, the leading organization of colored women in America. At Oakland, California, in August, 1926, she was re-elected to this position, and as president, represents 200,000 of the women of the race. She has served as president of the National Association of Teachers in colored schools, and is (1926) an active member in the Inter-Racial Council of America.

Another outstanding woman of South Carolina who differs from Mrs. Bethume in that most of her work has been done in this state where she has always lived and labored for the uplift of the race is Mrs. Marion Birnie Wilkinson. Mrs. Wilkinson was born in Charleston, S. C.

Her family is an old and well known one in the state and members of it have been very prominent in many of the lead-

ing movements among the colored people of the state. Mrs.
Wilkinson has been especially prominent in social uplift work
of all kinds in the state. She began to show this interest
in the uplift of those farthest down even while a student in
high school at Avery in her native city. We are told by her
father that most of the money she earned as a school teacher
soon after graduation was spent in various charitable projects. All through the years of her life she has continued
to share the material prosperity which has come to her and
hers with the less fortunate. She has achieved more than
ordinary success in inspiring other women of the state to
share their material resources for the promotion of worth-
while programs for social uplift. She has inspired the young
girls at State College, where she has long made her home as
wife of the president, to work for the promotion of the causes
in which she is interested. Through her leadership the young
women of the State College Y. W. C. A. have constructed
the only Y. W. C. A. building on the campus of any Negro
college in the country at the present time (winter 1928) and
made it one of the show places of the country in this line of
work.

For a number of years Mrs. Wilkinson has been the
president of the State Federation of Colored Women's Clubs.
She has unquestionably shown able leadership at the head of
this organization and the various projects of great social
worth to the Negro race in this state which have been sponsored by this organization under Mrs. Wilkinson's leadership
cannot be fully accounted for here on account of space limitations. Not only has Mrs. Wilkinson successfully led and
inspired the rank and file of women in the state in the projects of the State Federation of Colored Women's Clubs but she
has shown tact and skill in getting the co-operation of the
male and female members of the college community to help in
these practical matters. Students, teachers, and workers have
all generally shown willingness to co-operate with Mrs. Wilkinson in practically all her uplift programs. The chief interest
of the State Federation for some years has been the Home
for Girls who are maladjusted and have few friends and no

proper family protection. The Fairwold School has been carried by the women of this organization at great sacrifice. This institution, we hope, will in the near future become a state supported institution, but until that day comes the clubs are performing an indispensable service in this connection.

Although this work we have been describing is of vital importance, we are of the opinion that the finest contribution Mrs. Wilkinson has made to the state is that of her life as a model mother for her family of four children. Mrs. Wilkinson has demonstrated in her life the possibility of a woman taking an active part in the work of the world and yet being true to her family obligations and bringing up a family in the way that it should go. She has been of inestimable aid to her husband as executive of the college at the same time that she has trained her sons and daughters. We have taken this opportunity to emphasize the home-making achievement of this distinguished South Carolina woman not because her accomplishments in this connection are unique or unequaled, but because we feel that such an example is worth placing before the world at this time when the conception of larger freedom for women is understood by many as an argument against the effectiveness of motherhood. We feel that the career of Mrs. Wilkinson and others like her in this state proves that the progressive colored woman has shown herself capable of using the new freedom in such a way as to preserve the old family life and at the same time give the woman a chance to function as a productive member of the social order.

Some one has said that "history is biography written large." This statement has much of truth in it; that is, it suggests, as Doctor Wilkinson puts it, that "the greatest values of history are human values." Yet we must not overlook the fact that an overemphasis on the biographies of a few great leaders may cause us to overlook the importance of the life and work of the common people. In this book we have endeavored to emphasize the achievements of the Negro masses and we do not plan that this chapter shall be an exception; therefore we shall not write at length of any more individuals among the colored women of the state. The two that we have already mentioned serve to emphasize and illustrate the main facts. There are dozens of other women in the state who have achieved positions of honor and trust in the churches, secret orders, in industry, in business, and in social service. There are thousands of them who have fulfilled the great mission of women in the world—the privilege and duty of motherhood in a wonderful way. All these without thought of financial reward or earthly honors commensurate with their labors have given their gifts of love and made their contribution to the progress of the race here in this state. We here pay tribute to womanhood in ebony of the state of South Carolina without regard to position, class or station in life. It may seem that "full many a flower is born to blush unseen and waste its sweetness on the desert air" of ingratitude and obscurity; but, as another poet has said, "no life can be pure in its purpose and strong in its strife and all life not be purer and stronger thereby." Therein lies the secret of the conservation of goodness and the assurance of the everlasting blessing of the nobility of Negro womanhood in South Carolina.

In speaking of the life and work of Mrs. Marion Wilkinson, we mentioned the State Federation of Colored Women's Clubs to which organization we must revert in order to discuss the methods colored women of this state have used to do their charitable work and make other contributions to the welfare of the state. The South Carolina Federation of Colored Women was organized about 1910.[6] Its main purpose at the beginning seems to have been the founding and support of a reformatory school for delinquent girls. This was established near Columbia. Since its organization the federation has taken on other objectives, one of these being the support of a worthy girl student of scientific social service in the Atlanta School of Social Service. The federation has grown until there are now about seventy local organizations. These local organizations engage in various

---

[6] Information obtained largely from Mrs. Etta Rowe of Orangeburg.

projects for social welfare and uplift, the total value of which would be difficult to overestimate. As examples of the worthy work of these local organizations we may quote the following reports of local clubs as printed in the minutes of one of the annual convention reports of the federation:

CAMDEN—UPLIFT CLUB

Another annual meeting finds the Uplift Club struggling, but still alive. On Christmas day the father of our president suffered a stroke of paralysis which kept him a suffering, helpless invalid over five months and her a faithful and devoted nurse, who was constantly at his side. Two weeks ago God mercifully removed him and released her. Since that time she has been and still is under the care of a physician. We all know what it means to have the head of any organization away for a long time, but like the woman of the Bible, we have done what we could. We have paid taxes on, and so saved, the home of two mentally afflicted sisters. We also sent out at Christmas forty-one baskets to the poor. We sold tags to the amount of $7 for Fairwold. On several occasions, we sent committees with fruit and flowers to the hospital. We are chagrined that we have not been able to raise anything for the various enterprises of the national.

Number of members............................... 17
Membership dues ....$ 8.50
Ways and means................................... 2.00
Education 2.00
Fairwold 40.00
                                                 ———
                                                 $52.00

Already sent for Fairwold $7 and $3.

Mrs. L. D. Spaulding, President.
Mrs. L. Dibble, Secretary.
Mrs. J. D. Wright, Delegate.

CHARLESTON—LOUISE F. HOLMES LITERARY AND ART CLUB

We are submitting our first annual report. This club consists of twenty-four members. Under the leadership of our efficient and intensely interested president, Mrs. Leila H. Drayton, we have accomplished some good work in the various branches for which our organization stands.

The following contributions were given during the Christmas season: Family Welfare Association, $5. The members also assisted during the Avery drive at which time $10 was donated, and tubercular seals for Pine Haven were sold.

Fairwold	$100.00
Membership	12.00
National dues	12.00
Ways and means	1.00
Education	1.00
Delegates' fee	.50

$126.50

Mrs. Leila Drayton, President.
Mrs. Erma L. Pequette, Secretary.

ORANGEBURG—SUNLIGHT CLUB

The club numbers thirty-five live and active members. Meetings are held twice per month.

Means of raising money for the past year: Recital by Miss Marion Anderson; play by members of the club assisted by students of Claflin and State College and directed by Mr. and Mrs. Bryant; having a booth at both the white and colored county fairs; and by a doll contest.

The club operates a help directory for men and women; it expects to secure a house to demonstrate the home improvement plan for the coming year. We are alive to the issues of the federation and stand ready and willing to help carry them through.

Delegates (seating of same)	$ 4.00
Education	3.00
Membership	17.50
Ways and means	3.00
Fairwold	300.00

$327.50

We have already sent $325 to Fairwold.

Minutes of the South Carolina Federation.

Mrs. Marion B. Wilkinson, President.
Mrs. Etta B. Rowe, Secretary.

If one knows the officers and leaders of the South Carolina Federation of Colored Women's Clubs, he knows most of the women in the state who are doing most for the uplift of the Negroes so far as the colored women are concerned.

We therefore list here the officers, "heads of departments," and organizers of the federation as given in the latest annual report:

Mrs. Marion B. Wilkinson, president, Orangeburg; Mrs. Ida E. Green, first vice-president; Mrs. Maggie O. Levy, vice-president, Pee Dee District, Florence; Mrs. Martin Menafee, vice-president Orangeburg District, Denmark; Mrs. Nina Littlejohn, vice-president Piedmont District, Spartanburg; Mrs. Allonia L. Frederick, recording secretary, Sumter; S. M. Morrison, assistant recording secretary, Charleston; Mrs. Etta B. Rowe, corresponding secretary, Orangeburg; Mrs. Celia D. Saxon, treasurer, Columbia; Mrs. Susie J. Butler, chairman ways and means committee, Columbia; Mrs. Louise F. Holmes, chairman executive committee, Florence; Mrs. Carrie W. Thompson, state editor, Greenville; Mrs. Phyllis Gibbes, associate editor, Charleston; Miss Anna J. Dickson, auditor, Aiken; Mrs. Laura Spaulding, chaplain, Camden.

Heads of Departments: Mrs. Mabel K. Howard, suffrage, Darlington; Mrs. Susie Dart Butler, education, Charleston; Mrs. Julia Stephenson, temperance, Florence; Mrs. Emma Andrews, home economics, Sumter; Mrs. Effie Strother, music, Florence; Miss Rosa DeLorme, girls' work, Sumter; Mrs. Mary Kirvin, business, Syracuse; Mrs. M. B. Wright, health, Spartanburg; Mrs. Belle Vincent, mothers' department, Columbia; Mrs. C. R. Brown, chairman club presidents, Florence; Mrs. M. Alice LaSaine, rural education, Charleston. *Organizers:* Mrs. Jennie Jackson, special organizer, Orangeburg; Mrs. Mary E. Gordon, Dillon; Mrs. Annie Saunders, Sumter; Mrs. Nina Littlejohn, Spartanburg; Mrs. M. O. Rodolph, Charleston.

The State Federation, under Mrs. Wilkinson's leadership, is interested in bettering inter-racial relationships in the state as shown by the fact that its president is a member and officer of the state inter-racial committee, and by the following resolutions, passed at the last annual meeting:

Whereas, Discrimination and segregation work an embarrassment and a hardship upon our people all over the South;

Whereas, Paying equal fare for unequal accommodation, as often expressed in wooden coaches, unclean surroundings; the intrusion by others upon segregated portions of trains in the South;

Whereas, Our people have been largely intimidated and denied the privilege of seeking sleeping car accommodations all over the South;

Whereas, Inconvenient changes of trains and long layovers between trains, without the privilege of sleeping car accommodations, make for much inconvenience for us all and invite temptations for our daughters going to and fro to boarding schools;

Be it resolved: That we the colored women of South Carolina in our state federation assembled, do hereby wish to go on record as expressing our deepest gratitude to Dr. Alexander, chairman of the inter-racial committee of the southern states, for his manly Christian courage, his fine sense of fair play and justice for all his broad humanitarian program for our people as evidenced by his utterances at the Interdenominational Sunday School Convention in Birmingham.

And be it resolved: That we express the hope that Dr. Alexander be encouraged to continue his constructive and progressive program in our behalf; that criticism and opposition will not cause him to falter or his enthusiasm and courage to wane in a cause that needs the vision of a prophet and the soul of a martyr;

Be it further resolved: That this body of women go on record as rejoicing in the work of the inter-racial committee all over the country, and that we hereby express our gratitude especially for the kind and hopeful words of Mrs. Celia P. McPherson, Dr. Mills, Judge Hicks and Mrs. Parker as expressed to us in our inter-racial session.

Respectfully submitted,

JEANNETTE KEEBLE COX, Chairman,
LILLA L. WHITTAKER,
OLIVIA M. RODOLPH,
MAGGIE O. LEVY.

In the chapter on the educational efforts and achievements of South Carolina Negroes we have mentioned the wonderful work of the colored women as teachers in the colored schools rendering invaluable service for a mere pittance—in many instances far less than a living wage. Certain individuals stand out in this connection, especially Miss Wilson, founder of the Mayesville Institute, and the founder of Voorhees.

An excellent form of social service not common enough in this state is that represented by the Phyllis Wheatley Center at Greenville. Its program somewhat resembles the work of a Y. M. C. A. and a Y. W. C. A. combined. It also has achieved no small amount of inter-racial co-operation. This work was founded by Mrs. Hattie Logan Duckett.

A host of Negro women have rendered remarkable service for the uplift of the race through the churches of all denominations; especially through their missionary and charitable organizations. Outstanding among these was Mrs. Cora Boykin. Mrs. Boykin was for a time dean of women at the State A. and M. College at Orangeburg and, in the opinion of the writer, was one of the most able occupants of that position which has appeared at the college during the decade within which she has served here.

As we said of Mrs. Wilkinson we should say of the entire Negro womanhood of the state, that their greatest contribution to the uplift of their people has been through their service as wives and mothers. It is not possible to name the great number who have made a reasonable success of this common though exceedingly difficult work of home building. It is remarkable that Negro womanhood has achieved what it has in this connection when we realize the resources and training at their command. In spite of all handicaps they have done so well that the Negro, old and young, has been able to sing "be it ever so humble, there is no place like home" with as much zeal and feeling as any other people in the civilized world. This is a great achievement and is a more eloquent testimonial to the nobility of Negro womanhood in South Carolina than anything we shall be able to write.

By no means have we exhausted the subject, but we must pass on to other matters; however, before we do so, we wish to present at the conclusion of this sketch a tribute to "womanhood in ebony," written by the author while serving the colored soldiers as a Y. M. C. A. secretary during the recent World War. It describes one of the remarkable traits of Negro womanhood which has enabled it to "stand the

storm" here in South Carolina and make these wonderful
contributions to which we have referred:

HEALING HOPE

"Hope! of all the ills that men endure,
The only cheap and universal cure;
Thou captive's freedom and thou sick man's health,
Thou loser's victory, and thou beggar's wealth,
Thou manna which from heaven we eat,
To every taste a several meat!
Thou strong retreat, thou sure entailed estate,
Which naught has power to alienate."

It was not necessary for the late Bert Williams to write
an article for the American Magazine on the "Comic Side
of Trouble" in order that the world might discover that the
Negro is somehow an unusual optimist. History had already
demonstrated it. In bondage, the Jew "hung his harp upon
the willows" and slaved away in silence. Enslaved, the Negro
smiled and sang with wonderful harmony: "I want to be more
loving in my heart," "I ain't got long to stay here," and
"By and by I'm going ter lay down my heavy load."

The ultimate argument of the optimist is hope. Negro
manhood has always apparently had an inexhaustible supply
of hope. With darkness, doubt, and failure all around, the
Negro has ever sung:

"Out of the night which covers me,
Black as the pit from pole to pole,
I thank whatever gods there be
For my unconquerable soul!"

The secret, hidden spring of this perpetual stream of hope
has been within the heart of Negro womanhood. So when
we saw the Negro forever discovering the comic side of
trouble in the army of the recent World War, when we heard
the colored soldiers sing as they marched, when we enjoyed
the inspiration of their eternal smile, we ought to have taken
off our hats to "womanhood in ebony." The Negro soldier
couldn't descend into the Slough of Despond because in so
doing he would desecrate the very soul of his mother—the
embodiment of hope. Not only was his mother filled with
this hope, but his sweetheart wrote to remind him: "Behind

the darkest cloud the sun is still shining."[7]   She may not have agreed with Ella Wheeler Wilcox that "Whatever is is best," but she had a vastly more true, though evidently less poetic, philosophy; namely, "whatever shall be will be better."   The extent to which this hopefulness of Negro womanhood influenced the life of the Negro soldiers is a fine tribute to that womanhood.   The way in which colored womanhood was reflected through our manhood in the army, is very beautifully suggested in some lines of poetry which I read in Collier's Weekly Magazine some time ago:

> I have not heard her voice, nor seen her face,
>   Nor touched her hand;
> And yet some echo of her woman's grace
>   I understand.
>
> I have no picture of her lovelihood,
>   Her smile, her tint;
> But that she is both beautiful and good
>   I have true hint.
>
> In all my friend thinks and says, I see
>   Her mirror true;
> His thought of her is gentle; she must be
>   All gentle too.
>
> In all his grief and laughter, work and play
>   Each mood and whim,
> How brave and tender, day by common day,
>   She speaks through him!
>
> Therefore I say I know her, be her face
>   Or dark or fair—
> For when he shows his heart's most secret place
>   I see her there!

and in this reflection of the Negro woman the most conspicuous and characteristic element is *hope*, hope eternal and sublime.

A friend of men who lived in a house by the side of the road asked an ancient traveler: "Is there any balm in Gilead?"   The Negro poet with characteristic optimism and hope answers: "There is a balm in Gilead to heal the wounded soul."   Hope has a healing influence.   It is the never-failing balm that restores the wounded soul.   The recent triumph of

---

[7]Direct quotation from a letter to a soldier at Camp Gordon, Georgia.

the spirit of war and the present prevalence of gross material-
ism have wounded, in many ways, the soul of civilization. Indeed we have again "times that try men's souls." Each man
who was in the army, and each man or woman who was back
home, feels that he has suffered the violation of some right,
the ruthless breaking of some sacred tie. All about us are
the open, bleeding wounds. These wounds, if not healed,
will destroy our world. Among no people are the wounds
so deep as among our colored people. Yet those wounds are
ever healing rapidly. The balm that is healing is the hope
of our mothers, sisters and sweethearts who are telling us to
trust for the best. They are telling us that we must believe
that it all means a better day for us and for them. Their
contagious hope is binding up our broken hearts.

Wounded as we are we scarcely care to ask whence this
healing. Yet at the end of each sentence we learn stands that
eternal little word "why." The hopefulness of Negro womanhood is a remarkable phenomenon. Its existence is evident.
But when we try to explain it we are baffled. We shall
leave the problem to occupy the attention of some future
social philosopher. For us it is permitted not to explain but
to enjoy and honor it.

We may peruse the pages of history carefully, but we
shall search in vain for an example of womanhood more consummately hopeful and charmingly beautiful than Negro
womanhood. Down in the shadows of old Egypt there was
womanhood, beautiful in body, but fickle and false in soul.
Within the seclusion of ancient China there was a womanhood silent and suffering. Crowning the beauty of philosophi-
cal Greece and military Rome we find a womanhood noble
and free, chiefly in marble and oil. Robed in the golden
laces of Teutonic, Nordic and Anglo-Saxon wealth we find
womanhood too often either a flower or a novelty. The pearl
of great value, hidden "within the veil," is womanhood in
ebony, beautiful and strange, tried and true!

* * * *

A hero in ebony went over the top one day. Out there
in "No Man's Land" he lay, wounded within the shadows

of the night. He had gracefully given his best for the truth as he saw it. His face was upturned to the silent stars. Back home his sweetheart, little "Lingering Love," was watching and waiting. The moonlight revealed a smile on his face. Why that smile? It came not from the philosophy of his profoundest teachers. It came not from the "faith" of the chaplain so near. As he lay there wounded, bleeding in body and soul, he was willing to believe that he would recover, that he would ere long walk again in the land of the living. That beautiful smile of faith was bestowed by the most wonderful gift of his "Lingering Love"—Healing Hope!

CHAPTER IX

THE NEW NEGRO CHALLENGES THE OLD ORDER

By B. E. Mays[1]

"HE IS NEW, he is old as the forests primeval.
Stark in their nakedness of limb,
His forebears roamed the jungle and led the chase.
Crystallized by the heat of Oriental suns,
God made him a rock of undecaying power,
To become at last the nation's corner stone.
Rough hewn from the jungle and the desert's sands,
Slavery was the chisel that fashioned him to form,
And gave him all the arts and sciences had won.
The lyncher, mob, and stake have been his emery wheel,
TO MAKE A POLISHED MAN of strength and power.
In him, the latest birth of freedom,
God hath again made all things new.
Europe and Asia with ebbing tides recede,
America's unfinished arch of freedom waits,
Till he, the corner stone of strength,
Is lifted into place and power.
Behold him! dauntless and unafraid he stands.
He comes with laden arms,
Bearing rich gifts in science, religion, poetry and song.
Labor and capital through him shall find
The equal heritage of common brotherhood,
And statesmanship shall keep the stewardship
Of justice and equal rights and privileges for all.
HE KNOWS HIS PLACE, to keep it
As a sacred trust and heritage for all,
To wear God's image in the ranks of men
And walk as princes of the royal blood divine.
ON EQUAL FOOTING everywhere with all mankind.
With ever-fading color on these shores,
The oriental sunshine in his blood
Shall give the winning touch of brotherhood
And love, to all the fused races in our land.
He is the last reserve of God on earth,
Who, in the goodly fellowship of love,
Will rule the world with peace."[2]

THIS chapter shall be written without any effort to define terms. Whether the Negro is "new" or "old" shall, in a technical sense, exercise no influence in this discussion. Anyone who is familiar with the *Crisis*, *Opportunity*, the *Messenger*, the *Chicago Defender*, the *Pittsburgh Courier*, and many other race papers and magazines, must have formed

---

[1]Benjamin E. Mays, Executive Secretary of the Tampa (Florida) Urban League, 1926-8, is a native South Carolinian, having been born

some conception of what is meant by the term "New Negro." Furthermore, Negro expressions in art, literature, and in such organizations as the National Association for the Advancement of Colored People, the Equal Rights League, and the Urban League, help us to interpret and understand the New Negro.

Rather than attempt to define the New Negro, present him in art and literature, or represent him in terms of living personalities, this treatise shall point out *how the New Negro reacts as he faces concrete and specific situations.* From these reactions one can easily determine the meaning of the term as used in these pages. It is hoped that this method of approach will lend life to the chapter, and at the same time will reveal in no small degree the transformation that is going on in the Negro's mind. Likewise the "old order" is to be understood in the light of the things challenged in this discourse.

It must be admitted that the number of Negroes developing a new race psychology with respect to inter-racial affairs is very small. The New Negro is still a "rara avis." He who reads the leading Negro publications finds it easy to conclude that we have an enormous number of New Negroes; but the most casual observations, as we come in contact with leading Negroes in various communities, will prove that this is not the case. To the average Negro, schooled and unschooled, young and old, the white man is still a little god— to be honored, revered, and idolized; or to be feared and obeyed. Ignorance and age do not adequately account for it. It does not necessarily follow that the young college Negro is "new" nor the aged and untrained Negro is backward and nonprogressive—"old."

---

thirty-odd years ago near Ninty Six, in Greenwood County. He attended school at the State A. and M. College at Orangeburg where he completed his high school work. He attended Virginia Union, was graduated at Bates College in Maine and received his M. A. at Chicago University. He has taught at Morehouse College, and the S. C. State College.—Editor.

²The poem entitled "The New Negro" by Reverdy C. Ransom was not used by Mr. Mays but was placed here by the editor because it seems to him to be in harmony with the ideas of the writer. Quoted from *Negro Year Book,* 1926, page 77.

These attitudes just described defy localization. They hold not only in sections where opportunities are few and conditions less favorable, but in communities where discrimination and inequalities are less pronounced. Therefore, it can only be said that increasing numbers of Negroes are beginning to be "new" and are reacting to their environment in a way that distinguishes them from the Negro of tradition.

There is no denying the fact that on the whole the Negro, and the Southern Negro in particular, the South Carolina Negro, has accepted as true and without question the white man's point of view in matters that vitally concern his own (the Negro's) welfare. More and more, however, the white man's interpretations are being questioned and challenged by the New Negro here in South Carolina as elsewhere. Take for example the famous statement that runs something like this—"as long as the Negro stays in his place, he gets along all right." Formerly this was a common expression not only among white people, but leading Negroes accepted the statement as true and urged their people to stay in their places. It was not many months ago that the writer heard an argument on this subject between two Negroes in this state representing two schools of thought. The conservative Negro said, "I know my place, and I stay in it." The less conservative of the two (also a South Carolina Negro) admitted that he was finding it exceedingly difficult to know his place. He argued that the Negro's place varies to such an extent that one can never know when he is in it.

"On the train," said he, "it is in front; on the ship, it is below; on the street car, it is in the rear; and in the theatre, it is above." The former Negro insisted that the white man is boss, and that the thing for the Negro to do is to find his place and stay in it. The latter Negro concluded his argument with the statement that the Negro who attempts to stay in his place as defined by another will be compelled to accept without petition or protest every imposition placed upon him by each individual white man; that the Negro who is constantly looking for his place can never assert his manhood; for the reason that the Negro who differs or takes issue with some white people is out of his place, even if the white man is robbing him of his house and land or insulting his wife. Here we have two Negroes born and reared in South Carolina, yet living in two separate worlds.

A white man representing a dry cleaning establishment stepped into the parlor of a respectable Negro woman. "Anything today?" said he. The lady of the house: "You forgot to remove your hat—didn't you?" Without comment, without removing his hat, without waiting to see if there were clothes to be cleaned, he left the house. The next week the same man returned, leaving his hat in the car.

Again and again, certain white dealers lose trade and patronage because of their traditional method of discrimination and disrespect. A Negro man and his wife went to a Cantilever shoe store to buy a pair of shoes for the wife. It was a small store and evidently the man who served them was both clerk and proprietor. On the whole, he was courteous and polite. In the process of the sale, however, he made one slip. Mrs. A had just about decided on the pair she wanted and the husband had approved. Anxious to make another sale, the proprietor said, "We carry men's shoes, too, boy," speaking to Mrs. A's husband. Mrs. A to her husband: "Boy!" Mr. A to his wife: "Boy!" Mr. A to the proprietor: "Do I look like a boy to you?" The proprietor to Mr. A: "Yes. I am a boy, don't I look like a boy?" Mr. A: "No, you look like a man to me." Mr. A to Mrs. A: "Do not buy them." Proprietor now asks Mrs. A which pair to wrap up. Mrs. A said to him, "Neither pair." He then commented on the beauty and quality of the shoes she was examining and offered to order a pair similar to the pair she had on if she preferred that. She informed him again that she did not care to buy. Failing in this, the proprietor turned to the husband and said, "This is a Cantilever I have on, wouldn't you like a pair?" The husband: "No, I wear Edwin Clapp and Florsheim." Mr. and Mrs. A walked out as the proprietor invited them to come again. The shoes were ordered from Chicago.

Many Negroes refuse to buy shoes from certain stores

scattered throughout the South on account of their refusal to fit shoes for colored customers. White business men have often failed to land their sale because in the process of selling, the Negro has been called "Big Boy," "Jack," "George," and other names that are offensive to colored people. Some resent openly; others resent by not patronizing stores where discourteous treatment is accorded Negroes.

This resentment on the part of the Negro manifests itself in various ways. Less than three months ago an intelligent Negro walked into a Western Union office to send a telegram. The office is located just a little inside the white waiting room of a great southern city. The Negro, though southern, was not familiar with the customs of that place. The Negro picked up a pencil and began to write. He was abruptly informed that he would have to go to the window outside; that he could not be served in the white waiting room. The Negro walked out, went to a booth, and called the Postal. A messenger from the Postal came and the telegram was sent. The Negro vows not to use Western Union again. When questioned as to what he hoped to gain by his reaction, the Negro replied: "Maybe nothing except I have kept my self-respect in refusing to accept discrimination that I was not obliged to accept. Then, too, my opportunity may come, and I will take this matter up with an official of the Western Union."

Equally objectionable to the New Negro is the continued practice on the part of some white people of calling Negro men "uncle" and Negro women "aunt." To the white man, and the southern white man in particular, it may be considered a title of respect and a mark of good breeding; to the new Negro, it is a title of disrespect, and not infrequently the Negro gets it across to white people that to call him "uncle" is to insult him.

A new day is likewise dawning among Negro women. A good percentage of Negro women will not give their first names to white folk. They object to being called "Mary," "Sallie," "Jane," etc. If the given name is Mary Ann, she gives the initial, M. A. Commenting on this point one Negro man has this to say: "In case my wife allows herself to be called Jane or Sallie by men who have no right to do so, the way is paved for insult. A man will insult and disrespect Jane much quicker than he will Miss Jane." Another comment comes from an unschooled Negro woman: "I resent the familiarity with which white men approach Negro women. It hurts my pride to be addressed by my first name. We are respected in proportion as we respect ourselves. Negro women should not accept anything less than proper respect from men—be they white or colored."

The following incident will present still another side of this subject: A representative white woman made a business call to see a trained Negro social worker in the interest of her servant who was in need. As she presented the case she called her servant "Susie" and the trained social worker "Mabel"—all in the same breath. The social worker to Mrs. X: "Pardon me. I hope you will not be offended in what I am about to say. I note that you call your cook 'Susie' and you address me 'Mabel.' It seems to me, Mrs. X, that white people should not place all Negroes in the servant class." Mrs. X apologized and promised not to offend again. Thereafter, she called the social worker "Miss."

In like manner, Negro men desire to be treated as other men are treated. It often happens that a Negro man who has no title at all, except Mr., is addressed "Reverend," "Professor," and "Doctor." Rather than call him "Mr.," many white people prefer to give the Negro an unearned title. Three years ago this incident occurred in a Negro college: A white salesman interviewed a college teacher who had charge of the Chapel exercises of the college. The salesman wanted an opportunity to present his goods to the student body. Throughout the interview the salesman called the teacher "Doctor." At the end of the conversation the Negro calmly asked the salesman: "Why do you call me Doctor?" The salesman replied: "You deserve it. A man of your intelligence should be called Doctor." The teacher informed the salesman that he was not entitled to this honor, that he had not earned a doctor's degree, and that no school had conferred the title upon him. He requested the salesman not to call him doctor. The salesman then asked: "What is your title?" The teacher: "Mr."

A representative of the largest insurance company in the world called to see a Negro who has in force with that company $8,000 worth of insurance. The object of the call was to get the Negro to increase this amount to $10,000. In the course of the conversation, the agent called the prospect by his first name as if he and the Negro had known each other for some time. The Negro to the agent: "Were I inclined to increase my insurance, I would not do it now. You have never seen me before, and yet you call me by my first name."

The writer was greatly surprised a few days ago as he talked with an aged Negro who has almost reached his seventieth birthday. This old man has never ridden in a "Jim Crow" street car. He is a carpenter and stands well in his community. He states that before buying an automobile he walked miles to work, carrying his tools on his shoulder. The old man, with a steady and continuous shake of the head, said that he never intends to degrade his soul by riding in a Jim Crow street car. He differentiates between the discrimination on the train and that of the street car: "In going to Washington, it is almost compulsory that I go on the train. If I take the train, the law says that I must be Jim Crowed. I am a law-abiding citizen, and Washington is too far for me to walk; it may be necessary that I do not drive my automobile. Even in the latter case," says the old man, "my spirit has never been Jim Crowed. I have never believed that discrimination is right; hence I cannot accept it." Hundreds of Negroes feel this way. They do not attend Jim Crow theaters and churches on the ground that no compulsion is attached and Negroes should not voluntarily segregate themselves.

Attitudes usually displayed by white people in their contact with Negroes are noted most critically by the New Negro. It is said that the white man in his dealing with Negroes invariably assumes the role of master or teacher. A cartoon recently published in a southern newspaper illustrates the point at issue. Two boys, one Negro and the other white, were planning to run a train. The Negro boy said to the white boy: "You'll be the engineer and I will be the conductor." Instantly, the white boy replied, "No! I will be engineer and conductor. You will be porter." A friend of mine pictures this another way. A white boy walks up to a Negro boy, touches him, and says, "Let's play tag." Without waiting to see whether the Negro boy wants to play the white boy begins the game from the moment he touches the Negro. The Negro boy has nothing to do but play. The white boy has decided for him.

The New Negro contends that he has a right to help determine the time and place of the game. For example, a Negro professor holding a United States treasury certificate went to the vice-president of a reputable bank. He explained to the vice-president that the president of the bank knew him; but inasmuch as the president was busy, he would appreciate it, if he (vice-president) would sign the certificate, a necessary procedure before sending the certificate to Washington. Immediately the vice-president informed the Negro that he (the Negro) did not understand. "You will have to take your certificate to the post office," said the vice-president. "Not necessarily," replied the Negro, "it must be signed by a postmaster or by an official of an incorporated bank or trust company. I do not know the postmaster; I am known here at your bank." The Negro then pointed to the directions on the back of the certificate. The vice-president: "We cannot cash it for you after it is signed." "I know it," said the Negro. "On the other hand before I can get a check which you can cash, this certificate must be properly signed, sent to Washington, and the treasury department in Washington will send me a check which you can cash." The certificate was eventually endorsed by the vice-president.

The Negro students are becoming equally critical. In most Negro colleges the white man who tells a "Negro joke" which in any way reflects discredit on the Negro, or who introduces himself with a story of his "Beloved Black Mammy" is almost certain to lose his audience. The speaker does not understand. He feels that this is the way to win his Negro audience. This, however, is not the case. Almost invariably, he loses his audience when he relates Negro jokes or talks about his "black mammy." True this is, not only of students but of other groups as well. The manager of a leading Negro insurance company gives a specific example. A certified public accountant and actuary delivered a speech to seventy-five members of a Negro insurance company. In order to make clear his point on speculative sick claims he related a story about his "black mammy." He got up one morning, went and found his "black mammy," who occupied a room over his garage, sick in bed. He was fond of her for she nursed him and his children. The accountant, suspecting "mammy" to be faking, asked how much money did the insurance company give her in weekly benefits. She replied, "ten dollars." The employer gave her ten dollars and instantly she became well enough to prepare the meals. He told this at the beginning of his speech. The manager says that without a doubt the accountant made an excellent address; but his reference to "mammy" destroyed its effectiveness. "He sat down and not a man applauded. The silence was so conspicuous that it was embarrassing."

A word might be said here about Negro melodies. Some Negro college students have been severely criticized for their attitude toward Negro spirituals. Out of fairness to the students who, in some form, resent singing the melodies, an expression from a student should throw light on the subject. "It is not that students are ashamed of melodies. They are not. They represent a period in our racial history, express yearnings, an aspiration that we cannot afford to lose; on the other hand, we resent singing melodies for white people who merely want to be entertained, consider them as something to be laughed at, and who do not have a sufficient background to appreciate the hope, courage, pathos, and often despair depicted in these spirituals. Then, too, there is a feeling among some white people that Negroes can sing nothing else."

The whole question of distributing the public school funds is being challenged. The argument that white people pay more taxes is no longer accepted as justification for the unjust distribution of the school money. A college professor relates the analytical approach made by a sophomore in one of his classes. It was clearly outlined by the student that under a democratic form of government public education is not based on race nor upon the amount of taxes paid. "The theory is, that in public education the poorest child will enjoy the same privileges that are accorded the richest child. In South Carolina the white child is protected by the theory; the Negro child is not. The poorest white child does enjoy the same public school advantages as those shared by the richest white child by virtue of the fact that the poor white child is a member of the white group. Were it a matter of taxation, many Negro children would enjoy better schools than some white children." This student further pointed out in his paper that the Negro who rents and pays no taxes often pays enough overcharge in rent to pay the taxes; and that, according to economic theory, the Negroes and others who rent pay the taxes anyway and not those who own the houses and land.

Quite often we complain that the boys and girls from the country, after receiving their education, do not go back and help develop their communities. There is considerable truth in the complaint. Of the boys the writer has questioned during his four years as teacher in two southern colleges (including a South Carolina college), most of them gave three reasons for their not returning: (1) field of activity limited in country and small towns; (2) economic reason— nothing to do; cannot get sufficient returns for your labor to compensate for time and money spent in preparation; (3) willing to sacrifice, but cannot endure the treatment accorded them by white people in small communities. These boys and girls contend that in order to get along in their home communities, they must assume the same role assumed by the fellow who has never had school advantages. They maintain that the Negro school boy or girl in a small community is looked upon with suspicion because he or she appears in a manner different from that of other Negro boys and girls; and straightway the schooled Negro becomes the object of attack. Therefore, the least assertion of manhood on his part is considered to mean that "much learning has made him mad." These are the testimonies of scores of students with whom the writer has talked concerning their life work.

The New Negro is beginning to assert his right to choose his own leaders and spokesmen. For a long time, Negro leaders have been chosen by white people. The New Negro is questioning the ability of his white-chosen leader to represent properly the Negro's interests. When he should be strong, when he should be courageous and stand for a principle, he has to remember the hand that made him; he staggers and often sells his soul in the most crucial hour. In addition to this, the Negro is resenting one-man leadership. It is nothing strange to hear Negroes say that "the day of one-man leadership is over. We are developing leaders in various fields of endeavor."

Finally, as never before, the New Negro is questioning the white man's Christianity. There was a time, not very long ago, when most Negroes accepted the white man's Christianity in good faith in spite of discriminations and other injustices that they received at the white man's hands. That day is rapidly passing. It is not the eloquence of his speech; nor his brilliant talks about the "Jesus way." The New Negro is watching the white man's activities. He is watching the inability of America to stop lynching; the unjust distribution of school funds; the robbery on the railroad in accepting the same fare from Negroes as from whites and according the Negro inferior accommodation; the discriminations in the courts; and the injustices in the social and economic worlds—these are the things that concern the New Negro and he includes them in religion.

ADDRESS DELIVERED AT OLDER BOYS'
CONFERENCE[3]

Benedict College, Feb. 26, 1926

Subject: "The Goal"

Were I to talk to you about the physical goal, that little white line that contending teams defend and fight to cross; were I to speak of the home plate in baseball, that little rubber cushion that every runner seeks to touch; you would readily and clearly understand what I mean by the goal. In fact, the football goal can be seen with the naked eye. It can be touched with the physical hand. No doubt, you have seen Benedict College defend that white line as the Allies defended Verdun; perhaps you have seen Allen University fight as though the sky would fall if they crossed not the goal. You must have heard the cheers, the roars, and the yells of the grand stand, urging its team to victory. Surely you have seen the excited multitude go wild with enthusiasm as someone made a "touchdown." These things are too familiar to be further explained.

But this goal of life, this goal that you have asked me to speak about, is not so easily defined. It cannot be seen with the naked eye; neither can it be touched with the physical hand. It cannot be thoroughly demonstrated; thus, if I do not make clear to you just what the goal of life is, you must sympathize. The task is just too difficult, that's all.

Were I white, and held a professor's chair in the University of South Carolina; were you white, and represented the best white schools of this commonwealth; my task would not be so difficult. We would then be clothed in that skin that gives perpetual protection. We would represent that group that presumes to hold the destiny of this nation in its hand, and to whom the doors of opportunity are never closed. Were this true, I would define the goal without limitations. I would recommend that you aspire to be governor of your native state. I would point the way to the president's chair.

---

[3] We present the address as an example of the type of advice given by and to the New Negroes.

As it is, Americans though we be, I must speak to you not as an American to Americans but as a Negro to Negroes. It is this regrettable fact that makes the goal most difficult for me to define.

Yes, we are Americans; we are South Carolinians; we are Negroes; and I make no apologies for being any. I am proud to be an American citizen. Neither do I make any apologies for being a South Carolinian. I tell that everywhere I go. I cannot and would not apologize for being a Negro. We have a great history; we have a greater future. Be this as it may, there can be no denying that the rules of this game, though laid down for Americans, we must play with handicaps and restrictions. It is this thing that makes the goal difficult for me to define. Nevertheless, whatever the restrictions are, we have a rendezvous with South Carolina; we have a rendezvous with America; we must not fail that rendezvous.

Though the game of life may be compared with a football game, in many respects, the two games differ. For example in the football game, we know when the goal is crossed. In life's game, the goal is never crossed. The goal we set for this generation will not be the goal for the next generation. The goal of our fathers is not ours. Already, my father and I live in two separate worlds. His creed is not my creed; his ideals are not my ideals; and his philosophy of life differs widely from my philosophy of life. Forty years from today, a youth reading my speech will perhaps call it "old timey" and out of date. Thus the goal moves on. The goal of life, like the ideal in Lowell's poem, is never overtaken. In that poem, Lowell pictures most beautifully the pursuit of a lofty ideal. The chaser finds the rock where the ideal sat and left footprints on the moss of the rock; but the ideal was not there—it had fled. "In dimples still the water slips where thou has dipt thy fingertips;" the ideal was not there—it had fled.

> "Just, just beyond, forever burn
>   Gleams of a grace without return;
>   Upon thy shade I plant my foot,
>   And thru my frame strange raptures shoot;

All of thee but thyself I grasp;
I seem to fold thy luring shape;
And vague air to my bosom clasp
Thou lithe perpetual escape."

The ideal was not there—it had fled. It leads the chaser onward and upward to higher and nobler planes; but he never attains.

The goal of life may also be compared with the "Ideal" portrayed in Emerson's "Forerunners." "The Forerunners," in that poem "are those eternal mysteries that forever beckon but forever elude." Emerson, like Browning, emphasizes the unseizableness of the ideal.

"Long I followed happy guides,
I could never reach their sides;
Their step is forth, and, ere the day,
Breaks up their leaguer, and away.
Keen my sense, my heart was young.
Right good-will my sinews strung,
But no speed of mine avails
To hunt upon their shining trails.
On and away, their hasting feet
Make the morning proud and sweet;
Flowers they strew—I catch the scent;
Or tone of silver instrument
Leaves on the wind melodious trace;
Yet I could never see their face."

The ideal was not there. It was gone. To understand further what I mean, when I compare the goal of life with an ideal, read Emerson's "Forerunners," Longfellow's "Excelsior," Whittier's "The Vanishers," Tennyson's poem, "The Voyage," and Lanier's "Song of the Chattahoochee." In these poems the ideal of life is not static. It leads upward to truth, onward to virtue, through perils to right, and through bitter experiences to the plain of justice.

Thus life's goal is an ideal. It lures us onward and upward and makes it possible for successive generations to stand on the shoulders of the generations that precede; the real goal, however, is never reached. This is as it should be. When the ideal is reached, it ceases to be an ideal. When the ideal is reached, satisfaction comes; when satisfaction comes, stagnation appears; and when stagnation appears, death is at hand. I pity the satisfied youth.

We are told that when Thorwaldsen, the great Danish sculptor, unveiled his statue of Christ, he wept. His friends congratulated him; Thorwaldsen continued to weep. As he wept, he was heard to exclaim: "My genius is decaying." "What do you mean?" his friends asked. He replied, "This statue is the first of my works that I have ever felt completely satisfied with—I can never create a great work of art again." You are also familiar with the tradition of Alexander the Great. He wept because there were no more worlds to conquer. If Alexander had truly reached his goal, it was time for him to weep. If there is one individual in this room who is completely satisfied, who has reached his goal, who sees nothing beyond—his is a pathetic case. He needs to weep.

Young men, I am trying to define your goal. But Longfellow has defined it far better than I could ever do it:

> "Not enjoyment, and not sorrow
> Is our destined end or way;
> But to act that each tomorrow
> Finds us farther than today."

Do your bit in order that those who come after you may enjoy a larger freedom and receive a greater heritage. Not only is this the goal of Negro youth, it is the goal of America. It was the goal of the Pilgrim Fathers. They suffered; they bled; they died. They did it in order that those who followed would enjoy a larger religious freedom. It was the goal of those who fought in the Revolutionary War. They fought that we might enjoy a larger political freedom. It was the goal of America in the great World War. We fought that the world might enjoy the freedom of democracy. It was the goal of the Negro, Crispus Attucks, the first to shed his blood that America might be free. It was the goal of the immortal Abraham Lincoln who freed four million slaves. It was the goal of those black boys who fought and died in Flanders Field. They did it, partly in the hope that discrimination, segregation and lynching would soon disappear. It was the goal of our enslaved parents, for they prayed and endured the lash in order that their children might some day be freed. Your sitting here tonight is an answer to their prayers, their toils, and their sacrifices. Young men, the goal of life is something like this.

Only a few years separate you from me. As you see, I am a young man. Yet I will live in vain, if I do not live and so act that you will be freer than I am—freer intellectually, freer politically, and freer economically. I must make it possible for you to become citizens of the world. I owe it to you to make fine, wholesome, racial contact; sell my personality to white men who do not believe in us, in order that you may enjoy what I will never enjoy.

May my right hand forget its cunning, and my tongue cleave to the roof of my mouth, if I do not make it possible for my unborn son to live more completely than I am now living. I owe it to my silver-haired mother who picked cotton in the cold winter days on the hills of South Carolina in order that I might go to school. I was seventeen years old before I was able to stay in school more than four months a year. The school in my section ran only three or four months yearly. A longer term would not have helped for the farm was calling me. God grant that my unborn son may share a larger freedom and a richer heritage than I enjoy. This little poem, "The Bridge Builder," will illustrate just what I have in mind:

> "An old man going a lone highway
> Came at the evening cold and gray
> To a chasm vast and deep and wide.
> The old man crossed in the twilight dim;
> The sullen stream had no fear for him
> But he turned when safe on the other side
> And built a bridge to span the tide.
> 'Old Man' said a fellow pilgrim near,
> 'You are wasting your strength building here.
> Your journey ends with the ending day;
> You never again will pass this way.
> You've crossed the chasm deep and wide,
> Why build you here at the evening tide?'
> The builder raised his old gray head,
> 'Good friend in the path I've come,' he said,
> 'Here followeth after me today,
> A youth whose feet must pass this way;
> The chasm that held no fear for me,
> To the fair haired youth may a pitfall be,
> He too must cross in the twilight dim;
> Good friend, I am building this bridge for *him*.'"

Young men, this is the goal—build the bridge for those who come after you.

I must hasten on to something more definite. As I have already indicated, Lincoln, with one stroke of his pen, broke the chains of physical slavery; but there is another chain that Lincoln could not break. This chain is not physical; it is mental. The Negro, though freed by Lincoln, emerged from slavery with a slave's psychology, an inferiority complex. In the main, he thought like a slave; he acted like a slave; he crouched, cringed, and cowered like a slave. To him the white man was God, and sixty-three years is a comparatively short time in which to breed out this inferiority complex.

How could it be otherwise? For more than two hundred years the Negro was in physical slavery. The white man did his thinking. The white man acted for him. The white man even gave him his form of religion. Excepting the free Negro, he did not develop any sense of responsibility for he had no need to. His duty was to obey and carry out the dictates of his master. It was inevitable, then, that along with the physical slavery there was being developed a slave's psychology. Lincoln did not, and Lincoln could not break the mental chains.

During the period of slavery the Negro to a large extent learned to disrespect the personality of the Negro. He had no confidence in his fellow slaves, and his white masters encouraged this distrust. There was no opportunity for co-operation, and as long as the slave system worked well, there was no need of co-operation. Thus, in the main, the Negro emerged from slavery with little or no confidence in himself and with little or no confidence in his brother in black.

You would be surprised to know that there are intelligent Negroes today who do not believe in the inherent possibilities of the Negro race. They have unconsciously, perhaps, accepted the erroneous, unscientific propaganda that the Negro is inherently inferior. They have accepted this philosophy in spite of the fact that the best scientists of the world have agreed that there is no such thing as an inferior race; that there is an equal amount of inherent potentiality and power in all races. It is clear that inferiority is not a racial trait; it is an individual trait. The intelligence tests prove this to be a fact. For the most brilliant white child, there can be found a Negro child equally brilliant; and for the most stupid colored child, there can be found a white child equally as stupid.

Of course, we do not deny that, on the whole, the white man and the Negro parent stand on two different planes—two different levels of civilization. Neither do we deny that on the whole, the white man has attained more culture than the Negro has attained; we have already indicated that this is due to environmental factors rather than to inherent qualities.

As a result of this psychology and lack of training on the part of the average Negro parent, the Negro youth has suffered. He has not received the stimulus from his parents and teachers that the white child has received. Too often the Negro child has been led to believe that he cannot do the things that the white child does. This clips his ambition, crushes his genius, and often a great mind goes undeveloped.

This is a challenge to Negro teachers. Help the Negro boy find himself. Encourage ability wherever you find it— be it in art, science or industry. Drive home the fact that the old Palmetto State is expecting him to make his contribution to civilization—his contribution in agriculture, in industry, in the arts and sciences—in fact, in every phase of human endeavor.

Young men, you must strive to be an agriculturist, not a Negro agriculturist—just an agriculturist! Strive to be a doctor, not a Negro doctor—just a doctor! Seek to serve your state, not as a Negro but as a man. Aspire to be great—not among Negroes, but among men! God knows I want to be a great teacher; not a Negro teacher—just a great teacher. I want no racial adjective modifying it. I want to preach the gospel of peace, good will, justice, and brotherhood—not to Negroes and for Negroes, but to men and for men. I want to act so that each tomorrow will find us farther than today—not the Negro race, the human race. It seems to me that this is our goal.

Still another challenge comes to you—yes, to all of us. We represent one of the suppressed groups in America. We are constantly being reminded that we are Negroes. The temptation is that we will use our minds, our energies, and our time fighting this ever present race problem. We may become narrow, one-sided, and warped in our thinking— never thinking beyond the confines of race. I know brilliant Negroes who are capable of making a greater contribution; but the race problem wears and tears on them so heavily that they find themselves fighting for that justice which should be ours without the asking. This being true, most of the time of our great Negroes is used up in things racial.

I am necessarily conscious though that we must contend for justice; must never relinquish our claim until the mind and character become the standard of the man—not race, not color. Yet we must produce a larger number of Negroes who can lose themselves in their work and think the thoughts of the world, undisturbed. After all the best thing that I know to convince the world that we are not inferior is to do what the greatest men of the world do, and do it as well as they do it, or do it better than they do it. No amount of argument will convince the world that we are not inferior. The burden of proof is on us, and we must prove our equality by producing great scientists, great artists, great business men—in fact, whatever man has done, we black men must do if we are to take our place in the world of competition. I thank God tonight that within sixty-three years we have produced men that the world is forced to recognize.

You young men are going to be able to forget the race problem far better than I. A new day has already begun to dawn. The white people of the South are more interested in race relations than ever before. It is difficult to estimate the great good that the Inter-racial Commission is doing to promote good will between the races. All over the South Inter-racial Committees are at work—bringing the two races together on a mutual basis. Equally meritorious is the daring, uncompromising work of the National Association for the Advancement of Colored People.

The white southern students are aroused and many are determined to face frankly and discuss honestly problems of racial character. Last November white and colored students from four southern states—South Carolina, Georgia, Florida and Alabama—met in Atlanta and discussed in common the great problem of war. Just this year, the white students of the South sent telegrams to the governor of Florida, urging him to bring to justice the guilty parties who lynched a Negro early in the new year. Mississippi declares that lynching must go. These things mark the dawn of a new era. The Negroes of the next generation will be able to give themselves more freely to the great problems of the world.

Even in our own age, a few Negroes have been able to do this. Roland Hayes is an artist—not a Negro artist. When Hayes sings, the world listens; Europe bows to do him homage, the North is thrilled, and some southern towns hear him gladly. Earnest Just, a South Carolinian, is a scientist—not a Negro scientist. When Just writes, the scientists of the world read. Tanner is an artist—not a Negro artist. Many painters prior to Tanner had painted the picture, "Daniel in the Lions' Den," but when Tanner touched it with his master hand, no painter has dared touch it since. The master of masters had painted it. If these men in their age rose above race, you in your day will be able to do it, with far more ease. This is my challenge to you.

Finally, you must guard your health. To be able to do these things I have outlined, you must lead clean, wholesome lives. You must, during these plastic years, form correct habits. The habits you are now forming will follow you through life. They will be your enemy or your ally. You cannot advance the thoughts of the world unless you pass on to future generations sound minds in sound bodies.[4]

---

[4]There was terrific applause following Mr. Mays' address but, outside, the Editor heard a representative of the "Old Negro" saying: "The young man has much to learn; he is quite radical."

THE CREED OF THE NEW NEGRO

1. I believe in God as the embodiment and the expression of all the goodness of the universe, material and immaterial.

2. I believe in Youth as the recurrent, perennial, external spirit of progress.

3. I believe in Humanity, the humanity that transcends color, feature, geography or social and political organization.

4. I believe in the Negro race as in any other race, only as an element, and perhaps an episode, of this humanity.

5. I believe therefore in Unsegregated Justice as the only justice, and the unqualified equality as the only equality.

6. I believe in Individual Liberty, which is possible only in a society of essential individual equality.

7. I believe in Tolerance which is possible only in a society of liberty.

8. I believe in Eternal Progress, which is possible only in a society of tolerance.

9. I believe in the Divine Destiny of Man, which is thinkable only as progressive purpose of evolution.

10. I believe therefore in the present, as the all Mother of the illimitable Future; in happiness limited only by other happinesses and by the legitimate claims of future happiness.   Selah.[5]

---

[5]This "Creed" was written by William Pickens (a South Carolinian, representative of the "New Negro") under the title, *Creed of the American Negro Youth.* Mr. Pickens wrote it at the request of the American Student Federation, one of our "Youth Movements." The editor has taken the liberty to quote it here under a slightly different heading but we think it expresses the creed of the New Negro for the youth movement embraces him.

CHAPTER X

MANHOOD IN EBONY FACES THE FUTURE

Night is for sorrow and dawn is for joy,
Chasing the troubles that fret and annoy;
Darkness for sighing and daylight for song,
Cheery and chaste the strain, heartfelt and strong.
All the night through, though I moan in the dark,
I wake in the morning to sing with the lark.

Deep in the midnight the rain whips the leaves,
Softly and sadly the wood-spirit grieves.
But when the first hue of dawn tints the sky,
I shall shake out my wings like the birds and be dry;
And though, like the rain-drops, I grieved through the dark,
I shall wake in the morning to sing with the lark.

On the high hills of heaven, some morning to be,
Where the rain shall not grieve thro' the leaves of the tree,
There my heart will be glad for the pain I have known,
For my hand will be clasped in the hand of mine own;
And though life has been hard and death's pathway been dark,
I shall wake in the morning to sing with the lark.

Paul Laurence Dunbar.

Look not mournfully into the past; it comes not
back again. Wisely improve the present; it is thine.
Go forth to meet the shadowy future without fear
and with a manly heart.

Henry W. Longfellow.

THE poem quoted from Dunbar at the beginning of this
chapter and the quotation from the writings of the lovable Longfellow suggest the eternal optimism of the Negro's
soul ever flowing fresh and clean from the deepest springs of
his heart, which is the principal power, aside from his great
power of adaptability, that brought the colored race through
the hell of slavery in South Carolina and other states of the
union and lifted it to this wonderful hour of modern civilization in a mighty country among the most progressive people
of all human history. Thus, in spite of all discouraging
appearances in the environment, the observer and recorder
of contemporary Negro life and history in this state must
note the Negro's faith in his future as one of the outstanding
facts of the group life of these struggling people. In spite

of hardships, handicaps and discouragements the colored people can "see the triumph from afar" and "by faith they bring it near" though experience teaches them that their "place in the sun," like the goal of perfection in all things human, is "infinitely receding."

This confidence of the Negro in the greatness of his future is not without justification in the realms of reality. There are some tangible facts which support and promote this belief. The first of these is the fact that the Negro himself has not lost what Doctor DuBois calls his "Gift of the Spirit."[1] One of the qualities of this spirit of the Negro, the quality of optimism, we have already emphasized. There then is the quality of unconquerable friendship, fellowship and love. Without a doubt the spiritual Good Samaritan of American civilization is the Negro. The Negro has faith in his future because he believes that love will win in the long run. He believes that love is the great solvent of the world's unhappiness. The Negro's fellowship or neighborliness is founded upon a kind of naïve faith in the evolutionary potentiality of human nature. This friendliness or confidence on the part of the colored people disarms their enemies now as it did in slavery. It will procure for the Negro a chance to exist and develop in the future as it enabled him to pass through slavery and keep the friendship of a large number of his white fellow citizens. This is true because the white man of South Carolina, like any other man, will tend to strive to live up to the fine and noble ideals that others have set for him. The fact that the white people of South Carolina are meeting the challenge of the Negro's persistent friendship is shown by the growth of the inter-racial work in this state and the increasing value of its efforts. The Inter-racial Commission began its work in Atlanta, Georgia, under the leadership of Mr. Will W. Alexander, its present (1928) national director. The work was at first financed largely by the War Work Council of the National Young Men's Christian Association. Such an organization came at the psychological

---

[1]DuBois, W. E. Burghardt: *The Gift of Black Folk* (Stratford), Chapter 9.

moment for then the people of all the South, white and black alike, were looking for some agency to bring healing hope and the balm of peace in the post-war reactionary period when feeling against the returned Negro soldiers was running high partly because some of the white people felt that the Negro's contact with the equality of races practiced in France had made him anxious for "social equality" and restless under the restrictions of southern proscriptions. The assumptions as to the Negro soldier's anxiety for forced social association with the white people, which is their idea of what they call "social equality," were mostly imaginary but there was a new note of dissatisfaction within the Negro group on account of the continuation of the undemocratic manifestations of race prejudice in this state. The Negro had enlisted or had been conscripted into a war which he was told was being fought "to make the world safe for democracy." Very naturally and logically he thought the process of democratization should begin at home, in South Carolina, or at least be applied after the war was over and he had done his bit "to save civilization." But, alas! the South Carolina he found when he returned from the trenches of blood-stained France was very much the same as the South Carolina he had left singing "We'll hang Bill Kaiser on the sour apple tree." He returned to find his white fellow citizens ready to hang him without a trial on the limbs of the pines of his native state if he made the slightest signs of resisting "the old order." Indeed it was another time which tried the souls of men—both white and black. At such a time as this it was providential, or certainly highly fortunate, that the Inter-racial Commission with its director, Will Alexander, a southern white man, a Gentile of the Gentiles, came saying:

The Negro is not a menace to America. He has proved himself worthy of confidence. He has been and may continue to be a blessing. In the years that are to come he needs the help of those who have voices of influence. He needs only that we remove unnecessary barriers out of his way, and give him a chance to demonstrate that under God he is a man and can play a man's part.

These sentiments found a sincere echo in the hearts of hundreds of native white South Carolinians of both sexes. This olive branch offer was met by the colored people of the state. And the colored man's answer is well expressed in the words of a native South Carolina black woman who, because of her present position, speaks not only for all the colored people of her native state of South Carolina but for the Negroes of the country. We refer here to Mrs. Mary McLeod Bethume, president of the Bethume-Cookman Collegiate Institute of Daytona, Florida, a woman whom all the world delights to honor:

The Negro asks simply for a fair chance to develop, unfold, possess and live as other American citizens. He seeks no special consideration; only to be dealt with as a man. He does not wish to become a white man or a yellow man; he is entirely content to be himself; but he does desire the opportunity to become the best self of which he is capable.

These leaders have inspired other leaders to take up the work which is creating better feeling between the races and promoting the "Better Day" which is revealed in the vista of the future. The work is being carried on by such leaders as Mrs. R. S. Wilkinson, Mr. T. B. Lanham, executive secretary of the state committee of the Y. M. C. A.; Mrs. McGowan, chairman of the State Inter-racial Committee; Dr. D. H. Sims; the writer, and dozens of others scattered all over the state.

Another fact which gives the Negro faith in the future and confidence in his destiny in South Carolina is the knowledge that he himself is mobilizing, organizing and supporting certain agencies for his uplift which insure the perpetuity of his progress.

One of the most effective organizations efficiently functioning in America today for the general uplift of the colored people is the militant National Association for the Advancement of Colored People. This organization came into being as a result of the inspiration of Dr. W. E. B. DuBois, who procured the co-operation of a few men and women of both races to form this organization to work for the realization of complete democracy for all American citizens including the Negroes. In 1910 Dr. DuBois gave up his position as professor of sociology and history at the Atlanta University where he had gained a national and international reputation by editing the only series of truly scientific studies which, up to that time, had ever been made on the vexing "Negro Problem."[2] Giving up this valuable work Dr. DuBois accepted the position of director of publicity and research for the N. A. A. C. P., which position involved editing its official organ, the new colored magazine called *The Crisis*. This association, from its beginning, has maintained a competent staff of men to carry on its work in an honest, scientific and progressive way. It is by far the most effective and altruistic effort being made in this country today to fight segregation, Jim Crowism, disfranchisement, lynching, etc., in every legal way. In addition to Dr. DuBois the association now has on its staff of workers some of the ablest men of the country; particularly of the colored race. It is difficult to think of a stronger combination among Negroes than Robert Bagnall, Walter White, William Pickins, a South Carolinian, and James W. Johnson, perhaps the most versatile Negro of genius America has yet produced.

All this has a very vital influence upon the life and history of the colored people of South Carolina. All over the state there are individual Negroes who have joined the N. A. A. C. P. and contribute regularly toward its support financially and otherwise. The circulation of *The Crisis* is itself an influence of no mean importance. This magazine, speaking in a frank and manly way in the "King's English," helps to encourage those who read it to believe in the future security of the race because it has such an organ through which to find expression. Just to illustrate how *The Crisis* is used by thoughtful Negroes to help in the cause we may mention the custom which Mrs. R. S. Wilkinson[3] has adopted.

[2]Atlanta University studies of the Negro in the South. Publications 1 to 20 are available at Atlanta University Press, Atlanta, Ga.
[3]Wife of President Wilkinson of the State A. & M. College and herself president of the State (S. C.) Federation of Colored Women's Clubs.

She sees that this magazine is put into the hands of white people of power and influence so that they may see that the Negroes are fighting for full manhood rights. Mrs. Wilkinson circulated, through the State Federation of Colored Women's Clubs, about a hundred copies of *The Crisis'* report on Negro education in the public schools of South Carolina.[3a] A complimentary copy of this magazine was sent to each county school superintendent in the state so that he might know just what the Negroes knew about what was being done and how they felt about it. Just as *The Crisis* is being used in this way, other Negro magazines and newspapers, such as *Opportunity* and *The Messenger*, serve to carry on the good work.

There are local organizations or chapters of the N. A. A. C. P. in the larger cities such as Columbia and Charleston. The local branch of the N. A. A. C. P. in Columbia is, at this writing, headed by the Negro lawyer, N. J. Frederick, who gained national reputation on account of his able and successful defense of the Bowmans before the Aiken lynching. It is true that in this case the effort of the National Association, co-operating with the local branch-president, Lawyer Frederick, proved abortive on account of the violence of a savage mob, but its effort assures the Negroes of the state— even the most ignorant and humble ones—that there is some organization which is interested in their welfare and willing to help them in their fight for freedom and justice.

The local branches of the N. A. A. C. P. have before them the hard task of procuring the full confidence and co-operation of the white people of the state. It must be admitted that South Carolina is somewhat of a "clannish" state. A good many South Carolinians, colored as well as white, do not freely and enthusiastically co-operate with an organization such as the N. A. A. C. P. because it is "foreign" in its origin and in its leadership. The white people of the state especially do not easily become enthusiastic over an organization largely controlled by Negroes who live in the North. This attitude, however, is not justifiable. Although the

---

[3a]Issue of December, 1927.

N. A. A. C. P. is headed by Negroes who now live at northern addresses, many of the leaders and perhaps the majority of its members are southern Negroes. Walter White, the efficient assistant secretary, was born in Atlanta, Georgia. William Pickins, one of the greatest of contemporary Negro orators, the field secretary, is a South Carolina Negro. Dr. Du Bois, the Director of Research and Publicity, while not born in the South, spent over a decade as a teacher of history and sociology in a Southern Negro college. While in Atlanta he applied the best talent he possessed to the careful, scientific study of the colored man and his life in the South to which we referred above. Thus a little study will show that the N. A. A. C. P. is an organization prepared to work sympathetically and understandingly with the progressive people of South Carolina, white and black, who desire to promote democracy and apply brotherhood in this state. But the unusual frankness of Dr. DuBois and the enthusiasm of his fellow workers tend to cause some to look askance at their program. This is not as it should be. The frankness of Dr. DuBois should be appreciated for the courage that it represents and the enthusiasm of a Walter White should be commended by every fellow southerner whether he be in South Carolina or elsewhere. Especially should the Negro of South Carolina feel proud and honored to co-operate with her illustrious son, William Pickins, in his effort to "carry on" for the realization of complete democracy in America. All this some of the white and black people of South Carolina are beginning to see and appreciate and thereby help us to face the future without fear. We believe that our white fellow-citizens of South Carolina will be willing in ever increasing numbers to join with any movement, whether its base of action be North or South of the Mason and Dixon line, if that organization is working to assure the development or salvation of American democracy, which all agree must not perish from the earth on account of lack of support. We cannot afford to let a petty sectionalism keep us from co-operating with any and all forces working for human betterment in this commonwealth. That this spirit is really developing in the

South is shown by this extract from the pen of Clark Howell, editor of a leading southern newspaper, the *Atlanta Constitution*:

It is up to us to teach the Negro to be a better citizen and to support those who are engaged in this laudable work.

By rendering such service we not only help the Negro but we help ourselves.[4]

Another most encouraging factor in the present situation pointing to the better day is the fact that the white women of this state are, along with their colored sisters, developing a social conscience which demands "even-handed justice" for all and are too womanly to accept a chivalry proffered them on the theory that they are innocent of the great transgressions only because protected and shielded by the infamous Judge Lynch who presides over the disgraceful court of mob violence. The white women of the state of South Carolina are beginning to speak out in favor of the truth even if it is favorable to the Negro and contrary to an age-old libel upon the character of the black race. The white women's Committee on Race Relations in South Carolina have passed a resolution in substantial agreement with these words published by the director of publicity of the Commission on Inter-racial Co-operation:

We protest against mob violence by any race for any crime; against the claim that lynching is necessary for the protection of white womanhood; against a double standard of morals which tends toward amalgamation of the races and threatened racial integrity.[5]

We place ourselves on record as unalterably opposed to mob murder. The barbaric practice of lynching arouses unchristian passions, violates the sovereignty of our State, brings Mississippi into disrepute in the eyes of the world, and brutalizes all those who come within its evil influence.

As Southern women, we hold that no circumstances can ever justify mob action and that in no instance is it an exhibition of chivalric consideration for the honor of womanhood.

---

[4] Pamphlet called *Southern Opinion and Race Relations*, edited by the director of publicity of The Commission on Inter-racial Co-operation, Atlanta, Ga.

[5] Ibid.

All that these ladies have said of lynching have long been recognized in some civilized parts of America and the world. In fact, even in the states that imagine that lynching is a better process than that of duly enacted laws, the hypocrisy of the excuses given is understood. Lynching is nothing more than the inability to appreciate the standards of civilization on the part of the majority of those who engage in such cruel and cowardly act and an outright reversion to a savage state by others who have a thin veneer of civilization. Lynching is tolerated only in those regions where ignorance, prejudice and intolerance have the upper hand over intelligence, Christianity, refinement and fine sensibilities. There would be no lynchings and burnings if the preachers, teachers, lawyers, doctors and other citizens of intellect and courage did not look with complacency upon the practice. Maybe, though, the southern white ladies can bring about a change in the barbaric practice. Certainly, the lynchers will have to find some other excuse if the ladies keep telling them that "in no instance is it an exhibition of chivalric consideration for the honor of womanhood." Perhaps, even mere man will become bold enough to denounce the practice without at the same time apologizing therefor. Even the president of the country may become bold enough to utter a word of condemnation, instead of giving a fine imitation of one afflicted with lockjaw. These ladies have certainly furnished an example of straight from the shoulder—or should we say heart?—denunciation of a practice that has no place among a Christian people.

Under the progressive, courageous leadership of Mrs. McGowan of Charleston, the white women of the state are slowly coming to a state of mind which means justice and fair play for colored men and women so far as they are able to exert influence.

Another influence which is encouraging the Negroes of South Carolina today is the new attitude of the white daily and weekly press. In the civilization in which we live today, one of the best and truest indicators of public opinion is the newspaper press. The news, including the advertisements which a paper of large circulation carries, unmistakably shows the chief interests and opinions of the people in the community it serves. There was a time, not long since past, when every white paper in the state delighted to play up the news which described the Negro as a criminal or played him up as a comedian. Today we find the large daily papers often anxious to present any news about the Negro which shows his progress or unusual achievement in any line. Even the smaller papers in the rural districts and small towns are often willing to present good as well as bad news about the Negro. In a word, these papers are more and more coming to the place where they can treat Negro news in accordance with the general principles governing news.

One notices, too, a great improvement in the editorial attitude of these papers. More and more the editors of the white papers of South Carolina are showing a disposition to challenge the people of their respective localities to repudiate mob violence, peonage and petty discriminations against the Negro.[6] This is very encouraging to any one who knows anything at all about the genius of the modern American newspaper. It shows that there is not an inconsiderable body of public opinion represented in the constituency of these papers which supports these ideas of the editors. A newspaper, like a politician, cannot get far ahead of its supporters; it must lead by emphasizing the better ideas of its subscribers and advertisement purchasers. We insert here an editorial appearing recently in one of the leading white papers of South Carolina. It speaks for itself:

Suspect Proves Innocence

A rebuke to the mob spirit that seems to prevail in the South to a remarkable degree of late was lately administered by one near victim—that is he might have been lynched for the murder of a 15-year-old girl.

We refer to the release of Conrad Sharp at Gaffney, the other day, after Morganton, N. C., officers verified his statement that he is not Broadus Miller, wanted at Morganton, for the alleged murder of a girl.

---

[6] *The State* and *The Record* of Columbia, *The News and Courier* of Charleston and *The Daily Item* all stand for a liberal attitude toward the Negro though "there is room for improvement."

The mob, never caring for nor considering the evidence of guilt, apparently is content to kill its victim. If it discovers that it made a mistake in the aftermath of the tragedy, it merely remarks that it was a bad day for suspects.

We have often wondered if any criminal anywhere ever committed a greater crime than the mob commits when it murders the helpless without trial or mercy.[7]

In this connection the Negro newspapers are not to be ignored. From time to time the papers published by Negroes in the state serve as mediums of expression for those who wish to criticize the present order or publish a prophecy of the new day. Nearly every Negro newspaper in this state and out of it is a "propaganda sheet." It is natural that this should be so. The average Negro paper has to struggle for existence because of the keen competition of white papers. This competition is overwhelming in the field of pure news as the white papers have unlimited resources of capitalization and advertisement at their disposal whereas the colored papers are very limited in these particulars. The colored newspaper must therefore live upon its subscriptions to a greater extent than most regular newspapers. It therefore undertakes to serve not only as a newspaper but as an advocate of Negro rights and opportunities which are nowhere else defended.[8] Then, too, it is still true, in spite of much improvement mentioned above, that much news which would be inspiration to Negroes is ignored by the white people because the majority of them are not yet vitally interested in the true progress and advancement of Negroes in all phases of civilization. Therefore such colored papers in this state as *The Palmetto Leader, The Charleston Messenger* and others furnish the Negro of the state with agencies of free speech and so help him to face the future with assurance and happiness. A few brief editorials from colored papers of the state illustrating their outlook and service may not be out of place. We have selected the following because they deal with typical problems in a characteristic way:[9]

---

[7]*Columbia Record,* June 30, 1927.
[8]Eugene Gordon: In *The Messenger Magazine.*
[9]From *The Palmetto Leader.*

"The Hickory Grove Hoax, as the matter is now referred to here, has passed into history." This is the way a news dispatch described the calm after a two or three days' man hunt in and about that little country village way up on the northern border of South Carolina. The excitement was caused by a white woman suffering, as the dispatch says, with a "hallucination or hysterical imagination" which made her cry out that an assault had been attempted on her by a Negro youth of about eighteen years of age. The report caused men and boys "to lose their reason"—if they had any; guns and pistols flashed and the man hunt was on, on for the imaginable Negro. The governor, determined that, if possible, there should be no lynching, called out a company of militia. But after all the excitement, the more intelligent thought that a check up on the story was the sensible thing to do. The check up was made and lo and behold! only a "hallucination or hysterical imagination" was found.

Some time before that, in Greenville City, the county sheriff was foully and brutally murdered at midnight; shot down at his garage door. At once, the cry was raised that the deed was done by a Negro. Any and every Negro was liable to be arrested. For was it not at first said that a Negro was seen running from the place? But some folks began to think. Deliberate deeds of that character are not usually committed by Negroes. Skillful detectives got on the job—well, the arrests were made, but the arrested ones are not colored.

Still further back, a destructive race riot was precipitated at Coffeyville, Kansas, by the story of a white high school girl who claimed that she and her chum were assaulted in her house while alone at night by Negroes. After much rioting in which a few lives were lost and much property destroyed, a sensible investigation was made. It was revealed that the girl who cried "wolf" was a party to the assaulting party—only the assailants were white men. The girl and one man are in jail awaiting trial.

But in the meantime, is it not fair to ask just how many Negroes have not been the victims of mobs because of "hoaxes," "hallucinations" or plots?

* * * * * *

The Vandals in America[10]
A Menace to Our Civilization
(From *Charleston New Era*)

When we first thought of presenting to our readers the thoughts in this editorial, the first subject that suggested itself to us was "American Vandals." But after a little thought we

---

[10]Written by the author as "special contributing editor."

decided that such a wording of the subject would be an injustice to this great country of ours. No country on the face of the globe, we believe, has higher or finer ideals than the United States of America. We have always believed that Wilson in Europe fighting for "open diplomacy," "a world made safe for democracy," and similar noble ideals that Lloyd George and other "hard-headed" Old World so-called statesmen couldn't appreciate was really standing by the soul of America. Wilson was not mistaken in the ideals of his country but he made his great mistake in the methods he employed with his colleagues. We believe that this will be the ultimate judgment of history upon the work of this remarkable man.

So Vandals are not American because America, in her traditions and ideals, does not stand for vandalism. However, no one who reads the newspapers and so is familiar with the lynchings, burnings, and general lawlessness in our country today can doubt for a moment that there are Vandals between the Atlantic and the Pacific and south of the Great Lakes and north of the Gulf of Mexico. A vandal may be defined as one who has little regard for the finer things of civilization including especially its laws and courts. Vandals are essentially barbarians. The Vandals in this country are responsible for the mobs, lynching, etc. The Ku Klux Klan seems to us to be an organization of Vandals.

These Vandals in America, both unorganized and organized, are the chief menace or danger to the stability of American civilization and institutions and the final greatness of America. These Vandals are a much greater menace to our future than the Japanese, the English, the Germans, or any other foreign governments. The great, though cynical, essayist, Macaulay, made a statement to this effect that "America, like Rome of old, will finally be destroyed by Vandals, with this difference: the Vandals who destroyed Rome came from without; those who will destroy America will come from within." There are many, working with the Ku Klux Klan, to make the pessimistic prophecy of the cynical Englishman come true in the not far distant future.

* * * * * *

THE DANGER OF DIPLOMACY[11]

The presence and progress of the Negro race is a great tribute to the power and worth of diplomacy. If the Negro had not been diplomatic in practically all his relationships and contacts with the proud, self-conceited, self-satisfied Anglo-Saxon, he, the Negro, would most assuredly have come to an early and

---

[11]Ibid.

tragic end in this western civilization. But because the Negro was willing to smile when frowns seemed appropriate, because he was willing to show charity when his nature called for hatred, because he was outwardly respectful when his soul saw only unworthiness, because he was diplomatic, the Negro largely disarmed the destructive power of the white people and today is rapidly becoming a part of this mighty civilization whereas the American Indian, for some reason not diplomatic, has little part in it.

The fact that diplomacy has led us to some successes causes us as a race to unconsciously put a great deal of stress on that quality. Then, too, it fits into our peace-loving character. It was no accident that the American Negro produced, in the person of Booker T. Washington, one of the greatest diplomats that the modern world has yet produced. We have often thought that if the great modern German empire had possessed one single diplomat of the quality of Booker T. Washington they would have conducted the international affairs so successfully that the World War would never have been thought of and Germany would today be the most powerful industrial society in the world.

Nevertheless there are dismal dangers that lurk beneath the shadows of too much diplomacy. The Negro race is suffering from the presence of some of those dangers now.

One of the dangers of diplomacy is that it tends to be too successful. For example, one element of Negro diplomacy in this country has been the attempt to disarm hatred by laughing in the face of mean, discouraging, and damaging acts from our neighbors. The danger of that diplomacy was that the white people would be fooled into thinking that we are a care-free, "happy go lucky" people without any serious purpose in life. Our diplomacy has been successful to the extent that they largely believe that today. That is very dangerous for us. We are not a joke; we are deserving of the same serious consideration as other men and the same rights and honors and rewards.

Another danger of diplomacy is that it will decrease one's self-respect. In plain words, diplomacy is largely made of lies; pleasing and flattering lies to be sure, but lies nevertheless. No person can tell lies perpetually and maintain his self-respect. The inexorable power of psychological influences finally works to convince the diplomat himself that there must be some truth in the things he says and practices. So the Negro has about convinced himself in many instances that he is inferior, or unworthy, or at least vastly different from other people.

Finally let us say that if we are to avoid the danger of diplomacy we must use it as sparingly as possible.

Another encouraging feature of recent Negro history in this state is the rise and practice of a new form of diplomacy between the races. It must be admitted that diplomacy is of vast importance in bringing about a satisfactory solution of our complex inter-racial problems in this state. As has been pointed out in several other instances in this book, the old type of diplomacy as between the white man and the colored man in this state, is rapidly passing away. The old diplomacy was characterized by a hypocritical, bootlicking sycophancy on the part of the Negro who tried to get what he wanted by flattering the vanity of the white man through an insincere but blatant recognition of the white "superiority complex." The white man's answer to this was a tolerant attitude toward the Negro's shortcomings coupled with the precarious promise to protect the "good Negro" as long as he was satisfied and contented to "remain in his place" and not disturb the status quo. The trouble with the old diplomacy was that it went too far. It paid too big a price for the things it purchased. Diplomacy ceases to serve its legitimate purpose when it goes beyond certain definite limits. In human relationships it goes beyond its proper limits when it sacrifices manhood and tolerates injustice; when it degrades human character and dwarfs the human soul.

The new diplomacy accomplishes finer results by nobler methods. This new diplomacy as practiced by "the New Negro" in South Carolina is characterized by at least two methods of procedure: First, it frankly faces the facts; secondly, while recognizing the evil present in the situation, it conscientiously emphasizes the potentiality of the good. Mr. B. E. Mays has excellently brought this out in the chapter entitled "The New Negro Challenges the Old Order." We have a large number of Negroes in this state, devotees of the new diplomacy, who, without ignoring the evil, are continually accomplishing the better because they speak well of the good. A very good example of this is the excellent progress in procuring opportunity for "higher education" at public expense through the diplomatic efforts of President R. S. Wilkinson of the State A. and M. College at Orangeburg. Examples of less conspicuous but very necessary and worth while accomplishments of a similar nature could be given from every community in the state of South Carolina.

As regards the white South Carolinian, the new diplomacy expresses itself in a frank admission of the past errors and weaknesses of both white and black alike coupled with a sincere effort to work *with* the Negro rather than *for* him to the end that all may live together as brothers. These two fundamental principles of the southern white man's "new diplomacy"—the honest confession of past wrongs and the sincere promise of future co-operation are excellently expressed in the two following quotations published in the leaflet referred to before, distributed by the Southern Commission on Inter-racial Co-operation.

The race problem is a human problem. Until we think of all citizens as human beings, with human rights, human interests, and human possibilities; until we insist on equality of opportunity, equality before the law, equal sanitary provisions, equal protection of persons and property . . . until we become conscious of a common brotherhood and cease to exploit the weak, we are not even in sight of our goal.

There must be real sympathetic co-operation between the leaders of the two races . . . frank interchanges of opinions . . . earnest effort to understand . . . prompt and positive condemnation of all acts of injustice . . . the developments of plans for larger sympathy and closer co-operation.

We feel that there are many white people in South Carolina who will subscribe to these sentiments without mental reservations. This means that the new diplomacy has come to bring its healing balm to this wounded state.

Perhaps the most encouraging fact of all is the growing number of educators in the white colleges or higher schools of South Carolina who are encouraging young white men and women to approach the so-called Negro problem in the modern scientific spirit—the spirit of open minded, courageous search for the truth. In the University of South Carolina, Wofford College, Clemson College, the Citadel, and most of the other state institutions we find social science courses offered and taught in which the students are acquainted to some extent with the real truth about the Negro. They are introduced to his literature and his leaders and many learn for the first time that not all Negroes are of the domestic servant type. The Young Men's Christian Association and the Young Women's Christian Association are working through their local branches in these institutions to bring about a clearer understanding between the white and colored students who are to be the future leaders of both races. Thus these organizations have become vital forces in promoting the new day. It is practically impossible to overestimate the tremendous influence exerted upon the future of the state by the various conferences of these organizations such as the Blue Ridge conference of the student leaders of the Young Men's Christian Association in the South. Young white men from the schools of South Carolina and other colleges go to these conferences and come into contact with their own leaders, such as Mr. Bergthold, who have liberal views and they are greatly helped toward an acquisition of those attitudes necessary for the new diplomacy referred to above. At these conferences the white students come in contact with Negro leaders of national importance. For example, Mrs. Mary McCloud Bethume was once a speaker at Blue Ridge. Through the agency of the Y. M. C. A. white students on their local campuses have been made familiar with the work of Negroes who are making worth while contributions. This is accomplished by recommending lists of books to be read or studied in connection with "Bible Study Groups" or "World Problems Forums." The Y. M. C. A., co-operating with the Southern Commission on Inter-racial Co-operation, has encouraged the colleges to establish regular courses of study in the social science departments which deal with the Negroes in a scientific way. One of the books suggested as a text for such courses was prepared by one of the outstanding leaders of the Y. M. C. A., the president of the southern Y. M. C. A. College at Nashville.[12]

A good example of some of the excellent work done by the students themselves in the local Y. M. C. A. organizations is

---

[12]W. D. Weatherford: *The Negro from Africa to America.*

the organization and conduct of an Inter-racial Forum at
Columbia containing representatives from all the leading
white and colored colleges of the city.   The young college
students of both races meet and discuss the problems con-
fronting their state.   They meet as fellow students on terms
of mutual self-respect seeking the truth as revealed to both.
They are pioneering in the new diplomacy.   We have time
and space here to present only one example of constructive
work of this Columbia Inter-racial Forum of students.
Through this agency the Negro representative of the National Council of the American Y. M. C. A. in its African
work came to Columbia and presented his marvelous message
and challenge of courageous, sacrificial service as a pioneer
for the Kingdom of Heaven in far off Africa.   Max Yergan
is the outstanding Christian layman of the Negro race today
having received the Harmon medal (1927) for distinguished
service in the field of religion, which means that in the opinion
of a committee of distinguished Americans, white and colored,
he had done more during that year to promote the interests
of religion than any other Negro of American descent.   This
fact had been so much impressed upon the white students of
Columbia by the colored members of the inter-racial forum
that they looked upon the visit of Max Yergan as the opportunity to see and hear "one of the outstanding Christian
statesmen of this generation"; even before they met Yergan
these young white men began to think of this young Negro
pioneer as a man worthy of honor and respect.   Therefore
when he arrived at Columbia he was met by a joint committee
of white and colored students and as it happened, we are
told, one of the white students was first to greet him, take
his baggage and welcome him to South Carolina as a great
Christian leader.   One must recognize that this is quite a
deal of progress since the ancestors of Yergan, black slaves,
were brought into the South in chains driven by the ancestors
of this same young white man who owned human beings and
thought of them as a special order of inferior men only a
little higher than the beasts of the field and deserving no
more consideration.   Certainly the young colored and white

men who saw this had a view of a better day dawning in Dixie.

At the inter-racial meeting held at one of the largest Negro churches in Columbia a large audience heard this prophet in brown, a contemporary Paul, deliver what was doubtless the greatest challenge to constructive Christian service they had ever heard, for such is the message of Yergan.

One might think from our description so far that all the work is being done in the colleges, but this is far from true.

Although the Negro naturally has a friendly, forgiving disposition there is a human limit to his forbearance and love. The Negro in South Carolina is facing a situation in which many of the younger men are truly "getting weary" of the injustice, etc., which the race must suffer in this state. There is beginning to develop a hatred for the white people as a race on the part of some of the younger generation of colored youth. The program of the Y. M. C. A. in the colleges is successfully combating this tendency and, if the work continues, will, we believe, practically eradicate it altogether. The writer has noticed this increasing loss of confidence in all the white people in the young men and women he has met, and he has seen many of them get a new faith in all mankind, including the southern white people, when at a Y. M. C. A. conference or some similar meeting they have met young white men and women of the new school. These contacts have caused the young colored skeptics to believe that, perchance, it is possible for the white man to develop a brotherly spirit. Jesus Christ taught the fatherhood of God and the brotherhood of man but the white churches failed so miserably to practice this, their profession, that the young Negroes were beginning to believe that they would never try it. Thus the Negroes were about to agree with many of the white people that the story of the Good Samaritan is impracticable in a world such as ours. They were about to throw the philosophy of the brotherhood of man overboard as an unnecessary weight upon the progress of a struggling people handicapped by their white competitors. But, with their attention called to the fact that here and there are still found young white men and women who are willing to sacrifice life itself if need be and what is more, live courageously for the principle of love, these "doubting Thomases" of the black race have been encouraged to "carry on" toward the goal of universal love a little longer. We have dwelt at considerable length on this question of development of the right ideas of inter-racial co-operation, a sound social philosophy, for the young white men and women now in colleges are makers of the future civilization of our state—they are the prophets and pioneers of the coming "new social order."

Although in this last chapter we have seen fit to emphasize certain tendencies in contemporary life which indicate progress in particular lines which are very influential in giving the Negroes of this state a basis of fact to face the future without fear, yet the reader is asked to keep in mind the fact that every chapter in this book reveals progressive evolution in the life and history of Negroes in this state and so assists manhood in ebony to have faith in its future here in South Carolina and in the world at large.

It happens that a distinguished son of South Carolina to whom we have referred before several times has expressed this idea in classic prose which some have even called poetry:[13]

I See and Am Satisfied

The vision of a scion of a despised and rejected race, the span of whose life is measured by the years of its Golden Jubilee, and whose fancy, like the vine that girdles the tree-trunk, runneth both forward and back.

I see the African savage as he drinks his palmy wine, and basks in the sunshine of his native bliss, and is happy.

I see the man-catcher, impelled by thirst of gold, as he entraps his simple-souled victim in the snares of bondage and death, by use of force or guile.

I see the ocean basin whitened with his bones, and the ocean current running red with his blood, amidst the hellish horrors of the Middle Passage.

---

[13]Kerlin: *Negro Poets and Their Poems.*

I see him laboring for two centuries and a half in unrequited toil, making the hillsides of our southland to glow with the snow-white fleece of cotton, and the valleys to glisten with the golden sheaves of grain.

I see him silently enduring cruelty and torture indescribable, with flesh flinching beneath the sizz of angry whip or quivering under the gnaw of the sharp-toothed bloodhound.

I see a chivalric civilization instinct with dignity, comity and grace rising upon pillars supported by his strength and brawny arm.

I see the swarthy matron lavishing her soul in altruistic devotion upon the offspring of her alabaster mistress.

I see the haughty sons of a haughty race pouring out their lustful passion upon black womanhood, filling our land with a bronzed and tawny brood.

I see also the patriarchal solicitude of the kindly hearted owners of men, in whose breast not even iniquitous system could sour the milk of human kindness.

I hear the groans, the sorrows, the sighings, the soul striving of these benighted creatures of God, rising up from the low grounds of sorrow and reaching the ear of Him who regardeth man of the lowliest estate.

I strain my ear to supernal sound, and I hear in the secret chambers of the Almighty the order to the Captain of the Host to break his bond and set him free.

I see Abraham Lincoln, himself a man of sorrows and acquainted with grief, arise to execute the high decree.

I see two hundred thousand black boys in blue baring their breasts to the bayonets of the enemy, that their race might have some slight part in its own deliverance.

I see the great Proclamation delivered in the year of my birth of which I became the first fruit and beneficiary.

I see the assassin striking down the Great Emancipator; and the house of mirth is transformed into the Golgotha of the nation.

I watch the Congress as it adds to the constitution new words, which make the document a charter of liberty indeed.

I see the new-made citizen running to and fro in the first fruit of his new-found freedom.

I see him rioting in the flush of privilege which the nation had vouchsafed, but destined, alas, not long to last.

I see him thrust down from the high seat of political power, by
fraud and force, while the nation looks on in sinister silence
and acquiescent guilt.

I see the tide of public feeling run cold and chilly, as the vial of
racial wrath is wreaked upon his bowed and defenceless head.

I see him writhing in the agony of death as his groans issue
from the crackling flames, while the funeral pyre lights the
midnight sky with its dismal glare.   My heart sinks with
heaviness within me.

I see that the path of progress has never taken a straight line,
but has always been a zigzag course amid the conflicting
forces of right and wrong, truth and error, justice and injustice, cruelty and mercy.

I see that the great generous American Heart, despite the temporary flutter, will finally beat true to the higher human
impulse, and my soul abounds with reassurance and hope.

I see his marvelous advance in the rapid acquisition of knowledge and acquirement of things material, and attainment in
the higher pursuits of life, with his face fixed upon that light
which shineth brighter and brighter unto the perfect day.

I see him who was once deemed stricken, smitten of God and
afflicted, now entering with universal welcome into the patri-
mony of mankind, and I look calmly upon the centuries of
blood and tears and travail of soul, and am satisfied.[14]

Perhaps Mr. Mays, the writer of the chapter on "The
New Negro Challenges the Old Order" would demur at
Doctor Miller's conclusion of satisfaction. If so, the writer
would be in sympathy with him, but we think that Doctor
Miller wrote that passage to convey to the readers his pro-
found faith in the Negro's future.

It seems fitting and proper to close this chapter and this
book with a favorite expression of one of South Carolina's
greatest educators, Doctor R. S. Wilkinson:

We are to go the road which we see to be the straight
one, not looking backward, but following a constructive, far-
sighted policy, to be loyal, just, sympathetic and useful to others;
finally to accomplish our tasks with greater determination and
finer finish than ever.

---

[14]Miller, Kelly: *"Out of the House of Bondage,"* pages 240-242
(quoted by permission of Thos. Y. Crowell Co., New York.)

APPENDIX

In Re: Chapter II—"The Slaves' Fight for Physical Freedom." The following notes show how the fight developed the agitation that led to the Civil War.

NOTE 1.

Calhoun, South Carolinian, champion of the slaveholding interests and a fearless defender of the justice of slavery, thus commented on abolition in 1837:

As widely as this incendiary spirit* has spread, it has not yet infected this body, or the great mass of the intelligent and business portion of the North; but unless it be speedily stopped, it will spread and work upward till it brings the two great sections of the Union into deadly conflict. This is not a new impression with me. Several years since, in a discussion with one of the senators from Massachusetts [Mr. Webster], before this fell spirit had showed itself, I then predicted that the doctrine of the proclamation and the Force Bill—that this government had a right, in the last resort, to determine the extent of its own powers, and enforce its decision at the point of the bayonet, which was so warmly maintained by that senator—would at no distant day arouse the dormant spirit of abolitionism. I told him that the doctrine was tantamount to the assumption of unlimited power on the part of the government, and that such would be the impression on the public mind in a large portion of the Union. The consequences would be inevitable. A large portion of the northern states believed slavery to be a sin, and would consider it as an obligation of conscience to abolish it if they should feel themselves in any degree responsible for its continuance,—and that this doctrine would necessarily lead to the belief of such responsibility. . . .

They who imagine that the spirit now abroad in the North will die away of itself without a shock or convulsion, have formed a very inadequate conception of its real character; it will continue to rise and spread, unless prompt and efficient measures to

---

*As we stated in Chapter II, the "incendiary spirit" of abolition was encouraged and kept flaming by the Negro's manly fight for physical freedom through the Underground Railroad, etc.

stay its progress be adopted. Already it has taken possession of the pulpit, of the schools, and, to a considerable extent, of the press; those great instruments by which the mind of the rising generation will be formed.

However sound the great body of the non-slaveholding states are at present, in the course of a few years they will be succeeded by those who will have been taught to hate the people and institutions of nearly one-half of this Union, with a hatred more deadly than one hostile nation ever entertained toward another. It is easy to see the end. By the necessary course of events, if left to themselves, we must become, finally, two peoples. It is impossible under the deadly hatred which must spring up between the two great sections, if the present causes are permitted to operate unchecked, that we should continue under the same political system. The conflicting elements would burst the Union asunder, powerful as are the links which hold it together. Abolition and the Union cannot co-exist. As the friend of the Union, I openly proclaim it—and the sooner it is known the better. The former may now be controlled, but in a short time it will be beyond the power of man to arrest the course of events. We of the South will not, cannot, surrender our institutions. To maintain the existing relations between the two races, inhabiting that section of the Union, is indispensable to the peace and happiness of both. It cannot be subverted without drenching the country in blood, and extirpating one or the other of the races. Be it good or bad, it has grown up with our society and institutions, and is so interwoven with them, that to destroy it would be to destroy us as a people. But let me not be understood as admitting, even by implication, that the existing relations between the two races in the slaveholding states is an evil—far otherwise; I hold it to be a good, as it has thus far proved itself to be to both, and will continue to prove so if not disturbed by the fell spirit of abolition. . . .

I feel myself called upon to speak freely upon the subject where the honor and interests of those I represent are involved. I hold then, that there never has yet existed a wealthy and civilized society in which one portion of the community did not, in point of fact, live on the labor of the other. Broad and general as is this assertion, it is fully borne out by history. . . . I fearlessly assert that the existing relations between the two races in the South, against which these blind fanatics are waging war, forms the most solid and durable foundation on which to rear free and stable political institutions. It is useless to disguise the fact. There is and always has been in an advanced stage of wealth and civilization, a conflict between labor and capital. The condition of society in the South exempts us from the disorders and dangers resulting from this conflict; and which explains why it is that the political condition of the slaveholding States has been so much more stable and quiet than that of the North. The advantages of the former, in this respect, will become more and more manifest if left undisturbed by interference from without, as the country advances in wealth and numbers. We have, in fact, but just entered that condition of society where the strength and durability of our political institutions are to be tested; and I venture nothing in predicting that the experience of the next generation will fully test how vastly more favorable our condition of society is to that of other sections for free and stable institutions, provided we are not disturbed by the interference of others, or shall have sufficient intelligence and spirit to resist promptly and successfully such interference. It rests with ourselves to meet and repel them. I look not for aid to this government or to the other states; not but there are kind feelings toward us on the part of the great body of the non-slaveholding states; but as kind as their feelings may be, we may rest assured that no political party in those states will risk their ascendance for our safety. If we do not defend ourselves none will defend us; if we yield we will be more and more pressed as we recede; and if we submit we will be trampled under foot. Be assured that emancipation itself would not satisfy these fanatics—that gained, the next step would be to raise the Negroes to a social and political equality with the whites; and that being effected, we would soon find the present condition of the two races reversed. . . . *Calhoun, Speeches (N. Y., 1856), II, 628-633 passim.*

NOTE 2.

Answering Calhoun and other apologists for slavery, William H. Seward upheld "The Higher Law":

There is another aspect of the principle of compromise which deserves consideration. It assumes that slavery, if not the only institution in a slave state, is at least a ruling institution, and that this characteristic is recognized by the constitution.† But slavery is only one of many institutions there. Freedom is equally an institution there. Slavery is only a temporary, accidental, partial, and incongruous one. Freedom, on the contrary, is a perpetual, organic, universal one, in harmony with the constitution of the United States. The slaveholder himself stands under the pro-

---

†Of course, the constitutionality of slavery would not have become a burning issue if the slaves in South Carolina and elsewhere had not continued to fight for their freedom.

tection of the latter, in common with all the free citizens of that state. But it is, moreover, an indispensable institution. You may separate slavery from South Carolina, and the state will still remain; but if you subvert freedom there, the state will cease to exist. But the principle of this compromise gives complete ascendancy in the slave states, and in the constitution of the United States, to the subordinate, accidental, and incongruous institution, over its paramount antagonist. To reduce this claim of slavery to an absurdity, it is only necessary to add that there are only two states in which slaves are a majority, and not one in which the slaveholders are not a very disproportionate minority.

But there is yet another aspect in which this principle must be examined. It regards the domain only as a possession, to be enjoyed either in common or by partition by the citizens of the old states. It is true, indeed, that the national domain is ours. It is true it was acquired by the valor and with the wealth of the whole nation. But we hold, nevertheless, no arbitrary power over it. We hold no arbitrary authority over anything, whether acquired lawfully or seized by usurpation. The constitution regulates our stewardship; the constitution devotes the domain to union, to justice, to defense, to welfare, and to liberty.

But there is a higher law than the constitution, which regulates our authority over the domain, and devotes it to the same noble purposes. The territory is a part, no inconsiderable part, of the common heritage of mankind bestowed upon them by the Creator of the universe. We are His stewards, and must so discharge our trust as to secure in the highest attainable degree their happiness. How momentous that trust is we may learn from the instructions of the founder of modern philosophy:

"No man," says Bacon, "can by care-taking, as the Scripture saith, add a cubit to his stature in this little model of man's body; but, in the great fame of kingdoms and commonwealths, it is in the power of princes or estates to add amplitude and greatness to their kingdoms. For, by introducing such ordinances, constitutions, and customs as are wise, they may sow greatness to their posterity and successors. But these things are commonly not observed, but left to take their chances."

This is a state, and we are deliberating for it, just as our fathers deliberated in establishing the institutions we enjoy. Whatever superiority there is in our condition and hopes over those of any other "kingdom" or "estate" is due to the fortunate circumstances that our ancestors did not leave things to "take their chance," but that they "added amplitude and greatness" to our commonwealth "by introducing such ordinances, constitu-

tions, and customs, as were wise." We in our turn have succeeded to the same responsibilities, and we cannot approach the
duty before us wisely or justly, except we raise ourselves to the
great consideration of how we can most certainly "sow greatness
to our posterity and successors."

And now the simple, bold, and even awful, question which
presents itself to us is this: Shall we, who are founding institutions, social and political, for countless millions; shall we, who
know by experience the wise and the just, and are free to choose
them, and to reject the erroneous and unjust; shall we establish
human bondage, or permit it by our sufferance to be established?
Sir, our forefathers would not have hesitated an hour. They
found slavery existing here, and they left it only because they
could not remove it. There is not only no free state which would
now establish it, but there is no slave state, which, if it had had
the free alternative as we now have, would have founded slavery.
Indeed, our revolutionary predecessors had precisely the same
question before them in establishing an organic law under which
the states of Ohio, Indiana, Michigan, Illinois, and Wisconsin
have since come into the Union, and they solemnly repudiated
and excluded slavery from those states forever. I confess that
the most alarming evidence of our degeneracy which has yet been
given is found in the fact that we even debate such a question. . . .

The senator proposes to expel me. I am ready to meet that
trial, too; and if I shall be expelled, I shall not be the first man
subjected to punishment for maintaining that there is a power
higher than human law, and that power delights in justice; that
rulers, whether despots or elected rulers of a free people, are
bound to administer justice for the benefit of society.—*William
H. Seward, Works (N. Y., 1853), I, pp. 74-129.*

NOTE 3.

AN EARLY INCIDENT OF THE CIVIL WAR**

*Robert Smalls of Beaufort, S. C., achieved the greatest dis-
tinction of any Negro during the Civil War by turning over to
the United States the steamer, Planter. The facts of this incident are set forth in reports by committees of several Congresses
as follows:*

On May 13, 1862, the Confederate Steamer, *Planter,* the
special dispatch boat of General Ripley, the Confederate post
commander at Charleston, S. C., was taken by Robert Smalls,

**Here we have recorded an example of physical fighting for physi-
cal freedom.

under the following circumstances, from the wharf at which she was lying, carried safely out of Charleston, S. C., harbor, and delivered to one of the vessels of the Federal fleet then blockading that port.

On the day previous, May 12, the *Planter,* which had for two weeks been engaged in removing guns from Cole's Island to James Island, returned to Charleston. That night all the officers went ashore and slept in the city, leaving on board a crew of eight men, all colored. Among them was Robert Smalls, who was virtually the pilot of the boat, although he was only called a wheelman, because at that time no colored man could have, in fact, been made a pilot.

For some time previous he had been watching for an opportunity to carry into execution a plan he had conceived to take the *Planter* to the Federal fleet. This, he saw, was as good a chance as he would ever have to do so, and therefore he determined not to lose it. Consulting with the balance of the crew, Smalls found that they were willing to co-operate with him, although two of them afterwards concluded to remain behind. The design was hazardous in the extreme. The boat would have to pass beneath the guns of the forts in the harbor. Failure and detection would have been certain death. Fearful the venture, but it was made. The daring resolution had been formed, and under command of Robert Smalls wood was taken aboard, steam was put on, and with her valuable cargo of guns and ammunition, intended for Fort Ripley, a new fortification just constructed in the harbor, about two o'clock in the morning the *Planter* silently moved off from her dock, steamed up to North Atlantic wharf, where Smalls' wife and two children, together with four other women and one other child, and also three men, were waiting to embark.

All these were taken on board, and then at 3:25 A. M., May 13, the *Planter* started on her perilous adventure, carrying nine men, five women, and three children. Passing Fort Johnson, the *Planter's* steam whistle blew the usual salute and she proceeded down the bay. Approaching Fort Sumter, Smalls stood in the pilot house leaning out of the window, with his arms folded across his breast, after the manner of Captain Relay, the commander of the boat, and his head covered with the huge straw hat which Captain Relay commonly wore on such occasions.

The signal, required to be given by all steamers passing out, was blown as coolly as if General Ripley were on board, going out on a tour of inspection. Sumter answered by signal, "All right," and the *Planter* headed toward Morris Island, then occupied by Hatch's light artillery, and passed beyond the range of

Sumter's guns before anybody suspected anything was wrong. When at last the *Planter* was obviously going toward the Federal fleet off the bar, Sumter signaled toward Morris Island to stop her, but it was too late. As the *Planter* approached the Federal fleet, a white flag was displayed, but this was not at first discovered and the Federal steamers, supposing the Confederate rams were coming to attack them, stood out to deep water. But the ship, *Onward,* under Captain Nichols, which was not a steamer, remained, opened her ports, and was about to fire into the *Planter,* when she noticed the flag of truce. As soon as the vessels came within hailing distance of each other, the *Planter's* errand was explained. Captain Nichols then boarded her and Smalls delivered the *Planter* to him. From the *Planter* Smalls was transferred to the *Augusta,* the flagship off the bar, under the command of Captain Parrott, by whom the *Planter,* with Smalls and her crew, were sent to Port Royal to Rear Admiral DuPont, then in command of the Southern Squadron.

Smalls was made pilot and did service on the *Crusader,* the *Planter* also, and the monitor, *Keokuk,* on which he was during the memorable attack on Fort Sumter April 7, 1863. The *Keokuk* was struck ninety-six times, nineteen shots passing. Feeling very keenly the sting sustained in the loss of the *Planter,* the Confederates made a very hot fire upon her. The same report from which the findings are extracted says:

"Upon one occasion Captain Nickerson became demoralized and left the pilot house and secured himself in the coal bunker. Smalls was on the deck and finding out that the Captain had deserted his post, entered the pilot house, took command of the boat and carried her safely out of the reach of the guns. For this conduct he was promoted by order of General Gilmore, commanding the department of the South, to the rank of captain of the *Planter,* which was used as a supply boat along the coast until the end of the war. In September, 1866, he carried his boat to Baltimore; there she was put out of commission and sold." —*House of Representatives, 55th Congress, 2d Session, Report No. 120.*

The following extracts from *"The Status of the Negro in South Carolina, 1822-1823,"* have an obvious bearing on his fight for freedom:

(A) Every slave who shall raise, or attempt to raise an insurrection in this province, or shall endeavor to delude or entice any slave to run away and leave the province, every such slave and slaves, and his and their accomplices, aiders and abetters, shall, on conviction thereof, as aforesaid, suffer death. Provided

9

always, that it shall and may be lawful, to and for the justices who shall pronounce sentence against such slaves, by and with the advice and consent of the Freeholders as aforesaid, if several slaves shall receive sentence at one time, to mitigate and alter the sentence of any slave, other than such as shall be convicted of homicide of a white person, who they shall think may deserve mercy, and may inflict such corporal punishment (other than death) on any such slave, as they in discretion shall think fit, any thing herein contained to the contrary thereof, in any wise notwithstanding. Provided, that one or more of the said slaves who shall be convicted of the crimes or offence aforesaid, where several are concerned, shall be executed for example, to deter others from offending in the like kind.—*A. A. 1740. P. L. 167.*

(B)* *Examination of Sally, a Negro woman belonging to Mr. Alexander Howard.*

I know Jesse, and heard him speak several times about it; one day in particular, he was anxious to see his brother, who has my mother for his wife, and waited until he came, when they conversed together. Jesse said, he had got a horse to go into the country, to bring down men to fight the white people; that he was allowed to pass by two parties of the patrol on the road, but that a third party had brought him back and that, if there were but five men like him, they would destroy the city. This was on last Sunday week (the 16th of June), he said, that before three o'clock, that night, all the white people would be killed. That, if any person informed, or would not join in the fight, such person would be killed or poisoned. He frequently came into the yard to see his brother, and I threatened to inform, if he came there, and spoke in that way, to get us all into trouble. We never had any quarrel.

Examination of Lot, a Negro man belonging to Mr. Forrester.

I knew Jesse; he met me last Sunday week (16th June) at the corner of Boundary Street, as I was coming into town; he said, he was going to get a horse to go into the country. From what my master had told me the Thursday before, I distrusted his errand, and gave him a caution. When, as I was going down into town towards Mr. Hibben's ferry ship, and conversing with him, he said, you shall see tonight, when I come down, what I am going up for, and, if my own father does not assist, I will cut off his head. He said, he was going as far as Goose Creek Bridge, and would get a horse if it cost him nine dollars. The

---

*"B," "C" are extracts of testimony of several witnesses in the trial of Denmark Vesey.—Ibid.

church bells were then ringing, and at half past eleven o'clock, same day, I saw him at Mr. Howard's, and afterwards understood from Sally, that he had set off for the country, and had been brought back by the patrols.

(C) *Examination of Frank, a Negro man belonging to Mrs. Ferguson.*

I know Denmark Vesey, and have been to his house; I have heard him say that the Negro's situation was so bad he did not know how they could endure it; and was astonished they did not rise and fight for themselves, and he advised me to join, and rise. He said, he was going about to see different people, and mentioned the names of Ned Bennett and Peter Poyas, as concerned with him; that he had spoken to Ned and Peter on this subject, and that they were to go about and tell the blacks, that they were free, and must rise and fight for themselves; that they would take the magazines and guard houses, and the city, and be free; that he was going to send into the country to inform the people there, too; he said he wanted me to join them. I said I could not answer. He said if I would not go into the country for him he could get others; he said himself, Ned Bennett, Peter Poyas and Monday Gell were the principal men, and himself the head man. He said they were the principal men to go about and inform the people, and fix them, etc.; that one party would land on South Bay, one about Wappoo and about the farms; that the party which was to land on South Bay was to take the guard house and get arms, and then they would be able to go on; that the attack was to commence about twelve o'clock at night; that great numbers would come from all about, and it must succeed, as so many were engaged in it; that they would kill all the whites; that they would leave their masters' houses, and assemble near the lines, march down and meet the party which would land on South Bay; that he was going to send a man into the country on a horse, to bring down the country people, and that he would pay for the horse. He gave two dollars to Jesse to get the horse on Saturday week last (15th June), about one o'clock in the day, and myself and witness (No. 8), also put in 25 cents apiece, and he told Jesse if he could not go he must send someone else. I have seen Ned Bennett at Vesey's. I, one night, met at Vesey's a great number of men, and as they came in, they each handed him some money. Vesey said there was a little man, named Jack, who could not be killed, and who would furnish them with arms; he had a charm and would lead them; that Charles Drayton had promised to be engaged with them. Vesey said the Negroes were living such an abominable life they ought to rise. I said I was living well. He said, though I was, others were not, and that it was such fools as I that were in their way and would not help them, and that, after all things were well, he would mark me. He said he did not go with Creighton to Africa because he had not a will, he wanted to stay and see what he could do for his fellow creatures. I met Ned Monday, and others, at Denmark Vesey's, where they were talking about this business.

The first time I spoke with Monday Gell it was one night at Denmark Vesey's house, where I heard Vesey tell Monday that he must send some one into the country to bring the people down. Monday said he had sent up Jack, and told him to tell the people to come down and join in the fight against the whites; and also to ascertain and inform him how many people he could get. A few days after, I met Vesey, Monday and Jack in the streets, under Mr. Duncan's trees, at night, where Jack stated he had been into the country, round by Goose Creek and Dorchester; that he had spoken to 6,600 persons, who had agreed to join. Monday said to Vesey, that if Jack had so many men, they had better wait no longer, but begin the business at once, and others would join. The first time I saw Monday at Vesey's, he was going away early, when Vesey asked him to stay, to which Monday replied, he expected that night a meeting at his house to fix upon and mature the plan, etc., and that he could stay no longer. I afterwards conversed with Monday in his shop, when he asked me if I had heard that Bennett's and Poyas' people were taken up, that it was a great pity. He said he had joined the business. I told him to take care he was not taken up. Whenever I talked with Vesey he always spoke of Monday Gell as being his principal and active man in this business.

(H) *Confession of Jesse, the slave of Thomas Blackwood, Esqr.; furnished to the Court by the Rev. Dr. D. Hall.*

I was invited to Denmark Vesey's house, and when I went, I found several men met together, among whom was Ned Bennett, Peter Poyas, and others, whom I did not know. Denmark opened the meeting by saying he had an important secret to communicate to us, which we must not disclose to any one, and if we did, we should be put to instant death. He said, we were deprived of our rights and privileges by the white people, and that our church was shut up, so that we could not use it, and that it was high time for us to seek for our rights, and that we were fully able to conquer the whites, if we were only unanimous and courageous, as the St. Domingo people were. He then proceeded to explain his plan by saying that they intended to make the attack by setting the governor's mills on fire, and also some houses near the water, and as soon as the bells began to ring for fire, that they should kill every man as he came out of his door, and that the servants in the yards should do it, and that it should be done with axes and clubs, and afterwards they should murder the women and children, for he said God had so commanded it in the Scriptures. At another meeting at Denmark's, Ned Bennett and Peter Poyas and several others were present in conversation; some said they thought it was cruel to kill the ministers, and the women and children, but Denmark Vesey said he thought it was for our safety not to spare one white skin alive, for this was the plan they pursued in St. Domingo. He then said to me, Jesse, I want you to go into the country to enlist as many of the Negroes as possible, to be in readiness to come down to assist us. I told him I had no horse and no money to hire one; he then took out two dollars and gave them to me to hire a horse, and told me to enlist as many as possible. I got the horse the next Sabbath, and started, but the guard was so strict I could not pass them without being taken up; so I returned and told Denmark, at which he expressed his sorrow, and said the business was urgent, for they wanted the country people to be armed, that they might attack the forts at the same time, and also to take every ship and vessel in the harbor, and to put every man to death, except the captains. For, said he, it will not be safe to stay in Charleston, for as soon as they had got all the money out of the banks, and the goods out of the stores on board, they intended to sail for St. Domingo; for he had a promise that they would receive and protect them. This Jesse asserted to me, was the truth, whilst the tears were running down his cheeks, and he appeared truly penitent; and I have reason to hope that he obtained pardon from God through the merits of Christ, and was prepared to meet his fate with confidence, and that he was accepted of God. At four o'clock on the morning of the execution I visited all the prisoners condemned, and found Jesse at prayers. He told me, his mind was placid and calm; he then assured me that what he had told me was the truth, and that he was prepared to meet his God.

(K) *Confession of Monday Gell.*

I come out as a man who knows he is about to die—sometime after Christmas, Vesey passed my door; he called in and said to me that he was trying to gather the blacks to try and see if anything could be done to overcome the whites; he asked me to join; I asked him his plan and his numbers; he said he had Peter Poyas, Ned Bennett and Jack Purcell; he asked me to join; I said no; he went up Wentworth Street, Frank Ferguson

met me, and said he had four plantations of people whom he was
to go for on Saturday, 15th June. How, said I, will you bring
them down; he said through the woods; he asked me if I was
going towards Vesey's to ask Vesey to be at home that evening,
and he would be there to tell him his success. I asked Jack
Purcell to carry this message and he said he would; that same
evening at my house I met Vesey's mulatto boy; he told me Vesey
wished to see me; I went with him; when I went into Vesey's I
met Ned Bennett, Peter Poyas and Frank Ferguson, and Adam
and Gullah Jack; they were consulting about the plan; Frank
told Vesey on Saturday 15th, he would go and bring down the
people and lodge them near town in the woods; the plan was to
arm themselves by breaking open the store with arms. I then
told Vesey I would join them; after some time I told them I had
some business of my own and asked them to excuse me; I went
away, and only then was I ever there. One evening Perault
Strohecker and Bacchus Hammett brought to my shop a keg,
and asked me to let it stay there till they sent for it; I said yes,
but did not know the contents; the next evening Gullah Jack
came and took away the keg; this was before the 16th June;
since I have been in prison I learnt that the keg contained powder.

Pharo Thompson is concerned, and he told me a day or two
after Ned and Peter were taken up, if he could get a fifty dollar
bill, he would run away; about two Sundays before I was brought
here, he asked me, in Archdale street, when shall we be like those
white people in the church, and took me into a stable in said street,
and told me he told his master, who had asked him, that he had
nothing to do in this affair, which was a lie. William Colcock
came to my shop once and said a brother told him that five hun-
dren men were making up for the same purpose. Frank said he
was to send to Hell-Hole Swamp to get men.

Perault Strohecker is engaged; he used to go of a Sunday on
horse back up the road to a man he knows on the same errand.
One Sunday he asked me to go with him; I went and Smart
Anderson; we went to a small house a little way from the road
after you turn into the ship yard road, on its left hand; they too
went into the stable with an old man that lived there; I remained
in the yard; they remained in the stable about half an hour; as
soon as they came out, I and Perault started to town to go to
church, and left Smart there; I was told by Denbow Martin, who
has a wife in Mr. Smith's house, that Stephen Smith belonged
to some of the gang.

Saby Gaillard is concerned; he met me on the bay, before the
16th of June and gave me a piece of paper from his pocket; this
paper was about the battle that Boyer had in St. Domingo; in

a day or two he called on me and asked if I had read it, and said if he had as many men he would do the same too, as he could whip ten white men himself; he frequently came to me to speak about this matter, and at last I had to insult him out of the shop; he and Paris Ball was often together. A week before I was taken up, Paris told me that my name was called.

Billy Palmer and Vesey were constantly together; there was once in my shop a long talk between them about this same matter; I begged them to stop it; Vesey told him to try to get as many as he could; he said he would.

John Vincent told me that Edward Johnson, a free man, had said, as he was a free man he would have nothing to do with slaves, but the night they began he would join them.

I told Charles Drayton what uproar there was about this business, and since we have been here we have talked together.

Albert Inglis came to me and asked if I knew anything about it; I said yes. He asked me if I had joined; I said yes; he said he was one also; he said Adam, a free man, wanted to see me; I went with him one night; Adam asked me how many men had joined; I told him what Frank Ferguson had said; he asked me if I believed it; I said yes; he said if he could only find men behind him he would go before. Previous to the 16th, Albert said to me, quit the business; I told him I was too far into it, so I must stick to it.

I never wrote to St. Domingo* or anywhere else on this subject, nor kept a list or books, nor saw any such things, but heard that Paul's William had a list nor did I hear anything about arms being in possession of the blacks. I don't know that Tom Russel made pikes, nor that Gullah Jack had any of them.

Lewis Remoussin called at my shop and asked me to call at his house, he had something to tell me, but I did not go; Jack Glen told me he was engaged.

I met Scipio Sims one Sunday coming from the country, who said he had been near the Savannah, to Mr. Middleton's place; I heard afterwards that his errand was on this business.

I know John, the cooper, who said he was engaged, too, in this business.

William Garner said he was engaged in it and had got twelve or thirteen draymen to join.

Sandy Vesey told me he belonged to it, too.

*Perault unhesitatingly stated to Monday's face, that he had written two letters to St. Domingo, and that he (Perault) had gone to Vanderhorst's wharf with him, in April or May last, to give them in charge of a black cook on board of a schooner bound to that island. After Monday was so charged, he confessed that the fact was so, and that he had been guilty of such an act.

At Vesey's house, Frank told Gullah Jack to put one ball and three buck shot in each cartridge.

Mungo Harth acknowledged to me that he had joined, and Peter Poyas told me so, too; he, Mungo, told me so several times; Mungo said he was to have his master's horse on the night of the 16th.

Lot Forrester told me frequently that he was one of the company, and I know that he had joined in the business myself. Isaac Harth told me once that he had joined; he knew I was in the business.

Morris Brown knew nothing of it, and we agreed not to let him, Harry Drayton or Charles Corr know anything about it. . . . . told me in my store that he was to get some powder from his master and give it to Peter Poyas; he seemed to have been a long time engaged in it, and to know a great deal. Joe Jore acknowledged to me once or twice that he had joined; he said he knew some of the Frenchmen concerned; he knew I was in it.

We present in the following pages details of the punishment of the leaders in Vesey's attempted insurrection—certainly documentary evidence of "The Slaves' Fight for Physical Freedom."[1]

---

[1] Taken from Yates Snowden's *Status of the Negro in South Carolina, 1822-1823.*

CLASS No. 1

Comprises those prisoners who were found guilty and executed.

Prisoners' Names	Owners' Names	Time of Commit.	How Disposed of
Peter	James Poyas	June 18	
Ned	Gov. T. Bennett	June 18	Hanged Tuesday, July 2,
Rolla	Gov. T. Bennett	June 18	1822, on Blake's lands,
Batteau	Gov. T. Bennett	June 18	near Charleston
Denmark Vesey	A free black man	June 22	
Jessy	Thos. Blackwood	June 23	
			Hanged on the lines near
John	Elias Horry	July 5	Charleston, Friday,
Gullah Jack	Paul Pritchard	July 5	July 12
Mungo	Wm. Harth	June 21	
Lot	...... Forrester	June 27	
Joe	P. L. Jore	July 6	
Julius	Thos. Forrest	July 8	
Tom	Mrs. Russell	July 10	
Smart	Robt. Anderson	July 10	
John	John Robertson	July 11	
Robert	John Robertson	July 11	
Adam	John Robertson	July 11	
Polydore	Mrs. Faber	July 11	Hanged on the lines near
Bacchus	Benj. Hammet	July 11	Charleston, Friday,
Dick	Wm. Sims	July 13	July 26
Pharaoh	...... Thompson	July 13	
Jemmy	Mrs. Clement	July 18	
Mauidore	Mordecai Cohen	July 19	
Dean	.... Mitchell	July 19	
Jack	Mrs. Purcell	July 12	
Bellisle	Est. of Jos. Yates	July 18	
Naphur	Est. of Jos. Yates	July 18	
Adam	Est. of Jos. Yates	July 18	
Jacob	John S. Glen	July 16	
Charles	John Billings	July 18	
Jack	N. McNeill	July 22	Hanged on the lines near
Caesar	Miss Smith	July 22	Charleston, Tuesday,
Jacob Stagg	Jacob Lankester	July 23	July 30
Tom	Wm. M. Scott	July 24	Hanged on the lines near
William	Mrs. Garner	Aug. 2	Charleston, Friday, Aug. 9

CLASS No. 2

Comprises those prisoners who were found guilty and sentenced to death, but recommended to the mercy of the executives by the Court of Magistrates and Freeholders.

They have been respited to the 25th day of October, 1822, with a view of the commutation of their punishment to banishment beyond the limits of the United States.

Prisoners' Names	Owners' Names	Time of Commit.	How Disposed of
Louis	...... Cromwell	July 12	Respited until October 25th; and now confined in the work house of Charleston
Seymour	...... Kunhardt	July 12	
Saby Gaillard	A free black man	July 13	
Isaac	Wm. Harth	July 13	
Paris	Mrs. Ball	July 15	
Peter	Mrs. Cooper	July 15	
Dublin	C. G. Morris	July 18	
George	...... Bampfield	July 18	
Sandy	Jacob Schnell	July 19	

CLASS No. 3

Comprises those prisoners who were found guilty and sentenced to death, but since respited by the executive, until the 25th of Oct. with a view to the commutation of their punishment, to banishment beyond the limits of the United States.

Prisoners' Names	Owners' Names	Time of Commit.	How Disposed of
William	Job Palmer	July 18	Respited until October 25th, and now in the work house
John Vincent	D. Cruckshanks	July 23	
Billy Robinson	P. Robinson	July 23	

CLASS No. 4

Comprises those prisoners who were found guilty and sentenced to be transported beyond the limits of the United States by their masters, under the direction of the city council.

Prisoners' Names	Owners' Names	Time of Commit.	How Disposed of
William	John Paul	May 31	Confined in the work house
Edwin	John Paul	June 24	
Monday	John Gell	June 27	Confined in the work house and sentenced to death, commuted to banishment out of U. S.
Charles	Hon. J. Drayton	July 2	
Harry	Davis Haig	July 5	
Frank	Mrs. Ferguson	June 27	
George	.... Theus	July 6	
Perault	.... Strohecker	July 10	
Billy	S. Bulkley	July 10	
John	Enslow	July 13	
Scipio	Wm. Sims	July 13	
Agrippa	Mrs. Perry	July 19	
Nero	Davis Haig	July 23	Confined in the work house
Sam. Bainsill	.... Bainstill	July 23	
Dembo	J. N. Martin	July 25	
Adam Bellamy	J. H. Merritt	Aug. 3	
Jack	Wm. Cattell	Aug. 5	
George	.... Evans	Aug. 5	
Harry	.... Butler	Aug. 5	
George	Sam. Parker	Aug. 5	
Pompey	Richd. Lord	Aug. 5	

Class No. 5

Comprises those who were found guilty and sentenced to be transported beyond the limits of the State of South Carolina.

Prisoner's Name	Owner's Name	Time of Commit.	How Disposed of
Prince Graham	A free black man	July 21	Sentenced to be imprisoned one month in the work house, and then transported beyond the limits of the state

This man will go out of the United States at his own request, under the direction of the city council.

Class No. 6

Comprises those prisoners who were acquitted by the court, their guilt not being fully proven. The court, however, has suggested to their owners, the propriety of transporting them beyond the limits of the United States.

Prisoners' Names	Owners' Names	Time of Commit.	How Disposed of
Buonaparte	Francis Mulligan	July 11	Acquitted by court; master desired to transport, and now in the work house at Charleston
Abraham	Dr. Poyas	June 22	
Butcher	Jas. L. Gibbes	July 11	
John	Mr. Taylor	July 13	
Prince	Miss Righton	July 19	
Quash Harleston	A free black man	July 29	By arrangement with council, gone out of the United States
Harry Purse	Wm. Purse	Not arrested	Arranged with owner to be transported
Panza	.... Mitchell		
Liverpool	Mrs. Hunt		

Class No. 7

Comprises those prisoners who were acquitted by the Court of Magistrates and Freeholders—and discharged.

Prisoners' Names	Owners' Names	Time of Commit.	How Disposed of
Amherst	Mrs. Lining	June 18	
Mungo	James Poyas	June 18	
Stephen	Tho. R. Smith	June 18	
Matthias	Gov. T. Bennett	June 18	
Jeffrey Grant	A free black man	June 20	
Brand	John Lucas	June 20	
Richard	John Lucas	June 17	
John	John Lucas	June 17	
Rob. Hadden	A free col'd man	June 22	
Sam. Guifford	A free col'd man	June 22	
Pompey	John Bryan	June 28	
Adam	Mrs. Ferguson	June 27	
Harry	.... Harleston	....	
Peter	Mrs. Ward	July 10	Acquitted
Sandy	Francis Curtis	July 11	and discharged
Isaac	Paul Trapier	July 11	
Charles	Mrs. Shrubrick	July 11	
Cuffy	Charles Groves	July 11	
Pierre Louis	Mons. Chapeau	July 18	
Caesar	Mrs. Parker	July 19	
William	Mrs. Colcock	July 12	
Pompey	David Haig	June 23	
Friday	Mrs. Rout		
Philander Michau	A free col'd man	Aug. 3	
Edward Johnson	A free black man	Aug. 3	
Stephen Walker	.... Walker	Aug. 5	
James	.... Walker	Aug. 5	
Harry	J. Nell	Aug. 6	

CLASS No. 8

Comprises those prisoners who were discharged after their arrest by the Committee of Vigilance, the testimony against them not being sufficient to bring them to trial.

Prisoners' Names	Owners' Names	Time of Commit.	How Disposed of
Hercules	.... Clark	June 20	Discharged June 28
Jim	J. H. Ancrum	June 22	Discharged June 25
Sandy	P. Holmes	June 25	Discharged June 26
Lemon	.... Houston	June 23	Discharged June 25
Robt. Nesbitt	A free man	July 3	Discharged July 5
Patrick	Mrs. Datea	July 4	Discharged July 6
Thomas	S. Magwood	July 5	Discharged July 8
Charles	F. G. Deliesseline	July 8	Discharged July 10
William	.... Adger	July 10	Discharged July 20
Smart	Mrs. Ward	July 10	Discharged July 27
Mungo	Wm. Lowndes	July 11	Discharged July 20
Thomas	A. Lord	July 11	Discharged July 13
Bob	.... Hibben	July 13	Discharged July 27
Albert	Thos. Ingles	July 15	Discharged July 17
Jim	.... Happoldt	July 15	Discharged July 29
John	.... Gates	July 15	Discharged July 29
Charles	.... Hasell	July 15	Discharged July 29
James	.... Dowling	July 17	Discharged July 29
Price	.... Dowling	July 17	Discharged July 29
Billy	.... Fordham	July 20	Discharged July 25
Ben	.... Cammer	July 22	Discharged July 27
William	.... Cromwell	July 22	Discharged July 27
Stephen	.... Harper	July 26	Discharged July 27
Louis	John Gell	July 18	Discharged July 20
Pompey	John Bryan	Aug. 5	Discharged Aug. 5

RECAPITULATION

Number of prisoners executed.......................	35
Number of prisoners respited until the 25th October, 1822, with a view to the commutation of their punishment....	12
Number of prisoners sentenced to be transported by their owners under direction of the city council..........	21
Number of prisoners sentenced to be transported beyond the limits of the state...........................	1
Number of prisoners acquitted, propriety of transportation suggested to their owners, and those whose masters have agreed to transport without trial..................	9
Number of prisoners acquitted and discharged by the court	27
Number of prisoners acquitted and discharged by Committee of Vigilance................................	25

Whole number arrested......................... 131

Respectfully submitted by

Fred. Wesner, Tho. D. Condy, Tho. Napier, ⎱ Com. of
Samuel Burger, Edward P. Simons,   ⎰ Vigilance

July, 1822—Jack, a slave belonging to Paul Pritchard, commonly called Gullah Jack, was brought up, and sentence pronounced by L. H. KENNEDY, Presiding Magistrate.

JACK PRITCHARD—The court, after deliberately considering all the circumstances of your case, are perfectly satisfied of your guilt. In the prosecution of your wicked designs, you were not satisfied with resorting to natural and ordinary means, but endeavored to enlist on your behalf, all the powers of darkness, and employed, for that purpose, the most disgusting mummery and superstition. You represented yourself as invulnerable; that you could neither be taken nor destroyed, and that all who fought under your banners would be invincible. While such wretched expedients are calculated to inspire the confidence, or to alarm the fears of the ignorant and credulous, they excite no other emotion in the mind of the intelligent and enlightened, but contempt and disgust. Your boasted charms have not preserved yourself, and of course could not protect others. "Your altars and your gods have sunk together in the dust." The airy spectres, conjured by you, have been chased away by the superior light of truth, and you stand exposed, the miserable and deluded victim of offended justice. Your days are literally numbered. You will shortly be consigned to the cold and silent grave, and all the powers of darkness cannot rescue you from your approaching fate. Let me then, conjure you to devote the remnant of your miserable existence, in fleeing from the "wrath to come." This can only be done by a full disclosure of the truth. The court is willing to afford you all the aid in its power, and to permit any Minister of the Gospel whom you may select to have free access to you. To him you may unburden your guilty conscience. Neglect not the opportunity, for there is "no device nor art beyond the tomb," to which you must shortly be consigned.*

* * * * * *

In Re: Chapter III—"The Negro's Part in the Reconstruction."

Speech on the Enforcement of the Fourteenth Amendment

By R. C. DeLarge

Mr. Speaker: I had supposed that in the consideration of this matter of legislation for the South, party lines would not have been so distinctly drawn, but that we would have at least first endeavored to ascertain whether or not there was any necessity for the legislation, and then decide what kind of legislation would be best. I say I did not expect that party lines would be drawn so distinctly while considering a matter of such grave import.

I believe that if there was a single gentleman upon the floor of this house who, before the commencement of this debate, doubted that lawlessness, confusion, and anarchy existed in some portions of the South, he is at least cured of that doubt by this time. Gentlemen upon both sides of the house have in their speeches acknowledged, and, by the evidence produced, proven to my satisfaction, and, I believe, to the satisfaction of a majority of the members of this house, that such a state of affairs does exist in some portions of the southern states.

I am free to say that none can bring the charge to my door of ever having acted in a manner that would be termed illiberal. I am also free to say that I, like other gentlemen upon the floor of this house, have the honor of representing a district in which no case of outlawry has ever occurred. Since the time of reconstruction no outrage has been committed in my district; and I say frankly to you today that until within the last few months no one upon the face of God's earth could have convinced me

---

*The above is selected out of the many sentences passed on this occasion, with a view to give the reader a general idea of them.

that any secret organization existed in my state for the purpose of committing murder, arson, or other outrages upon the lives, liberty, and property of the people; and, sir, I sincerely deplore and lament the abundance of that evidence which so plainly proves the existence of such an organization today. Would to God, sir, that the fair fame of the state of my birth, and which I have the honor in part to represent, had not been marred by the wicked deeds of these outlaws, who shrink from no cruelty, who spare no sex nor station to carry out their devilish purposes.

But, sir, I cannot shut my eyes to facts; I cannot refuse to yield my faith to tales of horror so fully proven; and I am thoroughly convinced that it is necessary to do something to cure these awful wrongs. I am free to admit that neither the Republicans of my state nor the Democrats of that state can shake their garments and say that they have had no hand in bringing about this condition of affairs. Both parties are responsible for it. As a member of the Republican party I may state, while demanding legislation on behalf of all the citizens there, that both parties to a considerable extent are responsible for this condition of things. Sir, it is necessary that we should legislate upon this subject. The governor of my state has called upon the executive of this country for assistance and protection. He has stated distinctly in that call that he is unable to preserve the public peace in some districts of that state. That is something which we must all admit. That is not denied by the Democrats of South Carolina. Some of them doubtless rejoice in this, because they can throw the blame, as they think, upon the administration of the state, which is in the hands of their political foes. It is now the question, what is the cause which has brought about this condition of affairs. It is useless, except for the purpose of gaining partisan credit or fixing partisan odium, now to charge the blame here or there. But, sir, the naked facts stare us in the face, that this condition of affairs does exist, and that it is necessary for the strong arm of the law to interpose and protect the people in their lives, liberty, and property.

Just here allow me to make a suggestion. If the gentlemen on this side of the house propose to legislate for the benefit of the people of the South, I tell them, and say it fully conscious of the responsibility that rests upon me in saying it, that while legislation is necessary, yet unless they are ready to concede along with this legislation for the protection of the loyal people of the South some accompanying measure to go hand in hand with this and remove as far as in our power rests some of the evils that have brought about the existing condition of things, neither this legislation nor any other that you may pass from

now until the hour of doom will be of any benefit. I speak knowing what I say.

Mr. Speaker, when the governor of my state the other day
called in council the leading men of that state to consider the
condition of affairs there and to advise what measure would be
best for the protection of the people, whom did he call together?
The major portion of the men whom he convened were men resting under political disabilities imposed by the fourteenth amendment. In good faith I ask gentlemen on this side of the house,
and gentlemen on the other side, whether it is reasonable to
expect that these men should be interested, in any shape or
form, in using their influence and best endeavors for the preservation of the public peace, when they have nothing to look for
politically in the future? You say they should have the moral
and material interest of their state at heart, though even always
to be denied a participation in its honors. You may insist that
the true patriot seeks no personal ends in the acts of patriotism.
All this is true; but Mr. Speaker, men are but men everywhere,
and you ought not to expect of those whom you daily call by
opprobrious epithets, whom you daily remind of their political
sins, whom you persistently exclude from places of the smallest
trust in the government you have created, to be very earnest to
co-operate with you in the work of establishing and fortifying
governments set up in hostility to the whole tone of their prejudices, their convictions, and their sympathies. What ought to
be is one thing, what in the weakness and fallibility of human
nature will be is quite another thing. The statesman regards
the actual and acts upon it; the desirable, the possible, and even
the probable furnishes but poor basis for political action.

If I had time I would enumerate some of the causes which
have brought about the existing state of affairs. I am not here
to apologize for murderers; I am not here to defend any one who
has committed any act of impropriety or wrong. But, sir, it is
a fact—I do not give it as any or even the slightest excuse for
the Democrats of my state, who, by their influence secretly or
by joining in armed organization, have brought about this condition of affairs—it is a fact, unfortunately for us, that our party
has done some things which give color to the charge that it is
responsible to some degree for the evils which afflict us.

When I heard the gentleman from New York [Mr. Cox] on
Tuesday last hurl his shafts against the members of my race,
charging that through their ignorance they had brought about
these excesses, I thought he should have remembered that for
the ignorance of that portion of the people he and his party
associates are responsible, not those people themselves. While

there may have been extravagance and corruption resulting from the placing of improper men in official positions—and this is part of the cause of the existing state of things—these evils have been brought about by men identified with the race to which the gentleman from New York belongs, and not by our race.

Many men like himself, in order to get a better position in society or officially, came down among us, and, not knowing them, we placed them in position. If we, through ignorance, have placed them in position, have placed them in power, and they have deceived us, it is no fault of ours. In this connection I desire to have read a part of the remarks of the gentleman from New York on Tuesday last.

The clerk read as follows:

"South Carolina has been infested by the worst local government ever vouchsafed to a people. Ignorance, bribery, and corruption are common in her legislature. Bonds by the million are issued, the public debt increased, and nothing to show for it. The debt in 1860 was but $3,691,574. It was last year $11,429,-711; and this year no one knows whether it is twenty or thirty millions, nor how much is counterfeit or genuine! Her rulers contrived new burdens in order to plunder more. On a full valuation of real and personal property of $183,913,367 the people pay this year sixteen mills on the dollar as a state tax and four mills county tax.

"This is for 1870 and 1871, and amounts in all to $4,095,-047, to which $300,000 is to be added for poll tax. In other words, the value of the property is reduced from $489,000,000 before the war to $188,000,000, and the tax raised from $400,-000 to $4,250,000, or ten times as much. It is two and a half per cent, or a full valuation, and only chronic insecurity and disorder as the consideration! This is done by those who pay no taxes, who squander what is paid, who use the means to arm Negro militia and create a situation of terror, from which men rush into secret societies for defense of homes, mothers, sisters, wives, and children.

"Add to these grievances the intolerable exactions of the Federal government, not only in taxes, but in laws, and it should give us pause before we place that people at the mercy of an inferior race, a vindictive party, a court-martial, and a hostile president."

I desire to correct the statement made by the gentleman from New York, that the state tax of South Carolina for 1870 is only nine mills on the dollar, for 1871, seven mills, not as he states, sixteen mills. I have already alluded to the ignorance referred to in the gentleman's remarks. Before closing I desire to say that I hope the house will adopt the substitute of the gentleman from Ohio. I am prepared to vote for the substitute, while I am free to admit that I did not intend to vote for the bill as originally reported.*

* * * * * *

As illustrative of the ability and attainments of some of the Negro statesmen of the reconstruction in South Carolina, we present:

A Speech Delivered at Charleston, March 9, 1871
By A. J. Ransier*

Gentlemen: It affords me pleasure always to meet my friends, and when under existing circumstances the compliment of this serenade has been paid me, it is an additional evidence of the confidence reposed in me, not only as a public man, but as your immediate representative. This, gentlemen, is not the only occasion upon which you have indicated an approval of my humble efforts in the field of politics. I remember, in the dark days of 1864, you indicated your confidence when you placed upon me the responsibility of pioneering certain movements looking to results that have been in great part attained. When, in 1865, the first Republican convention was held in South Carolina, where colored men met and expressed, without molestation, their opinions as to their condition, you invited me through the delegation to represent at Washington their grievances. In 1868, when, under the reconstruction acts of Congress, South Carolina was called upon to frame her constitution and government agreeably to those acts, you tendered me a unanimous nomination as a member of that convention; and subsequently, in 1870, through your representatives, you gave me a unanimous nomination as a candidate for the office of lieutenant-governor of the state of South Carolina; and at a still later period you again tendered me a unanimous nomination for the position of congressman for this district, and those are compliments of which any public man may well be proud and for which I am thankful. Gentlemen, I have tried to do my duty, and if at any time I have failed, it was not because I did not care to succeed, or that I was indifferent to your interests. Gentlemen, though the Republican party, as an organization, has achieved glorious victories in the past, though the majority of us as a race have, through trying ordeals, made marked progress, we are called upon today to pass upon

---

*Note: The above address shows that some of the Negroes who represented South Carolina in the national congress were not totally ignorant and depraved as some would have the world believe.

questions in which the entire past and the future are intimately wrapped up and interwoven. Holding the position which I do, gentlemen, and coming amongst you after an absence of nearly four months, at a time, too, when the gravest questions in which is wrapped up the good name of the Republican party, and the interests of all as a people are being discussed, it would seem proper that I should say a word in addition to the acknowledgment of the compliment you kindly tendered me.

All over the country the belief obtains that the situation of affairs in our state is most deplorable. No longer can it be said that these reports are traceable to Democratic sources alone. Representations of this kind have been made by good, bad and indifferent Republicans as well as Democrats: by those who look at everything through a sort of mental magnifying glass, and by others who are actuated by a variety of motives by which the country has been to some extent deceived. Representations are made against our party in a spirit of recklessness which to me is perfectly astounding. That things are not in a satisfactory condition in this state is too true; there are many things of which just complaint might be made. That it is possible, and has been so ever since the Republican party has held the ascendancy in the state to get along with lower rates of taxation by a more judicious expenditure of the public funds, and that we might have selected better men to fill our most important offices, cannot be denied; but neither do exaggerated representations made by our opponents, nor reckless and injudicious public speeches made by Republicans against their own party and public men, help the situation. I am in favor of a most thorough investigation of the official conduct of any and every public officer in connection with the discharge of whose duties there is anything like well-grounded suspicion; and to this effect have I spoken time and again. Nor am I lukewarm on the subject of better government in South Carolina than that which seems to be bearing heavily on all classes and conditions of society today. Still, recognizing that which I believe to be true that such is the determined opposition to the Republican party and its doctrines by our opponents that no administration of our affairs, however honest, just and economical, would satisfy any considerable portion of the Democratic masses in the state of South Carolina, and satisfied that the principles and policy of the great Republican party to which I belong is best adapted for the promotion of good government to all classes of men, our party leaders should be judicious in dealing with the situation. A leading public journal thus forcibly says: "A political leader should not be disingenuous with his own party friends; indeed, he should not 'run amuck' against the administration he is impliedly supposed to support. If there are causes of weakness or occasions for correction and amendment, these should be administered in the frankness and confidence of private counsel, and not in the wide forum of public debate. This is not the place to expose one's own weakness or unroll the calendar of defects which may be better corrected in the confidence of the caucus." In the spirit of this suggestion, I would ask for an advised action on the part of the Republicans throughout the state. I would ask you to calmly consider the state of affairs as they are presented to us today, and if you cannot reach those who have brought this ruin upon us through the medium of the courts instituted by us as a party, and by the officials whose duty it is to prosecute those who violate the law, then let them be forever discarded from the party. And, again, when you are called upon in your primary meetings in your country and state nominating conventions, let each man act as if, by his individual vote, he could wipe out the odium resting upon our party, and help to remove the evils that afflict us at present. Let him feel, black or white, that the country holds him responsible for the shortcomings of his party, and that it demands of him the elevation to public positions of men who are above suspicion. Let each man feel that upon him individually rests the work of reform; let each man feel that he is responsible for every dollar of the public money fraudulently used; for every school house closed against his children; for every dollar of taxation in excess of the reasonable and legitimate expenses of the state; in short, let every man feel that society at large will hold him and the party accountable for every misdeed in the administration of government, and will credit him with every honest effort in the interest of the people, and in the interest of good government, whereby the community as a whole is best protected and the equal rights of all guaranteed and made safe. (Applause.) This, gentlemen, is the line of argument which I had hoped to present to you. It is not for us to deny those charges which may be proven to be true, while it is for us to deal in the confidence of a caucus, and by other judicious means, without giving the Democrats weapons with which to beat out our brains (cheers—a voice cried "Good enough"). For I say tonight, with the full knowledge of the fact that what I may say here tonight will go out to the country, and in view of my responsibilities to my immediate constituents and to society at large, and in view of my responsibilities as a member of Congress, I say that Republicanism is best calculated for the welfare of the Democrats as well as Republicans. It is the government of the people made by the people and for the people, and you dare not, as a Republican, trample on any right of a Democrat, or trifle with the important interest of the people, while at the same time it is your duty to prevent them from trampling upon any of yours. (Applause.) And the best way to effect this is to keep the power within the party. (Applause. A voice—"That's so.") We must not think that because the colored people are in the majority now that we are privileged to be indifferent to the interest of others. As a country we have prospered, we have multiplied our vast resources from Maine to California, while we have increased our industries, and added vastly to our capital, and peopled our cities and towns with tenfold their number; we have rescued within the last ten years an entire race from bondage; we have not only emancipated, but we have enfranchised and clothed this race with the habiliments of citizenship.

But we find ourselves today, as a race, passing through a crisis. The colored people in the United States, with all the grand achievements of the past ten years, are today passing through the crisis of their political history in this country. We present to the world a noble spectacle, a record unparalleled in the annals of any people similarly situated. No race has been subjected to such a scathing fire of criticism; no people have had such tremendous disadvantages to labor under. And I feel free to say, no race in a similar position could have acquitted themselves more creditably; but now, in this trying epoch of our history, we seem to forget much that we should remember, we must not trifle with our responsibilities and let slip our best opportunities to prove our fitness for government. We are charged as giving evidence in some localities of unfitness in this direction; it is for us in this crisis to deny as best we may those allegations against the colored man as a race as to their ability to manage the affairs of government. The country accepts in a great part the representations made by our opponents as to the situation of affairs in this state. It rests with you to remove every just cause of complaint, remembering that by every unworthy man you elevate to office, by every scoundrel you keep in office, you justify the public opinion in the country adverse to the well-being of the Republican party in this state, and to the fitness of the colored man for franchise. The tax-payers' convention was composed of gentlemen, most of whom, I believe, I am acquainted with. As to politics, it seems we must ever differ. Their representations are founded, however false, to a considerable extent, upon the bad management of the Republican party, and I believe that many Republicans in the state of South Carolina are giving their movements strength and aid, in the hope of accomplishing certain results. They will be deceived, of course. If any Republican thinks that in any possible contingency they as a class are going to support him for office, he will be most woefully deceived. They are not going to do it. I read the reply to the memorial of the "Tax-Payers' Convention," and when the committee of distinguished gentlemen reach the national capital and present their memorial, they will find that President Grant has already received Mr. Cardozo's paper, and already understands the situation, and will be able to make up a just judgment. I do not want any one to misunderstand me. That I believe there is a necessity for a correction of abuses in the state I have already stated. I have already said we could have done better; that I believe we have elected some men to position who are corrupt, and who hold offices now to the disgrace of the party and to the injury of the state. We cannot and must not repeat this thing. Everybody, perhaps, knows that I am colored, and I am very naturally proud when we do well; and when we do not, I could wish that I was not one of it. My hopes and aspirations are wrapped up with the race to which I belong. I want to see it live and prosper as I believe God intended that it should. And while the country may hold the colored people in South Carolina responsible for bad government, I want to say, in the name of that Republicanism to which I belong and which I represent, that the country would be justified in so doing by virtue of the fact that the colored people in South Carolina are in the majority—the white vote being 50,000 and the colored vote 80,000; therefore, the colored people would justly be held responsible for the affairs of the government; and, to that extent, they ought to feel the necessity of wiping out every stain and of removing every wrong from self-interest, if not from a sense of decency, from the love of good government.

But to return to the subject. There are those who have devoted their lives to the doctrine of civil and political equality, and have given their time and labor to the promotion of the colored men, who are anxiously watching us, and bid us do our duty; who would feel mortification and regret should we trifle with our vast responsibility as citizens. I believe that there is sufficient virtue and common sense, and pride of race, and love of country, in the breasts of the rank and the file of the colored people to secure to us an improved condition of affairs. Let each man in our primary meetings, and in our conventions, feel that his country's welfare, and his own political salvation depends upon his actions and vote; and as I have previously exhorted you, act as if by your individual vote you could effect the reform so much needed, so much desired. And now, gentlemen, in conclusion, let me thank you most heartily for this compliment. As long as I am in possession of my senses, I shall try to deserve your confidence and support, and to the extent of my ability to work for your interests and your welfare. And when, in the next campaign you are called upon, as you will be, to select men for our important offices, see to it that they are men whom you can trust, men who will not deceive nor disgrace you. As to myself, I shall go against any man, be he black or white, whose past conduct in or out of office does not give us the assurance of better government, cost me what it may. Again, gentlemen, I thank you for your more than kind and cordial welcome.

* * * * * *

In Re: Chapter IV—"The Negro's Long War Against Ignorance."

SOUTH CAROLINA NEGRO COMMON SCHOOLS*

South Carolina during the eighteenth century forbade the teaching of slaves to read and write and forbade free Negroes to do any teaching at all. During the Civil War large numbers of refugees congregated at Port Royal and on the sea islands and systematic teaching began. During the early efforts at reconstruction every effort was made to reduce the Negroes to slavery again and to stop their schools. Negro suffrage in South Carolina meant the first definite establishment of a public school system for Negroes and whites and is perhaps the greatest gift of the Negro to South Carolina. The constitution of 1868 provided for free schools regardless of race or color. But schools were not actually opened until 1872 and then were partially closed again in the political revolution of 1876. By the laws of 1877 the control of the schools was placed in the hands of local elective officials and thus the system has continued until our day.

The Negroes have long formed a majority of the population of South Carolina, although that majority has been dwindling. In 1900, for instance, there were 557,807 whites and 782,321 Negroes. By 1920, there were 818,538 white, and 864,719 Negroes. The number of Negroes enrolled in the public schools were as follows:

1870	8,263
1880	72,853
1890	116,535
1900	157,976
1910	151,728
1920	235,569
1925	228,516

*This is a reprint of article published in the December (1927) issue of *The Crisis*. Consent of publishers.

The cost of the Negro schools was $203,033 in 1900 and in 1925, a quarter of a century later, this had increased to $1,800,-150. On the other hand, the cost of the white schools was $693,-807 in 1900 and in 1925 was $11,561,819. *In other words, South Carolina spent over three times as much on her white schools as on her Negro schools at the beginning of the century and at the end of the first quarter of the century, she was spending over six times as much.* And during all this time there were more Negroes to be educated than whites. All this is the deliberate action of the whites, as W. K. Tate, state supervisor of elementary rural schools said in 1912:

"The education of the Negro in South Carolina is in the hands of the white race. The white trustees apportion the funds, select the teachers and receive the reports. The county superintendent has the supervision of these schools in his hands. We have expended this year $349,834.60 in the support of Negro schools. I never visit one of these schools without feeling that we are wasting a large part of this money and are neglecting a great opportunity. The Negro school houses are miserable beyond all description. They are usually without comfort, equipment, proper lighting, or sanitation. Nearly all the Negroes of school age in the district are crowded into these miserable structures during the short term which the school runs. Most of the teachers are absolutely untrained and have been given certificates by the county board not because they have passed the examination, but because it is necessary to have some kind of a Negro teacher."

So wretched was the condition of South Carolina Negro schools that in the last ten years various outside philanthropic bodies have tried to help. The General Education Board has paid for a white state agent for colored schools. The Rosenwald fund has built school houses, aided by contributions from the colored people, white people and the educational authorities. The Jeanes fund has paid for teachers. These contributions have varied from $82,694 in 1922 to $92,514 in 1925. This has had comparatively little effect upon the state. The state agent for colored schools says in 1925: "The organization and development of these schools in any community depend absolutely upon the education and standard of the white folk." The local (white) board of trustees in each district uses in its discretion whatever school funds are expended for colored schools. Thus, the total amount of state aid for various counties was in 1922, $1,851,715. Of this every cent went to white schools except $15,000. In the case of school houses outside aid brought better results: From July 1, 1920 to June 30, 1922, they erected 89 school houses at a cost of $424,874. Notwithstanding this, in the latter year the state agent says: "Only about 10 per cent of the colored school houses in the state are respectable." Other facts for 1922 are as follows:

	Whites	Negroes
Teachers' salaries	$5,584,159	$818,248
Schools:		
Town	332	189
County	1954	2304
Enrollment	235,535	243,774
Average attendance	171,742	174,143
Average length of session:		
Town	172	127
County	134	74
Expense per capita of enrollment	$36.10	$4.17
Pupils per teacher	24	49

It is a little difficult to get the latest reports of South Carolina schools, so that conditions today must be illustrated mainly by figures from the year 1924-25:

1925

	Whites	Negroes
Schools	2181	2413
Teachers	7889	3677
Average salary	$885	$261
Total salaries	$6,982,989	$963,155
Furniture and apparatus	$319,948	$20,146
Fuel and incidentals	$1,012,492	$43,867
Average length of session	159	97
Per capita cost according to enrollment	$48.39	$6.13
Enrolled pupils to each teacher	30	62
Value school houses	$20,428,663	$2,268,287
Value of houses and grounds	$23,535,823	$2,661,499
Value of school furniture and apparatus	$1,988,821	$282,889
Cost of transportation	$173,805	$196
Grounds, repairs, buildings and rents	$2,156,296	$372,564
Total expenses	$11,561,849	$1,400,150

The state agent says that 90 per cent of the schools in 1924-5 "are still being accommodated and are attempted to be taught under very undesirable conditions."

The legislature which adjourned in April, 1927, appropriated $3,250,000 instead of the $3,512,000 which the superintendent of education asked. There was also a deficit of $473,000 in 1926. This means that the colored schools will undoubtedly suffer most.

There is only one bright spot in the South Carolina school situation and that is the building of the Rosenwald school houses.

There have been completed to date (November, 1927) in South Carolina, 381 Negro school houses paid for as follows:

Negro contributions	$ 418,356
White contributions	177,269
From public school funds	1,294,157
Rosenwald fund	357,800
Total	$2,247,582

These school houses house 57,105 pupils or 34 per cent of the rural Negro school population.

Excellent as this showing is and great as is the debt of South Carolina and the Negro to Julius Rosenwald, it has two unfortunate features.

First, nothing could be more astonishing than to see a proud southern commonwealth, which in the past protested loudly against the "interference" of philanthropists with its institutions, now on its knees before the organized philanthropy of the North for contributions toward the support of its public school system; and especially that part of the system which is chiefly necessary to increase the efficiency of labor and decrease the waste of crime, sickness and poverty. Second, we must not forget the injustice of the double taxation forced on Negroes to support their schools. The brunt of public taxation on real property, land and business falls heavily and chiefly, in the last analysis, on the black laborers. Yet from these school funds the whites get their school houses built for them while the Negro in his poverty must submit to $400,000 additional taxation to get his school houses. This may teach sacrifice but it is terribly unjust.

This gives a general picture of the Negro schools. To this may be added a word on local conditions.

Charleston is the metropolis of the state. It had in 1920, 35,585 whites and 32,326 Negroes in the city, while in the county, including the city, there were 44,214 whites and 64,236 Negroes. Of this population 14,178 are reported to be illiterate or 5,000 more than in any other county of the state; and, of course, the real facts are far in excess of this report. Charleston Negroes have always had an intelligent, striving group of educated leaders. The free Negroes supported their own schools for ten years, beginning in 1744 until the state law stopped them. In 1822, they attempted under Denmark Vesey, one of the most carefully planned insurrections against slavery made in the United States. On the other hand, they have received from their white fellow citizens a minimum of encouragement. The present conditions of their schools can be seen from the following figures:

	Whites	Negroes
Number of teachers	268	182
Total teachers' salaries	$341,660	$101,329
Average salary	$1,274	$556
Pupils to teacher and enrollment	31	60
Enrollment	8,416	10,919
Average attendance	6,845	8,005
Per cent of enrollment and attendance	81.3	73.3
Value school houses	$1,392,250	$423,335
Value of houses and grounds	$1,606,300	$483,475
Value of school furniture, etc	$78,450	$26,187
Furniture and apparatus	$23,421	$6,045
Fuel and incidentals	$88,103	$20,035
Average length session, days	179	110
Per capita, expense, attendance and enrollment	$99.77	$18.01
Libraries	$496	$127
Transportation	$28,301	....
Grounds, repairs	$304,474	$69,143
Total expense	$839,610	$196,681

In Charleston there are four schools. In the Simmonton School, which is in a low street which is easily flooded when it rains, there are five grades with 1,150 pupils; 27 teachers who receive from $50 to $62.50 a month. The term is nine months. The Buist school is in a good location and has five grades and an enrollment of 905 with 14 teachers. There are double sessions; that is, two sessions a day for the first and second grades. The principal personally has furnished the piano which is used in the school. The Shaw school is a frame building heated by stoves and has five grades and an enrollment of 890; there are 18 teachers for a nine-month school. The Burke Industrial School was built in 1910 near a dumping ground. It has from the fifth to eleventh grade and an enrollment of nearly 1,000 under 24 teachers. This is supposed to be the high school, but the real high school for the city is a private school, Avery institute.

The plight of Avery institute illustrates the school methods of South Carolina. It was established by the American Missionary Association and the association still pays about one-third of its $16,000 annual budget. Avery has 500 pupils of whom 200 are in high school and it employs eleven teachers. It has for years done all of the normal work and practically all of the high school work for the city. Nearly all the teachers in the city schools are graduates of Avery, yet the city, the county and the state have refused any aid to the school.

For the year 1926-27 Charleston made the following appropriations for its white and Negro schools:

	White	Colored
Teachers, county	$110,612	$38,073
city	284,610	71,285
Fuel and incidentals, county	26,149	15,307
city	63,868	29,226
Grounds and buildings, county	207,171	3,313
city	32,374	4,141

In Columbia there is a nine-months' term and four schools. The Booker T. Washington school has eleven grades and two buildings. The buildings were put on land which was cheap but has proved expensive because it had to be buttressed. There is an enrollment of 1,286 pupils under 28 teachers. The salaries range from $60 to $90 a month. Five of the grades have double sessions and about 100 beginners were turned away at the opening of school. The old Howard school* is a very old wooden building across from the jail and in a bad situation. It has 840 pupils in seven grades under sixteen teachers. The salaries are from $55 to $80 a month and there are double sessions in first grade. The new Howard school is in a new brick building near a railroad on a dumping ground. It has 415 pupils in seven grades, under 12 teachers. There are double sessions in the first grade.

The salaries for white teachers in the grade schools begin at $900 and reach $1,400. In the high schools the salaries begin with $1,000 and go to $2,000. In the Negro graded schools the salaries range from $550 to $800 and in the high school from $600 to $850.

The white schools have ample space for their children with 40 or fewer pupils to a teacher in a classroom. But the superintendent says:

"The same contention can not be made for the Negro schools. Up to September, 1924, we have been compelled to take care of from 200 to 300 more Negro pupils than the two school buildings were equipped to accommodate. At that time we opened the third building, a new one, equipped to accommodate 450 pupils. We had such an inrush of new pupils that within two weeks after the opening of school, we had as many overcrowded rooms as ever. We are still compelled to run double daily sessions of pupils in several grades at two of the schools. One

---

*This school has now (1928) been replaced by a large brick building; formerly, in part, a white school. It is modern. A. H. G.

teacher in these cases meets two groups of pupils each day. The fourth year has been added to the Negro high school, and practically the entire third year class remained to enter the fourth year.

"It is but justice to say that our Negro teachers, almost without exception, have been patient, faithful and loyal throughout these years of crowded conditions."

This is the result of outrageous discrimination on the part of the city in the use of public taxes. By bond issues in 1922-25 they raised $375,000, which with other items made a total building fund of $438,645. Of this the Negroes, forming 47 per cent of the county population, received only $73,304, or 16 per cent.

There are similar conditions in Greenville, where two of the three schools are in old frame buildings. The third school is a new brick school, but in a poor situation. "There are no colored men in this school system as the superintendent is unfavorable to them." He defers entirely to the reactionary poor whites. A private school, housed in dilapidated frame buildings, does most of the high school work. In Orangeburg, the public school is terribly overcrowded, with as many as 100 in some classes and three in a seat. Nine miles from Orangeburg is a new Rosenwald school with teachers' home. Here conditions are much better, but the state pays for only six months' school, and gives the teachers from $50 to $55 a month, except the principal who receives a salary from the Smith-Hughes fund. In Sumter, there is one old and one new school. Both have double sessions through the fifth grades and are very much crowded. In many counties for 1927 the board of education has cut the Negro schools from five to three months, even when paying salaries as little as $42.50 a month. In Bennettsville, in 1926, we find a colored minister, praying to white people for a decent school building because visitors "look with laughter and indignation at what we call our school." And finally, perhaps this picture will do for rural South Carolina. It is written from Seabrook in Beaufort county in March, 1927:

"The school children are poorly provided for, having to walk long distances to school, an average of two to four miles a day. School term six months, November to May. The average persons 18 to 45 do not know the alphabet. School houses small, overcrowded. A number of children don't get any lessons for two or three days. Some parents get disheartened and keep their children away from school."

In Re: Chapter VII—"The Negro Farmer in South Carolina."

NOTE 1:

SCIENTIFIC FARMING BY NEGROES

Reports of Results of Experiment Station in Sumter County, South Carolina, Conducted by R. W. Westberry, County Demonstrator in Charge of Work Among Negro Farmers.*

Many different varieties of cotton and corn were planted on a farm at Horatio, S. C., to determine which would make the best yield. The several plots were planted in one field so as to give each about the same grade of land.

All of the cotton plots were planted the same time with the same amount and kind of fertilizers, and worked with the same implements and the same way. The plots were all planted April 10. The soil was dark gray. The first picking was August 21, the second was September 28, third was November 15. The different varieties were as follows: The Money-maker produced 1,800 pounds of seed cotton to the acre; the Toole produced 1,600 pounds of seed cotton to the acre; the Hites prolific produced 1,400 pounds of seed cotton to the acre; Cook's big boll, 1,500 pounds of seed cotton to the acre; Dillon wilt resistant, 1,350 pounds of seed cotton to the acre; the Bates, 1,750 pounds of seed cotton to the acre; Latents improved, 1,550 pounds of seed cotton to the acre; Peterkins, 1,400 pounds of seed cotton to the acre; Russell big boll, 1,600 pounds of seed cotton to the acre; Morse's improved, 1,525 pounds of seed cotton to the acre; "Bank Account," 1,200 pounds of seed cotton to the acre.

Among the different varieties of cotton mentioned, the Bates is the most favored, the yield of lint was 41 per cent. The Money-maker made the largest amount of seed cotton, but the lint was only 34 per cent. The Russell big boll makes the finest lint of any of the short staple cotton. The Columbia long staple was planted near the experiment station, June 1, after oats; a little more than two acres were planted, and the amount of seed cotton gathered from the same was 1,524 pounds, lint cotton 510 pounds. The amount paid for the lint was $73.50. The seed is being sold for $1.50 per bushel, which will amount to about $45.00, making a total of $118.50 for one bale of long staple cotton and seed. It would be a good idea if the farmers plant a portion of their farms with the good varieties of long staple cotton. There are factories in South Carolina that use no other

---

*Serves here as example of work being done in this state by farm demonstration agents.

cotton but the long staple, and whenever South Carolina farmers cannot supply the demands, it is ordered from other places.

Cotton coming in from foreign markets is very likely to bring pests into the state that would be very injurious to our cotton crops, such as the boll weevil and diseases, that have been kept out of the state thus far.

The names of the different varieties of corn were: Dr. Simms, Marlboro prolific, Strawberry, Hudson, Aldrich perfection, Sanders Improved, Jerry Moore, and Charlie Sanders. The number of bushels made per acre by each were as follows:

Dr. Simms	45
Marlborough Prolific	$43\frac{1}{2}$
Strawberry	49
Hudson	49
Aldrich Perfection	$40\frac{1}{2}$
Sanders Improved	$49\frac{1}{2}$
Charlie Sanders	$38\frac{1}{2}$
Jerry Moore	70

The Hudson variety is not a good seed for this section of the state, the weevils were in abundance on this plot. It is an early field variety, having matured nearly two weeks earlier than the other varieties. The Jerry Moore variety proved to be much heavier than the others, while Dr. Simms was more prolific.

Charlie Sanders variety has a great deal of nutrition, it will not decay or rot as easy as the other varieties, and the corn weevils do not affect it as much. The experiment station will be planted in the same plot this year with reference to the use of fertilizer.

NOTE 2.

THE FARMER'S OPPORTUNITY

*From an address before the Colored Business League of South Carolina, July 4, 1912**

Mr. President, Ladies and Fellow Farmers:

This opportunity which I now have to meet the farmers from all parts of the state is to me a great deal of pleasure.

The farmers have a great opportunity for permanent progress. No class of people does the world depend on as much as that of the farmers. Much responsibility rests upon their shoulders. They feed and clothe the world. There are many things a farmer must do to make the best success on the farm. The one thing that stands head and shoulders above them all is love for

---

*Address by R. W. Westberry.

work. To see a man plowing in the field and his wife carrying him a drink of cool water and the crops growing with a fresh and green color with all the surroundings of nature and art forms a noble picture of civilization. It was God's first commission to man, and his commission has never been discharged. He represents every element of human sustenance and progress. I shall ever be thankful that I learned to work on the farm. There are no short-cuts to riches, but there is a steady and substantial growth to wealth if you only know how to farm and then do what you know. We have the earth for our dwelling place, the blue sky for our canopy, the sun, moon and stars for our candles, the woods and flowers for our companions; the birds and breezes for our music, and the beasts for our helpers. As we toil we can sing, and as we eat we give thanks to God; as we sleep we rest from our labor and when the Sabbath day comes we can go to the house of worship and then we enjoy the old-time religion and it is good enough for anybody.

Agriculture is an absolute and fundamental necessity. Everything in commerce and manufacture, in peace, and in war, in progress and prosperity, depends upon the farm and the farmer. No man has yet discovered the art of manufacturing food and clothing except from the elements of nature. Let the famine and the drought come upon the farmer and all other industries will perish. If the farmer fails, the mighty steamers that plow the briny deep and bring the old world to the new and link the new world to the old world, would have to anchor in some harbor and the captains disband their crews.

The great engines that carry food and supplies to feed the nations of the world, would have to stop and not a wheel could turn. The great factories with their thousands of wheels and big engines that belch forth might and power would cease, their noise and their mighty plants would be still, and the people would inquire as to where is our Joseph. He was the greatest farmer the world has ever seen before or since his day, for he made and stored away in store houses and bins enough grain to last the world seven years. No man before or since has fed so many people from the farm during a famine. I have seen some farmers who were unable to feed their families from their own barn seven weeks after harvest, with forty years experience on the farm. Joseph made enough on Pharaoh's farms in seven years to feed the Egyptians fourteen years and the world seven years. Let the wisdom of Joseph be the wisdom of our farmers and we will clothe and feed the world with ease. Paralyze the hand of the farmer and you paralyze the world. If there is a human being under heaven whose interest should be protected, supported and honored at the hands of our great government, it is the farmer.

The trouble has been that most people look upon farming as a sort of common drudge. I once had occasion to ask a man what business he followed, and he replied with apparent sincerity, "I have no business, have never had any; I am a farmer."

Now, that man's opinion, like a great many people's opinion, sadly needs revising. For I assert and the facts will compel you to agree with me, that the most important business of man is that of farming. Compare the business of farming with the best business of the world, and put it just a little ahead and you will put farming in its rightful place.

* * * * * *

In Re: Chapter IX—"The New Negro Challenges the Old Order."

We add to this chapter an address by William Pickens, a South Carolinian, on "The Kind of Democracy the Negro Race Expects," which we think fits into the idea of this chapter.

Democracy is the most used term in the world today. But some of its uses are abuses. Everybody says "Democracy"! But everybody has his own definition. By the extraordinary weight of the presidency of the United States many undemocratic people have had this word forced upon their lips but have not yet had the right ideal forced upon their hearts. I have heard of one woman who wondered with alarm whether "democracy" would mean that colored women would have the right to take any vacant seat or space on a street car, even if they had paid for it. That such a question should be asked, shows how many different meanings men may attach to the one word *Democracy*. This woman doubtless believes in a democracy of me-and-my-kind, which is no democracy. The most autocratic and the worst caste systems could call themselves democratic by that definition. Even the Prussian junker believes in that type of democracy; he has no doubt that he and the other junkers should be free and equal in rights and privileges.

Many have accepted the word *Democracy* merely as the current password to respectability in political thinking. The spirit of the times is demanding democracy; it is the tune of the age; it is the song to sing.

It is in order, therefore, for the Negro to state clearly what he means by democracy and what he is fighting for.

First. Democracy in education. This is fundamental. No other democracy is practicable unless all of the people have equal right and opportunity to develop according to their individual endowments. There can be no real democracy between two natural groups, if one represents the extreme of ignorance and the other the best intelligence. The common public school and the state university should be the foundation stones of democracy. If men are artificially differentiated at the beginning, if we try to educate a "working class" and a "ruling class," forcing different race groups into different lines without regard to individual fitness, how can we ever hope for democracy in the other relations of these groups? Individuals will differ, but in democracy of education peoples living on the same soil should not be widely diverged in their training on mere racial lines. This would be illogical, since they are to be measured by the same standards of life. Of course, a group that is to live in Florida should be differently trained from a group that is to live in Alaska; but that is geography and general environment, and not color or caste—the Negro believes in democracy of education as first and fundamental; that the distinction should be made between individual talents and not between colors and castes.

Second. Democracy in industry. The right to work in any line for which the individual is best prepared, and to be paid the standard wage. This is also fundamental. In the last analysis there could be very little democracy between multi-millionaires and the abject poor. There must be a more just and fair distribution of wealth in a democracy. And certainly this is not possible unless men work at the occupations for which they are endowed and best prepared. There should be no "colored" wages and no "white" wages; no "man's" wage and no "woman's" wage. Wages should be paid for the work done, measured as much as possible by its productiveness. No door of opportunity should be closed to a man on any other ground than that of his individual unfitness. The cruelest and most undemocratic thing in the world is to require of the individual man that his whole race be fit before he can be regarded as fit for a certain privilege or responsibility. That rule, strictly applied, would exclude any man of any race from any position. For every man to serve where he is most able to serve is public economy and is to the best interests of the state. This lamentable war that was forced upon us should make that plain to the dullest of us. Suppose that, when this war broke out, our whole country had been like Mississippi (and I refer to geography uninvidiously), suppose our whole country had been like Mississippi, where a caste system was holding the majority of the population in the triple chains of ignorance, semi-serfdom and poverty. Our nation would be now either the unwilling prey or the golden goose for the Prussian. The long-headed thing for any state is to let every man do his best all of the time. But some people are so short-sighted that they only see what is thrust against their noses. The Negro asks American labor in the name of democracy to get rid of its color caste and industrial junkerism.

Third. Democracy in state. A political democracy in which all are equal before the laws; where there is one standard of justice, written and unwritten; where all men and women may be citizens by the same qualifications, agreed upon and specified. We believe in this as much for South Africa as for South Carolina, and we hope that our American nation will not agree with any government, ally or enemy, that is willing to make a peace that will bind the African Negro to political slavery and exploitation.

Many other evils grow out of political inequality. Discriminating laws are the mother of the mob spirit. The political philosopher in Washington, after publishing his opinion that a Negro by the fault of being a Negro is unfit to be a member of Congress, cannot expect an ignorant white man in Tennessee to believe that the same Negro is, nevertheless, fit to have a fair and impartial trial in a Tennessee court. Ignorance is too logical for that. I disagree with the premises but I agree with the reasoning of the Tennesseean: that if being a Negro unfits a man for holding a government office for which he is otherwise fit, it unfits the same man for claiming a "white man's" chance in the courts. The first move therefore against mob violence and injustice in the petty courts is to wipe out discriminating laws and practices in the higher circles of government. The ignorant man in Tennessee will not rise in ideal above the intelligent man in Washington.

Fourth. Democracy without the sex-preferment. The Negro cannot consistently oppose color discrimination and support sex discrimination in democratic government. This happened to be the opinion also of the first man of the Negro race in America—Frederick Douglass. The handicap is nothing more or less than a presumption in the mind of the physically dominant element of the universal inferiority of the weaker or subject element. It is so easy to prove that the man who is down, deserves to be down and under. In the first place, he is down there, isn't he? And that is three-fourths of the argument of the ordinary mind; for the ordinary mind does not seek ultimate causes. The argument against the participation of colored men and women in self-government is practically one argument. Somebody spoke to the Creator about both of these classes and learned that they were "created" for inferior roles. Enfranchisement would spoil a good field-hand, or a good cook. Black men were once ignorant, women were once ignorant. Negroes had no political experience, women had no experience. The argument forgets that people do not get experience outside. But the American Negro expects a democracy that will accord the right to vote to a sensible industrious woman rather than to a male tramp.

Fifth. Democracy to church. The preachings and the practices of Jesus of Nazareth are perhaps the greatest influences in the production of modern democratic ideas. The Christian church is, therefore, no place for the caste spirit or for snobs. And the colored races the world over will have even more doubt in the future than they have had in the past of the real Christianity of any church which holds out to them the prospect of being united in heaven after being separated on earth.

Finally. The great colored races will in the future not be kinder to a sham democracy than to a "scrap-of-paper" autocracy. The private home, private rights and private opinion must remain inviolate; but the commonwealth, the public places and public property must not be appropriated to the better use of any group by "Jim Crowing" and segregating any other group. By the endowments of God and nature there are individual "spheres." Jesus' estimate of the individual soul is the taproot of democracy, and any system which discourages the men of any race from individual achievement, is no democracy. To fix the status on earth according to the physical group in which it was born, is the gang spirit of the savage which protects its own members and outlaws all others.

For real democracy the American Negro will live and die. His loyalty is always above suspicion, but his extraordinary spirit in the present war was born of his faith that on the side of his country and her allies is the best hope for such a democracy. And he welcomes, too, the opportunity to lift the "Negro question" out of the narrow confines of the southern United States and make it a world question. Like many other questions our domestic race question, instead of being settled by Mississippi and South Carolina, will seek its settlement finally on the battlefields of the world.*

*   *   *   *   *   *

In Re: The subject of the New Negro's challenge to the "Old Order," we quote below extracts from an address on "What the Negro Wants," by that illustrious South Carolina colored

---

*The above address delivered by Mr. Pickens during the great World War is certainly a challenge to the "Old Order" as much today (1928) as it was then.

woman, Mrs. Mary McLeod Bethume, as reported by a Negro weekly paper, *The Black Dispatch*:

"The Negro wants protection in the community from the menace and persecution by policemen and public officials. He wants protection from groups whether formed spontaneously or representing permanent organizations which attempt to regulate his conduct without the sanction of constituted law. He wants protection from petty insult at the hands of irresponsible youths who develop early in life and exercise an inadvisable attitude on race relations and are frequently used to precipitate local disturbances between race groups.

"He wants protection in travel, whether on public carriers, such as railways or in private conveyances on the public highway. He wants protection from trouble makers in certain communities where a local rule obtains that Negro passengers may not alight or raise their window sashes or shades while the train remains at the station. He wants protection from employees such as station agents, baggage masters and conductors who assume the right to demand unnatural subservience from the Negro patron or heap upon him with impunity any insult or put him to any inconvenience they may please.

"He wants relief from the nervous apprehension that at any moment he may be compelled to abandon his home, seeking personal safety in hasty flight or that any night his home, his church, or lodge hall may be consumed by fire applied by some unknown person to satisfy a private grudge. He wants assurance that his wife, his sister, and his daughter may sit in the home or walk on the street or go about their daily tasks without danger of insult or violence from the unmanly man who may desire to victimize them to gratify his own unspeakable lust.

"He believes that the only absolute guaranty of sure protection is a well organized court system, administered without fear or prejudice. He wants therefore the protection of the court and the assurance of impartial judgment in its administrations. He believes that properly qualified Negro barristers should be admitted to practice before the bar on a par with all lawyers and that registered Negro citizens should be drawn upon without discrimination for service on grand and petit juries. He wants therefore the privilege of rendering his share of this necessary and important function of citizenship duty.

"The Negro cannot understand the justice in spending eight dollars on each white child for every dollar spent on his own. He cannot understand the justice in giving the principal of a white school a salary of three or four thousand dollars, while the Negro in the same school system receives eight or ten hundred

dollars.   He cannot understand the justice of giving the white
teacher a monthly salary of two hundred dollars, while the
colored teacher congratulates herself upon receiving sixty; and
just why the school building for whites cost eight or ten times
as much as that for Negroes.

"If his child must adjust himself to the white man's civilization, fit himself into the white man's industrial scheme, be measured by the white man's standards of intelligence and answer to
the white man's law, he wants for his child an equal measure with
the white man's child in thoroughness of preparation.

"If it takes sacrifice, he wants to 'give until it hurts.'   He is
willing to suffer the aches and darts of 'growing pains' to change
from the thing he is unto the thing he ought to be.   If it takes
a finer home life, he wants but the opportunity in industry and
education to make his home appearance and atmosphere what it
ought to be.   If it takes a finer soldiery, he wants merely a better
opportunity to serve in the army and navy without embarrassment, without humiliation, without unfair repression; and just as
he has done in every past war of the nation's history, so again
will he make the supreme sacrifice to keep Old Glory floating—a
symbol of justice and democracy to the oppressed world.

"If it takes a finer citizenship, he simply wants to be taught,
not merely by the white man's example, of what the white man
conceives superlative citizenship to mean, but also he wants the
white man to urge upon his own son and neighbor to practice
that citizenship.   If it takes a finer religion, he is willing to tarry
as long as the most devout at the feet of the lowly Nazarene
until he has thoroughly incorporated the spirit of humility and
purity and service and love, until he is willing to put into operation among all men, all races, all nations actively and without
reservation or qualification a full free-hearted practice of the
golden rule.

"If these wants can be supplied, there will be not only an
immeasurably better Negro but there will be an immeasurably
better America, because this kind of Negro is in it."

INDEX

Abolition
  free Negro slave owners not in
    favor of, 30
  Negro slaves fought in Civil
    War to help cause of, 49
  Vesey's Insurrection helped, 48
Abolitionist(s), 20
  assisted by Underground Rail-
    road and Negro assistants, 23,
    25
  extreme radicalism of, 16
  "first one, a runaway slave," 17
  John Brown, 16
  William Lloyd Garrison, 16
Aboriginal Indians
  workers, 1
Accomplishments
  of Negro labor, 10; see also
    Negro
  of Reconstruction government,
    66–79
    adopted a constitution more
      democratic than any before,
      79
    building penal and charitable
      institutions, 66
    caused the state to be read-
      mitted to Union, 79
    demonstrated capacity of Ne-
      gro to produce political
      leaders of ability and char-
      acter, 79
    establishment of public school
      system, 66
    laws relative to finance, 66
    placed state on road to pros-
      perity, 67
    provided education for deaf
      and dumb, 67
    rebuilt bridges, 67
    re-established ferries, 67
    reformatory laws in every de-
      partment still on books, 66
    worked with Gov. Hampton's
      conservative Democrats in

Accomplishments—*Continued*
    1876 to complete money
      legislation already started,
      67
Adams Express
  received "Henry Box Brown,"
    21
Adaptability
  great power of Negro, 213
Advice
  address to Older Boys' Con-
    ference at Benedict College
    by B. E. Mays, 203–11
  by and to the "New Negro,"
    203–11
Africa
  black servants from, 4, 5
  fight for freedom started before
    leaving, 30
  Negroes from, 2
Africa Slave or Free
  by Harris, 117
African   Methodist   Episcopal
  Church
  Bishop Daniel Payne, 86
    taught in Bonneau school
      prior to becoming bishop, 86
  established Allen University in
    Columbia in 1880, 94
    under leadership of Bishop
      W. F. Dickerson, 94
Aftermath of Slavery, The
  by W. A. Sinclair, Negro writer,
    59
  quotes from, 57–59, 64–65
Alabama
  Negroes in War of 1812, 41
  under carpet-bag government
    during 3 or 4 years of re-
    construction, 58
Aldrich, Judge A. P.
  of S. C. Superior Court (1867),
    57
  order from Federal officer that
    he could no longer sit as
    judge, 57

Alexander, Dr. Will W.
chairman, inter-racial committee of southern states, 186
National Director (1928) of Inter-racial Commission, 214
quote, on Negro in America, 215
Alexander the Great, 206
Allen University
established 1880 by African Methodist Episcopal Church, 94
by Negroes under complete Negro control, 94
had theological course, 95
law department several years, 95
see "Negro, Colleges agree. . . ."
Allendale
Arthur Daniels, Negro teacher of agriculture, 164
Allendale County
Rosa Gibbs, home demonstration agent, 165
Alvord, J. W.
general superintendent of education, Freedmen's Bureau 1865, 91
A.M.A. Annual Report, 1864
Negro contributed to his own growth financially, out of great poverty, 100
America
fell heir to economic and political revolution, 5
land in, endless and fertile, 5
American
government, 16
History, Missing Pages, 13–54
Indians, servants, 45
social order, 16
American Baptist Home Mission Society
denominational organization, 91
supported Rachel Crome Mather in attempt to found school, 91
more social service organization, 90
American History, Missing Pages in
pamphlet by Laura E. Wilkes, 13–54

American Magazine: "Comic Side of Trouble," by Bert Williams, on Negro as optimist, 188
American Missionary Association
more or less associated with missionary service of Congregational Church, 91–92
pioneer in education for Negroes in southern states, 88
"semi-denominational," 91
American Negro Slavery
by Prof. U. B. Phillips, 2, 3, 120, 157, 159
American Student Federation
footnote, 212
Anders, Lymus
called "Black Yankee," 104
founded school with teachers from Mass., 104
full-blooded African, 103
illiterate until after war, 103
Anderson, Miss Marion
recital, in report of Orangeburg-Sunlight Club, 184
Anderson, S. C., school
established by Mrs. C. M. Hicks, 103
Negro teacher sent South by a New York society, 103
Andover Institution
sent volunteers to help Freedmen in 1862, 88
Andrews, Mrs. Emma
Sumter, head, department of home economics, S. C. Federation of C. W. C., 185
Anglo-Saxon
thinking of Booker T. Washington, 9–10
Anti-slavery office in Philadelphia, 21
received "Henry Box Brown" express, 21
Antisdel, Doctor
present president of Benedict College (1927), 94
Appendix
excerpts from references throughout text, 235–80
see footnote, 173

Apprehending fugitive slaves, 19

Aristocracy
mostly Charleston area, 76
servants· felt superior to other
Negroes, 76
caused rift among Negro
working classes, 76

Arkansas
under carpet-bag government
during 3 or 4 years of reconstruction, 58

Association for the Study of Negro Life and History
published education article by
Woodson 1919, 82

Atlanta University Press
published *The Negro American
Family* in 1908, 114
see also Atlanta University
Publications

Atlanta University Publication
No. 13
The Negro American Family,
113, 117, 124, 130, 131
No. 18, DuBois and Dill: *Morals
and Manners Among Negro
Americans* 128
Nos. 1 to 20, footnote, 217

Atlanta University studies of the
Negro in the South
Publications 1 to 20, footnote,
217

Attitude toward work
Negroes, 72
Negroes vs. Europeans, 10–11

Attucks, Crispus
first Negro to shed blood to free
America, 206

Author
a Y.M.C.A. secretary during
World War, 187
poem by, 188

Avery, E. L.
Negro teacher of agriculture,
Ft. Mill, 164

Avery Normal Institute
named for philanthropic minister Avery who gave $10,-
000 to build it, 93
present principal, B. F. Cox, 93

Avery Normal Institute—*Continued*
private high school in Charleston, 92
organized by F. L. Cardoza,
1865, 92
supported by Congregational
American Missionary Assn.,
92–93

Baddy (author)
"Negro Womanhood's Greatest
Needs," in Messenger Maga-
zine, Feb. 1928, 177

Bagnall, Robert
on N.A.A.C.P. staff, 217

Baker Theological Institute at
Charleston
consolidated with Claflin U. at
Orangeburg, 95

Banberg [Bamberg] County
E. D. Jenkins, county farm
agent, 165

Baptist Home Mission Society,
American
attempted to found school
through Rachel Crome
Mather, 90
more social service 90
denominational organization, 91

Barnett, Amelia
taught on Mary St., 86

Barnwell
H. E. Sutton, Negro teacher of
agriculture, 164

Barnwell, B. B.
graduate of Hampton Institute,
156
prepared statement on Negro
farmer of S. C., 165–69
Smith-Lever agent in Beaufort
Co., 165
state farm demonstration agent,
Frogmore, St. Helena Island,
156
wrote part of Chap. VII of this
book, 156, 158, 161

Barnwell, Benjamin B., and Mabel Price
county farm and home demon-

Barnwell, Benjamin B., and Mabel
Price—*Continued*
    stration agents, Beaufort Co.,
    165
Batesburg
    T. F. Curry, Negro teacher of
    agriculture, 164
Battle of Ft. Wagner
    described, 52
Beard, Edward
    taught in school on Coming St.,
    86
Beard, Simeon
    taught in school on Wall St., 86
Bearer, burden, 1, 3
    black man, in S. C. immortalized
    his work through jazz or
    "spirituals," 12
    Negro, superior physical fit-
    ness, general adaptability, 8
    who established S. C.'s leader-
    ship in rice industry, 3
    not intended for participation
    in business matters, 135
Beaufort
    County, Benjamin B. Barnwell
    and Mabel Price, county farm
    and home demonstration
    agents, 165
    developed Negro businesses sim-
    ilar to Charleston, 142
    Hilton Head cotton, 4
    training school, 169
Bee, Capt.
    led men from church to meet and
    overcome insurrectionists, 33
Benedict, Mrs. Bethsheba A.
    white northern philanthropist
    who made Benedict Institute
    (College) possible, 93–94
Benedict College
    address to Older Boys' Confer-
    ence by B. E. Mays, 203–11
    both white and colored on fac-
    ulty, 94
    economics class helped make sur-
    vey of Negro businesses, 143
    originally Benedict Institute, 93
    some leaders named, 94
Benedict Institute
    founded by Baptist Home Mis-

Benedict Institute—*Continued*
    sionary Society in 1870 for
    Negroes, 93
    later Benedict College, 93
    made possible by northern white
    philanthropist, Mrs. Beth-
    sheba A. Benedict of Paw-
    tucket, R. I., 93–94
    private school in Columbia, 93
    purpose of Institute, 94
Bennett, Battean
    a chosen leader in Vesey's In-
    surrection, 46
Bennett, Ned
    a chosen leader in Vesey's In-
    surrection, 47
Bennett, Rolla
    brother to Ned, a chosen leader
    in Vesey's Insurrection, 46
Berkeley, St. John's
    cotton area, 4
Bethume, Mrs. Mary McLeod
    attended Goodwill School at
    Mayesville, 98
    greatest woman of color to come
    out of S. C., 178
    once a speaker at Y.M.C.A.
    Blue Ridge Conference, 229
    orator and educator of interna-
    tional reputation, 98
    president of Daytona-Cookman
    College, Daytona, Fla., 98
    president of National Federa-
    tion of Colored Women's
    Clubs, 98
    quote, from 1927 "Who's Who in
    Colored America," 179
        on inter-racial aims, post
        World War period, 216
    sent to Scotia Seminary by Miss
    Mary Crissman of Denver, 98
    taught at Goodwill by Miss
    Emma Wilson, 98
Bettis Institute or Academy
    founded at Trenton by Rev.
    Alexander Bettis, Negro ex-
    slave, 98
Bettis, Rev. Alexander
    Negro ex-slave, founded Bettis
    Institute or Academy at
    Trenton, 98

"Big House"
   domestic service by slaves, 5
   home of plantation master, 5
Bigelow, A. M.
   teacher of colored school at
     Aiken, 101
     compelled to leave town to
       save life, 101
Biologist Ernest Just
   graduate of State A. & M. Col-
     lege, 111
   great work at Howard Univer-
     sity, 111
Birnie, Dr. C. W.
   Education of the Negro in
     Charleston, South Carolina,
     Before the Civil War, The,
     Journal of Negro History, 82
   footnotes, 84, 85, 86
   in Journal of Negro History, 83
Birnie, Charles
   leader in cotton shipping, 140
Birnie, Richard
   leader in cotton shipping, 140
"Black-and-tan" Constitution of
   1868, of S. C.
   allowed state back in Union, 55
"Black Codes,"
   legislation prejudicial to inter-
     ests of white people, 55, 78
   provisions, 72
Black Man's, Burden, 1
   contribution to S. C.'s economic
     and industrial advancement,
     12
   cotton, 3
   physical labor, 3
   immortalization of his work
     through jazz or "spirituals,"
     12
"Black Soldiers"
   chapter in DuBois publication,
     38
   "the American Negro always
     fought for his own free-
     dom . . . ," 39
Blacks in South
   Sherman issued first order for
     help in 1862, 87

Blackville
   J. B. Reddish, Negro teacher of
     agriculture, 164
Blackwood, Jessie
   not allowed out of Charleston
     June 15, day before plot to
     be carried out, 47
   Vesey's messenger in insurrec-
     tion, 47
Blythewoods in Orangeburg
   leading undertakers, 147
Bondage, House of, 23
Bonneau, Fannie
   taught on Coming St., 86
Bonneau Library Society
   school for Negro children, 84
Bonneau, Thos. S.
   kept a school from about 1803
     to his death, 1828 or 1829, 85
   had two assistants, 85
   one of most famous colored
     teachers of his time, 85
   school later carried on by
     Daniel Payne, 85
Boston
   Crafts, fugitive slaves, lived in,
     22, 23
Boston, Miss Dora E.
   office at State A.&M. College
     for Negroes, 165
   state extension service supervis-
     ing agent (1927–28), 165
Botume, Elizabeth Hyde
   established industrial school at
     Beaufort for New England
     Freedmen's Aid Society, 90
Bowen, T. T. W.
   Negro teacher of agriculture,
     Latta, 164
Bowler, R. F.
   Negro teacher of agriculture,
     Darlington, 164
Boykin, Mrs. Cora
   once dean of women, State
     A.&M., 187
Bradley, E. J.
   Negro teacher of agriculture,
     Wisacky, 164
Brainerd Institute at Chester
   supported by Board of Missions
     of Presbyterian Church, 97

Brawley, Prof. Benjamin
author of, *History of the American Negro,* 2, 3
Social History, 18
footnote, 49
native South Carolinian, writer,
44
on warlike slaves, 31
short story on Vesey Insurrection, 44
Brazil, accomplishments of Negro
labor in, 10
Brent, T. J.
trustee for Mrs. E. L. Hart, 27
on Kibby slave sale contract,
27
Brewer, H. G.
Negro agriculture teacher,
Hartsville, 164
Brewer, J. L.
Negro teacher of agriculture,
Timmonsville, 164
Brewer Normal, Industrial and
Agricultural Institute
project of Congregational
American Missionary Assn.,
97
secondary school at Greenwood,
97
"Bridge Builder, The"
quote, 207
Brier, Thomas
State College senior (1927),
compiled and analyzed figures
on survey of Negro business
in S. C., 144–45
Brisbane, William
cotton planter, 4
British fleet
attacked and repulsed June 15,
1776, 40
May 31, 1776, 20 miles from
Ashley River at Charleston,
40
unsuccessful attacks off coasts
of Va. and N. C., 40
Brown, Mrs. C. R.
of Florence, chairman, club
presidents, S. C. Federation
C.W.C., 185

Brown, John
abolitionist, 16
white martyr, 48
Brown Fellowship Society
later Centenary, from Rev.
Thomas Frost's suggestion for
society to maintain school for
Negro children, 84
oldest of secret societies in
Charleston, 142
still maintains an office (1927),
142
Brown Institution
sent volunteers to help Freedmen in 1862, 88
Browning, 205
Browning Industrial Home and
Mather Academy for Girls
in Camden, for Negroes, 97
first owned by Mrs. Mather of
Boston, 97
later given to Woman's Home
Missionary Society of the
Methodist Episcopal Church,
97
Bryant, William Cullen
helped sponsor American Missionary Assn., 88
Building and Construction
one of early business successes
for S. C. Negroes, 141
Bull, Governor
met armed company of slaves,
spread alarm, and took slaves,
33
Bull, William, Junr. Speaker
signed "Petition and Representation to His Majesty . . ."
covering colony's ills in 1740,
34–38
Bunch, W. C.
county farm agent, Spartanburg
Co., 165
Burcell, Jack
a chosen leader in Vesey's Insurrection, 46
Burden
bearer, 1, 3, 8
black man immortalized his
work through "spirituals,"
12

Burden—*Continued*
    not intended for participation in business, 135
    Negro who established S. C.'s leadership in rice industry, 3
    black man's, 1
    for black man, cotton, 3
    physical labor, 3
    Negro slave's, rice cultivation, 2
Bureau, Freedmen's, Act of Congress, 90–91
Burton, Foster
    Negro teacher of agriculture, Neeces, 164
Burton
    J. S. Shanklin, Negro teacher of agriculture, 164
Business
    Mrs. Mary Kirvin, Syracuse, head of department of, S. C. Federation of C. W. C., 185
    Negro in, in S. C., 135–155
    first woman in, "Joe Cole and Wife—Fish," 139
Butler, Mrs. Susie Dart
    Charleston, head of education department, S. C. Federation of C. W. C., 185
Butler, Mrs. Susie J.
    Columbia chairman ways and means committee, S. C. Federation of C. W. C., 185

Calhoun [John C.]
    of S. C., 16
Cambridge Institution
    sent volunteers to help Freedmen in 1862, 88
Camden
    Browning Industrial Home and Mather Academy for Girls, 97
    later given to Woman's Home Missionary Society of Methodist Episcopal Church, 97
    had been owned by Mrs. Mather of Boston, 97
    insurrection of 1816, 42
    date set for July 4, 43
    foiled by gathering under pretense of fox chase, 42–44

Camden—*Continued*
    informer given freedom and pension for life, 44
    Negro teacher Frank Carter founded school to which whites contributed, 103
    training institute consolidated with Claflin U. at Orangeburg, 95–96
Camden—Uplift Club
    officers listed, 183
    Report to State Federation of C. W. C., 183
Camp Gordon, Ga.
    footnote, 189
Campbell, William B.
    Negro teacher of agriculture, McCall, 164
Cardoza, Francis L.
    educated at universities in England and Scotland, 60
    Negro, long time leader of legislature, 60
    organized Avery Normal Institute, private school, in 1865, 92
    "the brightest light among Negro teachers," 104
Carney, Sgt. William H.
    saved flag in siege of Petersburg, 52
Carpentry and contracting
    one of early business successes for Negroes, 141
"Carpet-bagger"
    and Negro legislature problems, 59–68
    government, covered 11 southern states during reconstruction, 58
    in Journal of Negro History, 56
    less harmful than northern bondholders, 58
    of Reconstruction days mostly white, 63
    self-styled, white man, Post, on S. C. rejoining Union in 1868, 55
    Tweed ring in New York City stole more than all "carpet-

"Carpet-bagger"—*Continued*
  baggers" in South combined,
    58
*"Carpet-Bagger" in South Caro-
lina, A*
  by Louis F. Post, 78
Carter, Frank
  Negro teacher, founded school
    at Camden to which whites
    contributed, 103
Cato
  fomented slaves' insurrection
    (*see* footnote 1), 2
Centenary Society
  school for Negro children sug-
    gested originally by Rev.
    Thomas Frost, 84
  still maintains office (1927), 142
Challenge
  of Old Order by "New Negro,"
    192–212
Chapelle, Bishop W. D.
  chancellor of Allen University,
    95
  did great service collecting
    money from Negroes, 95
Chaplin, Ben
  Negro of St. Helena Island,
    Beaufort Co., 168
  started with 3 acres, now has
    40, making money, 168
Chapman, J. H.
  Negro agriculture teacher,
    Plezer, 164
Character of Negro, 28–29
Charleston
  County, Connie N. Jones, home
    demonstration agent, 165
  Crafts couple, fugitive slaves
    from Georgia, 22
  traveled first class hotels, 22
  Daily News, editorial on free
    labor, 71
  decided to fortify against prob-
    able attack, 39
    Negro labor brought in from
      plantations to help, 39
  Gov. Bull returning to, when he
    met insurrectionists' army, 33
  Mayor took steps against
    Vesey's Insurrection, 47

Charleston—*Continued*
  Negroes of
    freed, some had ideas of aris-
      tocracy, 69
    getting some education in
      1700's, 83–84
    in business, center of early
      efforts, 142
    prominent business and pro-
      fessional men, 77
  slave purchases similar to
    Kibby, 27
Charleston College
  in connection with Episcopal
    church school, 86
Charleston *Courier*
  on Rev. Porter's visit to How-
    ard and President Johnson:
    "much more substantial and
    lasting token of friendship
    to colored race . . . ," 102
Charleston Harbor
  a fascine battery erected, 40
  a fort built in 4 bastiles, 40
  British attacked June 15, 1776,
    and driven back, 40
  erect breastworks on Sullivan's
    Island in Harbor, in 1776, 39
  Negro labor brought in from
    plantations to help, 39
Charleston Messenger, The
  Negro newspaper, serves as
    newspaper and advocate of
    Negro rights, 223
Charleston New Era
  Negro newspaper, quotes from
    "special contributing editor,"
    224–226
Charleston—Louise F. Holmes
    Literary and Art Club
  Report to State Federation of
    C. W. C., 183–84
  officers, 184
Chase, S. P.
  Fed. Gov. official, sympathized
    and encouraged work of
    American Missionary Society,
    89
Chattel slaves
  became wage slaves after Civil
    War, 72

Cheap labor
large supply, 1
Chestnut, Col., of Camden
aide-de-camp to Gov. Williams, 42
with governor and others foiled 1816 insurrection by gathering under pretense of fox chase, 42–44
Chicago Defender
publication, gives concept of "New Negro," 192–93
Chiles, H. A.
Negro teacher of agriculture, Traveler's Rest, 164
Chosen leaders in Vesey's Insurrection, 46
Christian
religion, and the Negro, 28–29, 81
Protestant, had early slave owners teach slaves to read and write, 81
fellowship from Negroes from North in schools during and after Civil War, 90
Christianity
and rudiments of civilization, 87
to be taught blacks under Sherman's Order No. 9, of 1862, 87
of white man being doubted by Negroes, 202
Church schools before Civil War
Methodist, Roman Catholic, Episcopal, 85, 86
Churches
Negroes very active in, 141
Citadel, The
social science courses teaching real truth about the Negro, 228–29
Civil Rights Bill
embraced by "Congressional Plan," 55
giving freed men all civil rights of citizens, 55
Civil War, 13–54
for economic, not humanitarian, reasons, 13–54
partly brought on by Fugitive Slave Law, 25

Civil War—*Continued*
Emancipation Proclamation, 53, 54
fight for freedom just begun, 54
free Negro slave-owners in hopeless minority among Negroes in war, 30
Negroes fought in, 49
did not rebel in South—"playing safe," 50
joined Union armies, 50, 51
soon after start many Negroes attached to Federal armies in S. C., 87
many were fugitives, 87
Civilization, rudiments of, and Christianity, 87
American, Negro spiritual Good Samaritan of, 214
to be taught blacks under Sherman's Order No. 9 of 1862, 87
Claflin, Lee
generous northern friend (Mass.) gave name to Claflin, 96
Claflin University, Orangeburg
consolidated with smaller schools, 95
founded by S. C. Conference of Methodist Episcopal Church, 95
normal school established with, in 1877, 96
obtained charter in 1869, 95
one of best known colleges for Negroes in America, 95
purchased property of old white school known as Orangeburg Female College, 96
see "Negro, Colleges agree. . . ."
State College of Agriculture and Mechanic's Institute, established as division of in 1872, 96
Clarendon County
William Thompson, county farm agent, 165

Clement, Bishop
  prominent Columbia Negro business man, 77
Clemmons, F. N.
  Negro teacher of agriculture, Jefferson, 164
Clemson College
  social science courses teaching real truth about the Negro, 228–29
Cleveland, Prof. C. D.
  in anti-slavery office to receive "Henry Box Brown," 21
Clinton, Bishop Isaac
  Negro, treasurer of town of Orangeburg, 60
Clinton (British officer)
  attacked Charleston June 15, 1776, and was repulsed, 40
  crippled, sailed away to New York, 40
  Negroes and whites defended Charleston, 40
  not able to land at Sullivan or Ft. Moultrie, 40
Colby, Lewis
  among leaders of Benedict College, 94
Collier, R. C.
  Negro teacher of agriculture, Minturn, 164
Colony of S. C., 1
  government of, 1
Colored
  race, mission of, 1
  slaves, 12,220 in colony in 1720, 1
Columbia
  developed Negro businesses during and after Reconstruction, 142–55
  Negroes getting some education in 1700's, 84
  quoted from New York Times "whites extended every possible facility and encouragement in . . . education," 102
  survey of Negro businesses made, 143
Columbia Phoenix
  quoted on school, 93

Columbia schools
  first in basement of Negro church, 1865, by Freedmen, 93
  several others soon founded, 93
  white and colored faculties, 93
Columbia State
  letter to Editor by author concerning editorial on numbers of Negroes leaving state, 162–63
"Comic Side of Trouble"
  by Bert Williams, 188
Commission,
  land, of Reconstruction Government
    given $750,000 to buy lands for Freedmen, 70, 158
    fund misused, government and Freedmen defrauded, 70, 158
  on Inter-racial Co-operation, footnote, 220
Committee on Race Relations in S. C.
  white womens', 220
Common humanity
  in Southern white people, 28
  slaves appealed to this for freedom, 28
Commonwealth of South Carolina
  called Military District No. 2 from 1867 to 1874, 57
  from 1868 to 1874 known as time when S. C. was under "Rule of the Robbers," 57
  Negro reconstruction government, 55–79
Confederacy
  planned to use large numbers of slaves just before close of war, 50
  white men who had helped, could not vote during reconstruction, 57
Confederate
  description of battle of Ft. Wagner, 52
  Negroes prominent in, 54

Confidence
  of Negro in greatness of his future, 214
Congregational Church
  more or less associated with
  American Missionary Association, 90–91
  project: Brewer Normal, Industrial and Agricultural Institute, secondary school, Greenwood, 97
  supported Avery Normal Institute, private high school in
  Charleston, 93
Congress
  Gen. Hunter's statement on
  Negro soldiers read in, 51
Congress, United States
  placed state under military control during reconstruction,
  "Congressional Plan," 55
  embraced Civil Rights Bill,
  Fourteenth Amendment, 55
"Congressional Plan"
  embraced Civil Rights Bill, 55
  Fourteenth Amendment, 55
  Negroes given power to vote, 55
  some Negro leaders, 60–62
  state put under military control
  during reconstruction, 55, 178
Constitutional Convention of S. C.
  members received copies of
  N. Y. Tribune from Francis
  L. Cardoza, 60
  of 1890, Mr. Tillman's argument
  answered by Thos. E. Miller,
  65–68
"Constitutions
  Black-and-Tan" of 1868, 55
  allowed state back in Union,
  55
  Fundamental," 1
Construction and Building
  one of early business successes
  for S. C. Negroes, 141
Contracting and Carpentry
  one of early business successes
  for Negroes, 141
Contribution
  of black man to S. C.'s economic

Contribution—*Continued*
  and industrial advancement,
  12
Cooke, Edward
  effective president of Claflin U.,
  96
Coolidge, Calvin
  quote: "No man was ever
  meanly born . . ." 174
Cooper, T. W.
  Negro teacher of agriculture,
  Russellville, 164
Cotton
  as material for clothing, 5
  boll weevil, one reason for decrease in Negro farmers 1920–
  25, 165–66
  cheap labor, 1
  crowned "King," 3, 5
  English market, 4
  first success, 4
  Negro physical labor necessary,
  3
  plantations, 1–5
  planters: William Brisbane,
  William Elliott, Peter Gaillard, General Moultrie, John
  Screven, William Seabrook,
  James Sinkler, 4
  sampling and shipping, one of
  first Negro successes in business, 140
County farm agents, 165
County home demonstration
  agents, 165
Cox, B. F.
  present principal of Avery
  Normal Institute, 93
Cox, Jeannette Keeble
  chairman, inter-racial committee, S. C. Federation C. W. C.,
  186
Craft, Ellen, 20
  fair, dressed as young white
  planter, ailing and dependent
  on servant, William, 22
  slave from Georgia, 22
Craft, William, 20
  dark, went as slave, 22
  fugitive slave from Georgia, 22

Craft, William and Ellen, 20
after emancipation, returned, bought plantation near Savannah, Ga., 23
lived in Boston until Fugitive Slave Law passed, 22
sent by friends to England, 23
slaves from Georgia, 22
traveled first class hotels Charleston, Richmond, Baltimore to Philadelphia, 22

Creed
of New Negro, 212

"Creed of the American Negro Youth"
see footnote, 212

Crisis, The
circulation of, 217
edited by W. E. B. DuBois (1910– —), 217
publication gives concept of "New Negro," 192–93

Crisis, The Impending
by Helper, 16

Crissman, Miss Mary
dressmaker in Denver, Colo., sent Mary McLeod to Scotia Seminary, 98

Critics, of S. C. Negroes
during Reconstruction, 59
general impression given false, 59
prejudiced writers, 59
John S. Reynolds also presented many facts, 59

Crogman, Nichols and: *The Progress of a Race*, 22–23
footnote, 22–23

Crogman, Dr. William
from *"Uncle Tom's Cabin,"* 129

Cromwell, John W.
The Negro in American History, 118

Cultivation
of cotton, Negro labor necessary, 3
of rice, Negro labor necessary, 2, 3

Curry, T. F.
Negro teacher of agriculture, Batesburg, 164

Daily Item, The
changing toward news of Negroes, 222
white newspaper, 222

Daily News
editorial, 73

"Danger of Diplomacy, The"
quoted from *Charleston New Era,* 225–26

Daniel, H. E.
contributed to Chap. VII, 169–72
state extension service supervising agent (1927–28), 165
office at State A. & M. College for Negroes, 165

Daniels, Arthur
Negro teacher of agriculture, Allendale, 164

Daniels, G. W.
county farm agent, Orangeburg, 165

Darkwater
by W. E. B. DuBois, 175, 176

Darlington
R. F. Bowler, Negro teacher of agriculture, 164

Darlington County
Mabel Howard and S. C. Disher, county home demonstration and farm agents, 165

Davis, Mr.
in "Henry Box Brown" escape, 21
in mercantile business in Philadelphia, 21

Daytona-Cookman College, Daytona, Fla.
Mrs. Mary McLeod Bethume, 98

Dean, Robert D.
Negro teacher of agriculture, Saluda, 164

Deane, Major E. L.
successively state superintendent of education under Freedmen's Bureau, 1865, 91

Decrease in number of Negro farmers, 1920–25, 165–67
average Negro farmer not able to take advantage of Federal Land Bank aid, 166

Decrease in number of Negro farmers—*Continued*
  big wage opportunities in Northern industries, 167
  cotton boll weevil probably first reason, 166
  failure to, adapt to farming without cotton, 166
  co-operate, work in groups, 167
  obtain credit, 166
  fluctuation in prices of other crops after losing cotton, 167

Defense of Ft. Moultrie
  as described by Laura Wilkes, 39–41

Defenses built
  Charleston Harbor, Sullivan's Island, Ft. Moultrie, 40
  British attacked June 15, 1776, and driven back, 40

Deliesseline, Esq., Francis G.
  description of Camden insurrection of 1816, 42
  reproduced here as published by Holland, 42

DeLorme, Miss Rosa
  Sumter, head of girls' work, S. C. Federation C. W. C., 185

Democrats
  conservative, Gov. Hampton's government, 67
  political party, Southern whites, 67

Denmark
  home of Voorhees Normal and Industrial School, 98–99

Dennison, Chaplin
  on Ft. Wagner battle, 52

Dibble, Dr. Eugene, of Camden
  director of Hospital at Tuskegee Institute (1927), 142
  recently toured world with Principal R. R. Morton, 142

Dibble, Mrs. L.
  Sec., Camden Uplift Club, 183

Dibble, Negro family
  educated children, 142
  financially successful, 142
  in Camden, 142

Dibble, Negro family—*Continued*
  known for achievements in mercantile business, 142
  Mr., helped sum up present status of Negro business in S. C., 143

Dickerson, Bishop W. T.
  A.M.E. Church, helped establish Allen University, 1880, 94

Dickson, Miss Anna J.
  Aiken, auditor, S. C. Federation of C. W. C., 185

Dickson, J. E., and Francis Thomas
  county farm agents, Richland County, 165

Diplomacy
  new, of white man to work *with* Negro rather than for him, 228
  new type practiced by "New Negro" in S. C., accomplishes much, 227
  old type: hypocritical, bootlicking, degrading, passing away, 227

Discrimination, 206
  attacked by S. C. Federation of C. W. C., 185

Disfranchisement
  The Crisis most effective against, 217

Disrespect
  of white man for Negro as a person, 195–202

Dill, DuBois and,
  Morals and Manners Among Negro Americans, 128
  Atlanta University Publication No. 18, 128

Disher, S. C., and Mabel Howard
  county and home demonstration agents, Darlington, Co., 165

Dodge, Timothy
  among leaders of Benedict College, 94

Domestic service
  by ex-slaves, mostly for whites, 76
  by slaves at "Big House," 5

Domestic service—*Continued*
 Negroes preferred working for whites, not Negroes, 75
Douglass, Frederick
 free Negro of North, helped finance and push movement of Am. Missionary Assn., 89
Dowd
 The Negro Races, 116
Dowd, Jerome
 The Negro in American Life, 123, 125, 126, 159
Drayton, Mrs. Leila
 Pres., Charleston—Louise F. Holmes Literary and Art Club, 183–84
Dry goods business
 Negroes of French extraction engaged·in as early as 1805, 140
DuBois, W. E. B.
 Atlanta University studies of the Negro in the South, Publications 1 to 20, 217
 "Black ·Soldiers," chapter in a publication, 38
 contributions of Negroes to labor, 10–11
 Darkwater, 175, 176
 director of department of history and sociology, Atlanta University, 114, 216–17
 director of publicity and research for N.A.A.C.P. (1910), 217, 219
 edited *The Crisis* for N.A.A.C.P., 217
 footnotes, 5, 31, 49, 51, 52, 56, 68, 88, 128, 175, 176, 214
 John Brown, on process of selection of slaves, 31
 leader in organizing N.A.A.C.P., 216
 Miller speech quoted from occasional papers of Negro Academy, No. 6, 65–68
 on Negro suffrage, 56
 on warlike slaves, 31
 physical resistance not the way out, 41

DuBois, W. E. B.—*Continued*
 philosopher, on Christian fellowship, 90
 published the pamphlet, "The Negro American Family," 114
 quote, 152
 some slaves fought for freedom by "appeal to reason," buying themselves, 25
 The Gift of Black Folk, 4, 5, 51, 56, 214
 The Souls of Black Folk, 88, 114
DuBois and Dill
 Morals and Manners Among Negro Americans
 Atlanta University Publication No. 18, 128
Duckett, Mrs. Hattie Logan
 founder of Phyllis Wheatley Center, Greenville, 187
Dunbar, Paul Laurence
 poem quoted, 213
Dunton, Dr. L. M.
 prominent educator, 96
 white, wise president of Claflin, served nearly half-century, 96
Duty
 on imported slaves, 1749, 2

Early settlers, 1
Easley
 J. T. Simpson, Negro teacher of agriculture, 164
Eastover
 L. N. Scott, Negro teacher of agriculture, 164
Ebony, Gifts of Womanhood in, 174–91
Economic
 and, industrial advancement, contributions to by black man, 12
 political revolution in America, 5
 psychological aftermath of war, 100
 social phases attracted less attention than political during reconstruction, 55
 interest vs. laws, 2

Economic—*Continued*
  Negroes tried to gain status and power by owning land after Civil War, 70–71
  not humanitarian, reason for Civil War, 13–54
  sharecropping and renting farm land uneconomical, 75
Edie, Col. J. R.
  successively assistant commissioner of Freedmen's Bureau, 1865, 91
Editors of S. C. newspapers
  changing attitudes toward Negroes in news, 222
Education
  "Black Code" provisions prohibiting Negroes from certain trades, 72
  college men criticized as not being well trained for business,—probably valid claim, 154
  colleges adding more commercial, economics, and other departments, 154
  curtailed after Vesey Insurrection in 1822, 84
  development of during Reconstruction, 77
  hope lies in colleges furnishing trained, efficient, constructive leadership graduates, 155
  law of 1740 prohibiting teaching of S. C. slaves, 83
  law of 1835 did not stop schools, 85
  many children of ex-slaves educated by parents' hard work and self-denial, 77
  Mrs. Susie Dart Butler, head of department of, for S. C. Federation of C. W. C., 185
  Negro justified help from Northern whites in rebuilding and building schools after Civil War, 99–112
  Negroes being taught in Columbia and Orangeburg as well as Charleston, 84

Education—*Continued*
  new law forbidding teaching of slaves in 1835, 84
  of S. C. Negroes in spite of great disadvantages, 80
  Rosenwald plan for rural Negro in South, 108
  rural, Mrs. M. Alice LaSaine, head of department of, S. C. Federation of C. W. C., 185
  schools on increase later in 1700's, 84
  widespread by 1790, 84
  seriously crippled after 1822 Vesey Insurrection, 84
  state school appropriation and budget report for 1924, 106–7
  State Supt. of, Report of 1924, on Negro women and girls working, 176
  students do not have educational background to make good in business, 154
Education of the Negro in Charleston, South Carolina, Before the Civil War
  by Dr. C. W. Birnie, 82
Education of the Negro Prior to 1861, The
  by Carter G. Woodson, 82
"Educational Efforts of the Freedmen's Bureau and Freedmen's Aid Societies in S. C., The"
  by Luther Jackson, *Journal of Negro History*, 87, 89, 90–91, 104
  Negroes in South helped finance schools established by Bureau, 103
  money from patrons, 103
  tuition and service from students, 103
Educational extension work
  centered at State A. & M. College, Orangeburg, 111
  includes farm demonstration, home economics and vocational education, 111
  largely procured through Smith-Hughes and Smith-Lever agencies, Gen. Education

Educational extension work—
Continued
  Board, Rosenwald Fund, etc.,
    111
Elliott, William
  first success in S. C., cotton, 4
Ellis
  Yoruba Speaking Peoples, 117
Eloree
  Roy Gordon, Negro agriculture
    teacher, 164
Emancipation
  allowed the Crafts to return to
    Georgia, 23
  just beginning at end of Civil
    War, 54
  Proclamation, 31, 53, 54
  ultimate aim of fugitives, 25
Emerson
  quote from "Forerunners," 205
English market for cotton, 4
Episcopal church
  opened St. Stephen's school
    about 1840, 86
  still in use, 86
  Rev. Toomer Porter on aid to
    Negro education, 102
  Sunday Schools for Negro child-
    ren, 86
  took active part in Negro edu-
    cation, 86
Equal Rights League
  Negro expressions in, 193
Equality of races, 100
European workman vs. Negro
workingman
  in attitude toward work, 10–11
"Even handed justice"
  Woodrow Wilson, 108
"Evolution of the Negro Home,
The (In South Carolina)"
  Chap. V, 113–34

Fair Forest
  Thos. F. Hill, Negro teacher of
    agriculture, 164
Fairbanks, Calvin
  imprisoned for helping slaves
    escape in Kentucky, 24
  mistreatment in prison, 24

Fairfield County
  Negro representatives and sena-
    tors, 61
  quote from Kelly Miller, 61–
    62
Fairfield Normal Institute, Wins-
boro
  supported by Northern Presby-
    terian Church, 98
Fairwold School for delinquent
girls
  established near Columbia by
    State Federation of C. W. C.,
    184
Farm demonstration agent
  B. B. Barnwell of Frogmore, St.
    Helena Island, 156
Farming Methods in state after
Civil War
  backward, uneconomical, ineffi-
    cient, with few exceptions, 75
Federal Government
  through officials, sympathized
    with and encouraged Ameri-
    can Missionary Assn., 88–89
Federal Army
  in battle of Ft. Wagner, 52
  many Negroes, 54
  many fugitive slaves joined at
    beginning of Civil War, 87
Feerette, Wm.
  taught on Market St., 86
Fellowship
  quality of Negro, 214
Felton, J. B.
  state agent for Negro schools,
    1927, report, 109
    outside agencies rendered
      vast assistance to Negro
      education, 109
Fenwicke, John
  signed "Petition and Represen-
    tation to His Majesty . . . "
    covering Colony's ills in 1740,
    34–38
Ferguson, Frank
  a chosen leader in Vesey's In-
    surrection, 46
Fetichism in West Africa
  by Nassau, 117

Fight
  slaves, before leaving Africa, 30
  for freedom by buying them-
      selves, 25
  for physical freedom in S. C.,
      13-54
Fish business
  one of earliest successful Negro
      businesses (C. C. Leslie), 139
  sign: "Joe Cole and Wife—
      Fish," first Negro woman in
      business, 139
Fladger, G. B.
  Negro teacher of agriculture,
      Latta, 164
Fladger, R. A. E.
  Negro teacher of agriculture,
      Lake View, 164
Flanders Field
  black boys in, 206
Fleming, E. T.
  Negro teacher of agriculture,
      Lynchburg, 164
Florence County
  Jessie J. Wilson, county farm
      agent, 165
Florida
  railroad construction, 24
      Capt. Walker, white engineer,
          branded "S.S." on right
          hand for helping slaves es-
          cape, 24
  under carpet-bag government
      during 8 years of reconstruc-
      tion, 58
Floyd, E. F.
  Negro teacher of agriculture,
      Newberry, 164
Forrester, Lot
  a chosen leader in Vesey's In-
      surrection, 46
Ft. Mill
  E. L. Avery, Negro agriculture
      teacher, 164
Ft. Moultrie
  British attacked June 15, 1776,
      and driven back, 40
  defense of, described by Laura
      Wilkes, 39-41

Ft. Wagner
  battle of described, 52
  Negroes prominent in, 54
"Forty acres and a mule"
  myth kept many freed slaves
      from working after Civil
      War, 157
Foster, Charlotte S.
  graduate of Salem, Mass., State
      Normal School, 89
  outstanding teacher in Port
      Royal Experiment, 89
Fourteenth Amendment
  each ex-Confederate required to
      approve and accept before be-
      ing readmitted into Union, 55
Fox Chase
  pretense of, foiled insurrection
      of 1816 in Camden, 42-44
Frasier, E. Franklin
  in *Opportunity* (Magazine), 115
  on Negro home and civiliza-
      tion, 115
Frederick, Mrs. Allonia L.
  Sumter, recording Sec., S. C.
      Federation of C. W. C., 185
Free Negroes
  education for, 81-86
  from Islands of Atlantic, par-
      tially educated before arriv-
      ing, 81
  hard time making living after
      Civil War, 73-75
  organizations formed in North
      to help them during Civil
      War, 87, 91
  saw great value of education
      and provided schools, 81
  some owned slaves before Civil
      War, 30
      believed their standing hurt
          by Vesey's Insurrection, 48
  volunteers in relief organiza-
      tions called "Gideonites," 88
Freedmen
  aid organizations, 87, 91
      non-sectarian, denominational,
          and semi-denominational, 91
  education for, 81-86
  faced serious handicap in at-
      tempting business because of

Freedmen—*Continued*
   attitude of whites, 135
   volunteers in relief organizations called "Gideonites," 88
   's Aid Bank failed, 152–53
   Negroes suffered financial loss and faith in banks, 152–53
   's Aid Society, The New England, formed early in Civil War, 87, 91
   's aid societies, 82–111
   's Bureau, Act of Congress 1865, 90–91
   's efforts for education during and after Civil War, 91–112
   's Relief Association, N. Y. National, formed early in Civil War, 87, 91
   's Relief Association, Pennsylvania, formed early in Civil War, 87, 91
Freedmen's Aid Bank
   failed, 152–53
Freedmen's Aid Society of Methodist Episcopal Church
   denominational organization, 91
Freedmen's Bureau
   Act of Congress 1865, 90–91
   schools founded and fostered by, 92–112
   success with private organizations in educational work, 91
Freedom
   and idleness not synonymous, Negroes learned during Reconstruction, 71
   by buying themselves, 25
   fight just begun at end of Civil War, 54
   physical, slaves' fight for in S. C., 13–54
Friendly Society of Charleston, 1808, 77
Friends Association of Philadelphia for the Aid and Elevation of the Freedmen, 91
   denominational organization, 91
Friends of Pennsylvania
   supported Schofield school at Aiken, 97

Friendship
   quality of Negro, 214
Friendship College
   property of Negro Baptists of the state, 99
   supplements work of Benedict and Morris Colleges, 99
Frost, Henry
   taught on Magazine St., 86
Frost, Rev. Thomas
   Charleston in 1790, 84
   suggested organization of a society to maintain schools for Negro children, 84
     Brown Fellowship Society formed, later Centenary, 84
Fugitive slaves
   aim for Mason-Dixon Line, 18
   and Indians, 18
   apprehending, 19
   assistance from many whites, 24
   dangers compared to Lindbergh's flight, 20
   intermarriage with Indians, 18
   Law, 17, 20
   many joined Federal Armies at beginning of Civil War, 87
   Underground Railroad, 19, 20, 23, 25
   Virginia Slave hunters, 21
Fugitive Slave Law, 17, 20
   helped bring on Civil War, 25
   made property in slaves uncertain and uneconomical, 25
"Fundamental Constitutions," 1
   prepared by John Locke to guide Lords Proprietors, 1
   recognized slavery in 1669, 1
Furniture business
   one of early successes of S. C. Negroes, 140
Future, Manhood in Ebony Faces the, 213–34
   confidence of Negro in greatness of his future, 214·

Gaillard, Peter
   cotton planter, 4
Garden, Rev. Alexander
   opened school in 1743 with help

Gardner, Rev. Alexander—*Continued*
of S.P.G. and F.P., reported, 83

Gardner, Job
London, certified Richard Holloway on board the *Catherine* near 10 months, with sobriety and good conduct, 138

Garrison, William Lloyd
abolitionist, 16
helped sponsor American Missionary Assn., 88

Gates of toil, 1

Gell, Monday
a chosen leader in Vesey's Insurrection, 46

General Education Board
help to State A. & M. College in continuing extension service, 111

General Shipping at Charleston
one of earliest successes in Negro business, 140

Georgia
under carpet-bag government during reconstruction, 58

Gibbes, Mrs. Phyllis
Charleston, associate editor, S. C. Federation of C. W. C., 185

Gibbs, Rosa
home demonstration agent, Allendale County, 165

"Gideonites"
applied to volunteers who helped teach Freedmen in 1862, 88

Gift of Black Folk, The
by W. E. B. DuBois, 4, 5, 51, 56, 214

"Gift of the Spirit"
of Negro, 214

Gifts of Womanhood in Ebony, 174–91
see Negro, womanhood

Girls' work
Miss Rosa DeLorme, Sumter, head of department, S. C. Federation of C. W. C., 185

Gladden, R. F.
Negro teacher of agriculture, Newberry, 164

Glover, Sam
Negro, Orangeburg Co., story of, 172
working with extension agent from 1916 to 1928, 172
25 acres to 125 acres and success, 172

"Goal, The"
address by B. E. Mays at Benedict College, 203–11

Goal(s)
of life, 207
of the Negro, 203–11

Good Samaritan
spiritual, of American civilization is Negro, 214

Goodel: *Slave Code,* 121

Goodspeed, E. J.
among leaders of Benedict College, 94

Goodwill School at Mayesville
supported by Board of Missions, Presbyterian Church, 97

Goose Creek Parish
Rev. Samuel Thomas began teaching Negroes about 1695, 82

Gordon, Eugene
describes Negro newspapers in *The Messenger Magazine,* 223

Gordon, Mrs. Mary E.
Dillon, organizer for S. C. Federation of C. W. C., 185

Gordon, Roy
Negro agriculture teacher, Eloree, 164

Government
almost all white people in state cut off from taking part in government, 57
Negro, formed in 1868, 57
of S. C. Colony, 1
reconstruction, all Negro except governor, 61
quote from Kelly Miller, 61–62

Gray Court
W. A. White, Negro teacher of agriculture, 164
Green, Mrs. Ida E.
first vice-president, S. C. Federation of C. W. C., 185
Greener, Prof. Richard R.
only Negro appointed professor at S. C. State University, 61
Greenville
County, Delphenia Wilkinson, County home demonstration agent, 165
Negro teacher Charles Hopkins conducted school to which whites contributed, 103
survey of Negro businesses made, 143
Greenwood
Brewer Normal, Industrial and Agricultural Institute, secondary school, 97
Gregory
old colored citizen of Charleston (1927), 73
said Negroes worked for very low wages, poor condition after Civil War, 73
Gresham,
D. T. Taylor, Negro teacher of agriculture, 164

Hagood, Gen.
conservative Democrat, 67
helped pass money legislation started by Negroes, 67
Hale, Edward Everett
helped sponsor American Missionary Assn., 88–89
Hammond, Mr.
late Negro farmer of Anderson, 167
left well-equipped 600-acre farm, nice home, and educated children, 167–68
Hampton, Governor
conservative Democrat, 67
Hampton Government
came into power 1876, 67
helped pass money legislation started by Negroes, 67

Hancock, Cornelia
founded Laing Normal and Industrial School for Negroes at Mt. Pleasant, 97
owned and supported by Pennsylvania Quakers, 97
Harleston, E. G.
father of the artist, 140
in active shipping business many years, 140
Harriot, George
Negro, superintendent of education in his county, 60
Harris: *Africa Slave or Free,* 117
Hart, Mrs. E. L.
recipient of funds on Kibby slave contract, 27
trustee for funds, T. J. Brent, 27
Hart, Henry C., and Elizabeth L.
sold Susan, slave, to George Kibby for wife, 26–27
T. J. Brent, trustee for Mrs. E. L. Hart, 27
Hartsville
H. G. Brewer, Negro teacher of agriculture, 164
Harvard
educated many children of slaves, 76
lecture: "History of Ante-Bellum South," by Prof. Phillips, 1921, 16
sent volunteers to help Freedmen in 1862, 88
Harvesting of rice, 2, 3
Hayes, Roland
artist, great singer, 211
Haynes, C. D.
head of agricultural department of State A.&M. College, 163
Health
advice in B. E. Mays' address, 211
Mrs. M. B. Wright, Spartanburg, head of department of, S. C. Federation of C. W. C., 185
Negro slaves in rice cultivation, 2

Heart of Africa
by Sweinfurth, 117
Helper (author) of North Carolina
The Impending Crisis, 16
see footnote, 3, 16
Henry, Patrick
Negro slaves as true in "Give
me liberty or give me death,"
8, 41
"Henry Box Brown," 20
boxed up and expressed to
Philadelphia, 21
entertained in Boston, 22
first words from psalm: "I
waited patiently for the Lord
and he heard my prayer," 21
from Richmond 26 hours, 21
James A. Smith, shoe dealer,
shipped him, 21
Mr. Davis, merchant in Philadelphia, 21
Mr. McKim, engineering program, 21
received by Adams Express, 21
shipped to Wm. Johnson, Arch
St., 21
stayed in home of Lucretia
Mott, 21
Hewitt
on slave insurrection, in S. C.,
32–33
fomented by Spaniards, 32
some armed, formed army,
killed whites, looted, and
burned, 33
some taken, tried, and hanged
at Charles Town, 33
"Hickory Grove Hoax"
quoted from *The Palmetto
Leader,* 223–24
Hicks, Mrs. C. M.
established school at Anderson,
103
Negro teacher sent South by a
New York society, 103
praise from *The Anderson Intelligence,* 103
Hicks, Judge
on inter-racial committee, S. C.
Federation of C. W. C., 186

Hill, Thos. F.
Negro teacher of agriculture,
Fair Forest, 164
Hilton Head
cotton, 4
History of Mankind
by Ratzel, 117
History of the American Negro
by Brawley, 2, 3
"History of the Ante-Bellum
South"
Harvard lecture by Prof. Phillips in 1921, 16
Holland
A Refutation of Calumnies, etc.,
31, 130
on insurrection in S. C., 32
published Deliesseline's description of Camden Insurrection
of 1816, 42
"The Status of the Negro in
S. C." (1882–23), 44
Holloway, Charles, 137
Holloway, Miss Mae
lived in house in her family over
100 years, 133
on free Negroes owning slaves
before Civil War, 30
on Negro efforts in business,
own records, 136–38
permitted use of scrap book
containing original documents
on Negro in S. C., 115
Holloway, Richard
about 20 years old, 1797, 138
free man, 137, 138
Holman, J. A.
Negro teacher of agriculture,
McClellanville, 164
Holmes, Mrs. Louise F.
Florence, chairman executive
committee, S. C. Federation
of C. W. C., 185
Home
most important function—to
provide a proper place for
nurture and development of
children, 114
not just buildings, possessions,
113

Home—*Continued*
  physical environment important, 114
Home economics
  Mrs. Emma Andrews, Sumter, Head of Department of, S. C. Federation of C. W. C., 186
Hope, Hon. J. H.
  state superintendent of education in 1924, 106
  report, 106–7
Hope
  perpetual stream of from Negro womanhood, 188
  ultimate argument of Negro optimist, 188
Hopkins, Charles
  Negro teacher, conducted a school at Greenville to which whites contributed, 103
House of Bondage, 23
Howard, Mabel, and S. C. Disher
  home demonstration and county farm agents, Darlington County, 165
Howard, Mrs. Mabel K.
  Darlington, head, suffrage department, S. C. Federation of C. W. C., 185
Howard, Gen. O. O.
  Commissioner of Freedmen's Bureau, 1865, 91
Howard School
  Columbia, opened 1867, 93
  Columbia Phoenix quoted, 93
  effort of N. Y. Society and Freedman's Bureau, 93
  long time only public high school in state, 93
  Prof. I. M. A. Myers, principal, sec. of Negro State Teachers Assn. (1927), 93
Howard University
  great biologist Ernest Just, 111
  graduate of State A.&M. College, 111
Howell, Clark
  editor of the *Atlanta Constitution,* quote from, 220

Hubert, B. F.
  established a morale for development of scientific agriculture at State A.&M., 164
  head of agricultural department at State A.&M. College nearly 10 years, 163
  now president of Ga. State Industrial College, 164
Huger, Benj.
  on Board of Trustees, Wilburn school, 86
Humane and Friendly Society
  maintained School for Negro children, 84, 142
Hunter, Gen.
  had numerous Negro volunteers, 51
  in Union Army, 51
Hunters
  slave, Virginia, 21

Ignorance
  after Civil War, aid from Northern aid societies, missionaries, philanthropists, 99–112
  fight against ignorance by Negroes just begun (1927), 112
  law of 1740 prohibiting teaching of slaves, 83
  Negro's long war against, 80–112
  slaves were taught until 1740, 80–83
  state giving financial aid by 1896, 109
  teaching continued after 1740, schools widespread by 1790, 84
Illiterate Among Colored Population
  U. S. Census Reports, 1890, 106
Impending Crisis, The
  by Helper of N. C., *see* footnote, 16
"In his place"
  Negro, various opinions among Negroes about where that is, 194–95

Indians
  aboriginal, workers, 1
  American, servants, 4, 5
  and black fugitive slaves, 18
  intermarriage with Negroes, 18
  Negro, wife of Osceola, 18
  not as well suited to S. C. labor
    as Negro, 6
  numbered 1400 in colony in 1708,
    1
  slaves, could escape to tribes
    easily, 6
  S. C. Negroes fought in all
    wars with, 41
  West Indies, 4, 5
Industrial and economic advancement in S. C.
  contribution to by black man, 12
Inferiority
  Negro, theory of, 13, 14
  proven fiction by individual
    slaves, 28
Influences on Negro home life
  economic and social influences,
    115-16
    all wages for Negroes low in
      this state, injures home life
      beyond estimation, 127
    below living wage makes
      stealing tempting, 127
    children, neglected, often un-
      derfed, when mothers work,
      125-26
    early marriage leads to mal-
      adjustments, large families,
      more poverty, 128
    female member of family,
      usually mother, is in domes-
      tic service, 125
    hard to escape poverty cycle,
      128
    poverty and immorality go
      hand in hand, 127
    small income of Negro largely
      responsible for early mar-
      riages in S. C., 128
  houses he has built and used,
    116-34
    better housing for Sea Islands
      slaves, 130

Influences on Negro home life—
  Continued
    crudest of one-room huts or
      cabins, 119
    freed men began to build own
      houses before Abolition,
      132-33
    since Emancipation Procla-
      mation, Negroes have built
      and owned more and better
      homes, 134
    some domestics lived in "Big
      House," learned home life,
      131-32
    some nothing but shelter, 131
  moral and idealistic principles,
    115
    African, customs, traditions
      and practices differ from
      American, 116
      great variety of civiliza-
        tions, 116
      polygamy widely practiced
        custom, 116
    built on ideals of love, court-
      ship, marriage, 116
    customs and traditions in-
      herited from Africa still
      apparent in some American
      Negroes, 117
    elevation of Negro home life
      commended, 124
    have made much progress in
      sex behavior, as agreed by
      white teachers and leaders,
      123
    immorality of some masters of
      slaves, 120
    monogamous relationship of
      America not prized in Af-
      rica, 116
    Negro colleges agree sexual
      ideals are improving and
      sex behavior better (1927),
      123
    Negroes in S. C. were moral
      in so far as they lived up to
      their ideals, 117-18
    slavery placed stumbling
      block in path of S. C. Ne-

Influences on Negro home life—
Continued
    groes struggling to achieve
    new ideals, 118–19
    no legal marriages among
    slaves, 118
    housing, one-room, crude
    air-less huts, 119
  slavery weakened Negro's
    true morality since it de-
    stroyed African morality
    and put nothing in its place,
    122
  with good masters slaves ben-
    efitted by example, 121
  wives of masters taught mor-
    als and religion, 120
Insurrection, of slaves, 2, 31–33,
38, 42–44, 44–47
  Camden, 1816, 42–44
    date set for July 4, 43
    foiled by gathering under
      pretense of fox chase, 42–44
    informer given freedom and
      pension for life, 44
  caused Negro Act of 1740 to
    discourage importation of
    slaves, 38
  fomented by Spaniards, 32
  intended, by Vesey, 44
  known as Vesey's Insurrection,
    44
    date changed to June 16, 1822,
      47
    set for July 14, 1822, 47
"Intended Insurrection" by Vesey,
  44
  first set for July 14, 1822, 47
  prevented by informer, 47
  second date June 16, 1822, 47
Inter-racial
  work, growth of in this state,
    214
Inter-racial Commission
  began its work in Atlanta, Ga.,
    214
  first financed by War Work
    Council of National Y.M.C.A.,
    214
  Will W. Alexander, National
    director (1928), 214

Inter-racial Committee
  Dr. Alexander, chairman of
    southern states, 186
  Jeannette Keeble Cox, chair-
    man, 186
  Mrs. M. B. Wilkinson, officer of,
    S. C. Federation, C. W. C.,
    185
  members listed, 186
  s, at work all over South,
    210
Inter-racial Forum, Columbia
  organized by Y.M.C.A. students,
    229–30
Islands of the Atlantic
  free Negroes partially educated
    before they came, 81

Jack, Gullah
  a chosen leader in Vesey's In-
    surrection, 46
Jackson, Mrs. Jennie
  Orangeburg, special organizer,
    S. C. Federation, C. W. C.,
    185
Jackson, Luther P.
  "Educational Efforts in S. C.,"
    Journal of Negro History,
    101–2
  Educational Efforts of the
    Freedmen's Bureau and
  Freedmen's Aid Societies in
    S. C., *Journal of Negro His-
    tory,* 87, 89, 90–91, 104
Jazz, plantation songs, "spirituals"
  immortalized by black man
  "burden bearers," 12
Jefferson
  F. N. Clemmons, Negro teacher
    of agriculture, 164
Jefferson, Thomas, 16
  20,000 Negroes deserted colonies
    for English in Revolutionary
    War, 39
Jenkins, E. D.
  county farm agent, Ba[m]berg
    County, 165
Jennings, William
  Negro teacher of agriculture,
    Orangeburg, 164

Jeweler McCall
  one of first S. C. Negroes in this business, 141
Jim Crowism
  and Race pride, 146
  helps some businesses, 146–47
  "Jim Crow" service and "regulations," 151
  The Crisis, most effective against, 217
John Brown
  W. E. B. DuBois quote on process of selection of slaves, 31
Johnakin, Milbia
  Negro teacher of agriculture, Orangeburg, 164
Johnson, Chancellor
  of Marlboro, describes his sharecropping arrangements, 74–75
Johnson, D. J.
  Negro teacher of agriculture, Johnston, 164
Johnson, James W.
  on N.A.A.C.P. staff, 217
Johnson, Wm.
  to receive "boxed" Brown in Philadelphia, 21
Johnston
  D. J. Johnson, Negro teacher of agriculture, 164
Jones, Connie N.
  home demonstration agent, Charleston County, 165
Jones, James M.
  Negro teacher of agriculture, Trenton, 164
Journal of Negro History
  "Educational Efforts in S. C.," by Luther P. Jackson, 101
  Educational Efforts of the Freedmen's Bureau and Freedmen's Aid Societies in S. C., by Luther Jackson, 87
  on Freedmen's Bureau, 90–91
  Post on Negroes in S. C. Legislature, 59–60
  Post (white writer) self-styled "Carpet-bagger," on S. C. rejoining the Union in 1868, 56

July 4, 1816
  set for Camden insurrection, 43
Just, Ernest
  great biologist at Howard University, 111
  most illustrious graduate of State A.&M. College, 111
  scientist, 211

Kegney
  a white Roman Catholic had a school at corner of Radcliffe and St. Phillip Sts., 86
Kentucky prison
  persecution of Calvin Fairbanks for helping slaves escape, 24
Kerlin
  Negro Poets and Their Poems, 232–34
Kibby, George and Susan
  George purchased Susan for wife from Henry C. Hart and wife Elizabeth, 26
  of St. Louise, 26
  story of, as told by Trexler, 26–27
"King Cotton," 5
Kingsley
  Travels in West Africa, 116, 117
Kirvin, Mrs. Mary,
  Syracuse, head business department, S. C. Federation, C. W. C., 185
Ku Klux Klan
  spirit must disappear before renaissance of Negro agriculture in S. C., 160–61
  through dirty work, unjustly and unnecessarily eliminated Negroes from state politics, 79

La Saine, Mrs. M. Alice
  head of department of rural education, S. C. Federation, C. W. C., 185
Labor
  cheap on plantations, 1
  free, quote from *The Charleston Daily News* editorial, 71

Labor—*Continued*
necessary for cotton cultivation, 3
for rice cultivation, 3

Laing Normal and Industrial School (for Negroes)
at Mt. Pleasant, 97
founded by Cornelia Hancock of Philadelphia, 97
here Abbey D. Monroe helped Freedmen, 97
supported by Pennsylvania Quakers, 97

Lake View
R. A. E. Fladger, Negro agriculture teacher, 164

Land
American, endless and fertile, 5
Commission of Reconstruction Government, 158
given $750,000 to buy lands for Freedmen, 70, 158
fund misused, government and Freedmen defrauded, 70, 158

Lanham, T. B.
white, state secretary of Y.M.C.A., agrees with other authorities that Negroes have made much progress in sex behavior, 123
post World War work on interracial problems, 216

Lanier
"Song of Chattahoochee," 205

Latta
G. B. Fladger, T. T. W. Bowen, Negro teachers of agriculture, 164

Laurens, Henry
attitude helped free many Negroes, 29
S. C. statesman and leader, letter to son, 29

Law,
Fugitive Slave, 17, 20
vs. economic interest, 2

Law of 1740
prohibiting the teaching of S. C. slaves, 83

Lawrence, Robert
Negro in Beaufort Co., very successful potato grower, making money, 168

Leaders
Negro, under Congressional Plan, 60–62

Leadership
in rice industry established by Negro, 3

Lee, Joseph
unrest not economic, but spiritual, 12
World's Work, footnote, 11

Lee, Robert E.
surrender, kept large number of slaves out of war, 50

Lee, Samuel J.
Negro legislator and among best criminal lawyers of state, 60

Leggette, P. C.
Negro teacher of agriculture, Marion, 164

Legislature
Negro and "carpet-bagger" problems, 59–68
Reconstruction, of S. C., 57–79

Leonard
The Lower Niger and Its Tribes, 117

Leslie, C. C.
owned wholesale fish business, 139
one of earliest of Negro efforts, 139

Letter to Editor of *Columbia State*
concerning editorial on numbers of Negroes leaving state, 162–163

Levy, I. S.
Negro business man of Columbia who helped sum up present status of Negro business in S. C., 143

Levy, Mrs. Maggie O.
Florence, Vice-Pres., Pee Dee District, S. C. Federation of C. W. C., 185

Levy, Mrs. Maggie O.—*Continued*
member inter-racial committee,
S. C. Federation, C. W. C.,
186
Lewis, T. W.
influential in founding Claflin,
96
S. C. Methodist Episcopal minister, 96
Lindbergh's flight
not as dangerous as that of runaway slaves, 19–20
Lincoln, Abraham, 16
diplomat, 49
Emancipation Proclamation, 31,
53, 54
goal of, 206, 208
Great Emancipator, 17
Negro ballot fulfilled Lincoln's
prophesy, 58
Little Rock
Robert McBryde, Negro teacher
of agriculture, 164
Littlejohn, Mrs. Nina
Spartanburg, organizer for S. C.
Federation, C. W. C., 185
vice-president Piedmont District, S. C. Federation of
C. W. C., 185
Livery Stables
one of early businesses of S. C.
Negro, 141
probably led to success in
undertaking business, 141
Locke, John, 1
prepared "Fundamental Constitution" for S. C. government
in 1669, 1
to guide Lords Proprietors, 1
London Freedmen's Aid Society
non-sectarian organization, 91
Longfellow, Henry W.
"Excelsior," 205, 206
quote, 213
Lords Proprietors, 1
Louisiana
Negroes in War of 1812, 41
under carpet-bag government
3 or 4 years of reconstruction, 58

Love
quality of Negro, 214
Low lands
Negroes naturally adapted to, 3
Lowell
quote from poem, 204
Lower Niger and Its Tribes, The
by Leonard, 117
Luxuries
Old World trade, 5
Lynchburg
E. T. Fleming, Negro teacher
of agriculture, 164
Lynching, 206
The Crisis, most effective
against, 217
white women opposing through
Committee on Race Relations
in S. C., 220–21

McBryde, Robert
Negro teacher of agriculture,
Little Rock, 164
McCall
a jeweler and did considerable
work in this line, 140
eccentric, never passed a bar-
gain, bought own coffin on
sale, 141
first Negro to have mercantile
business, Charleston, 140
had a furniture store soon after
Civil War, 140
said to be first Negro to ride a
bicycle in S. C., 140
McCall
William B. Campbell, Negro
teacher of agriculture, 164
McClellanville
J. A. Holman, Negro teacher of
agriculture, 164
McCottry, Eugene
Negro teacher of agriculture,
Ridge Spring, 164
McDuffy, D. C.
Negro teacher of agriculture,
Marion, 164
McFall, Dr. John A.
has old and valuable records of
Negro efforts in business in
Charleston, 136, 139

McFall, Dr. John A.—*Continued*
McFall Drug Store, one of oldest of pharmacies, 141
third man in state to put considerable capital in pharmacy, 141

McGowan, Mrs.
of Charleston, white chairman of state interracial committee, 123
agrees with others on much progress by Negroes in sex behavior, 123
post World War work on Interracial Committee, 216
work on Committee on Race Relations, 221

McKim, J. M.
in office to receive "Henry Box Brown," 21
Philadelphia, in anti-slavery office, 21

McKinlay, Wm.
assistant teacher to Mr. Thos. S. Bonneau, 85
on Board of Trustees, Wilburn School, 86

McPherson, Capt.
owned slaves who wounded his son, killed another man, and escaped, 32

McPherson, Mrs. Celia P.
on inter-racial committee, S. C. Federation, C. W. C., 186

Making of South Carolina, The
by White, 2, 57

Malaria
Africans generally immune, 3
in rice plantations, 3
whites susceptible, 3

Maloney, J. C.
county farm agent, Sumter Co., 165

Mance, Dr. Robert W.
president of Allen University for several years, 95

Manhood in Ebony Faces the Future, 213–34
assisted by progress revealed in this book to have faith in

Manhood in Ebony Faces the Future—*Continued*
its future in S. C. and the world, 232

Marion
D. C. McDuffy and P. C. Leggette, Negro teachers of agriculture, 164

Market
for cotton, English, 4

Mason-Dixon Line
aim of many fugitives, 18

Massachusetts, 54th Brigade
composed of Negroes, 52
in battle of Ft. Wagner, 52

Mather Academy for (Negro) Girls, Camden
see Browning Industrial Home

Mather, Mrs., of Boston
see Browning Industrial Home and Mather Academy for (Negro) Girls

Mather, Rachel Crome
attempted to found school for American Baptist Home Mission Society, 90
was more social service, 90

Maxwell, John M.
Negro business man of Orangeburg, 143
helped sum up present status of Negro businesses in S. C., 143

Mayesville school (Institute)
founded by Miss Emma Wilson, 98, 186

Mayor of Charleston
took measures to protect people of Charleston and prevent Vesey's Insurrection, 47

Mays, Benjamin E.
address to Older Boys' Conference at Benedict College, 203–11
executive secretary, Tampa, Fla., Urban League, 1926–28, 192
perhaps would demur with Dr. Miller's conclusions, 234
short biographical sketch by editor, footnote, 192–93

Mays, Benjamin E.—*Continued*
"The New Negro Challenges the Old Order," 192–212
Menafee, Mrs. Martin
Denmark, vice-president Orangeburg District, S. C. Federation of C. W. C., 185
Mercantile business
one of early successes of S. C. Negro, 140
Messenger Magazine
carries on Negro work, 217
concept of New Negro, 192
Eugene Gordon in, 223
"Negro Womanhood's Greatest Needs," by Baddy, 177
Methodist Episcopal Church
Freedmen's Aid Society, 91
denominational organization, 91
Woman's Home Missionary Society of, 97
given Browning Industrial Home and Mather Academy for (Negro) Girls, Camden, 97
Michigan Freedmen's Relief Association
non-sectarian organization, 91
Mickeys
leading undertakers of Charleston, 141, 147
Miller, Andred
kept school about 1830, 86
Miller, Kelly
article in *The Messenger,* 69–70
Negro native of S. C., quoted on reconstruction government, 61–62
Out of the House of Bondage, footnote, 234
"These Colored United States—South Carolina," *New York Messenger,* footnote, 62
Miller, Thomas
elected to Congress after overthrow of reconstruction government, 61
Miller, Thos.
prominent Beaufort Negro businessman, 77

Miller, Hon. Thos. E.
first president of State A.&M. College, Orangeburg, 109
remained in office until disfranchisement of his people, 60
speech on reconstruction government in answer to Mr. Tillman, made in Constitutional Convention of 1890, 65–68
quoted from DuBois, 65–68
Minors Moralist Society
School for Negro Children, 84
Minturn
R. C. Collier, Negro teacher of agriculture, 164
Miscegenation
natural possibility, 59
of immoral nature of decline in this state (1927), 124
Missing Pages in American History, 13–54, 55
by Laura E. Wilkes, 13
Mission,
of colored race, 1
Missionaries
to help Indian and Negro slaves in America, 1701, 82
The Society for the Propagation of the Gospel in Foreign Parts, 82
most effective work in early history in S. C., 82
Missionary Association, American
pioneer in education for Negroes in southern states, 88
Mississippi
planter found it paid to allow slaves to purchase themselves and their families, 26
under carpet-bag government during 3 or 4 years of reconstruction, 58
Mitchell, J. H.
(2 No.), Notary Public in Charleston, S. C., 1797, 138
signed certificate of entry into S. C. of Richard Holloway, Mulatto seaman, 138

Mobley, James S.
  prominent Columbia Negro businessman, 77
Monroe, Abbey D.
  at Laing Normal and Industrial School for Negroes at Mt. Pleasant, 97
Monuments of Civil War
  to Gen. Shaw with tribute to Negro soldiers, in Boston Commons, 53
  to many Confederate soldiers, 53
Mood
  taught on Beaufain St., 84
Moore, Benjamin
  Vice Council, British Consul's Office, State of S. C., 138
  certified J. H. Mitchell's authority as Notary Public, for Richard Holloway, 138
Morals and Manners Among Negro Americans
  DuBois and Dill, Atlanta University Publication No. 18, 128
Morris, J. W.
  early president of Allen University, 95
  studied law at U. of S. C. when it was democratic, 95
Morris College
  Negro Baptist school, 99
Morris Street School
  Charleston, 93
Morrison, S. M.
  Charleston, asst. recording sec., S. C. Federation of C. W. C., 185
Morse, Prof. Josiah
  of U. S. C., agrees with others of prominence that Negroes have made great progress in sex behavior, 123
Morton, R. R.
  Principal at Tuskegee Institute (1927), 142
Mosquitoes
  in rice fields, 3

Mother's department
  Mrs. Belle Vincent, head of, S. C. Federation, C. W. C., 185
Mott, Lucretia
  took Henry Box Brown into her home, 21
Moultrie, Col.
  directed defense building, 40
Moultrie, Ft.
  in Charleston Harbor, defended in Revolutionary War, 40
Moultrie, General
  cotton planter, 4
Mount Pleasant
  Laing Normal and Industrial School (for Negroes), 97
Mullins
  J. S. Roberts, Negro teacher of agriculture, 164
Munns, or Munz, school for Negroes
  popular for a time, 85–86
Munz, or Munns, school for Negroes
  popular for a time, 85–86
Murray, George W.
  elected to Congress after overthrow of reconstruction government, 61
Music
  Mrs. Effie Strother, Florence, head of department of, S. C. Federation of C. W. C., 185
Myers, I. M. A., Prof.
  principal Howard high school, 93
  sec. Negro State Teachers Assn. (1927), 93

Nash, Beverly
  Negro, S. C. state senator, 60
Nassau
  Fetichism in West Africa, 117
National Association for the Advancement of Colored People
  chapters in Columbia and Charleston, 218
  Columbia chapter headed by Negro lawyer, N. J. Frederick, 21

National Association for the Advancement of Colored People —*Continued*

considered "foreign" in S. C., to Negroes and whites, 218

militant effect organization, post World War, 216

Negro expressions in, 193

organized under leadership of W. E. B. DuBois, 216–17

strong Negro staff of Robert Bagnall, Walter White, William Pickins (of S. C.), and James W. Johnson, 217

uncompromising work of, 211

National Federation of Colored Women's Clubs

Mrs. Mary McLeod Bethume, president, 98

Neeces

Foster Burton, Negro teacher of agriculture, 164

Negro

enter South Carolina, 1

forced into U. S. against his will, 1

free ones, 30

some owned slaves before Civil War, 30

believed their standing hurt by Vesey's Insurrection, 48

farmer, in S. C., 156–73

began after war with handicaps of poverty, lack of credit or assistance, 158

also handicapped because of ignorance, 159

this condition by no means yet eliminated, 158

being aided by agricultural education in state, 159

discouraged when educated children do not return to farming, 160

some girls return to teach, 160

some young men return to teach agriculture, 160

few before Civil War but have become independent

Negro—*Continued*

business men in agriculture, 156

has made progress in acquiring land, building homes, starting in scientific farming, 163

hundreds of successful farmers in state, 167

labors under difficulties of both races in farming plus race prejudice, 156

leaving state in great numbers, 162, 163

number in state decreased between 1920 and 1925 census, 165

reasons for decrease, 165–67

outstanding examples of antebellum days are James Pendarvis and Mrs. Persons, 156–57

suggestions for improvements for successful and unsuccessful farmers, 168–69

freed

Gregory, old Charleston citizen (1927), said wages low and conditions poor, 73

hard time making living after Civil War, 73–75

learned freedom and idleness not synonymous, 71

listed in U. S. Census Report, 1890, by profession or trade, 78

lost social status over slaves, 69–70

prominent business and professional men in Charleston, Columbia, and Beaufort, 77

removed from politics unjustly by Ku Klux Klan, 79

some educated their children, 76

home, 113–34

developed peculiar dialects when not in contact with whites, 122

Negro—*Continued*

colleges agree sexual ideals are improving and sex behavior better (1927), 123

has made much progress in sex behavior, agreed by white teachers and large group of Southern white people, 123

influence of slavery on, 115–34 experienced difficulty in mastering English due to slavery and poor education, 122

in business in S. C., 135–55

active in general shipping in Charleston, 140 some owned their boats, 140

as slaves unconsciously learned some business methods of Western white man, 135–36

Beaufort developed similar to Charleston, 142

building and construction, carpentry and contracting, 141 built for white people, too, 141

Charleston center of all early business, efforts made in other places, 142

Columbia, especially successful after Civil War, from Government connections, 143

cotton shippers were free, rose to prominence, built homes, educated children, 140 leaders in cotton shipping, Richard and Charles Birnie, Joe Wilson, 140

Dibble family, in Camden, 142 known for achievements in mercantile business, 142

E. G. Harleston, father of the artist, active in shipping for many years, 140

early start in Charleston in undertaking, 141

Negro—*Continued*

probably grew out of livery stable business, 141 Mickeys, present leaders in undertaking, 141

Evans Pharmacy, in Columbia, second in state, 141

faced serious handicap as free man to try business for himself, by attitude of whites, 135 handicap within himself for becoming business man, 135 like Oriental people, not naturally fitted for western type business, 135–36

first in mercantile, McCall, who had furniture store soon after Civil War, 140 also a jeweler, 141 learned business by responsible assignments as slaves, 136

fish business, one of earliest, 139 first woman in business in S. C.: "Joe Cole and Wife—Fish," 139

helped make Charleston prominent cotton shipping center, 140

in Charleston, some French extraction, some West Indies engaged in business, 139 successful in cotton sampling and shipping, 139–40

McFall Drug Store, of Charleston, one of oldest, 141

most kinds except manufacturing and banking, 143

of French extraction, engaged in dry goods business as early as 1805, 140

operated 49 stores in S. C. in 1880, 143

Negro—*Continued*
Peoples' Pharmacy of Charleston, first of kind in state, 141
present status (1927) and progress from contemporaries, 143
survey of present business, 143–45
achievement comparatively insignificant in state, 150
race prejudice plays great part, 150
"Toy Business Men" to white "Board of Trade," 151–52
assistance from economics classes in Benedict and State Colleges, 143
banking and insurance have begun with hope of economic improvement, 152–53
"not prepared for banking," Rosenwald, 153
college graduates criticized as not being well trained in business, probably valid claim, 154
figures compiled and analyzed by Thomas Brier, senior (1927) of State College, 144–45
gets Negro trade while whites get both races, 146–55
handicapped, by lack of capital, 152
by lack of trust in each other, 152
hope lies in colleges' furnishing trained, efficient, constructive leadership graduates, 155
made in Orangeburg, Greenville, Columbia, 143
race prejudices a handicap? many variations in

Negro—*Continued*
answers (*see* Race prejudice), 145
treated with disrespect, such as not using title "Mrs.," "Miss," etc., 149
types of businesses surveyed, 145
will trace with white companies, whites do not trade much with them, 146–55
some have profitable shops serving whites only, 147
seems inferior to whites, 136
shipping, organized a Negro pilot's association, 140
still active after over 50 years (1927), 140
some before Civil War, 136–38
especially in Charleston, 136–38
took part in effort to establish silk culture, 140
very active in church business and secret societies, 141
was conscripted burden bearer, not intended to participate in business, 135
in U. S. Wars, 13–54
always fought for his own freedom, 39
fought on both sides Revolutionary War, 38
in Civil War, 49–54
monument to Gen. Shaw in Boston Commons, 53
of S. C. fought in all wars with Indians, 41
not as prominent in War of 1812 as those of Ala. and La., 41
see also under specific war
"New Negro," 192–212
goals of, 203–11
"in his place," but where? great difference of opinion, 194–95

Negro—*Continued*
 is doubting white man's
  Christianity, 202
 newspapers, 223–26
 qualities: optimism, friendship, fellowship, love, 214
 real truth about, being taught
  in white colleges in state,
  228–29
 spiritual Good Samaritan of
  American civilization, 214
 younger generation beginning
  to develop a hatred of white
  people as a race, 231
  Y.M.C.A. helping combat
   this tendency, 231
  "doubting Thomases" en-
   couraged to carry on,
   231
 of North
  helped finance American Missionary Association during
   Civil War, 89
 of South
  helped finance schools established by Freedmen's Bu-
   reaus, 103
   students by tuition and
    service, patrons with
    money, 103
   teachers helped schools by
    working for small pay,
    103
  fared badly educationally
   from beginning of Wade
   Hampton regime, 105
  rural education, Rosenwald
   plan for, 108
  state College closed to Negroes when Negroes eliminated from state politics,
   105
 optimist
  as in "Comic Side of Trouble," by Bert Williams, 188
 problems after Civil War
  added to own by referring to
   "Rebels" and such, 102
  contributed to financial
   growth out of great poverty, 100

Negro—*Continued*
 help from North, educational
  and financial, 100
  justified through faith, co-
   operation, hard work, 100
  moral, religious, mastered
   themselves, 100
  white Northerners also added
   to difficulties by references
   to war, 102
  see also under specific problem
 reconstruction participation, 55–
  79
  and "carpet-bagger" legislature problems, 59–68
  ballot, fulfilled Lincoln's
   prophesy, 58
  quote from white and Negro
   writers, 57–58
  given power to vote under
   "Congressional Plan," 55
  government, formed in 1868,
   57
   some mistakes inevitable,
    57, 58
  humanly imitative of white
   people, especially in social
   life during Reconstruction,
   68
  in S. C. admitted to State
   University during Reconstruction, 61
  leaders in S. C. under Congressional Plan, 60–62
  lost power on overthrow of
   reconstruction, 61
  more Negroes than whites
   could vote during Reconstruction, 57
  some elected to Congress after
   downfall in 1876, 61
   had ideas of aristocracy,
    especially in Charleston,
    69
  suffrage, DuBois quote, 56
 slave(s)
  always fought for his own
   freedom, 39
  and Christian religion, 28–29

Negro—*Continued*
    attitude toward work, 9–10, 72
    better suited to S. C. labor than Indians, 6
    character of, 28–29
    conscripted, 1
    contribution to work philosophy ignored, 11
    established leadership in rice industry, 3
    fight for freedom started before leaving Africa, 30
    from Africa, 2
    fugitives, assistance from many whites, 24
    health in rice cultivation, 2
    helped build harbor defenses at Charleston, 39–40
    in Civil War, 13–54
    intermarriage with Indians, 18
        wife of Osceola descendant of Indian-Negro parents, 18
    labor, accomplishments of, 10
    naturally adapted to low lands, 3, 6
    North sold last of its slaves to South, 15
    numbered 4120 in colony in 1708, 1
    officially defined 1682, 1
    philosophy of, 7, 8
    population increased faster than whites, 1
    prominent in Civil War, 49–54
    runaways, 8, 17
        as true as Patrick Henry in "Give me liberty or give me death," 8
    sang at work, 11
    soldier, paid tribute by Charles Pinckney, 40
    theory of inferiority of, 12, 13, 28
    war against ignorance, 80–112
    law of 1740 prohibiting teaching of S. C. slaves, 83
    many from Islands of Atlantic partially educated before they came and encouraged it, 81
    through tremendous sacrifices, great disadvantages, 80
    was taught to read and write by early slave owners of Protestant Christian faith, 81
    see also School(s), Education
womanhood
    first, gift of greatness, transmitted through inheritance to Negro manhood, 175
    gifts of, 174–91
    influence on soldiers of World War, 188–91
    loyal love to Negro manhood, 177
    perpetual stream of hope, 188
    philosophy, "whatever shall be will be better," 189
    physical fitness and labor, 175
        giving labor, wages so low, 175
    's Greatest Needs, by Baddy, 177
    supreme gift, motherhood, 174
        Calvin Coolidge: "No man was ever meanly born . . . " 174
women
    exploited immorally by white men, 178
    feel less dependent upon marriage for support than white women, 176–77
    outstanding, of S. C., Mary McLeod Bethume, Mrs. Marion Birnie Wilkinson, 178, 179
    self-supporting, more independent than white women, 176
    see also Business, Education, Home, S. C. Federation of Colored Womens' Clubs, Womanhood
Woodson
    The Negro in Our History, 38, 159

Negro Act of 1740
caused by insurrections to discourage importation of slaves,
38
Negro American Family, The
Atlanta University Publication
No. 13, footnotes, 113, 124,
130, 131
little on subject for 20 years
after 1908, 115
published in 1908 for history
and sociology of Atlanta University, 114
Negro Baptists of the state
own Friendship College, 99
*Negro from Africa to America,
The*
by Weatherford, 117
Negro Home, in S. C.
is African Negro home as
adapted to civilization of
S. C., 115
like his civilization, did not originate in U. S., certainly not
S. C., 115
literature of Atlanta University
press of some value, 115
little known or published on it,
115
unpleasant influence of slavery
on, 115, 118–19
see Influences on Negro home
life
Negro in American History, The
by John W. Cromwell, 118
Negro in American Life, The
by Jerome Dowd, 123, 125, 126,
159
Negro in Our History, The
by Woodson, 38, 159
*Negro in South Carolina During
the Reconstruction, The*
by A. A. Taylor, 55, 143, 157,
158
Negro Pilots' association
organized from Negro shipping
businesses, 140
Negro Poets and Their Poems
by Kerlin, 232–34
Negro Race, The
by Dowd, 116

"Negro Womanhood's Greatest
Needs"
by Baddy, in *Messenger Magazine,* 177
Negro workingman vs. European
workman in attitude toward
work, 10–11
Neide, Major Horace
successively state superintendent of education under
Freedmen's Bureau, 1865, 91
New England Freedmen's Aid
Society, The
established industrial school at
Beaufort, S. C., 90
formed in early Civil War to
help needy blacks in South, 87
non-sectarian organization, 91
New Negro
age, education, not factor in
"New Negro," 193
creed, 212
written by William Pickens,
212
how he faces concrete and
specific situations, 193–212
"in his place," where? is problem, 194–95
is doubting white man's christianity, 202
very small number developing
new race psychology re inter-
racial affairs, 193
New Negro Challenges Old Order,
192–212
by B. E. Mays, 192–212
"New Negro, The"
poem by Reverdy C. Ransom,
192
New York Freedman's Relief
Association
Annual Report, 1866, 88
non-sectarian organization, 91
New York National Freedmen's
Relief Association
formed in early Civil War to
help needy blacks in South,
87, 88
non-sectarian organization, 91
New York Times
reported Columbia "whites ex-

New York Times—Continued
tend every possible facility and encouragement in . . . education," 102

Newberry
E. F. Floyd, R. F. Gladden, S. M. Young, Negro agriculture teachers, 164

News and Courier
white newspaper of Charleston, 222
changing toward news of Negroes, 222

Nichols and Crogman
The Progress of a Race, footnote, 22, 23

Nigeria
accomplishments of Negro labor, 10

Nix, Prof. N. C.
of State College, 124
has dealt with Negro students in S. C. for 25 or 30 years, 124

North
bond holders during reconstruction, 58
got more of the money for southern government than "carpet-baggers," 58
people of, began organizations to help Negroes in South soon after Civil War began, 87
sold last of its slaves to South, 15

North Carolina
under carpet-bag government during 6 years of reconstruction, 58

Northern Presbyterian Church
supports Fairfield Normal Institute at Winnsboro, 98

Northern white people
partly responsible for difficulties they faced in south, 102
referred to "Old Jeff Davis" disrespectfully, 102
taught children "Marching through Georgia," "John

Northern white people—*Continued*
Brown's Body," and other songs, 102

Oberlin
educated many children of slaves, 76

Odom
Social and Mental Traits of the Negro, 127

"Old Jeff Davis"
referred to disrespectfully by Northerners in south, 102
added to difficulties after Civil War, 102

Old Order
challenged by New Negro, 192–212

Old World trade
for luxuries, 5
to world-wide trade in necessities, 5

Opportunity (Magazine)
carries on work for Negroes, 217
concept of "New Negro," 192–93
E. Franklin Frasier, on Negro home and civilization, 115

Optimism
eternal, principal power of Negro, 213

Optimist, Negro
as in "Comic Side of Trouble," by Bert Williams, 188
ultimate argument is hope, 188

Orangeburg
Claflin University for Negroes, one of best known in America, 95
farm workers made 50¢ a day or about $8 a month, 74
Female College, sold to Claflin U., 96
G. W. Daniels, county farm agent, 165
Milbia Johnakin, Negro agriculture teacher, 164
Negroes getting some education in 1700's, 84

Orangeburg—*Continued*
survey made of Negro businesses, 143
where State A.&M. College located, 109
William Jennings, Negro agriculture teacher, 164

Orangeburg—Sunlight Club
officers, Mrs. Marion B. Wilkinson, Pres., Mrs. Etta B. Rowe, Sec., 184
report to State Federation of Colored Women's Clubs, 184

Organizations
educational help, 87
in North to help southern Negroes during Civil War, 87
physical help, 87
volunteers called "Gideonites," 88

Organized rebellion
first in S. C. against masters, 31–33

Orr, Gov. of S. C.
to colored people at Charleston: "prepared to stand by the colored man who is able to read the Declaration of Independence and Constitution of U. S. . . . " 102

Outten, Acy
Negro teacher of agriculture, Summerville, 164

Oven, Chandler
"The Passing of Private Houses," editorial in *The Messenger,* 1927, 129

Palmetto Leader, The
Negro newspaper, 223
serves as newspaper and advocate of Negro rights, 223
quote from, 224

"Palmetto State"—South Carolina, 105
Negroes in business in, 136

Pamlico
Easterling Walker, Negro teacher of agriculture, 164

Panama Canal
accomplishments of Negro labor, 10

Parish, St. Luke's
cotton area, 4

Parker, Mrs.
on inter-racial committee, S. C. Federation of C. W. C., 186
"Passing of Private Houses, The"
Chandler Oven editorial in *The Messenger,* 1927, 129

Paul, William
domestic slave, 47
revealed Vesey plot to slave of Col. Prioleau on May 25, 1822, 47
insurrection date changed, 47
Mayor of Charleston informed and took measures to protect white people, 47

Payne, Daniel
Bishop A.M.E. Church, took over Bonneau school, 85

Payne Institute
consolidated with Allen University, 93

Pendarvis, James
at one time held 200 slaves, 157
before Civil War was large planter, 157
free Negro in St. Paul's parish, 157

Penn Normal and Agricultural Institute
aftermath of Penn School, 89–90

Penn School
founding helped by Luna [Laura] M. Towne, 89
St. Helena Island, 169

Pennsylvania Freedman's Relief Assn.
formed early in Civil War to help needy blacks in South, 87
non-sectarian organization, 91

Pennsylvania Quakers
supported Laing Normal and Industrial School for Negroes at Mt. Pleasant, 97

Pennsylvania Quakers—*Continued*
supported Schofield secondary
school at Aiken, 97

Peonage
elimination of, before renaissance of Negro agriculture in
S. C., 160–61
in Georgia—Williams Farm incident, 159
in Mississippi, 160
small town merchants backbone
of system, 160
some whites wanted ex-slaves
reduced to peonage, 73
still practiced in S. C., 159, 160

Pequette, Mrs. Erma L.
Sec., Charleston—Louise F.
Holmes Literary and Art
Club, 183, 184

Percell, Mr.
old resident of Charleston, 140
reported colored men of French
extraction in dry goods business as early as 1805, 140

Persons, Mrs.
census of 1780 reports 136 slaves
for her, 157
free Negro, large planter before
Civil War, 157

Petersburg
hardest fighting by black troops,
52
praised by Gen. Smith, 52
Sgt. Wm. H. Carney saved flag,
52
praised by Sec. of War Stanton, 52
siege of, in Civil War, 52

Petition and Representation
reporting state of unrest and
discord with French, Spaniards, Indians, and insurrection of Negro slaves, (reprinted in full), 34–38
signed by John Fenwicke for
Upper House of Assembly, 38
William Bull, Junr. Speaker,
26 July 1740—for Commons
House of Assembly, 38
to His Majesty of the Present
state of the Province, 34–38

Pharmacy
early business of S. C. Negro,
141

Philadelphia
anti-slavery office, 21
"Henry Box Brown" boxed
up and expressed to, 21
from Richmond, 26 hours
by express, 21
Crafts, from Georgia, safe, 22

Phillips, Prof. U. B.
American Negro Slavery, 2, 3,
4, 120, 157, 159
cotton industry, 3
footnote, 14
Harvard lecture, 1921, on "History of Ante-Bellum South,"
16
rice harvesting, 2, 3

Philosophy
of Negro womanhood, "whatever shall be will be better,"
189
of S. C. Negro slaves, 7, 8
on work ignored, 11

Phyllis Wheatley Center
Greenville, founded by Mrs.
Hattie Logan Duckett, 187

Physical freedom in S. C.
slaves' fight for, 13–54

Physical labor
black man's burden, 3

Pickens, William
distinguished younger Negro
leader, 17

Pickens, Wm.
N.A.A.C.P. field secretary, one
of greatest Negro contemporary orators, 219
Negro leader, given start by
hard-working parents, 76–77
of S. C., on N.A.A.C.P. staff,
217
wrote *Creed of the American
Negro Youth, see* footnote,
212

Pilgrim Fathers
goal of, 206

Pinckney, Charles
distinguished South Carolinian,

Pinckney, Charles—*Continued*
  paid tribute to Negro soldiers,
  41–42
Pineville
  J. H. Rumph, Negro teacher of
  agriculture, 164
Pittsburgh Courier
  publication, gives concept of
  "New Negro," 192–93
Plantation
  owners, 2
  home: "Big House," 5
  slavery profitable, 2
  rice prosperous industry, 2
  songs: jazz, "spirituals," immortalized by black man "burden
  bearer," 12
Planters
  began summering in "pine land"
  villages, 3
  cotton, names of, 4
  wealthy ones, town houses, 3
Plezer
  J. H. Chapman, Negro teacher
  of agriculture, 164
Political
  and Economic, revolution in
  America, 5
  intimidation of Negro must be
  eradicated before renaissance
  of Negro agriculture, 160–61
  leaders among Negroes unjustly
  removed from state politics by
  Ku Klux Klan, 79
  phase of reconstruction attracted more attention than
  social and economic, 55
Poor whites
  workers, 1
Population
  early colony, Indian, Negro,
  white, 1
  increase in Negro, caused concern, 2
  more Negroes than whites during reconstruction, 57
  Negro, in S. C., still mostly
  rural (1927), 156
Port Royal Experiment
  Charlotte S. Foster, outstanding
  Negro teacher, 90

Port Royal Experiment—*Continued*
  most teachers white, from
  North, some Negroes from
  North, 90
  to educate and modernize
  Freedmen, 90
Porter, Rev. Toomer
  Charleston *Courier:* "much more
  substantial and lasting token
  of friendship to colored race
  . . . " 102
  of Charleston Episcopal Church,
  went North to solicit educational funds, 102
  visited Howard and President
  Johnson, 102
Post, Louis F. (white man)
  "A Carpet-Bagger in South
  Carolina," in *Journal of Negro History,* 60
  in *Journal of Negro History,* 56
  on Negroes in S. C. Legislature,
  59–60
  Lt. Gov. A. J. Ransier of S. C.
  presided with dignity, 60
  self-styled "Carpet-bagger," on
  S. C. rejoining Union in 1868,
  56
Poyas, Peter
  a chosen leader in Vesey's Insurrection, 46
  convicted, died "silently," 47
  spread advice for Vesey to
  leaders, 46
Prejudice, race
  see Race prejudice
Presbyterian
  Board of Missions, Brainerd
  Institute at Chester, secondary school, 97
  Goodwill School at Mayesville, 97
  church at Wiltown, whose congregation met and overcame
  insurrectionists, 33
  Committee of Missions for
  Freedmen, 91
  denominational organization,
  91

Price, Mabel, and Benjamin B.
Barnwell
county home demonstration and
farm agents, Beaufort Co.,
165
Prioleau, Col.
learned of Vesey's intended insurrection from slave, 47
revealed plans to Mayor of
Charleston, 47
Proprietors, Lords, 1
Protestant Episcopal Freedmen's
Commission
denominational organization, 91
Protestant religious faith
as drive in early slave owners'
teaching the slaves to read
and write, 81
Psalm
"I waited patiently for the
Lord, and he heard my
prayer," Henry Box Brown,"
21
Psychological
and economic aftermath of Civil
War, 100
Psychology
of slavery remained with freed
men, 208
race, small number of "New
Negroes" involved with inter-
racial affairs, 193
Public School System
in name only until funds provided by Reconstruction Government, 63
Punishment
for run-away slaves, 8
Puritans
opposed to slavery, 15
Putnam, Col.
commander of brigade under
Gen. Seymour, 52
in Ft. Wagner battles, 52

Quaker(s)
Martha Schofield, who estab-
lished school at Aiken, 97
opposed to slavery, 15
Pennsylvania, supported Laing
Normal and Industrial School

Quaker(s)—*Continued*
for Negroes at Mt. Pleasant,
97
"Queen Rice," 5

Race
colored, mission of, 1
problem, 192–212
papers and magazines, 192–93
*Crisis, Opportunity, Messen-
ger, Chicago Defender,
Pittsburgh Courier,* 192–93
give concept of "New Negro,"
192–93
Race prejudice
a handicap to Negro business?
asked on survey in 1927, 144–
45
many varied answers, 145–46
according to some whites it is
proper for Negro to be servant to whites but outrageous
for whites to serve Negroes,
148
some indication (1928) that
this attitude slowly changing, 148
forced Negroes to work together
and set up own businesses,
such as restaurants, 146
most business men think it helps
rather than hurts their business, 146
Negroes cannot function on
U. S. Chamber of Commerce,
152
own National Business
League a "huge joke," 152
"Toy Business Men" to
white "Board of Trade,"
151–52
reason for educated children
from farms not to come back
to work, 160
Race pride
each serves his own in such
things as undertaking, eating
places, barbering, etc., 146–
47
of Negroes, 146

Race pride—*Continued*
 separation of Negroes and
  whites, especially on services,
  146–47
Race psychology
 remained with freed slaves, 208
 small number of "New Ne-
  groes" involved in inter-
  racial affairs, 193
Railroad construction
 Capt. Walker, white engineer,
  branded "S.S." on right hand
  for helping slaves escape, 24
 Florida, with slaves, 24
Railroad, Underground
 for fugitives, 19, 20
 some of bravest and best officers were Negroes, 23
 Wm. Still officer, 23
Randolph, Mr. J. B.
 colored, president of Claflin
  College, 96
Ransier, A. J.
 Negro, lieutenant governor of
  S. C., 60
 poor financial manager, 60
Ransom, Reverdy C.
 poem, "The New Negro," 192
Ratzel
 History of Mankind, 117
Rebellion in S. C.
 first organized against masters,
  31–33
Reconstruction, of S. C., 55–79
 "Carpet-baggers," mostly white,
  63
 Congress placed state under
  military control during reconstruction, "Congressional
  Plan," 55
  embraced Civil Rights Bill,
   55
  Fourteenth Amendment, 55
 government, accomplishments
  of,—*see* Accomplishments
  found it necessary to provide
   funds for public school
   system, 63
  overthrow of, 1876, 61
  quote of Kelly Miller, 61–62
  all Negro except governor, 61

Reconstruction, of S. C.—*Continued*
 land commission given $750,000
  to buy land for Freedmen,
  70, 158
  fund misused, government
   and Freedmen defrauded,
   70, 158
 legislature, 59–68
 Negro farm laborers make valuable contribution to, 71
 period, Negro was able to
  "carry on" with characteristic courage, fortitude, and optimism, 79
 political phase of, more attention than social or economic,
  55
 "scalawags" real government
  leaders, all white, 63
 state put under military control, 55
  military District No. 2, 57
 "under rule of Negroes and adventurers from North" from
  1868 to 1876, 56
*Reconstruction in South Carolina,
 The*
 by A. A. Taylor, 73
Record, The
 changing toward news of Negroes, 222
 quote from, 222–223
 white newspaper, Columbia, 222
Reddish, B. J.
 Negro agriculture teacher,
  Blackville, 164
Redpath, James
 appointed in 1865 by Col.
  Woodford, Commander of
  Charleston, to open schools
  for Negro and white children,
  92
 teachers white and colored, 92
Refutation of Calumnies, A
 by Holland, footnote, 31
Religion, Christian
 and the Negro, 28–29, 81
 development of during Reconstruction, among Negroes, 77

Renaissance of Negro agriculture in S. C.
  obstacles to, 160–61
Renters, farm
  after Civil War, 74–75
    did nothing to keep property livable, 75
    system unsatisfactory, 75
Report of S. C. State Supt. of Education, 1924
  numbers of Negro women and girls teaching for little pay, 176
Republicans
  Northerners and Negroes in Reconstruction government, 67
  political party, 67
Revolutionary War
  goal of, 206
  Negroes fought on both sides, 38
Reynolds, John S.
  Reconstruction critic, 59
  presented many facts among criticisms, 59
Rice
  cultivation, prosperous with Negro slaves, 2
  in swamp lands, 2
  harvesting, 2, 3
  mosquitoes, 3
    malaria, 3
  in economic organization, 5
  industry, leadership established by Negro, 3
  plantations, cheap labor, 1
Richland County
  J. E. Dickson and Francis Thomas, county farm agents, 165
Richmond to Philadelphia
  Crafts traveled first class hotels in, 22
  for "Henry Box Brown," 26 hours by express, 21
Ridge Spring
  Eugene McCottry, Negro teacher of agriculture, 164
Roberts, J. S.
  Negro teacher of agriculture, Mullins, 164

Robinson, D. T.
  Negro teacher of agriculture, Society Hill, 164
Rodolph, Mrs. M. O.
  Charleston, organizer, S. C. Federation of C. W. C., 185
Rodolph, Olivia M.
  member inter-racial committee, S. C. Federation, C. W. C., 186
Roman Catholic school
  Kegney teacher, Charleston, 86
Rosenwald, Julius
  became interested through Booker T. Washington, 108
  "Negroes are not prepared for banking," 153
  philanthropic multi-millionaire interested in rural education for Negroes in the South, 108
Rosenwald Fund
  for Negro rural education, 108–9
  S. C. leaders in procuring it, 109
  State A. & M. College, assistance from, on extension service, 111
Rowe, Mrs. Etta
  furnished information on establishment of State Federation of Colored Women's Clubs, 182
Rowe, Mrs. Etta B.
  corresponding sec., S. C. Federation of C. W. C., 185
  sec., Orangeburg—Sunlight Club, 184
"Rule of the Robbers"
  known of S. C. during period 1868 to 1874, 57
Rumph, J. H.
  Negro teacher of agriculture, Pineville, 164
Runaway, Negro Slaves, 8, 17
  punishment for, 8
  to join opposing forces in war against S. C., when promised freedom, 8
  undertook journey more dan-

Runaway, Negro Slaves—*Contin-
ued*
  gerous than Lindbergh's flight,
    19–20
Russellville
  T. W. Cooper, Negro teacher of
    agriculture, 164
St. Andrews Parish
  Rev. E. Taylor gave Negroes
    religious instruction as well
    as other branches, 83
St. Helena school
  taught by "Uncle Cyrus," prom-
    inent Negro teacher, 104
St. John's Berkeley
  cotton area, 4
St. Luke's parish
  cotton area, 4
St. Paul's
  cotton area, 4
St. Thomas
  in slave trade with Capt. Vesey,
    44
Saluda
  Robert D. Dean, Negro teacher
    of agriculture, 164
San Domingo
  in slave trade with Capt. Vesey,
    44
Sasportas, F. K.
  assistant teacher to Mr. Thos. S.
    Bonneau, 85
Sasportas, Joseph
  on Board of Trustees, Wilburn
    school, 86
Saunders, Mrs. Annie
  Sumter, organizer, S. C. Feder-
    ation, C. W. C., 185
Saxon, Mrs. Celia D.
  Columbia, treasurer, S. C. Fed-
    eration of C. W. C., 185
Saxton, Rufus, Gen.
  successively assistant commis-
    sioner of Freedmen's Bureau,
    1865, 91
"Scalawags"
  real leaders in Reconstruction
    government, all white, 63
Schneider, Wilhelm
  quote from *The Negro Amer-
    ican Family,* 113

Schofield Normal and Industrial
  School
    at Aiken, 97
  secondary school established by
    Marcha Schofield, Quaker, for
    Friends of Pennsylvania, 97
School Appropriation and Budget
  State of S. C. in 1924, 106–7
School Board of Trustees
  for Wilburn school, 86
Schools for Negro Children
  Bonneau Library Society, 84
  Brown Fellowship Society, later
    Centenary, 84
  Humane and Friendly Society,
    84
  Minors Moralist Society, 84
  Munns or Munz popular for a
    time, 85–86
  Other schools, 86
    Stromer, Mrs., woman of
      color, had school from 1820
      until Civil War, 86
Scotia Seminary
  attended by Mrs. Mary McLeod
    Bethume, 98
Scott, L. N.
  Negro teacher of agriculture,
    Eastover, 164
Scott, Gen. R. K.
  successively assistant commis-
    sioner of Freedman's Bureau,
    1865, 91
Screven, John
  cotton planter, 4
Sculptor, Thorwaldsen
  Danish, on success, 206
Seabrook, William
  cotton planter, 4
Secession of S. C., 14
Secondary Schools in S. C., *see
  also* by name
    founded 1868–70, 97–98
    Bettis Institute or Academy,
      98
    Brainerd Institute, at Ches-
      ter, 97
    Brewer Normal, Industrial
      and Agricultural Institute,
      Greenwood, 97

Secondary Schools in S. C.—*Continued*
> Fairfield Normal Institute, 98
> Goodwill School, at Mayesville, 97
> Schofield Normal and Industrial School at Aiken, 97

Secret societies
> in Charleston, 141
> Negroes active in, 141
> oldest, Brown Fellowship Society, 142

Segregation, 206
> attacked by S. C. Federation of C. W. C., 185
> laws of state of S. C., separate races, especially on services, 146–47
> Negroes find some businesses more profitable because of it, discrimination, "Jim Crowism," legal or customary, 146–47
> *The Crisis,* most effective effort against, 217

Sense of fair play
> in Southern white people, 28
> slaves appealed to this for freedom, 28

Servants
> American Indians, 4, 5
> black from Africa, 4, 5
> Negroes after Civil War, 76
> of aristocracy, 76
> West Indies Indians, 4, 5
> white bond, from Europe, 4, 5
> some educated children, 76–77

Settlers, early, 1

Seymour
> taught on George St., 86

Seymour, Gen.
> commander of division of Federal Army in battle of Ft. Wagner, 52

Shakespeare, Wm.
> quoted beginning of Chap. III, 55

Shanklin, J. S.
> Negro teacher of agriculture, Burton, 164

Share-croppers
> arrangements with Chancellor Johnson of Marlboro, 74–75
> did nothing to keep up property, 75
> ex-slaves, made very poor living, 73–75

Shaw, Col.
> in 54th Mass. Brigade, 52
> killed in battle of Ft. Wagner, 52

Shaw, Francis G.
> helped sponsor American Missionary Assn., 88–89

Shaw, Gen.
> monument to, including Negro soldiers, in Boston Commons, 53

Shaw Memorial Institute
> of Charleston, named for Col. Robert G. Shaw, hero of Morris Island, 93

Sherman
> issued first order for help for freedmen, or Negroes, in south, 1862, 87

Shipping
> general, at Charleston, 140
> one of earliest successes of S. C. Negroes in business, 140

Sicilian Vespers
> horrors of, in plans for Camden insurrection of 1816, 43
> date set for July 4, 43

Silk culture
> failed because climate and conditions not suitable, 140
> Negro took part in effort to establish business, 140

Simms, Dr. David H.
> a graduate of Oberlin College, 95
> present president of Allen University (1927), 95
> youngest college president in state, 95

Simonton, Judge
> conservative Democrat, 67
> helped pass money legislation started by Negroes, 67

Simpson, J. T.
  Negro teacher of agriculture,
    Easley, 164
Simpsonville
  Roosevelt White, Negro teacher
    of agriculture, 164
Sims, Dr. D. H.
  inter-racial work during post
    World War period, 216
Sinclair, W. A.
  quote from *Aftermath of Slav-
    ery,* 64–65
  quote on Negro ballot and gov-
    ernment after reconstruction,
    57–59
  The Aftermath of Slavery, foot-
    note, 59
Singing
  natural while Negro works, 11
Sinkler, James
  cotton planter, 4
Slater Fund
  John F. Slater co-operated to
    publish *The Negro American
    Family* through Atlanta Uni-
    versity Press, 114
Slave Code
  by Goodel, 121
Slavery
  in colony, 1
  in S. C., very profitable, 3
  Negro, in S. C., 14
    economic consideration, 13–54
    Helper, of N. C., *The Im-
      pending Crisis,* 16
    opposed by Puritans, 15
      and by Quakers, 15
  recognized in colony in 1669, 1
  remained in freed man's psy-
    chology, 208
Slavery as It Is
  by Angelina Grimpe Weld, 119
"Slaves Carry on in Civilization,
  The"
  article by Negro writer, 70
Slave(s)
  Indians, 6
    could escape to tribes easily, 6
    not as well suited to S. C.
      labor as Negro, 6

Slave(s)—*Continued*
  Negro
    after Civil War became wage
      slaves instead of chattel
      slaves, 72
    attitude toward work, 9–10
    Camden insurrection of 1816,
      42–44
      date set for July 4, 43
      informer given freedom and
        pension for life, 44
    conscripted, 1
    contribution to work philos-
      ophy ignored, 11
    domestic service at "Big
      House," 5
    ex-, had hard time making
      living, 72–75
    health in rice cultivation, 2
    import duty on, 1749, 2
    insurrection, 2, 31–33
      fomented by Spaniards, 32
      caused Negro Act of 1740
        to discourage importation
        of slaves, 38
    Law of 1740 prohibiting
      teaching of, 83
    managed more and more man-
      ual labor of business,
      learned trades, 139
    myth of "40 acres and a mule"
      kept many ex-slaves from
      working right after Civil
      War, 157
    North sold its last slaves to
      South, 15
    not originally intended to
      participate in business, 135
    numbered 4120 in colony in
      1708, 1
      32,000 in 1724, 1
    officially defined 1682, 1
    owned by some free Negroes
      before Civil War, 30
    owners, early encouraged
      slaves to get some educa-
      tion, 81
    philosophy of, in S. C., 7, 8
    renting not satisfactory, 74–
      75

Slave(s)—*Continued*
  rice cultivation, 2
  sang at work, 11
  share-cropping practices, 73–75
  unconsciously learned some business methods of Western white man, 135, 136
  Negro fugitives
  apprehending, 19
  danger of fugitives compared to Lindbergh's flight, 20
  fight for physical freedom, 13–54
  help from many whites to escape, 24
  hunters, Virginia, 21
  intermarriage with Indians, 18
  Law, 17, 20
  punishment for run-aways, 8
  received in anti-slavery office, Philadelphia, 21, 23
  welcome in Philadelphia, 21, 22
  run-away, 8, 17
  Underground Railroad for fugitives, 19
  with Indians, 18
  trade
  beginning of great commerce, 5
Small, Robert
  Negro S. C. state senator, 60
  elected to Congress after overthrow of reconstruction, 61
Smalls, Robert
  prominent Beaufort Negro business man, 177
Smith, James A.
  shoe dealer in "Henry Box Brown" story, 21
  expressed Brown to Philadelphia, 21
  imprisoned for 7 years, mistreated and persecuted, 22
  shipped two others who were apprehended, 22
  when released went North and married, 22

Smith-Hughes and Smith-Lever agencies, 111
  see Smith-Lever and Smith-Hughes agencies
Smith-Lever and Smith-Hughes agencies
  Act, Mr. H. E. Daniels, state supervising agent for men and boys' work, 165
  Miss Dora E. Boston, state supervising agent for women's and girls' work, 165
  headquarters for state agents at State Agricultural College for Negroes, 165
  help State A. & M. College carry on extension services, 111
Snowden, Prof. Yates
  of U. S. C., 44, 100
Social
  and economic phases attracted less attention than political during reconstruction, 55
  life of Negroes, in Reconstruction, imitative of white people, 68
  democratized to certain extent, 68
  freed Negroes lost social status over slaves, 69–70
  some had ideas of aristocracy, especially in Charleston, 69
Social and Mental Traits of the Negro
  by Odom, 127
Social History
  by Brawley, 18
Society for the Propagation of the Gospel in Foreign Parts
  organized in London in 1701, 82
  Missionary to Indian and Negro slaves in America, 82·
  An Account of the Endeavors Used by, 83
  most effective early work in S. C., 82
  report from, quote, 83
Society, Friendly
  of Charleston, 1808, 77

Society Hill
D. T. Robinson, Negro teacher of agriculture, 164
Sociology
by Spencer, 116
"Sojourner Truth"
grand old warrior, 24
Solomon, Kittie
teacher, said to have been Haytian refugee, 86
"Song of Chattahoochee"
by Lanier, 205
Souls of Black Folk, The
by DuBois, 88, 114
South Africa
accomplishments of Negro labor, 10
South Carolina
colony, 1
Commonwealth, 57
known as Military District No. 2, 1867–74, 57
Constitutional Convention, received copies of *N. Y. Tribune* from Francis L. Cardoza, 60
of 1890, Mr. Tillman's argument answered by Thos. E. Miller, 65–68
contribution to economic and industrial advancement of black man, 12
end of reconstruction government, 1876, 61
Federation of Colored Women's Clubs, *see* State Federation of C. W. C.
first success in cotton, 4
known as under "Rule of Robbers" from 1868 to 1874, 57
laws against intermarriage of races in state, 178
Negro, entered, 1
farmers in, 156–73
see Negro, farmer
in business, 135–55
see Negro, in business
leaders under Congressional Plan, 60–62
population in state predominantly rural, 156

South Carolina—*Continued*
slaves, attitude toward work, 9–10
joined opposing warring forces when promised freedom, 8
suffrage, DuBois quote, 55
given right to vote, 55
not as prominent in War of 1812 as those of Ala. and La., 41
part in reconstruction, 55–79
only state to admit Negroes to State University during reconstruction, 61
whites left, 61
"Palmetto State," 105
received back in Union under "Black-and-Tan" Constitution of 1868, 56
Reconstruction legislature, 59–68
secession of, 14
slavery very profitable, 3
slaves fight for physical freedom, 13–54
first insurrection in, 31–33
caused Negro Act of 1740 to discourage importation of, 38
fomented by Spaniards, 32
fugitives with Indians, 18
state, leader in procuring Rosenwald rural schools, 109
put under military control during reconstruction, Congressional Plan," 55
embraced, Civil Rights Bill, 55
Fourteenth Amendment, 55
school appropriation and budget for 1924, 106–7
Supt. of Education, 1924 Report, on Negro women and girls working, 176
The Making of, by White, 2
under carpet-bag government 8 years of reconstruction, 58
"under rule of Negroes and ad-

South Carolina—*Continued*
venturers from North" from 1868 to 1876, 56

Southern
Statesmen, before Civil War, 16, 17
S. C. Henry Laurens, 29
view, vs. Yankee on Negro-white situation in South after Civil War, 100
Negroes fundamentally inferior, 100

Southern Commission on Interracial Co-operation
co-operates with Y.M.C.A., 229

Southern Opinion and Race Relations
pamphlet, *see* footnote, 220
quote from, 228

Southern white people
had sense of fair play and feeling of common humanity, 28
slaves appealed to this for freedom, 28

Spaniards
fomented S. C. insurrection of slaves, 32

Spartanburg County
W. C. Bunch, farm agent, 165

Spaulding, Mrs. L. D.
Camden, chaplain, S. C. Federation of C. W. C., 185
pres., Camden—Uplift Club, 183

Spencer
Sociology, 116

Spiritual Good Samaritan
of American civilization is the Negro, 214

Spirituals
also jazz music and plantation songs, 12
immortalized by work of S. C.'s "burden bearers," 12

Staley, F. M.
head of agricultural department at State A. & M. College, 163

Stanton, Sec. of War
praised Negroes for conduct in siege of Petersburg, 52

State A. & M. College at Orangeburg
adjoining but no longer division of Claflin after 1896, 109
center of educational extension work in farming, home economics, vocational education, for state, 111
created as independent institution by Act of 1896 legislature, 109
Dr. Robert Shaw Wilkinson, elected president in 1911, 110
economics class helped make survey of Negro businesses, 143
faculty of colored men and women, 109
Hon. Thos. E. Miller, first president, 109
Mrs. Cora Boykin, once dean of women, 187
most illustrious graduate, great biologist Ernest Just, at Harvard University, 111
new legislative support for college began under administration of Cole L. Blease, 110
Pres. Wilkinson gets results in "higher education" by use of new diplomacy, 227
see Negro, Colleges agree . . ."
six trustees elected, 109
"the capstone of the public school system for Negroes in state," 111

State College of Agriculture and Mechanic's Institute
established in 1872 by Federal and State government, as division of Claflin, 96
100-acre experimental farm included, 96
state legislature passed act in 1896 to create State A. & M. College at Orangeburg adjoining but independent of Claflin, 109

State Extension Service
under Smith-Lever Law of 1914, 164

State Extension Service—*Continued*

County farm and home demonstration agents, 164–65

State, The

white newspaper, Columbia, 222

changing toward news of Negroes, 222

State Federation of Colored Women's Clubs, 180–85

attacked discrimination and segregation, 185

Inter-racial committees all over South, 210

in beginning, main purpose to support reformatory for girls, 180, 181, 182

established (Fairwold) near Columbia, 181, 182

organized about 1910, 182

information from Mrs. Etta Rowe of Orangeburg, 182

heads of departments, 185

officers of, 185

organizers of, 185

reports from, 183–84

Camden—Uplift Club, 183

Charleston—Louise F. Holmes Literary and Art Club, 183

Orangeburg—Sunlight Club, 184

State of S. C.

school appropriation and budget for 1924, 106–7

Statesmen, Southern

before Civil War, 16, 17

S. C., Henry Laurens, 29

Status of the Negro in South Carolina, The (1822–23)

by Holland, little book loaned to A. H. Gordon by Prof. Yates Snowden of U. S. C., 44

footnote, 100

Stephenson, Gen.

commander of reserve brigade in battle of Ft. Wagner, 52

Stephenson, Mrs. Julia

Florence, head, department of temperance, S. C. Federation of C. W. C., 185

Still, Wm.

in anti-slavery office to receive "Henry Box Brown," 21

officer in Underground Railroad, 23

wrote book on Underground Railroad, 23

Stobo, Archibald

Presbyterian minister at Wiltown, the men of whose congregation met and took insurrectionists, 33

Stories

of "Henry Box Brown," 20, 21

of William and Ellen Craft, 20

Stowe, Harriet Beecher, 19, 20

Straker, O. A.

professor of law and dean of Allen University, 95

Stroman, Mrs.

woman of color, had school from 1820 until Civil War, 86

Strong, Gen.

commanded brigade under Gen. Seymour, 52

in Ft. Wagner battle, 52

Strother, Mrs. Effie

Florence, head, department of music, S. C. Federation of C. W. C., 185

Success

cotton growing, 4

rice production, 2

Sudan

accomplishments of Negro labor, 10

Suffrage

Mrs. Mabel K. Howard, Darlington, head of department of, S. C. Federation of C. W. C., 185

Sugar cane, 5

Sullivan's Island

a fort built in 4 bastiles, 40

British attacked June 15, 1776, and driven back, 40

decided to erect breastwork there in Charleston Harbor, 39

Negro labor brought in from plantations to help, 39

Summerville
Acy Outten, Negro teacher of agriculture, 164
Sumter
J. C. Maloney, county farm agent, 165
Sunday Schools
for Negro children, Episcopal church, 86
Superior Court
Judge A. P. Aldrich received order from Federal officer that he could no longer sit as judge, 57
a Negro government formed in 1868, 57
Sutton, H. E.
Negro teacher of agriculture, 164
Swamp lands
in rice cultivation, 2
Sweinfurth
Heart of Africa, 117

Tanner
great painter of "Daniel in the Lions' Den," 211
Taylor, A. A.
Reconstruction politics only part of history, 68
The Negro in South Carolina During the Reconstruction, 55, 75, 78, 90
The Reconstruction in South Carolina, 73, 143, 157, 158
Taylor, D. T.
Negro teacher of agriculture, Gresham, 164
Taylor, Rev. E.
St. Andrew's parish gave Negroes religious instruction as well as other branches, 83
Taylor, Joseph and William
Negroes in business in Columbia after Civil War, 143
Taylor, William
especially successful in grocery business, 143
prominent Columbia Negro businessman, 77

Teachers
Civil War and after, 89-112
helped schools by working for small pay, 103
in early colony days to Civil War many named, 82-86, 103-4
Telemaque
original name of Denmark Vesey, 44
Temperance
Mrs. Julia Stephenson, Florence, head of department of, S. C. Federation of C. W. C., 185
Tennessee
under carpet-bag government during reconstruction, 58
Tennyson
"The Voyage," 205
Texas
under carpet-bag government during reconstruction, 58
Theory of Negro inferiority, 13, 14
proven fiction by individual slaves, 28
These Colored United States— South Carolina
by Kelly Miller, quote, 61-62
Thomas, Francis, and J. E. Dickson
county farm agents, Richland County, 165
Thomas, Rev. Samuel
Goose Creek Parish, began teaching Negroes about 1695, 82
Thompson, Asa
Negro teacher of agriculture, Whitney, 164
Thompson, Mrs. Carrie W.
Greenville, state editor, S. C. Federation of C. W. C., 185
Thompson, Lewis
in anti-slavery office to receive "Henry Box Brown," 21
Thompson, William
county farm agent, Clarendon County, 165

Thorwaldsen
  great Danish sculptor, on success, 206
Tillman
  Leonard P. Young, Negro teacher of agriculture, 164
Tillman, Senator
  (white) leader in movement to disfranchise Negroes, 60
  S. C. Constitutional Convention of 1890 argument answered by Thos. E. Miller, 65–68
Timmonsville
  J. L. Brewer, Negro agriculture teacher, 164
Tobacco, 5
Toil, gates of, 1
Tombs, of Georgia, 16
Tomlinson, Reuben
  successively state superintendent of education under Freedmen's Bureau, 1865, 91
Towne, Luna [Laura] M.
  of Philadelphia, important part in founding Penn School, supported by Pennsylvania society, 89
  continues today, 90
Traveler's Rest
  H. A. Chiles, Negro teacher of agriculture, 164
Travels in West Africa
  by Kingsley, 116, 117
Trenton
  Bettis Institute or Academy, 98
    founded by Negro ex-slave, Rev. Alexander Bettis, 98
Trenton
  James M. Jones, Negro teacher of agriculture, 164
Trexler
  The Negro from Africa to America, 26–27
  quoted by Weatherford, 26–27
"Truth, Sojourner"
  grand old warrior, 24
Turnbull, Robert J.
  about 1822, on better housing for slaves, on Sea Islands, 130

Tweed Ring
  in New York City, actually stole more of people's money than "carpet-baggers," 58

"Uncle Cyrus"
  prominent Negro teacher at St. Helena, 104
Uncle Tom's Cabin, 19, 129
  "Liza", escape, 19
Underground Railroad
  assisted abolitionists, 23, 25
  for fugitives, 19, 20
  some of bravest and best officers were Negroes, 23
  William Still officer, 23
  wrote book on, 23
Undertaking business
  leaders, Mickeys of Charleston, 147
    Blythewoods in Orangeburg, 147
  one of growing business successes in S. C. for Negroes, 141
  probably naturally followed livery stable business, 141
Union Army
  Gen. Hunter in S. C. with small force, 51
  in siege of Petersburg, 54
  Negroes volunteered, under Gen. Hunter, 51
  were praised by Gen. Hunter, 51
United States
  accomplishments of Negro labor, 10
  Congress, placed state of S. C. under military control during reconstruction, "Congressional Plan," 55
    embraced, Civil Rights Bill, 55
    Fourteenth Amendment, 55
  Negro forced in against his will, 1
  Negroes in wars of, 13–54
U. S. Census Report
  illiterates among colored population, 106

U. S. Census Report—*Continued*
in 1925, S. C. had 18,336 Negro owners of farms, 163
showed decrease in number of Negro farmers in state, 165
Negroes listed, 1890, by types of profession or trade, 78
population in U. S. 1890–1915, 134
houses owned by S. C. Negroes, 134

University of South Carolina, 44
only State college to admit Negroes during reconstruction, 61
whites left when Negroes admitted, 61
Prof. Yates Snowden, 44
social science courses teaching real truth about the Negro, 228–29

Unrest
not economic but spiritual, 12

Urban League
Negro expressions in, 193

"Vandals in America, The"
quoted from *Charleston New Era,* 224–25

Vesey, Capt.
home in Charleston, 45
owned Denmark Vesey, 44
slave trader between St. Thomas and San Domingo, 44

Vesey, Denmark (original name Telemaque)
handsome, intellectual, favorite with officers on Capt. Vesey's ship, 44
in 1800, won $1500 in lottery, 45
bought freedom for $600, got start in freedom, 45
insurrection, helped hasten Civil War, 45
to free Negroes and bring vengeance on whites, 46
native of St. Thomas, 44
planned and led "Vesey Insurrection" 1822–23, 44
slave of Charleston, 44

Vesey, Denmark—*Continued*
spread insurrection advice through Peter Poyas, 46
Vesey Insurrection, first set for July 14, 1822, 47
date changed to June 16, 1822, 47
last important physical fight in S. C. before Civil War, 48
Negro education curtailed after 1822, 84
forbidden by law in 1835, 84
plot killed, 47
Vesey started destroying all papers, 47
Vesey, one of 34 sentenced to death out of 131 arrested, 48
among world's great martyrs for human freedom, 48

"Vigilance Committee"
to receive fugitives in Philadelphia, 21

Vincent, Mrs. Belle
Columbia, head of mothers' department, S. C. Federation of C. W. C., 185

Virginia
under carpet-bag government during 3 or 4 years of reconstruction, 58

Virginia slave hunters, 21

Vocational teachers
under Smith-Hughes Act, 164

Voorhees Normal and Industrial School, Denmark
established by Elizabeth E. Wright, 98–99, 186
got help from Northern whites, 99

Vote
all Negroes could vote during reconstruction, 57
given Negroes under "Congressional Plan," 55
white men who had helped Confederacy could not vote during reconstruction, 57

Wade Hampton regime
from that time on Negroes fared badly, 105

Wade Hampton regime—*Contin-ued*
Negroes not given fair share of state's money for education, 105
professed to be friendly to Negroes, but only politicians' platitudes, 105
Wage slaves
better living than share-cropping or renting, 74
in Orangeburg Co., were paid 50¢ a day or about $8 a month, 74
not chattel slaves after Civil War, 72
some educated their children, 76
Walker, Capt.
branded "S.S." on right hand for helping slaves escape, 24
white engineer in Florida railroad construction, 24
Walker, Easterling
Negro teacher of agriculture, Pamlico, 164
Wallace (white man)
taught on Beaufain St., 86
Wallace, Judge
conservative Democrat, 67
helped pass money legislation started by Negroes, 67
Wallingford Academy
Charleston, founded by Jonathan C. Gibbs, 93
War(s)
against ignorance, Negro's, 80–112
against S. C. colony, Negroes joined opposing forces when offered freedom, 8
Civil, 13–54
Emancipation Proclamation, 54
Federals vs. Confederates, 52
Negroes fought in, 50
did not rebel against South —"playing safe," 50
joined Union forces, 50, 51
of 1812, S. C. Negroes not as prominent as those of Ala. and La., 41

War(s)—*Continued*
Revolutionary, Negroes fought on both sides, 38
U. S. Negroes in, 13–54
with Indians, S. C. Negroes fought in all, 41
World, 188–91
goal of, 206
War Work Council
of National Y.M.C.A. first financed by Inter-racial Commission, 214
Washington, Booker T.
Anglo-Saxon thinking, 9–10
chief ear-mark of his genius—diplomacy, 108
described as one of greatest diplomats, 226
interested Julius Rosenwald in education of rural Negro of South, 108
lost contact with Negro feeling on work, 9–10
on slaves' being allowed to purchase themselves—not a bad scheme, 26
The Story of the Negro Race, 26
Washington, J. I., Sr.
prominent Beaufort Negro businessman, 77
Waters, J. C.
early president of Allen University, 95
studied law at U. of S. C. when it was democratic, 95
Weatherford, W. D.
criticized Negroes in U. S. as having "inherited a loose moral life," because of different standards, 117
president, southern Y.M.C.A. College at Nashville, 229
suggested text for Y.M.C.A. courses, 229
The Negro from Africa to America, 26–27, 117
Webster, A.
S. C. Methodist Episcopal minister, 96

Webster, A.—*Continued*
influential in founding Claflin, 96
Weld, Angelina Grimpe
Slavery as It Is, 119
Wells, H. G.
definition of education, 80, 98
West Indies
accomplishments of Negro labor, 10
Indians, servants, 4, 5
"Whatever is is best"
Ella Wheeler Wilcox, 189
"Whatever shall be will be better" philosophy of Negro womanhood, 189
Wheatley, Phillis, 81
Wheatley, Phyllis, 187
White
(white writer) quote on ballot, 57
The Making of S. C., 2, 57
White, Ned L.
prominent Negro teacher, 104
White, Roosevelt
Negro teacher of agriculture, Simpsonville, 164
White, Walter
from Atlanta, 219
on N.A.A.C.P. staff, 217
White, W. A.
Negro teacher of agriculture, Gray Court, 164
White man's new diplomacy
to work *with* the Negro rather than *for* him, 228
White women's Committee on Race Relations in S. C., 220
opposing lynchings, 220–21
Whites
health in rice cultivation, 2
hired Negroes for domestic service after Civil War, 76
objected to Negroes in government or place of authority, 63
poor, workers, 1
population increase slower than Negro, 1
Whitney
Asa Thompson, Negro teacher of agriculture, 164

Whittaker, Lilla L.
member inter-racial committee, S. C. Federation, C.W.C., 186
Whittier, John Greenleaf
quoted from footnote, 22, 24–25
"The Vanishers," 205
Who's Who in Colored America, 1927 ed.
life of Mary McLeod Bethume, 179
Wilburn, W. W.
white man at school on Coming St., paid regular salary, 86
Wilcox, Ella Wheeler
"Whatever is is best," 189
Wilkes, Laura E.
defense of Ft. Moultrie, 39–41
Missing Pages in American History, 13–54
Wilkinson, Delphenia
county home demonstration agent, Greenville, 165
Wilkinson, Mrs. Marion Birnie
born in Charleston, especially prominent in social uplift work, 180
finest contribution: model mother, 181
officer of state inter-racial committee, S. C. Federation, C. W. C., 185
outstanding Negro woman of S. C., 179
president, Orangeburg-Sunlight Club, 184
president, State Federation of C. W. C., 180, 182, 185
through her leadership State College has only Y.W.C.A. building on any Negro campus in country (1928), 180
wife of president of State College, 180
Wilkinson, R. S.
Negro leader, given start by hard-working parents, 76–77
Wilkinson, Mrs. R. S.
president, State (S.C.) Federation of C. W. C., 217

Wilkinson, Mrs. R. S.—*Continued*
puts *"The Crisis"* in hands of
white people, 217–18
wife of Pres. Wilkinson of S. C.
State College, 217
work on inter-racial aims, post
World War period, 216
Wilkinson, Dr. Robert Shaw
a favorite expression of, 234
a professor of physics, 110
elected president of State
A. & M. College in 1911, 110
new diplomacy gets results in
"higher education," 227
outstanding leader of Negro
education in S. C., 110
Wilkinsonian, The, 1926
(State A. & M. College Annual)
footnote, 110
Williams, Bert
article in American Magazine,
"Comic Side of Trouble,"
on Negro as optimist, 188
Williams, Gov.
of S. C. in 1816, 42
with others foiled insurrection
with gathering under pre-
tense of fox chase, 42–44
Williams, Mr.
of Eloree, Orangeburg Co., 168
successful Negro farmer, owns
farm, nice home, educated
children, 168
Wilson, Jessie J.
county farm agent, Florence
Co., 165
Wilson, Joe
leader in cotton shipping, 140
Wilson, Miss
founder of Mayesville Institute,
186
Wilson, Woodrow (President)
"even handed justice," 108
Wiltown Presbyterian Church
whose congregation met and
overcame insurrectionists, 33
Winnsboro
Fairfield Normal Institute, 98
supported by Northern Presbyterian Church, 98

Wisacky
E. J. Bradley, Negro teacher of
agriculture, 164
Witzel, Mary
white woman, taught on Anson
St., 86
Wofford College
social science courses teaching
real truth about the Negro,
228–29
Woman in business
first in S. C., Negro woman, 139
sign: "Joe Cole and Wife—
Fish," 139
Womanhood in Ebony, Gifts of,
174–91
Woodson, Carter G.
footnotes, 14, 16, 49
on warlike slaves, 31
*The Education of the Negro
Prior to 1861,* 82
published by Assn. for the
Study of Negro Life and
History, 82
The Negro in Our History, footnotes, 38, 159
Work
attitude of, Negro slave, 9,
10–11
European slave, 10–11
Negroes, 72
World War
goal of, 206
Negro soldiers in, 188–91
post-war period for Negroes,
215
World-wide trade
slave trade, beginning of great
commerce, 5
transformed from Old World
trade in luxuries to necessities, 5
Worth, Nicholas
quote, 80
Wright, Elizabeth E.
attended Tuskegee Institute, 99
founded Voorhees Normal and
Industrial School at Den-
mark, 98, 186
interested Northern whites to
help build Voorhees, 98

Wright, Elizabeth E.—*Continued*
    sacrificial service cost her life,
        98–99
    tried to establish school in
        Hampton County, but build-
        ing burned, 99
Wright, Mrs. J. D.
    delegate, Camden—Uplift Club,
        183
Wright, Mrs. M. B.
    Spartanburg, head, department
        of health, S. C. Federation,
        C.W.C., 185

Yale
    educated many children of
        slaves, 76
    sent volunteers to help Freed-
        men in 1862, 88
Yankee view, vs. Southern view
    on Negro-white situation in
        South after Civil War, 100
    equality of races, 100
Yergan, Max
    Negro representative of Na-
        tional Council of American
        Y.M.C.A. in Africa, 230
    outstanding Christian layman,
        did great good in Columbia,
        230–31
    visited Columbia through Inter-
        racial Forum, 230
Yoruba Speaking Peoples
    by Ellis, 117
Young, Leonard P.
    Negro teacher of agriculture,
        Tillman, 164

Y.M.C.A., and Y.W.C.A.
    author secretary of Y.M.C.A.
        during World War, 187
    Bible Study Groups, 229
    Blue Ridge conference of stu-
        dent leaders of, 229
    had Mrs. Mary McLeod
        Bethume as speaker, 229
    leader, Mr. Bergthold,
        Y.M.C.A., 229
    co-operates with Southern Com-
        mission on Inter-racial Co-
        operation, 229
    Inter-racial Forum of Students,
        Columbia, 229–30
    brought Max Yergan, great
        Christian layman, from Af-
        rica to visit, 230–31
    National, War Work Council
        of first financed Inter-racial
        Commission, 214
    working through local bran-
        ches to bring understanding
        between races, 229
    Phyllis Wheatley Center a com-
        bination of the two, 187
    southern College at Nashville,
        229
    president, W. D. Weatherford,
        229
    World Problems Forums, 229
Young, S. M.
    Negro teacher of agriculture,
        Newberry, 164
Y.W.C.A. and Y.M.C.A.
    Phyllis Wheatley Center a com-
        bination of the two, 187
    see Y.M.C.A. and Y.W.C.A.